ALTERNATIVES
TO IMPRISONMENT
in Comparative Perspective

ALTERNATIVES
TO IMPRISONMENT
in Comparative Perspective

EDITED BY

Uglješa Zvekić

United Nations Interregional Crime
and Justice Research Institute

Nelson-Hall Publishers/Chicago

Library of Congress Cataloging-in-Publication Data

Alternatives to imprisonment in comparative perspective / edited by
  Uglješa Zvekić ; sponsored by United Nations Interregional Crime and
  Justice Research Institute.
       p.   cm.
    Papers from the Research Workshop on Alternatives to Imprisonment,
  held during the Eighth United Nations Congress on the Prevention of
  Crime and the Treatment of Offenders, Havana, Cuba, Aug. 27-Sept. 7,
  1990.
    Includes bibliographical references.
    ISBN 0-8304-1329-4 ——— ISBN 0-8304-1403-7(pbk.)
    1. Criminals—Rehabilitation—Congresses.   2. Alternatives to
  imprisonment—Congresses.   3. Imprisonment—Moral and ethical
  aspects—Congresses.   4. Prisons—Standards—Congresses.
  I. Zvekić, Uglješa.   II. United Nations Interregional Crime and
  Justice Research Institute.
  HV9276.5.A47   1993
  364.6'8—dc20   92-39832
                                                                              CIP

Copyright © 1994 United Nations Interregional Crime and Justice Research Institute

Manufactured in the United States of America

10   9   8   7   6   5   4   3   2   1

The paper used in this book meets the
minimum requirements of American
National Standard for Information
Sciences—Permanence of Paper for
Printed Library Materials, ANSI
Z39.48-1984.

Contents

Contents

Preface

This work originates from widely shared concerns about the negative effects that imprisonment has on society, the offender, and the criminal justice system. These concerns range from administrative and financial costs to doubtful effects of prison in terms of offenders' humane treatment and reinsertion in the community. These have generated a wide search for alternative sanctions, which in turn has resulted in a great amount of debate, legislation, projects, and research. While the search is still under way, many doubts have been raised as to the effectiveness, costs, and overall and particular benefits of the application of alternative measures. The United Nations has in general a favorable attitude toward development of alternatives to imprisonment. Part of this has been a highlighting of the need to promote research and exchange of information and experience in this field.

These are, then, some of the reasons that led the United Nations Committee on Crime Prevention and Control, and subsequently the Economic and Social Council, to approve the organization of the Research Workshop on Alternatives to Imprisonment, which was held within the context of the Eighth United Nations Congress on the Prevention of Crime and the Treatment of Offenders (Havana, Cuba, 27 August–7 September 1990). Following the practice of previous congresses, the United Nations Interregional Crime and Justice Research Institute (UNICRI, formerly UNSDRI) was entrusted with the responsibility for the scientific and organizational coordination of the workshop. This two-volume publication presents the results of the workshop.

The preparations for the workshop have involved close and active collaboration between the Crime Prevention and Criminal Justice Branch, the Helsinki Institute for Crime Prevention and Control, Affiliated with the United Nations (HEUNI), the United Nations Asia and Far East Institute for the Prevention of Crime and the Treatment of Offenders (UNAFEI), the United Nations Latin American Institute for the Prevention of Crime and the

vii

Treatment of Offenders (ILANUD), the United Nations African Institute for the Prevention of Crime and the Treatment of Offenders (UNAFRI), the Arab Security Studies and Training Center (ASSTC), and the Australian Institute of Criminology (AIC). In addition, the Department of Justice of Canada and a number of individual experts have provided information and reports. The preparations for the workshop lasted more than two years, and several expert meetings were held to develop methodology and review progress achieved.

This publication consists of two volumes. Volume 1 presents regional and case study reports; volume 2 presents a review of the literature and the *International Bibliography on Alternatives to Imprisonment, 1980–1989*. The introductory chapter to volume 1 presents and comments on the resolution on principles and directions for research on noncustodial sanctions that emerged from the research workshop and was adopted by the Eighth United Nations Congress.

The preparation and organization of the research workshop and this publication are indeed an example of fruitful, intensive, and well-targeted collaboration within the United Nations network of research institutions, which, in addition to the UN interregional and regional institutes, includes a number of leading national institutions. To all of them, and to UNICRI staff who collaborated in the preparation of the workshop and this publication, I wish to express my deep gratitude. Special gratitude goes to Nelson-Hall Publishers for making this rich comparative material available to international research and criminal justice communities.

It is UNICRI's hope that the presentation of this publication will indeed contribute to promote further development of credible noncustodial sanctions. It is also our belief that research into obstacles to the promotion and effectiveness of alternative sanctions has much to say and offer in this challenging and arduous journey toward increasingly humane and effective criminal justice systems.

Ugo Leone
Director, United Nations Interregional Crime
and Justice Research Institute

1

Noncustodial Sanctions: Comparative Overview

Matti Joutsen and Uglješa Zvekić

Imprisonment is the cornerstone of present penal systems. Those guilty of a broad range of offenses, and those otherwise fulfilling certain criteria, are deemed to be deserving of incarceration.

Despite the wide use of imprisonment, its drawbacks both to the offender and to society have become increasingly recognized. It is no exaggeration to say that a worldwide search is under way for noncustodial alternatives to imprisonment and for ways of otherwise alleviating the situation of prisoners. The search for such "credible noncustodial sanctions" has generated a considerable amount of legislation, projects, and research at both national and international levels.[1] Within the United Nations system, in 1980, the Sixth United Nations Congress on the Prevention of Crime and the Treatment of Offenders adopted a resolution recommending that Member States expand the use of alternatives to imprisonment and identify various new alternatives to prison sentences.[2] Five years later, the Seventh United Nations Congress adopted another resolution, recommending that Member States "intensify the search for credible non-custodial sanctions."[3] The Eighth United Nations Congress on the Prevention of Crime and the Treatment of Offenders held in 1990 devoted much attention to this issue, which was placed on the agenda of the congress but also discussed in the context of other of the congress's items; it adopted a number of decisions and resolutions.[4] Furthermore, the Research Workshop on Alternatives to Imprisonment considered issues of research and implementation of noncustodial sanctions in comparative perspective; a resolution regarding research was adopted, and it is presented in the Appendix herewith. Since the basic options open to the legislator and the judge are limited (to, for example, probation, deprivation of certain rights, community service, and fines), it is not surprising that parallel developments have taken place in many countries. It would therefore be in the general interest of policymakers and

1

practitioners to be informed of the experience and research results obtained elsewhere.

The present comparative overview is primarily based on documentation prepared for the Research Workshop on Alternatives to Imprisonment. However, this documentation should not be understood as providing an exhaustive global inventory or analysis of noncustodial sanctions. The regional reports present information on the basis of which the reader can form a relatively reliable picture of the different types of noncustodial sanctions in use today. The country-based case studies are illustrations of different types of noncustodial sanctions, ranging from traditional to modern, involving different degrees and forms of supervision, and in the context of different infrastructures.

Throughout this chapter, reference will be made to "noncustodial sanctions" and not to "alternative sanctions."[5] The latter implies that imprisonment is the norm and that all other measures are secondary. From the strict point of view of the law of some countries, this may be true for many serious offenses. In some jurisdictions, the so-called "alternative sanctions" are included in a scale of punishment that also includes imprisonment. In other jurisdictions, a sentence of imprisonment must be pronounced, and enforcement is suspended in favor of "alternative sanctions."[6] In yet other jurisdictions, offenders, offenses, and aggravating and mitigating circumstances are defined with such clarity and precision that a clear distinction is made between the circumstances in which imprisonment must be used and those in which a noncustodial sanction must be used.

The scope of the chapter is limited to noncustodial sanctions considered at the time of adjudication. A "sanction" is to be understood as a measure used for the deliberate punishment of the offender by the state in response to an offense. This limitation to noncustodial sanctions implies that the overview does not deal with the following:

a. Noncustodial *measures* in the broad sense. The purpose of measures may refer, for example, to the promotion of reintegration into the community and thus include assistance in obtaining housing, treatment, or employment;
b. Processes, institutions, or measures *preceding the adjudicatory stage* (with the exception of pretrial detention). This includes decriminalization, diversion, and discontinuance of proceedings. Such a limitation is understandable in light of the fact that a number of such processes, institutions, and measures are not directed toward a decrease in the use of imprisonment and inversely toward an increase in the use of noncustodial measures per se, but rather toward, e.g., reducing the number of cases burdening the criminal justice system or limiting the reach of the criminal justice system. Although their use may result in a decrease in the use of imprisonment, such use may also result in a decrease in the use of all forms of sanctions. It should be borne in mind that some preadjudicatory measures may be backed up with the threat that failure to

     abide with the conditions of the measures may lead to adjudication and even, in some cases, to imprisonment.

c. Measures imposed *outside of the criminal justice system.* Such measures (which may even involve institutionalization or other confinement) can be imposed, for example, on the basis of administrative law, military law, or social welfare law.[7]

d. *Alleviation of the enforcement of imprisonment* (for example, such sanctions as short-term imprisonment, semiliberty, or semidetention, and such measures as furlough and early release).[8] A strong argument can be made for considering such measures as alternatives to imprisonment in the basic sense. To the extent that they are deemed credible alternatives to full-term and full-force custody by the adjudicatory body, the public, and other parties concerned, their use should be encouraged. However, they remain essentially variants of imprisonment.[9]

e. Juvenile justice systems, for the most part. The overview primarily discusses measures that are applicable to adult offenders. In many juvenile justice systems, imprisonment does not have the same fundamental position it has in the adult criminal justice system. Where imprisonment is used, the issues involved are largely the same as where the offender is an adult.

This overview considers sanctions at the time of sentencing. The focus is on the possibilities open to the courts to apply noncustodial sanctions in cases where custodial sanctions would ordinarily be employed. However, it contains one significant exception to this focus, as it touches upon measures intended to limit pretrial detention. Pretrial detention and imprisonment are closely linked, and many of the problems connected with sentences of imprisonment are also evident with pretrial detention. As pointed out in the French response to the United Nations Survey,

> All thinking about alternatives to imprisonment is inseparable from thinking about detention pending trial; experience shows that a decision taken at the stage of preliminary examination to deprive a suspect of his freedom carries great weight when the time comes to pass sentence.

Moreover, in many countries, in particular in Latin America, a large proportion (or even the majority) of those held in prison are on remand.[10] Attempts to reduce the use of imprisonment should begin with the "front end" of the system, the decision to place a person in pretrial detention.

The Functions of Punishment—General Comments

The literature on punishment routinely distinguishes between two general purposes of punishment, general prevention and special prevention. General prevention is directed at society at large. Punishment is intended to warn the public against offending (deterrence) and to assist in the internalization of norms. The prioritization of norms and values is seen to require that the

3

more serious the offense is deemed to be in the opinion of the community, the greater the punishment should be.

Special prevention, in turn, is directed at the offender. In this case, the punishment serves as a concrete warning to the offender against further offending. Many commentators also argue that punishment should (ideally) have a rehabilitative effect in assisting with the integration of the offender into the community. Finally, in certain serious cases the offender is regarded as so dangerous to the community that he or she should be incapacitated (made harmless)—for example, by isolating the offender from the environment in which the dangerous offenses could be committed.

There is also a school of thought that argues that punishment should follow an offense as a matter of course, independent of the instrumental value of punishment: Punishment is retribution for an offense. This approach has passed through a period of disfavor in many countries, during which it was associated with vengeance. Now, however, punishment is increasingly regarded as an expression of society's reprobation of the offense, a function that is connected with the internalization of norms referred to above.

Finally, the growing interest in the protection and support of the victim has led to a resurgence of interest in the possible reparative and restitutive elements of punishment.[11] For example, the so-called Victim Declaration adopted by the United Nations urges governments to "review their practices, regulations and laws to consider restitution as an available sentencing option in criminal cases, in addition to other criminal sanctions."[12]

The Functions and Dysfunctions of Imprisonment—Imprisonment as a Sentence

With the exception of capital punishment and some forms of corporal punishment (where they exist), imprisonment is in general considered the most severe form of punishment in most present contemporary criminal justice systems. Even so, there appears to be considerable unanimity about what offenses "merit" imprisonment. Imprisonment is considered to be necessary with serious offenses, such as those involving serious danger to life, health, and well-being, serious trafficking in drugs, aggravated thefts, gross fraud, serious economic crime, serious offenses against the environment and offenses that seriously endanger national security.[13] Imprisonment is also considered to be necessary for certain kinds of offenders, but the characteristics of those offenders are often denoted in law or in legal practice in a broad and vague manner. The list of those for whom noncustodial sanctions are considered to be unsuitable in various countries includes for example, habitual offenders and recidivists, drug offenders, and violent and sadistic offenders. The most common background factors taken into consideration relate to previous criminal history and record.

For less serious offenses and for other types of offenders, there is considerably less unanimity as to whether or not imprisonment should be imposed. If imposed, the imprisonment would tend to be for a short term only.

When imprisonment is imposed, it can serve many of the functions of punishment referred to above. It is commonly justified in particular by its deterrent, rehabilitative, and incapacitative functions, as well as by the public demand for a severe response to serious offenses. The relative importance of these elements varies from jurisdiction to jurisdiction,[14] and the extent to which they are considered may even vary from one judge to the next.

Skepticism concerning the prison as a place of treatment has now been reflected in formal criminal policy in many countries. In Europe, for example, imprisonment is widely described as a sanction that cannot achieve any improvement in the great majority of prisoners or in their social situation. On the contrary, there is widespread awareness that the prospects for satisfactory adjustments in society are frequently made worse by imprisonment.[15] Reference can also be made to the high costs of running a prison system—both to the maintenance and the capital costs. Today, the economic resources available for necessary public services are subject to severe constraint. Moreover, to the extent that the prison system is required to take in more prisoners than it can deal with, overcrowding must result, thus further hampering the attempts to alleviate the negative consequences of imprisonment. For these reasons, imprisonment should not be used where a noncustodial sanction will do, except as a measure of last resort.

Pretrial Detention

Persons suspected of offenses of a certain level of seriousness, suspects who refuse to identify themselves, and suspects who the authorities fear will attempt to abscond, hinder the investigation of the offense, or commit new offenses can, under certain conditions, be held in remand even where the system of *habeas corpus* is applicable. The principle of the presumption of innocence, together with the principle of minimum necessary intervention, speak on behalf of as limited a use of pretrial detention as possible.[16]

Where and when criminal justice operates with dispatch, this period of remand, or pretrial detention, is generally quite brief. It is also generally taken into account when sentencing the convicted offender. In practice, however, the criminal justice systems of many countries operate slowly. Moreover, many persons held in pretrial detention are ultimately sentenced to a noncustodial sanction or even acquitted, or the time spent on remand may be longer than the sentence imposed.[17]

Functions and Dysfunctions of Noncustodial Sanctions

The arguments for noncustodial sanctions are essentially the mirror image of the arguments against imprisonment. First, they are considered more appropriate for certain types of offenses and offenders. Second, because they avoid "prisonization," they promote integration back into the community, promote rehabilitation, and are therefore more humane. Third, they are generally less costly than sanctions involving imprisonment. Fourth, by decreasing the prison population, they ease prison overcrowding and thus facilitate the administration of prisons and the proper correctional treatment of those who remain in prison.

The main arguments against the greater use of noncustodial sanctions is that they are not as effective as sentences of imprisonment in deterring other members of the public from committing offenses, that they do not incapacitate the offender, and that they do not sufficiently demonstrate the reprobation of the offense by society. Put simply, this argument is that noncustodial sanctions are overly lenient.

Appropriateness

For a wide range of petty offenses, imprisonment would not even enter the question; they are not seen to "merit" imprisonment. In addition, noncustodial sanctions are also deemed appropriate for certain types of offenders, or offenders with certain characteristics, such as first-time offenders, where there is little likelihood of recurrence, and those whose past behavior, repentance, status in the community, and some other factors give reason to believe that the offense was not typical. The assessment of appropriateness is also connected with the offender's willingness to participate in a noncustodial program, the ties of the offender to the community (for example, family and employment), and the availability of the necessary resources for noncustodial programs (e.g., supervisors, the availability of space in the programs, even the technological infrastructure). Further consideration is connected to the fact that noncustodial sanctions may provide a framework for a wider range of programs than institutional treatment. For these reasons, they are seen to serve the interests of the individualization of punishment and treatment.[18]

Rehabilitation

One of the main arguments for noncustodial sanctions is that they do not hinder readjustment to society and may indeed facilitate this. Prisons have difficulties in preparing offenders held in detention for life in the outside world. The ordinary method for assessing the success of rehabilitation is to study recidivism. The assumption is that the greater use of noncustodial sanctions will reduce recidivism. Problems in defining and measuring the link between recidivism and a type of sentence must immediately be stressed. A summary of the situation in England and Wales observes that "in general, research studies have failed to show that one type of sentence is more likely to reduce the likelihood that an offender would commit further offences than any other. The only measures which have been found to be consistently more effective than others were financial (usually fines, but sometimes compensation orders)."[19] The European regional report concluded that "recidivism is a measure of effectiveness which has to be handled with caution. Studies on the amount of recidivism at the end of a follow-up period following different disposals do not suggest that noncustodial alternatives lead to a significantly greater degree of recidivism than custodial sentences.[20] Another method to measure the effects of noncustodial sanctions is to consider the "success rate" of the program. It is based on the assumption that a successful completion of the program indicates a high likelihood of having achieved the purposes of the program, including rehabilitation.[21] The problem is that noncustodial sanctions tend to be used where there is a considerable likelihood of success (some programs have great control over admission); this means that the program is applied to a selective profile of offenders, and the consent of the offenders is requested. These factors tend to complicate the assessment of the achievement of the objectives of the program in question.[22]

Cost Reduction

A third argument often advocated in support of noncustodial sanctions is that they are less costly than imprisonment. Costs can, however, be variously defined and measured. One may speak of the immediate financial costs of the adjudication or the enforcement of sentences,[23] of the indirect financial costs resulting from an increase or decrease of crime, of the costs to the offender and to the victim, of the wider social costs, and so on. What is generally implied is that the wider use of noncustodial sanctions would allow the state to administer the enforcement of sanctions more cheaply. However, an assessment of the success achieved in reaching this goal requires an estimate of the savings that might be made with various changes in the rate with which different sanctions are used. Comparisons of per-diem costs alone would oversimplify the issue. Fines and penal warnings are cheap (fines even bring in revenue), but probation and community service require an organized, skilled, and often professional corps of workers to ensure their proper use.[24] Furthermore, minor cuts in prison rates would not reduce the maintenance costs of prisons. In addition, the possible net-widening effect of the adoption of noncustodial sanctions (more persons are processed and controlled, including those who in other circumstances would not have had sanctions imposed on them) may increase costs. Moreover, as suggested above, it would be unwise to concentrate solely on financial criteria as a measure of effectiveness. Also, the human and ethical factors (or "costs") or the social costs should be taken into consideration. For example, reliance on imprisonment as the "normal" punishment has clear humanitarian, ethical, and social costs. On the other hand, for example, home detention and electronic monitoring have been argued to place a burden on the immediate environment, such as the family of the offender; this can be deemed a social cost.[25]

Reduction of the Prison Population

The greater use of noncustodial sanctions is commonly expected to reduce the prison population. This can be understood in two ways: either such sanctions reduce the number of offenders in prison at any one time, or they reduce the number of offenders entering prison. The force of the first function is lessened by the fact that noncustodial sanctions generally replace only the shorter sentences of imprisonment and thus have little practical effect on the overall size of the prison population. Other circumstances (such as increased crime) could lead to more, and/or more severe, imprisonment sentences, making it difficult, if not impossible, to determine whether noncustodial sanctions actually have this function.[26] The effectiveness of noncustodial sanctions cannot be judged solely on the basis of whether their use reduces the size of the prison population.[27] Even if the greater use of noncustodial sanctions does not decrease the number of offenders in prison at any one time, it may reduce the number of persons entering prison. Such a function could have two benefits, one related to criminal policy and one to prison administration. If prison does indeed have a negative effect on offenders, then it is desirable to limit the use of imprisonment to the fewest possible offenders. Second, reducing the number of cases that have to be processed in prison decreases the work load of the prison administration.

Effect on Crime Rates

The main argument against noncustodial sanctions, as noted, is that, because of their leniency, they do not deter people from committing offenses. There are serious methodological difficulties in studying the effect that a change in sentencing policy may have on public attitudes and behavior and more specifically on the overall crime rate. The few existing attempts to study this point tend to conclude that the degree of use of imprisonment does not appear to be decisive for the general level of crime control in society. It may thus be that high rates of imprisonment do not curtail crime in general, nor do low rates encourage crime. There is also a lack of clear empirical evidence for asserting that the extended use of noncustodial sanctions leads to an increase, decrease, or stabilization of crime rates. It is generally held that other intervening factors such as the likelihood of detection and the certainty of punishment are probably more important. Taking into account the drawbacks of imprisonment, and in the absence of appreciable evidence to the contrary, it would appear that a wider use of noncustodial sanctions does not lead to any substantial increase in criminality, especially when such sanctions are properly planned and implemented and have the full support of the community and the public at large.[28]

Inventory and Classification of Noncustodial Sanctions[29]

Measures for the Avoidance of Pretrial Detention

In the previous section it was noted that pretrial detention will be used primarily in three cases: when the offense in question is a serious one, when the suspect refuses to identify himself or herself, and when the authorities fear that the suspect will attempt to abscond, hinder the investigation of the offense, or commit new offenses.

In the first case, the use of pretrial detention is conditioned on the severity of the probable sentence in the case. The law may state, for example, that if the minimum punishment for the offense is two years' imprisonment, the assumption will be that the suspect shall be detained. Release pending trial would be possible only if there were important grounds for release. In such cases, of course, the use of pretrial detention can be restricted by raising the minimum punishment stipulated or by granting the authorities more discretion over the decision whether or not to release the suspect pending trial.

In the second case, pretrial detention is only for the (presumably brief) period it takes to ascertain the identity of the suspect. The use of pretrial detention can be reduced by increasing administrative efficiency in the identification of suspects (i.e., through the use of mandatory identification documents or the computerization of fingerprints and other identifying characteristics).

It is in connection with the third set of criteria for pretrial detention that the greatest amount of discretion remains and correspondingly where there is the greatest potential for restricting the use of this measure. The success of the measures would thus lie in their ability to prevent the suspect from absconding, interfering with the investigation of the offense, or continuing to commit offenses.

The measures used for the avoidance of pretrial detention could be classified as follows: restriction of movement, supervision, payment of bail, and release on recognizance.

Restriction of Movement. In the most restrictive measure used to avoid pretrial detention, the suspect is required to stay within a certain area or within certain premises, most commonly his or her home. Violation of the conditions may lead to pretrial detention. Observance of the conditions is generally enforced through constant monitoring by the local police.[30] Such monitoring can also be carried out electronically.[31]

Supervision. A less restrictive measure requires that the suspect awaiting trial submit to supervision primarily in order to ascertain that he or she has not absconded. The suspect may be required to report to the police or another agency at intervals, or a representative of such an agency will make random checks on whether or not the suspect has adhered to the conditions. These conditions may include not only a prohibition against leaving the locality without prior permission, but also conditions more directly related to the offense being investigated. Examples would include disqualification from driving, in the case of a suspected traffic offense, or disqualification from engaging in certain business transactions, in the event of a suspected economic offense.[32]

Instead of a representative of an official agency, the supervisor may be another member of the collective at which the suspect works, a close relative, or simply a private citizen who agrees to act as a supervisor or as a guarantor that the suspect will come to trial.[33]

The Payment of Bail. "Bail" can be understood in a narrow and in a wide sense. In some jurisdictions, it is widely understood as release pending trial. In the more common, narrower sense, it is understood as the posting of property or money as surety that a person released from custody will appear in court at the appointed time. Some systems require the bailee to report at regular intervals to the local police station, while others require other types of supervision. Bail in the narrow sense is in common use in many countries throughout the world. Its primary drawback is that it can be discriminatory, since the poorer suspects cannot afford bail and often do not succeed in having a bondsman post bail for them.[34] An alternative to bail is "binding over." This involves a court order to keep the peace. Should the suspect violate the order, he or she may be fined or detained, or the order may be otherwise amended.[35]

Release on Recognizance. The most common measure used for avoiding pretrial detention is simple release on recognizance, whereby the suspect agrees to appear before the court when the case comes to trial. This is "bail" in the wide sense referred to above. Such simple release may be used even in more serious cases when the suspect is an established member of the community. Research in Costa Rica[36] reveals that while recognizance is frequently used for minor offenses, it is not applied for serious offenses (for example, more than three years' imprisonment). The main reasons lie in the attitudes of judges and defense lawyers and in the sentencing practices of higher courts. The research-monitored experiment on the application of this measure for serious offenses revealed that the main argument against its use was not sustained; as regards compliance with the obligation to appear before the court, there was a significant difference between suspects released on recognizance and those released on economic surety.

The Variety of Noncustodial Sanctions

The variety of noncustodial sanctions is immense, and there are many possible classification schemes that can be used in a synthesis overview of this nature. As pointed out, the one used here is based on the degree to which the state intervenes in the life of the offender. In addition, this overview could not present comparative statistics on the use of noncustodial sanctions. While reasonably comparative statistics can be presented on the use of imprisonment, the diversity in the classifications of noncustodial sanctions is so great that such statistics would raise more questions than they would answer. Instead of providing information, comparative statistics could be a considerable source of misinformation.

It is difficult to make generalizations regarding the extent to which the potential for noncustodial sanctions is being used in practice. This potential depends on a number of factors, including a clear policy regarding the purposes of noncustodial sanctions, legislative provisions, procedural provisions, attitudes toward the use of noncustodial sanctions, and the existence of the necessary infrastructure for the implementation of noncustodial sanctions.

However, the very fact that there is general agreement that wider use should be made of these sanctions suggests that there is a gap between the potential and the actual use of noncustodial sanctions, and that courts continue to sentence offenders to imprisonment even though a noncustodial sanction would be appropriate.[37]

Sanctions That Imply Supervision and Control

Probation and Suspended or Conditional Imprisonment with Supervision. Of measures that imply considerable supervision and control of the offender (suspended or conditional imprisonment with supervision, probation, community service, reformative and educational labor, special forms of treatment, and local banishment), the most common are probation and suspended or conditional incarcerative sanctions with supervision or the condition of treatment. The common element is that the offender is convicted but given the opportunity of not serving a sentence (which may or may not be specified) under certain conditions and directions, most commonly that he or she does not commit a new offense during the probationary period. This category of noncustodial sanctions is present in almost all criminal justice systems, in one or more variants. Although its use is increasing in some jurisdictions, in others it is decreasing, and in still other jurisdictions it is being combined with other categories of noncustodial sanctions. The supervision can range from intensive, through moderate, to minimum. Under intensive supervision, the offender is kept under close control in order to reduce the opportunities for recidivism, reintegrate the offender into society, and seek to ensure that the conditions of probation, or suspended or conditional imprisonment, are fulfilled. At the other end of the scale, minimum supervision entails only sporadic contacts between the offender and the supervisor, with little attempt to assist the offender in reintegration back into the community.[38] The supervision can be exercised by professionals, volunteers, or members of the collectivity in which the offender works or lives.[39]

In some countries, violation of probation does not automatically lead to obligatory and immediate revocation. Options may be a judicial warning, fines, an amendment of the conditions, or an extension of supervision.[40] Should the violation of probation lead to enforcement, various modalities for proceeding exist. In some jurisdictions, the term of imprisonment to be imposed in case of a violation is stated already at the time probation is ordered, and the court has no discretion as to how long a term to impose. In others, where the term of imprisonment is similarly stated at the outset, the court has discretion in whether or not to impose it in full. In yet other jurisdictions, the term is not determined until and unless a violation occurs.

Community Service. Community service is considered to be a fairly recent innovation.[41] In its present form it was first introduced in England and Wales in 1975. The sanction involves performance of a certain number of hours of unpaid work for the good of the community, usually during leisure hours.[42] In most systems, there are specific provisions regarding the prerequisites under which a community service order can be made; these include, for example, the type of offense and the consent of the offender. The use of this sanction has spread to a number of countries.[43] A corresponding sanction existed in a number of ex-socialist countries.[44] One of the arguments often made on behalf of community service is that it provides for community involvement in the reintegration of the offender. Little research exists to support such an argument. However, it can be presumed that the involvement of the community can be enhanced when community service is carried out within the context of the community organizations or structures already in place.

Home Probation. In home probation (home detention, home confinement, house arrest), the offender is required to stay at home for a certain period (generally, two or three months). The extent of the confinement may be limited to nighttime or to nighttime and leisure hours. It may also be full-time confinement for twenty-four hours a day. The conditions of home probation may include full or partial abstinence from alcohol, or counseling or treatment for substance abuse. The offenders are generally subject to strict and random surveillance, either face-to-face or electronic monitoring.[45]

In electronic monitoring, a tag is attached to the person under supervision. The passive tag responds to a signal, generally transmitted by telephone, thus informing the caller (the supervisor or a computer) that the person in question has not left the designated area. The active tag sends a continuous signal to a nearby telephone; should the person leave the designated area, the signal will stop, thus alerting the supervisor to a violation of the order.[46]

The special benefits of home probation are, first of all, that it incapacitates the offender: without violating the conditions of probation, with some exceptions (primarily abetting in offenses by offering advice) he or she cannot commit offenses other than against himself or herself (e.g., drug offenses) or against others in the household. Secondly, it is flexible: it can be implemented anywhere that the technology can reach (if, indeed, technology is necessary), and these conditions can be modified to allow for participation in different activities also outside the home. In common with other noncustodial sanctions, home probation allows the offender to maintain family ties and continue work or studies.[47] It is also less costly than prison, regardless of whether or not electronic monitoring is used. On the other hand, there are some technical difficulties involved with home probation combined with electronic monitoring, and its use may lead to inequities. Electronic monitoring is also said to involve some legal and ethical problems. In particular, it is regarded by some as an invasion of the offender's privacy at home. This last argument has been countered with reference to the fact that the sanction provides an alternative to imprisonment, where the offender would have considerably less privacy. Furthermore, the invasion of privacy is largely limited to the sending and receiving of electronic signals, while face-to-face surveillance requires either that the offender report to the supervisor or that the supervisor make random checks on the offender at home.

Open, Ambulant, or Contract Treatment. This form of treatment was noted in only a few countries.[48] This rehabilitative measure is used for specific offender categories, where medical or psychiatric expertise suggests that there is a connection between the offense and, for example, drug addiction or a drinking problem. As a result of, for example, the poor experiences with forced treatment for offenders during the earlier part of this century, the consent of the offender is often a condition for the order to treatment.

Sanctions That Do Not Require Supervision or Control

The State is less intervenient in the application of the noncustodial sanctions that, in essence, have the character of a warning. These are customarily used where the offense is not grave and especially where the offender is of previously good character. They are known by a variety of names, including *admonition, absolute discharge, conditional discharge, conditional sentence without supervision,* and *simple suspension of sentence.*[49]

The most common penal warnings are findings of guilt with no sanction imposed and conditional or suspended sentence with no supervision or control. Admonitions are possible in a great number of countries. The admonition may also be public; for example, it may be published in a local newspaper.[50]

Release on recognizance and release on a bail order after adjudication are related to penal warnings: the offender is convicted, but sentencing is postponed until a further date. His or her behavior in the interval is taken into consideration in deciding on the final sentence.[51]

Monetary Payments

Fines. In addition to penal warnings, the sanction that involves minimum state intervention in the offender's life is monetary payments. Fines are the best known and the most used of this category of sanction. They are economical in terms of both money and labor and practical in terms of management and administration. They are also humane, as they inflict a minimum of social harm. However, fines can create inequities by discriminating against the poor, for whom they are often converted into imprisonment because of nonpayment.[52] This disadvantage can be overcome through the use of the day fine.[53] It can also be overcome through limitations on the conversion of unpaid fines into imprisonment,[54] by granting reprieves of payments or the possibility of paying in installments, and by allowing the court discretion over whether or not conversion shall take place.[55] Fines can also be conditional. Furthermore, some jurisdictions use good-behavior bonds (the giving of security to keep the peace and be of good behavior, or to come up for judgment).[56] In the United States, certain states may also charge fees of offenders for various services, such as for supervision through electronic monitoring, drug testing, and other special needs.

Compensatory Payments. Compensatory payments (compensation orders and the like) as an independent sanction were noted in only a few countries.[57] In many countries, they can be imposed as one of several conditions of a conditional sentence. Generally, however, compensation or restitution is a civil matter, even if in many jurisdictions it is often imposed by a criminal court.[58] The United Nations has called for greater use of compensatory payments as a sanction. Restitution of the loss to the victim is deemed an appropriate aim of criminal justice and is in the interests of society as a whole.[59]

Reconciliation. Reconciliation, which is closely tied to compensatory payments, is generally considered an option only during the preliminary stages of the criminal process—for example, during the police investigation or as a measure implemented outside of the state-based criminal justice system. In the latter case, the structure in which reconciliation takes place can be traditional (such as the village courts in Papua New Guinea or the Lupong Tagapayapa in the Philippines) or of more recent origin (such as the social courts). However, some countries report that reconciliation is also an option at the adjudicatory stage, even for offenses in the medium range of seriousness, where imprisonment might be a possible sanction.[60]

Personal Reparation. Personal reparation predates imprisonment and is a common form of compensatory payment and a part of reconciliation procedures in almost all African societies.[61] It is widely used in customary law and, to a much lesser extent, in formal criminal justice systems. In the latter, it is frequently combined with restitution and a fine; default often leads to imprisonment. Research reveals that personal reparation, being culturally well established, could be more widely used by the formal criminal justice system.

Confiscation. Somewhat over half of the countries noted confiscation of personal property as an independent sanction.[62] This trend is encouraged by the 1988 United Nations Convention against Illicit Traffic in Narcotic Drugs and Psychotropic Substances. Generally, however, confiscation of the property derived from or used in the offense is considered a penal measure to be applied in addition to a sanction, and not as an independent penal sanction.

Diyya. Diyya, which originates from pre-Islamic common law,[63] bears the traits of compensatory payments, but there are important distinctions. It also has a deterrent and punitive component. It is a possible alternative to a retaliatory sanction for five Quesas (felony) crimes: premeditated murder, quasi-intentional murder, unintentional manslaughter, intentional physical injury or maiming, and unintentional physical injury or maiming. The Diyya is paid to the victim or to his or her family as compensation for bloodshed.

Furthermore, Diyya is based on collective responsibility, and thus also the family members of the offender may have the duty to pay Diyya. In some cases, it may be paid by the state. There are specific rules regulating the amount of Diyya, depending on the offense and the religious affiliation and sex of the victim. There are no definite rules for the division of the responsibility for payment of Diyya among the members of the family (the Aaqela) of the offender, although the general rule states that the amount depends on the degree of kinship and financial status of the family.

Withdrawal of Rights

Suspension of Driving or Other License. Suspension of licenses was noted by some countries as a sanction in criminal law; however, in most cases it is an ancillary criminal sanction or an administrative measure. *Deprivation of certain rights and/or removal of professional status* was also noted in a number of countries; examples of such rights include the right to perform certain functions or hold certain positions or public offices, the right to vote, and the right to act as an expert or a witness in court. In most countries, however, deprivation of such rights is an ancillary sanction. Furthermore, some forms of withdrawal of rights (such as dismissal from office) are reserved for certain special groups, such as civil servants.

Combination of Sanctions

Several systems have provisions allowing for the combination of custodial with noncustodial sanctions and the combination of different noncustodial sanctions. Where the offense is of a certain seriousness or where the offender's criminal record is serious, it may be deemed inappropriate to impose a single particular noncustodial sanction. A combination of sanctions may give the sentence more weight. In addition, a combination may be more successful in tailoring the sentence to the characteristics of the offender while meeting the expectations of the court and the community.[64]

Problems in Expanding the Use of Noncustodial Sanctions

There seems to be a strong interest throughout the world in replacing imprisonment by noncustodial sanctions, as also demonstrated by various United Nations resolutions and activities of other international bodies such as the Council of Europe and the international professional associations in the field of criminal justice. Even so, many of the reports submitted to the United Nations note that appropriate noncustodial sanctions are either simply not available or are used far less than they might be or, when used, are used as substitutes for other noncustodial sanctions and not for imprisonment.[65] The documentation presented in this volume suggests some reasons for this apparent inconsistency between policy and practice: even if the appropriate statutory changes are made, the courts may be either unwilling or unable to impose noncustodial sanctions, owing to factors related to sentencing, to a lack of suitable resources, or to attitudes.

Other problems in the use of noncustodial sanctions do not directly explain the slowness with which they are being put into effect, but should nonetheless be taken into consideration in the planning and implementation of these sanctions, since they affect the entire criminal justice system. For example, in addition to their net-widening effect (referred to above) and their supposed leniency, it has been also argued that, from the point of view of the offender, the noncustodial sanctions may raise problems of due process and legal safeguards, in particular in the case of an alleged violation of the conditions of the sanction.

Considerations of Penal Policy

The likelihood of the use of noncustodial sanctions depends first of all on the degree to which the penal policy is favorable to such sanctions and to the functions assigned to them. Punitive penal policy would tend to favor the wide use of imprisonment for a broad range of offenses. The policy orientation is also indicated by the legislators' attitudes to a breach of conditions of the noncustodial sanctions as well as by the legal prerequisites under which a court can impose noncustodial sanctions. Thus, direct commutation of a noncustodial sanction into imprisonment in the case of a breach of conditions indicates a greater degree of punitiveness than does the possibility of searching for other, more suitable noncustodial sanctions. Similarly, the requirement for express justification of a noncustodial sanction, as opposed to the requirement for express justification of the imposition of imprisonment, indicates a greater degree of punitiveness.

Statutory Provisions

There are few jurisdictions in which the courts have wide discretion in developing new noncustodial sanctions. In most jurisdictions, the courts can impose only sanctions that are expressly defined in statutory law. In the majority of jurisdictions, therefore, the law must first provide for the possibility of a range of appropriate noncustodial sanctions before they can be imposed by the court. It is noted in some reports contained in this volume that in some countries there is a lack of clear provisions in law regarding both the conditions for imposition of noncustodial sanctions and the methods of implementing them.[66] It is also noted that in some countries the range of noncustodial sanctions is quite restrictive, limited to a number of "classical" sanctions, such as fines, suspension of imprisonment, and probation.[67]

Legal Safeguards

Noncustodial sanctions have been and are being developed primarily with consideration for the position of the offender—for example, to improve the likelihood of social reintegration. Given this basic premise, the attitude may be taken that any noncustodial sanction is preferable to imprisonment, and legal safeguards are not seen to be an issue. Nonetheless noncustodial sanctions still remain punitive sanctions. Proper adjudication and implementation of noncustodial sanctions require the objective exercise of discretion. This may well lead to cases where the human, civil, and political rights of the offender are restricted beyond what is inherent in the sanction itself.[68] Among the more important safeguards against such a situation are that the application of the sanction should be based on law and established criteria, that the discretionary powers should be exercised by a competent authority, and that the sanction should be subject to review at the request of the offender. The offender should be properly informed of the conditions to be observed and the possible consequences of noncompliance with them. In an alleged breach of the conditions, the offender should have the right to be heard before a decision is taken on the consequence of such breach. Work on guidelines and standards in the area of noncustodial sanctions is under way in several countries as well as on the international level; for example, the Eighth United Nations Congress adopted the United Nations Standard Minimum Rules on Non-custodial Measures.[69]

Sentencing and the Establishment of Penal Value

Determination of the penal value of the noncustodial sanction presents a further problem. With existing sanctions, the penal value is generally well established. Thus, for example, a fine is generally deemed a lesser penalty than a suspended sentence, which in turn is deemed a lesser penalty than imprisonment. Established practice further guides the measure of each individual sanction: a fine of X amount for theft under certain circumstances, for example, and imprisonment for Y months for robbery under certain circumstances. When a new custodial sanction is introduced, it may be difficult for the legislator and/or the court to assign it its appropriate place in the scale of punishment and to decide, for example, whether forty hours of community service is the equivalent of one month of imprisonment and whether it is more or less severe than a suspended sentence.[70] The situation is further complicated if the legislator and the judge are to work within the framework of the noncustodial sanction as the per se referent point—in other words, if one is to establish a penal value of the noncustodial sanction as the normal sanction without reference to imprisonment.

In sentencing, therefore, the court must make a choice among a number of sanctions, using multiple criteria that relate the seriousness of the offense to what are deemed to be the relevant characteristics of the offender and the penal value of the noncustodial sanctions available, either singly or in combination. Furthermore, courts frequently work under pressure of time. For this reason, they tend to favor sanctions that do not require time for the collection, presentation, and assessment of social inquiries about the offender and his or her situation; in this, judges tend to find it easier to assess juridical information than data drawn from the social sciences.

Resources

Another problem relates to the availability of resources to implement the sanction. Obviously, the success of the sanction depends on the availability of resources for its enforcement. Just as imprisonment requires prison facilities, personnel, and a prison program, probation generally requires a suitable infrastructure for the arrangement of supervision, and community service requires not only a suitable organization but also designated places of work.[71] In addition, the general economic and political circumstances in a country may have a role in determining the extent to which noncustodial sanctions are used in general.[72]

Mere provision of the necessary resources is not enough. The resources must be of sufficient quantity and quality to ensure that the sanctions are successful in achieving their purpose, no matter how this purpose is defined. The courts tend to be cautious in imposing new noncustodial sanctions. If the court lacks confidence in the operational efficiency of the services responsible for the implementation of noncustodial sanctions, it will probably be less inclined to make use of such sanctions.[73]

Attitudes

In order for noncustodial sanctions to be implemented and effective, they must be regarded as legitimate, appropriate, and effective. The attitudes of various parties (including the public, the courts, professional groups, and the victim) toward noncustodial sanctions are therefore an important consideration. Noncustodial sanctions will not be used if the court regards them as ineffective or inappropriate. The sanctions will not be implemented properly if those responsible for their implementation (such as the supervisors) regard them as inappropriate; if this is the case, then the courts will adjust their sentencing policy accordingly. The opinion of the public will be instrumental both at the time when new sanctions are being considered by the legislature and when they are being incorporated into the general sentencing policy. Finally, in individual cases, the opinion of the victim (and, indeed, of the offender) may be of significance in selecting (and, sometimes, implementing) the sanction.

Of all these groups, it is the courts and the practitioners who occupy the key positions, as they decide on the imposition of a sanction and act on its implementation. In view of the results of research on the subject,[74] there is reason to think that precedents, general guidelines, and sentencing conferences are not fully adequate as measures for the introduction and establishment of new noncustodial sanctions. It is important to involve judges (as well as other professional groups) already at the stage of the drafting of new legislation on sanctions.[75]

Demonstrating the appropriateness of noncustodial sanctions to the courts and the practitioners is an ongoing process that by no means ends with the adoption of the requisite legislation and the arrangement of an initial training phase. Some experiments with noncustodial sanctions succeed because they are run by highly motivated individuals. Once the program is placed on a more general footing, there is the danger of falling into routines or meeting with unexpected difficulties in implementing the sanctions in light of local circumstances or with the help of persons who are not so committed to the original purpose of the program. Broad policy premises must be translated into practice, taking into account different environments and local contexts in a number of different environments, and by a number of practitioners who may have their own reasons for implementing the programs in a local context.[76]

Dysfunctions for the Operation of the Criminal Justice System

One area of concern relates to the possible dysfunctions of wider use of noncustodial sanctions, in particular the so-called net-widening effect.[77] Statistical evidence from various countries clearly suggests that noncustodial sanctions either are used far less than they might be or, when used, are used as substitutes for other noncustodial sanctions and not for imprisonment. In addition, when suspended sentences are pronounced, the period of imprisonment imposed may be longer than if an unconditional sentence to imprisonment were to be used. In the event of activation of the original sentence, the offender can therefore go to prison for longer than would otherwise have been the case.

Furthermore, if greater use of noncustodial sanctions does lead to a reduction of the use of short-term imprisonment, this may mean that there will be a corresponding greater proportion of offenders serving longer sentences in prison. This, in turn, may have an adverse effect on the security of the institutions. A "hard-core" prison population will lead to practical difficulties in prison management.

It is also possible that if no custodial sanctions are taken into wider use, this may lead to a dichotimization of sentencing. Those who receive a noncustodial sanction instead of imprisonment will benefit from a less restrictive sanction. However, the courts may balance this out by sentencing those for whom imprisonment sentences are imposed to even longer terms. The net result may be that the overall severity of sentencing will have remained about the same.

Promotion of Noncustodial Sanctions

A number of different ways were reported to be in use in the different jurisdictions for the promotion of the greater use of noncustodial sanctions. In the following, these measures are grouped primarily according to the source of the measure.

Statutory Measures

The fundamental statutory measure for promotion of noncustodial sanctions is legislation making a range of such sanctions available to the criminal justice system and clearly outlining the procedures and conditions for their imposition and implementation.[78]

Another statutory measure includes a statutory requirement of justification for the use of imprisonment.[79] Such a measure would compel the court to justify why none of the available noncustodial sanctions are appropriate in the case at hand.

Limiting conditions on the use of noncustodial sanctions could be eliminated or relaxed. For example, the maximum length of imprisonment that can be replaced by a noncustodial sanction could be raised, and existing absolute prohibitions against the use of noncustodial sanctions in case of recidivism could be replaced by statutory provisions allowing for court discretion. The possibility of imprisonment for certain offenses could be abolished. Changes in society are often reflected in the attitudes toward certain behavior. A review of criminal law may indicate that existing penal provisions on certain offenses were passed at a time when these offenses were deemed particularly reprehensible; in light of present attitudes, a noncustodial sanction may well be deemed more appropriate. At the same time, the public attitude toward the use of imprisonment may have changed; in many countries, its "penal value" has increased. Where imprisonment at one time was imposed in decades, it may now be imposed in years; where it was once imposed in years, it may now be imposed in months or even weeks.

Even so, in some countries there is a call for harsher punishment: instead of a response to this of expanding the use of imprisonment, it may be satisfied within the framework of noncustodial sanctions by allowing for combination of such sanctions. This end may also be achieved by making the existing noncustodial sanctions more attractive as sentencing options— for example, by allowing for the possibility of inserting additional requirements or conditions in, for instance, probation orders. In several jurisdictions, the elimination of imprisonment below a certain length has been proposed.[80] The rationale is that the courts would be compelled to seek alternatives to short-term custody. Other restrictions on the application of imprisonment could also be embodied in legislation.[81]

Measures Related to the Courts

Emphasis is often placed on the role of court precedents in guiding the practice of lower courts. This method was preferred over legislated guidelines in order to maintain the division of power between the executive and the judiciary. However, precedents remain decisions on *individual* cases, and the extent to which general conclusions can be drawn from them depends not only on the legal system but also on the case.

In some countries, the supreme court has the power to issue sentencing guidelines that extend beyond the scope of cases at hand. Such guidelines provide the judge with information on the usual sanction given for a specific type of offense. Also, judicial conferences or professional associations can assist in clarifying sentencing objectives and guidelines. For example, they could stipulate the criteria and principles that permit the comparison of various sanctions and the standardization of their use.[82] The conferences and associations need not be limited to judicial personnel; they could be expanded to include corrections personnel and other persons responsible for the administration of sentences.

The judicial conferences referred to above provide a special form of training. Other forms include the arrangement of special courses and seminars at which new legislation is introduced or at which the court personnel are acquainted with research on the effectiveness of various sanctioning options. Since the use of noncustodial sanctions depends on the professional legal culture of judges (as well as prosecutors and other practitioners involved in the imposition and implementation of the sanctions), the promotion of noncustodial sanctions to become the norm should start with the process of professional socialization. Consequently, for example, the curriculum of law schools should reflect these concerns.

Other strategies focus on drawing the attention of the courts to the official policy of favoring noncustodial sanctions (for example, through the adoption of an official statement of the purposes and principles of sentencing) or on increasing the credibility of such sanctions. Such credibility can be increased by providing the courts with information on a systematic basis regarding the effectiveness of sanctions.[83] It can also be enhanced through closer control over the enforcement of the sanction.

Where this would not be deemed a violation of the principle of the separation of the executive and the judiciary, the executive branch could consider the possibility of providing the court with sentencing guidelines, based, for example, on current court practice.[84] In turn, the judiciary could overview the implementation of the noncustodial sanctions, particularly in those countries where supervising judges have this function.

Measures Related to Prosecution

The selection of the sanction is often determined by the motion of the prosecutor or by the way in which the case is presented. For this reason, guidelines should also be developed for prosecutors on the selection of the appropriate sanction for presentation to court, and the appropriate prosecutorial training should be arranged. Such guidelines should include, in particular, criteria for nonprosecution.

Measures Related to Implementation

The most efficient route to increase the credibility of noncustodial sanctions and thus promote their use is for the state and local community to provide the necessary resources and financial support for the development, enforcement, and monitoring of such sanctions. Particular attention should also be paid to the training of the practitioners responsible for the implementation of the sanctions and for the coordination between criminal justice agencies and other agencies involved in the implementation of these sanctions in the community.

Because the success of many noncustodial sanctions depends to a large extent on the interaction between the community and the offender, special measures should be adopted to sensitize the community to the benefits and crime-control potential of noncustodial sanctions. Examples of such measures include the provision of information on noncustodial sanctions and the situations of offenders, greater use of the existing reconciliation or dispute-settlement mechanisms or institutions in the community, and increased reliance on volunteer and citizens' associations in the implementation of noncustodial sanctions (which may also decrease the costs of such implementation). Special target groups in the community for such measures include the victims of crime and the members of the family of the offender.

Conclusions

The problems associated with the use of imprisonment have led to a stronger interest in noncustodial sanctions. These are expected to combine many functions at the same time. For example, they are generally expected to help in reducing the prison population and the overall costs of the system. They are also believed to be more conducive to social integration, thus reducing recidivism and increasing the crime-control effects of the criminal justice system. They are also believed to act as a deterrent and just punishment for a certain range of offenses and for certain types of offenders, thus providing certain advantages to society if compared with imprisonment.

Some of these purposes conflict with one another, and they may not be adequate to all types of noncustodial sanctions. Some may be directed more toward treatment, some may have a bias toward integration, while others simply call for payment by the offender—a fiscal contribution to the state, compensation to the victim, or compensation to the community as a whole.

It has been noted that the actual experience with different sanctions in the different countries cannot be taken as a clear-cut demonstration that noncustodial sanctions have these benefits. For example, even when noncustodial sanctions do replace imprisonment, they generally replace quite short sentences, thus having little effect on the size of the prison population. The same negligible results are achieved if the noncustodial sanctions are used for a small number of offenders.

At the same time, other circumstances (such as increased crime) could lead to more, and/or more severe, sentences of imprisonment, thus giving the impression that the reform has on the contrary led to greater use of imprisonment. The evidence is also ambiguous as to whether or not the greater use of noncustodial sanctions succeeds in lowering costs or in promoting rehabilitation.

On the other hand, the evidence is at least as ambiguous on the argument that the extent of the use of noncustodial sanctions is linked to the structure and level of crime in society—for example, that noncustodial sanctions are used to a proportionately lesser extent when a country faces a "serious crime problem," or that "excessive" use of such sanctions would encourage more crime. No connection has been shown between more lenient sanctions and a greater amount of crime, or, correspondingly, between more severe sanctions and a reduction in crime.

On the basis of the material presented in this publication, the following general conclusions can be drawn.

1. *There is an interest throughout the world in increasing the use of noncustodial sanctions.* This can be seen on the level of penal philosophy and policy and, increasingly, on the statutory level (as in Australia and Europe). This trend, however, is not unidirectional. Many examples can be given of states where

there is a clear increase in the punitiveness of the criminal justice system and consequently an increase in the use of imprisonment and/or an increase in the use of punitive components in noncustodial sanctions, presumably as a reaction to an increase in crime.

2. Despite the increased theoretical interest in noncustodial sanctions, *a gap remains between policy and practice.* This is evident on several levels. On the statutory level, many governments (particularly of Arab and Latin American countries) report that they do not have an appropriate range of noncustodial sanctions or that the legislation does not provide clear guidance on the purposes, imposition, or implementation of these sanctions. On the level of sentencing practice, the gap is reflected in the continuing predominance of imprisonment as the norm or as the criterion for sentencing. Noncustodial sanctions are either used far less than the law would allow, or they are used as alternatives for other noncustodial sanctions. On the level of resources, the implementation of some noncustodial sanctions remains hindered because of the absence, for example, of the necessary personnel, support structures, and funds. The gap can be diminished only through a change in attitudes. The attitude of the legislator must be changed so that he or she has a greater awareness of the need for legislation supporting the goals of noncustodial sanctions. The attitudes of the judge and prosecutor (as well as the other practitioners involved) must be changed so that they become more aware of the need to seek the appropriate noncustodial sanctions and to apply them whenever possible. The attitudes of those who decide on resources must be changed in order to make them aware of the benefits to be derived through expanded use of noncustodial sanctions. Finally, the attitudes of the community must be changed to make the community aware of the importance of the reintegration of the offender into the community for the benefit of the offender, the victim, and the community as a whole.

3. In many jurisdictions (for example, in Australia, Canada, Europe, and the United States), there is a clear *development toward the diversification of noncustodial sanctions*, toward a greater range of these sanctions. This can be seen, for example, in the adoption of a greater number of different noncustodial sanctions, in the increased possibilities being provided for the adding of certain conditions to existing noncustodial sanctions, and in the increased possibilities for combining different noncustodial sanctions. These last two may be seen as a partial response to the demand for developing more appropriate and, indeed, in some cases, more punitive noncustodial sanctions.

4. In addition to the above general trends, some specific patterns can be noted, the strength of which varies from one jurisdiction to the next:

   a. The diversification of noncustodial sanctions has been paralleled in some countries by an *extension of noncustodial sanctions to a greater range of offenses and offenders* (for example in Europe).

   b. *A greater use of the classical noncustodial sanctions*, such as fines (in some countries of Europe and Latin America, in the form of day fines), probation (in many Asian, and in some African, countries), and suspended or conditional sentences (in some Arab and Latin American countries).

   c. *Development of noncustodial sanctions containing a number of*

conditions—in particular, one or a combination of the following components: work (as in community service), compensation/restitution, and
treatment (in Australia, Canada, Europe, and the United States).
   d. *Renewed interest in "traditional" sanctions and in sanctions that rely
   on traditional infrastructures* (in Africa and parts of Asia and the Pacific
   region).
   Totally new sanctions rarely appear. Among the few examples are
   community service and home probation, which in practice were unknown in many of the countries in which they have now been introduced on either a statutory or an experimental basis. Perhaps the most
   effective road toward greater use of noncustodial sanctions is to give life
   to "old" noncustodial sanctions. Indeed, most recent legislative action
   in this area has been toward expanding the scope of the already
   available sanctions or placing them on a statutory footing.
5. In some countries (such as Australia, Canada, and several countries of Europe)
   the use of noncustodial sanctions is being promoted through the *development
   of measures that provide guides for sentencing,* including attempts to standardize sentencing. This has been done, for example, through the introduction of
   statutory guidelines or guidelines adopted by judicial conferences and professional associations.
6. There is an *increased interest in national and international standard setting,
   with an emphasis on legal safeguards.*[85]
7. There is a *clear lack of statistical data and research on the effectiveness of
   noncustodial sanctions and problems met in promoting them.*

For the last reason, the Eighth United Nations Congress adopted the
earlier-mentioned resolution regarding research on noncustodial sanctions
(see the Appendix). What follows is a brief commentary on the resolution.

Research is needed on the normative structure that determines the
availability and application of noncustodial sanctions. Noncustodial sanctions cannot be imposed where the law does not allow for their imposition.
Furthermore, certain legal provisions related to noncustodial sanctions may
unintentionally deter their use in practice. For example, the procedural
requirements for the imposition of certain noncustodial sanctions may bar
their imposition in simplified proceedings.

Another example is that the greater use of noncustodial sanctions may
widen the statutory discretionary powers of certain authorities. This may be
in conflict with other policy goals, such as the goal of ensuring due process.
In addition, the introduction of noncustodial sanctions through legislative
action requires analysis of the proper place of the sanction in the normative
scale of punishments.

In regard to sentencing, research is needed on the factors considered
by the sentencing judge or tribunal. Unexpected factors may have a decisive
influence on the sentencing process. The little research that is available has

suggested, for example, that some judges will not consider noncustodial sanctions that require a social inquiry report.

Further in regard to sentencing, it is possible that the imposition of noncustodial sanctions is discriminatory, as has been argued to be the case with sentencing to imprisonment. For example, fines may be imposed only on those who are able to pay them; community service may be imposed only on offenders who have certain characteristics that were not necessarily envisaged by the legislator; or the milder forms of noncustodial sanctions may be imposed on offenders who have a high standing in the community.

An area of research that is related to sentencing concerns attitudes. Clearly, the attitudes of the sentencing judge affect his or her decisions on what available options to use. As important as the attitudes of the sentencing judge are the attitudes of other persons involved in the implementation of noncustodial sanctions. In particular, the degree to which a noncustodial sanction is "accepted" by professionals as well as by the community influences the probability that this sanction will actually be applied. Research on changes in attitudes (showing the causes and extent of such changes) might be of assistance in the planning of the introduction or expansion of noncustodial sanctions.

A key factor in the "success" achieved with the use of any noncustodial sanction is the extent to which the policymakers, courts, other practitioners and agencies, and the community are informed of the effectiveness of this sanction. Indeed, the effectiveness of noncustodial sanctions (and, indeed, the effectiveness of sanctions in general) has long been a popular subject of research. Regrettably, the research on effectiveness of sanctions has yielded relatively meager results. Yet it is indispensable and should pay special attention to criteria and methodologies for measuring the effectiveness of an adopted sanction, taking into consideration various interests and needs involved. Moreover, evaluation research must focus on the effectiveness of various noncustodial sanctions for various types of offenders with different characteristics and severity of crimes. It should also consider the relative effectiveness of noncustodial and custodial sanctions on successful completion of the conditions required, access to services, rate of recidivism, and a reduction of overall and specific costs of crime control. In the evaluation of noncustodial sanctions, attention must be paid to the consequences of their wider application on the reach, degree, and type of control exercised in the society, as well as on the processes of decriminalization/criminalization.

The problems faced by evaluation research on the effectiveness of noncustodial sanctions, and of evaluative research in general, are as great as expectations. Nevertheless, as noted, the promotion of noncustodial sanctions calls for research on effectiveness. This review of the available research and data on noncustodial sanctions throughout the world began with the observation that the different countries share much the same problems and concerns. This suggests that one promising approach to the issue is through comparative research and systematic exchange of experience drawn from different policy options.

Appendix

PRINCIPLES AND DIRECTIONS FOR RESEARCH ON
NONCUSTODIAL SANCTIONS

The Eighth United Nations Congress on the Prevention of Crime and the Treatment of Offenders,

Recalling resolution 8 on alternatives to imprisonment, adopted by the Sixth United Nations Congress on the Prevention of Crime and the Treatment of Offenders, held at Caracas from 25 August to 5 September 1980,

Recalling also resolution 16 on the reduction of the prison population, alternatives to imprisonment, and social integration of offenders, adopted by the Seventh United Nations Congress on the Prevention of Crime and the Treatment of Offenders, held at Milan, Italy, from 26 August to 6 September 1985, and in particular, its affirmation of the need to intensify the search for credible noncustodial sanctions and its call to United Nations interregional and regional institutes to strengthen their programmes in order to assist Member States in undertaking research on noncustodial sanctions,

Considering the need for promotion of action-oriented research, as highlighted by resolution 20 on research on youth, crime and juvenile justice, adopted by the Seventh Congress,

Expressing its appreciation for the reports of the Secretary-General on Alternatives to Imprisonment and the Reduction of Prison Population and on Research on Alternatives to Imprisonment,

Noting with satisfaction that the draft United Nations Standard Minimum Rules for Noncustodial Measures (the "Tokyo Rules") submitted to the Eighth United Nations Congress on the Prevention of Crime and the Treatment of Offenders emphasize the need for research and exchange of information on noncustodial measures,

Responding to Economic and Social Council resolution 1989/69 of 24 May 1989, by which the Council approved the organization of the Research Workshop on Alternatives to Imprisonment,

Considering also the policy and scientific significance of the findings resulting from the studies carried out by the United Nations Interregional Crime and Justice Research Institute, the Helsinki Institute for Crime Prevention and Control (affiliated with the United Nations), the United Nations Asia and Far East Institute for the Prevention of Crime and the

Treatment of Offenders, the United Nations Latin American Institute for the Prevention of Crime and the Treatment of Offenders, the United Nations African Institute for the Prevention of Crime and the Treatment of Offenders, the Arab Security Studies and Training Centre, the Australian Institute of Criminology, and experts in the preparation of the Research Workshop on Alternatives to Imprisonment,

Noting also with appreciation the results of the Research Workshop on Alternatives to Imprisonment, held at the Eighth Congress on 31 August 1990,

Aware of the importance of research and of the exchange of information on the results of research in facilitating the development of an appropriate response to pressing problems in criminal justice, such as the continuous increase, in many countries, of the prison population and overcrowding,

Aware also that the results of research studies should be used to promote a better understanding by the public at large of the advantage of noncustodial sanctions,

1. *Endorses* the principles and directions for policy-oriented research on noncustodial sanctions, as contained in the annex to the present resolution,
2. *Encourages* Member States, governmental and nongovernmental associations and the research community to provide policymakers, adjudicators and other practitioners with statistics and research results on the use and effectiveness of noncustodial sanctions in order to facilitate the making of informed decisions,
3. *Recommends* that the use of research findings on noncustodial sanctions as resource material in conferences and training courses for criminal justice personnel be encouraged,
4. *Calls for* a systematic exchange of information, experience and research findings on noncustodial sanctions between governmental and nongovernmental organizations and between researchers,
5. *Invites* Member States and the research community to promote research and the utilization of the results of research in the development of noncustodial sanctions,
6. *Encourages* the United Nations interregional and regional institutes for the prevention of crime and the treatment of offenders to provide technical assistance to Member States in implementing the principles and directions for research on noncustodial sanctions contained in the annex to the present resolution and to promote the coordination and conduct of evaluative and comparative research in this field.

Annex

PRINCIPLES AND DIRECTIONS FOR POLICY-ORIENTED RESEARCH ON
NONCUSTODIAL SANCTIONS

I. Role of Research in Policy Development and Sentencing Practice
  1. The systematic collection and exchange of information, together with the results of research and policy analysis, should be recognised as desirable for the evaluation and promotion of noncustodial sanctions.
  2. In order for research on noncustodial sanctions to have immediate policy relevance, it should focus on those areas and issues which present obstacles to the realization of the potential of noncustodial sanctions within a specific system, should address problems confronted by decision makers and administrators, ensuring their collaboration in all phases of the research process and should present its findings in an easily applicable form.

II. Adoption and Implementation of Noncustodial Sanctions
  3. Research on the appropriate place of specific noncustodial sanctions within the range of sanctions available for the treatment of offenders, including imprisonment and various types of noncustodial sanctions, provides a basis for the informed adoption and implementation of suitable noncustodial sanctions.
  4. Research should seek to determine the appropriateness of various noncustodial sanctions in view of criminal policy, socioeconomic, political, legal and organizational requirements and resources, and in view of the culturally specific contexts in which the noncustodial sanctions are to be applied.
  5. Research on the attitudes of the legislator, police officer, prosecutor, judge, administrator, victim, community and offender is desirable in order to reveal conditions which limit the adoption and implementation of any particular noncustodial sanction and to provide an appropriate basis for action aimed at increasing its acceptance.
  6. Research should investigate the possibility and outcome of the incorporation in noncustodial sanctions of various measures (such as, community work, compensation/restitution, treatment) and/or combinations thereof, and of utilizing traditional and culturally relevant noncustodial sanctions.

III. Evaluation Research
  7. Evaluation research is necessary for the promotion of practices in criminal policy, legislation and sentencing practice that are based on the informed appreciation of prerequisite conditions for, and benefits of, non-custodial sanctions.
  8. Such research should pay special attention to the criteria and methodologies for measuring the effectiveness of an adopted noncustodial sanction from the perspectives of the various interests and needs involved.
  9. Evaluation research could focus, *inter alia*, on *services to offenders while under sanction:*
      a. The effectiveness of particular noncustodial sanction for various types of offenders with different characteristics and severity of crime, and the

relative effectiveness of noncustodial sanctions and custodial sanctions on successful completion of the conditions of the sanction, access to different types of services, rates of recidivism and a reduction of the overall economic, human and social costs of the control of crime;

b. The consequences of a wider application of noncustodial sanctions on the extent of the use of imprisonment, and more generally, on the reach, degree and type of control exercised through the criminal justice system;

c. The consequences of a wider application of noncustodial sanctions on the processes of decriminalization/criminalization;

d. The effects of various means of expanding the use of noncustodial sanctions, such as the development of legislation, sentencing guidelines and the sentencing practice of the higher courts.

Notes

1. For research and related material, see volume 2.

2. Resolution 8, "Alternatives to Imprisonment," *Sixth United Nations Congress on the Prevention of Crime and the Treatment of Offenders* (A/CONF.87/14/Rev. 1), pp. 11–12.

3. Resolution 16, "Reduction of the Prison Population, Alternatives to Imprisonment, and Social Integration of Offenders," *Seventh United Nations Congress on the Prevention of Crime and the Treatment of Offenders* (A/CONF.121/22/Rev. 1), p. 85.

4. Topic II of the Congress dealt with criminal justice policies in relation to problems of imprisonment, other penal sanctions, and alternative measures. A number of background documents related to noncustodial measures were discussed, such as *Report of the Secretary-General on Alternatives to Imprisonment and the Reduction of Prison Population* (A/CONF.144/12) and *Report of the Secretary-General on Research on Alternatives to Imprisonment* (A/CONF.144/13).

The Congress adopted, in particular, *United Nations Standard Minimum Rules for Noncustodial Measures* ("The Tokyo Rules") and *Principles and Directions for Research on Noncustodial Sanctions.*

See *Eighth United Nations Congress on the Prevention of Crime and the Treatment of Offenders, Havana, Cuba, 27 August–7 September 1990* (A/CONF.144/28).

5. Other possible terms in wide use include *community sanctions, community-based sanctions,* and *intermediate sanctions.* The latter is used in the United States to refer also to those that fall between prison and noncustodial sanctions. See chapters 13 and 14.

6. For example, in the Netherlands a draft bill on community service provides that the judge has to state in his or her sentence the prison sentence he or she is considering imposing and for which the community service is a substitute.

7. It is difficult to distinguish among sanctions imposed in accordance with, respectively, administrative law, administrative criminal law, and criminal law. This limitation excludes from the scope of the study, for example, tax increases for tax offenses, the restriction or revocation of rights through administrative procedure, and

administrative custody (such as labor reform in labor correctional institutions, as used in China) or placement in special military units (such as assignment to a disciplinary battalion in the Byelorussian SSR).

8. In most countries, imprisonment can be alleviated through release on parole. The paroled offender is generally placed under supervision. It may be noted here that some countries combine sentences of imprisonment with a subsequent supervision order, thus combining custodial and noncustodial sanctions (for example, the split sentence, or shock incarceration, in the United States). Although in the first option, imprisonment is the main sanction and parole is the alleviation of the sanction, while in the latter option imprisonment is not necessarily considered the "main" sanction, the practical effect of the two options is much the same.

9. Two regional reports, those for Asia and the Pacific and for Latin America and the Caribbean, however, deal with these measures. See chapters 6 and 16.

10. For example, in the Philippines and in Indonesia, 80 percent of the inmates in prison or jail are on remand. In Argentina, many convicted persons will have spent between 50 to 90 percent of their time in remand centers without any correctional treatment, suffering all the negative by-products of prison and none of the benefits of treatment.

For the particular concern in the Latin American countries about the wide use of pretrial detention, see chapter 17.

11. This aspect of punishment has been a fundamental element of traditional and Islamic criminal justice.

12. "United Nations Declaration of Basic Principles of Justice for Victims of Crime and the Abuse of Power," paragraph 9, *Seventh United Nations Congress on the Prevention of Crime and the Treatment of Offenders* (A/CONF.121/22Rev.1), p. 46. See also, for example, Guideline 11 of Recommendation No. R(85)11 of the Committee of Ministers of the Council of Europe to Member States on the Position of the Victim in the Framework of Criminal Law and Procedure.

13. Legislation often specifies that noncustodial sanctions are not deemed appropriate, or are prohibited, when the offense in question is punishable by imprisonment of a certain length. Norman Bishop, *Noncustodial Alternatives in Europe,* HEUNI publication no. 14, Helsinki 1988, p. 50.

14. In China, for example, imprisonment combines productive labor with ideological education, and Japan views self-reformation efforts as indispensable to correction and rehabilitation. *Alternatives to Imprisonment and Measures for the Social Resettlement of Prisoners: Report of the Secretary-General* (A/CONF.121/13), para. 97. Furthermore, Japan notes that since no community-based treatment is able to provide the kind of programs given by institutional treatment, there will continue to be a great need for imprisonment.

15. This point was made, for example, in the regional report for the Arab countries. See chapter 4.

16. Pretrial detention is, in exceptional cases, also used in some jurisdictions to separate the parties to a conflict. The Philippines notes that there are certain additional advantages from pretrial detention, including the fact that the detention provides a "cooling-off period" that may lead to an informal settlement between the victim and the suspect.

17. The problem is by no means new. The preamble to Decree 110 of 27 June 1847 in the Dominican Republic noted that "with the present organization of our courts, the legislation in force is inapplicable in some procedures, with the result that a multitude of our fellow-beings and compatriots who, in view of the time for which they have been deprived of the previous and inestimable right of liberty without being tried in order to receive the penalties commensurate with their acts, have already purged them, lie almost in the night of oblivion, filthy and buried in living tombs." (Cited in the reply of the Dominican Republic to the secretariat survey.)

For example, in France, 16 percent, and in England and Wales, 40 percent of defendants who have been remanded in custody do not receive a sentence of imprisonment. P. Morgan, "Suggestions for Improvement," *Report on "Delays in the Criminal Justice System,"* prepared for the Ninth Criminological Colloquium of the Council of Europe, Strasbourg, 22 August 1989, p. 3.

18. This point was made in the regional report for Latin America and the Caribbean. See chapter 16.

19. This response was received to the European regional survey on the use of noncustodial sanctions. Bishop, *Noncustodial Alternatives in Europe*, p. 136,

20. See chapter 10.

A Dutch study compared offenders given community service in 1981 with those given short-term unconditional imprisonment for similar offenses in 1980. It emerged that 42 percent of the community service group, and 54 percent of the matched custodial group, reoffended during the three-year follow-up period. See chapter 12.

Norway also reported, in responding to the secretariat survey, that it would appear that no more crimes are committed by those receiving a community service order than by those imprisoned. An analysis of the experiences in Denmark (cited in William Rentzmann, "Erfarenheter av samhallstjanst i Danmark, in Alternative brottspafoljder i ett internationallet och skandinaviskt perspectiv," *BRA PM1* [Stockholm 1989], pp. 43–52, at p. 49) showed a 25 percent recidivism rate over a two-year follow-up period, as compared with 50–60 percent following imprisonment and 35 percent following a suspended sentence. However, the author notes that this was based on a small number of community service orders.

21. Thus, in the United States, some programs involving the use of electronic monitoring were deemed to be highly successful, while others had a success rate of only 50 percent. In Australia, the home detention order led to a success rate of 85 percent.

22. This is noted in, for example, the evaluation literature in the United States and Australia.

23. In a number of legal systems, simplified proceedings can be used where there is no threat of imprisonment involved.

24. See chapter 12. See also Christian Eliaerts, "The Use of Noncustodial Alternatives to Imprisonment: The Point of View of the Court," in *Alternatives to Custodial Sanctions*, Proceedings of the European Seminar, HEUNI publication no. 15, Helsinki 1988, pp. 194–227, at p. 205.

Some noncustodial sanctions are not applied because there is a near total lack of the necessary support infrastructure. For example, in Hungary, work duty has lost much credibility as a sanction along with the increased mobility of the labor force and consequently the decrease in the homogeneity of the work units in which the work duty is to be implemented. See chapter 11. Even the use of voluntary probation officers, as, for example, in Japan, brings in certain costs.

25. Chapters 9 and 15.

26. Bishop, *Noncustodial Alternatives in Europe,* pp. 126–28. Bishop cites statistics from England and Wales, as well as the Netherlands, suggesting such a development in these countries.

27. In responding to the Untied Nations survey, some countries explicitly stated that prison overcrowding was not a factor in their decision to expand the use of noncustodial sanctions. On the other hand, some countries (for example, Canada) note that since their prisons are not overcrowded nor are the costs of imprisonment prohibitive, there is no strong pressure to seek an expansion of noncustodial sanctions.

The USSR has noted that the increased use of noncustodial sanctions has led to a significant decrease in the prison population. As a result, not only is there no need to build new prisons, some two hundred existing prisons could be closed or converted into, for example, institutions for the treatment of alcoholics. Dusan Cotic, "Overpopulation of Prisons, Control of the Penitentiary Population, and the Use of Alternative Measures in Socialist Countries," paper presented at the Messina seminar for heads of European prison administrations, p. 14.

28. *Alternatives to Imprisonment and Measures for the Social Resettlement of Prisoners* (Report of the Secretary-General, A/CONF.121/13), para. 130.

29. In the following, the classification scheme is based on the degree to which the state intervenes in the life of the offender. Clear-cut classifications are impossible, since states use a seemingly limitless variety of measures that may have the same name, while different names may be used for essentially the same measure. It is very difficult to know, for example, whether *probation* is understood in the same way in two countries. The problems become even more complex when such hybrids as *limitation of liberty, controlled liberty,* and *supervised liberty* are considered. In addition, people will undoubtedly disagree on the extent to which any particular measure (such as suspended imprisonment with supervision, community service, or even a fine) intervenes in the life of the offender.

30. This measure is in use in, for example, China, Mexico, and Romania.

31. Electronic monitoring of persons released on bail is a very recent innovation, so far only to be found in a few jurisdictions in the United States. For a discussion of electronic monitoring combined with a noncustodial sanction see below.

32. France has instituted "judicial supervision" with the Act of 17 July 1970. This may be ordered by the examining magistrate when the suspect is liable to imprisonment or a more severe sanction. Among the possible conditions are periodic reports to the police, the posting of bail, disqualification from driving, and disqualification from writing checks. The conditions are strictly enumerated in law. The judicial supervisor may check in on the suspect and also seek to assist him or her. In practice, the reporting element has remained predominant. The Ministry of Justice is now seeking to expand socioeducational judicial supervision, primarily by securing the cooperation of various associations. The measure has been controversial. It has been criticized on the grounds that it violated the principle of the presumption of

innocence, that it contains the embryo of "social supervision," and that it expands the role of the examining magistrate to take in the social reintegration of the offender. However, this criticism has not been considered so serious as to require modification of the legislation.

Austria has instituted a form of supervised release known as "provisional probation" (section 197[a] of the Code of Penal Procedure).

33. Such a possibility exists in China, India, and the Philippines.

34. The report from the Philippines in the regional report for Asia and the Pacific drew particular attention to this drawback. It was noted that 75 percent of all criminal defendants in the Philippines belong to the lower socioeconomic level. The resulting high rate of detention is said to be the major cause of overcrowding in jails. See also the regional report for Latin America and the Caribbean (chapter 16).

35. Binding over is used, for example, in Fiji both during the pretrial stage and following conviction (sections 35 and 36 of the Penal Code, respectively).

36. See chapter 17.

37. Here, of course, it should be noted that considerable differences exist among jurisdictions in the proportional use of imprisonment. For example, Australia reports that one-third of the sanctions imposed are imprisonment, while Indonesia reports that over 80 percent of the offenders convicted by the district courts in 1986 were sentenced to imprisonment.

Some jurisdictions have dramatically lessened the gap between the potential and actual use of noncustodial sanctions. For example, in the USSR the proportion of custodial sanctions out of all sanctions imposed has decreased from 49 percent to 34 percent between 1984 and 1987.

A study in Belgium suggests that very little use was made of the possibilities to impose noncustodial sanctions; of possible cases, only 7 percent received a suspended sentence, 2 percent were put on probation, and 17 percent were subjected to a conditional custodial sentence. According to a later study, 73 percent of short-term prisoners could have been sentenced to a noncustodial sanction instead.

38. See chapter 14.

39. For example, in China the suspended sentence can be supervised both by the police and by so-called mass organizations of the community on a daily basis. A unique statutory sanction is Maatua Whangai in New Zealand, which is based on placement of the offender within the Maori extended family system, thus facilitating the social reintegration of the offender. This sanction was introduced by legislation in 1985. For probation in Japan, see chapter 7.

40. In Sweden, for example, the court has the option of imposing one or two weeks of custody in cases of violation of probation, after which the offender is returned to probation.

41. For example, Nigeria points out that community service as a criminal sanction is known to have existed in some traditional societies.

42. The work can involve, for example, maintenance and repair of social welfare institutions (as in the Netherlands), participation in a state-run project (as in Sri Lanka), or continuation of one's own employment in an enterprise or other entity (as in some socialist countries). In this last case, community service may result, in practice, in a withholding of part of the wages for the duration of the order, and thus it essentially corresponds to a monetary sanction. See chapter 11.

43. This development in Europe was encouraged in part by resolution (76) 10 of the council of Ministers of the Council of Europe. It is currently available in Australia, Canada, the Emirates, the Federal Republic of Germany, Fiji, France, Iraq, Ireland, Israel, Italy, Kiribati, Luxembourg, New Zealand, Northern Ireland, Papua New Guinea, Portugal, Scotland, Sudan, Tunisia, and the United States of America, and in an experimental stage in Denmark, Hong Kong, the Netherlands, Norway, and Sri Lanka. Barbados, Belgium, Cyprus, Finland, Sweden, and Switzerland are presently considering its adoption.

44. This was first introduced in the USSR in 1918. See chapter 11.

45. This option has been reported in, for example, Australia (North Territory, since 1987), Iraq, Thailand, and (combined with electronic tagging) the United States. Experiments with electronic monitoring have been reported from Canada (British Columbia) and the United Kingdom. In addition, sentences in Turkey of up to 60 days may be served at home if the offender is over 65 years old or if he or she is certifiably of ill health.

A variant of home probation is local banishment, where the offender is required to stay within a certain area. This sanction is used, for example, in the Emirates, Qatar, and Algeria. In Tunisia, it is used as a supplementary sanction for certain offenses.

46. This system was first used in Palm Beach County, Florida, in December 1984. According to early 1989 estimates, it is used in thirty-seven states in the United States, with about 7,200 offenders. The failure rate in the programs ranged from almost nil to almost half of the participating offenders. See chapter 15.

47. As noted in the study on home detention orders in Australia (see chapter 8), the involvement of the family in the implementation of the sanction is of crucial importance. A report prepared for the court as a basis for the decision on whether or not such a sanction is to be imposed must reflect the views of the members of the family. Furthermore, the home detention order program is now being implemented in the Aboriginal rural communities as a response to the fact that the majority of the prisoners (70 percent) in the Northern Territories are of Aboriginal descent and generally serve short-term sentences for offenses often related to alcohol abuse.

48. Among the countries where it is used is Sweden, where legislation that entered into force on 1 January 1988 allows the criminal court to order treatment (''civil commitment'') for drug or alcohol abusers where the offender consents to this and there is clear connection between the abuse and the offense in question.

Attendance programs, as the concept is used in Canada, denote programs based on sociological and psychological therapies, life skill training, and counseling. Such programs include those for impaired drivers, assaultive males, sex offenders, and shoplifters. Corresponding programs for impaired drivers, drug addicts, and sex offenders are to be found in the United States. Treatment programs for drug addicts are reported for the Emirates, and various treatment programs are reported for Bahrain and the People's Democratic Republic of Yemen. An impaired-driver program is currently being considered for drunken drivers in the Netherlands.

In most countries, treatment is an administrative matter, subject to the discretion of medical authorities. However, in some countries it is considered a security measure within the framework of criminal law. This is the case, for example, with Yugoslavia (articles 60 and 61 of the Criminal Code).

New Zealand uses a sanction called "community care," which is subject to the consent of the offender. It can include attendance at one or more medical, social, therapeutic, educational, or rehabilitative amenities or certain other types of placement.

The United States has various "community corrections" programs that are based on local, minimum security confinement. The offender lives at the center, where he or she is provided with treatment as needed, but continues to work at his or her usual job, or is helped in finding employment.

49. Here it should be emphasized that these modalities of penal warnings may have significantly different "penal values"; i.e., they are deemed to be of different severity. For example, conditional imprisonment without supervision is deemed a much more severe sanction than an admonition.

50. The public reprimand is used, for example, in Iraq and the USSR. In Tunisia, it is used as a supplementary sanction.

51. The royal commissioner of Belgium has proposed that, when dealing with continuing offenses, the judge may simply issue an injunction to put an end to the irregular situation and postpone the case until a later date, on which the judge may decide the case on the basis of compliance with the injunction. Putting an end to the irregular situation may be more important than imposing a penalty.

52. Commutation into imprisonment is often not an automatic consequence of nonpayment. In most jurisdictions, the judge may take the circumstances of nonpayment into consideration. As pointed out by Switzerland, the commutation of an unpaid fine into imprisonment is not a case of imprisonment for debt, since in this country only deliberate refusals to pay despite solvency can lead to commutation. Thus, the commutation is in effect a sanction for bad faith shown after the conviction of the offender.

Imprisonment for nonpayment of fines is a serious problem in certain countries. In Ireland, for example, 50 percent of all receptions into prison are made up of fine defaulters. Such nonpayment is not a serious problem in countries applying the day-fine method, where the size of the fine in itself is related to the ability of the offender to pay. In Sweden, for example, no fine-defaulters at all were sent to prison from 1984 on, despite the very widespread use of the day fine.

In Scotland, a new program to assist in increasing the effectiveness of the fine has been introduced into sheriff courts after an initial experimental phase. The Fines Officer Scheme is designed to reduce the number of persons going to prison because of inability to pay their fines. Fines officers visit defaulters at their homes to inquire about reasons for nonpayment and to obtain financial information in the light of which fine installments may be adjusted, and they may advise offenders how best to order their financial affairs so that their obligations may be met. The experimental scheme was evaluated by departmental researchers, and on the basis of the findings a national scheme was introduced. The effectiveness of the national scheme is subject to an ongoing review. A. R. Millar, *The Experimental Introduction of Fines Enforcement Officers into Two Sheriff Courts*, Central Research Unit Papers, Scottish Office, 1984.

For other research on fines, see, e.g., P. Softley, *Fines in Magistrates' Courts*, Home Office Research Study no. 46, HMSO, 1978; idem and D. Moxon, *Fine Enforcement: An Evaluation of the Practices of Individual Courts*, Research and Planning Unit Paper no. 12, Home Office, 1982.

Chapter 1

Tak notes that the large number of offenders defaulting on their fines and being sentenced to imprisonment was instrumental in promoting the search for other noncustodial sanctions, such as community service. See chapter 12.

53. The day fine is in use in Austria, Bolivia, Costa Rica, Cuba, the Federal Republic of Germany, Finland, France, Hungary, Iraq, Luxembourg, Peru, Portugal, and Sweden. It has been proposed in a number of other countries.

54. For example, Belgium's circular of 9 April 1984 provides that secondary prison sentences (i.e., imprisonment for unpaid fines) must not exceed three months and, in principle, are not to be enforced except where the person convicted can afford to pay his or her fines and legal costs but shows blatant contempt or is imprisoned on another charge. In March 1987, the minister of justice requested all judicial authorities to suspend the enforcement of all secondary prison sentences; although this order was originally to be in force only for four months, it was still in force in June 1988. The royal commissioner of Belgium has proposed elimination of secondary prison sentences for nonpayment of a fine.

55. In Bulgaria, Italy, and the USSR, for example, nonpayment cannot lead to imprisonment. In the USSR, nonpayment can result in an obligation to repair the damage caused by the original offense, a public reprimand, or (where the default was deliberate) work duty. In the Federal Republic of Germany, nonpayment can lead to community service. In some jurisdictions in Australia, fine-option orders require offenders to complete some community service in lieu of payment of a fine. This is also being considered in England.

56. This is the case in, for example, Australia, Cyprus, and Fiji.

57. Australia, Cyprus, Fiji, Greece, New Zealand, Papua New Guinea, Qatar, Scotland, Sudan, Turkey, the United Kingdom, and the USSR. Compensation orders are also being considered in the Netherlands. Barbados and Canada are currently considering a system of restitution and reparation of victims of crime as independent criminal sanctions. Qatar also applies a second sanction that is relevant here: the provision of a guarantor who would be liable in lieu of the offender for payment of compensation.

58. Matti Joutsen, *The Role of the Victim of Crime in Criminal Justice Systems*, HEUNI publication no. 11, Helsinki, 1987, pp. 235–40; see also pp. 192–96 and 231–35.

An experiment in France involves the use of the probation period for compensating the victims. Sentence is deferred in order to enable the offender to reimburse the victim and for the authorities to check that the reimbursement has taken place. The probation service monitors enforcement. For example, in the court of St. Etienne, a 90 percent level of overall reimbursement was reported in 1987. J.-P. Robert, *Alternative Measures to Imprisonment. Survey of the Present Situation and Prospects*, European Committee on Crime Problems, 23 January 1989, p. 4.

59. However, it has been noted in some countries that restitution programs are ineffective, inefficient, and inequitable. A study in the state of Pennsylvania in the United States, for example, noted that only 34 percent of the restitution ordered in a restitution program was actually collected from the offenders and that, furthermore, the program was inequitable to victims (in comparison with state compensation programs) in that only the apprehended offenders could be ordered to pay. See chapter 14.

60. In Qatar, mediation is used specifically as an alternative to imprisonment. In Fiji, section 160 of the Criminal Procedure Code permits reconciliation in the case of criminal trespass, common assault, assault causing actual bodily injury, and damage to or destruction of property. Furthermore, Fiji recognizes various traditional models of dispute resolution outside of the magistrates courts, such as "soro" or "bulubulu."

61. Adedokun A. Adeyemi, "Personal Reparations in Africa: Nigeria and Gambia" (chapter 3).

62. In some countries, confiscation may also be temporary. By the Act of 10 June 1983, France has empowered its courts, where an act is punishable by imprisonment, to impose as the principal penalty the immobilization for not more than six months of one or more of the vehicles owned by the defendant.

The regional report for Latin America and the Caribbean notes that general confiscation of all of the present and future property of the offender is regarded as unconstitutional. In many countries in this region, special confiscation (of a part of the property of the offender) is not an independent sanction.

63. Chapter 5.

64. Australia, for example, has developed a flexible sanction known as a "community-based order" that combines the elements of probation, community service, and the attendance center program. A somewhat similar sanction, the community supervision order, is under consideration in England. This sanction combines probation and community service, allowing the courts wide additional powers to add other requirements. In Canada, the so-called Daubney Committee has recommended that legislation be enacted to permit the judge to combine the community service order with other sanctions, provided that the judge is satisfied that a discharge, restitution, fine, or simple probation order alone would not achieve the purpose of sentencing. See chapter 13. For an account of developments along these lines in Australia and New Zealand, see chapter 8. For the United States, see chapter 14.

65. For example, in Poland, restriction of personal freedom was introduced in 1969 in order to reduce the rate of imprisonment. In fact, it has replaced fines and suspended sentences. A somewhat similar situation has been noted in Portugal. In England and Wales, there has been extensive research on this phenomenon in connection with community service.

66. This is noted, for example, in the regional report for Latin America and the Caribbean (chapter 16).

67. For example, in Arab countries. See chapter 4.

68. For example, in the Dutch experiments with community service, the Ministry of Justice laid down the requirement that community service should not conflict with the constitutional freedom of religion or political beliefs, or with provisions against forced labor. See chapter 12.

69. Examples on the national level include the work in Australia, Canada, and the United States, and, on the regional level, the Council of Europe.

70. In some jurisdictions, the criteria for assessing the appropriate place of a noncustodial sanction are laid down in law. For example, in Hungary the provisions on community service introduced in 1987 state that one day of community service corresponds to one day in prison. See chapter 11. A study in the Netherlands found

that judges and prosecutors consider 150 hours of community service to correspond to about three months of imprisonment, instead of six months as originally envisaged in the planning of the experiment. See chapter 12.

71. France reports that all courts have access to an adequate number and variety of jobs which are far from fully utilized; this is due, e.g., to court reluctance to use the sanction and to the fact that prosecutors and counsel rarely request it. Even so, its use is spreading. In the Netherlands, work is available, although finding it may be time-consuming for probation officers. Also, Norway notes that no difficulty has been experienced in obtaining suitable jobs, and neither the employers nor trade unions have shown a negative reaction to the sanction. In Hungary, however, the economic situation and the lack of suitable places have severely limited the use of community service.

72. As noted in the case study for Hungary, the newly established community service order may face difficulties in implementation, because the economic crisis and growing unemployment may result in firms being reluctant to provide jobs for those on whom a community service order is imposed. The case study for the Netherlands (chapter 12) notes that the idea of the extensive use of fines was linked to the favorable economic situation. With the advent of the economic recession, there was an increase in the number of offenders defaulting on their fines. However, due to the shortage of places in remand centers, the enforcement of sentences of imprisonment for those defaulting on their fines was restricted, resulting in pressure to find other, suitable noncustodial sanctions.

73. For example, in Portugal, with the adoption of probation and community service, it proved difficult to set up a wholly new probation service. This led to an overburdening of the probation services, which in turn decreased court confidence in these services. Helena Parada Coelho, "The Need for a Wide Understanding of Noncustodial Sanctions Imposed by the Courts," in *Alternatives to Custodial Sanctions*, Proceedings of the European Seminar, HEUNI publication no. 15, pp. 143–64, at pp. 146–47. See also chapter 11 for similar comments regarding Hungary; here the difficulties in introducing a new form of community service were compounded by the defamatory association the "work obligation" had previously carried.

74. Anna Alvazzi del Frate, Maria Luisa Fornara and Andrzey Siemazsko "Research on . . .", volume 2.

75. The development in France regarding community service is interesting in this connection: sentences are becoming more severe with time. This makes the sanction a more attractive option for a sentence. In New Zealand, on the other hand, a 1984 study noted that many judges regard community service as a "soft" option; the study suggested that this may be due to the fact that the judges had very limited knowledge of the placement and what it involved.

Eliaerts reports that judges who are more oriented toward resocialization or reintegration of delinquents will be more favorable to noncustodial sanctions. In contrast to the classical way of thinking, they will spend more time with the defendant, his or her lawyer, and probation services. They attach importance to full—not only juridical—information of the court, as a means for the individualization of the sanction. Research in Belgium shows that judges granting probation will less automatically resort to imprisonment in case of recidivism or violation of probation. More classically oriented judges regard noncustodial sanctions as a favor to occasional delinquents with less serious crimes—a favor that can seldom be granted twice. See Christian Eliaerts, "The Use of Noncustodial Alternatives to Imprisonment: The Point of View of the Court," in *Alternatives to Custodial Sanctions*, HEUNI, Helsinki, 1988. He cites S. Snacken, "L'application de la courte peine de prison en Belgique," *Revue de droit pénal et de criminologie*, 1986, pp. 555–75, at p. 572.

Research on attitudes toward community service has been undertaken, for example, in the Netherlands. According to the results, it was considered real punishment by two-thirds of the prosecutors, judges, probation officers, and offenders interviewed; 85 percent of the places in which community service was carried out had a positive view of the sanction; 90 percent of the prosecutors, judges, and probation officers considered the experiments at least reasonably successful. See Menke, W. Bol, *CSO's in the Netherlands*, Report no. 76, Research and Documentation Centre, Ministry of Justice, 1985; idem and J. J. Oerwater, *Dienstverlening. Eindrapport van het onderzoek naar de vervanging van de vrijheidsstraf in het strafrecht voor volwassen*, Research and Documentation Centre, Report no. 47, Ministry of Justice, 1984; idem, *Recidive van dienstverleners*, Research and Documentation Centre, Report no. 73, Ministry of Justice, 1985.

On public opinion in general, see Jan van Dijk and Philippe Robert, "L'opinion publique relative à la justice pénale," in Council of Europe, *Etudes relatives à la recherche criminologique*, vol. 17, 1979.

76. Michael C. Musheno, Dennis J. Palumbo, Steven Maynard-Moody, and James P. Levine, "Community Corrections as an Organizational Innovation: What Works and Why," *Journal of Research in Crime and Delinquency*, vol. 26, no. 2 (May 1989), pp. 136.-67, at p. 137.

77. "Whereas prison overcrowding is a matter of common knowledge and concern, relatively few people are aware that other sanctions . . . are equally overburdened. Over the past decade, the national prison population [in the United States] increased by 48 percent but the probation population grew by 63 percent" (Joan Peterselia, *Community Supervision: Trends and Critical Issues*, Crime and Delinquency, NCCD, July 1985, p. 339).

78. This point is made in the regional reports for Latin America and the Caribbean and the Arab countries (chapters 16 and 4). Its instrumentality is illustrated by the case of Cuba, where as a result of the new Penal Code of 1988, approximately 85 percent of offenses are punishable by noncustodial sanctions. The response from Cuba notes that during the first year of the application of the new Penal code, some 63 percent of the prison sentences pronounced have been suspended or replaced by noncustodial sanctions.

79. For example, section 11 of the Penalties and Sentences Act 1985 (Vic) promulgated in Victoria, Australia, states that "Where a Magistrates' Court passes a sentence of imprisonment on a person, the Magistrates' Court (a) must state in writing the reasons for its decision; and (b) must cause those reasons to be entered in the records of the court."

80. The elimination of short-term sentences of imprisonment is also often justified on the grounds that short custodial sentences have the negative effects of imprisonment but do not allow time for a reforming effect. Proposals have been

advanced in both Belgium and Switzerland, for example, for the elimination of prison sentences below six months. Such a policy would, however, meet with difficulties in countries where almost all sentences of imprisonment are quite short. For example in Finland, the median sentence is 3.2 months; in the Netherlands, it is 2.0 months.

81. Many countries noted that they have made efforts in their legislative provisions to ensure wider use of one particular sanction, the fine, as an alternative to imprisonment. Austria (section 37 of the Penal Code) and the Federal Republic of Germany (section 49 of the Penal Code) already emphasized the priority of fines over short-term imprisonment. Law 1419/1984 in Greece permits the commutation of every penalty not exceeding eighteen months into a monetary penalty.

82. For example, the Magistrates' Association of the United Kingdom has issued a provisional *Sentencing Guide for Criminal Offences (other than Road Traffic) and Compensation Table* (London, 1989).

83. This was recommended in the report of the Canadian Sentencing Commission (*Sentencing Reform: A Canadian Approach*. Minister of Supply and Services, Canada, 1986, recommendation 12.06). It was also noted in the European regional survey in the responses from the Federal Republic of Germany, Ireland, the Netherlands, and Romania.

84. An example here comes from England, where the Home Office regularly updates its handbook entitled *The Sentence of the Court* (London: HMSO, 1986). Guidelines have also been issued in Norway in connection with the introduction of community service. Belgium is considering the introduction of sentencing guidelines.

85. On the global level, the already mentioned United Nations Standard Minimum Rules for Noncustodial Measures exemplify this interest. Examples also include work done in Australia, Canada, and the United States and, at the regional level, the Council of Europe.

Part I
Africa

2

Alternatives to Imprisonment in Africa: An Overview

Elufemi Odekunle

The situation on alternatives to imprisonment in the African region[1] cannot be appreciated outside the context of the various operative criminal justice systems, and, in turn, the characteristics and problems of these systems cannot be understood without, first and foremost, some knowledge of the historical development of the present-day characteristics of the different types of socioeconomic organization in the region. This contextual prerequisite is particularly important because this report will be presented with reports on other regions of the world that have a relative advantage, in this respect, over the African region. For example, unlike the USA or Japan, which have monolithic criminal justice systems, the African region has at least three subregional, colonially inherited types of criminal justice systems; not to mention the internal or national subcultural differences in some of the countries. Again, while criminal justice policies and programs in other regions of the world have experienced the influence of institutions such as UNAFEI, the Council of Europe, and so on, for approximately two decades, Africa is just now "struggling" to establish such an institute (UNAFRI).

In terms of production, consumption, and associated social relations, the nature and characteristics of most precolonial African societies (state or stateless) manifested decentralization and democratization (e.g., the family, the ward). Generally speaking, the criminal justice systems and administrations had the following overriding features: community participation; emphasis on collective over individual rights and interests; consensual noncustodial and victim-centered sanctions of compensation, reconciliation, restoration, community service, exile or banishment, suicide, and the like of these. Prison and imprisonment were a rarity, if they were used at all.

However, with the Berlin Conference of 1884 and the European partitioning of Africa came the "amalgamation" of different nations into single "nations" and the imposition of British, French, Portuguese, or

Belgian ecosocial organization with (again, in general terms) the relative criminal justice systems and types of administration: criminalization of culturally accepted behaviors; emphasis on individual over collective rights and interests; adversarial and criminal-centered systems; formalization and technicalization of criminal justice administration and procedures; imprisonment and prisons as modal correctional tools; and so forth.

It is important and relevant to point out that the colonial powers promoted the creation of elites, particularly professional elites (e.g., lawyers), whose vested interests ensured the continuation of the essence and characteristics of colonially inherited criminal justice systems and administration.

The Current Situation

With the foregoing in mind, the findings of the most recent African seminar[2] should not come as a surprise to any observant African criminologist.

The following needs were considered to be overdue and urgent in order to usher in a responsive criminal justice system: penal reform and indigenization of the system; alternatives to institutional forms of punishment; reduction of the costs of servicing the system; and popular participation in the administration of justice.

With particular regard to alternatives to institutional forms of punishment, the report noted that even though prisons were an alien model and a form of punishment unknown to most societies of precolonial Africa in dealing with offenders, "there was little evidence to suggest that African countries had seriously considered and devised alternative measures to imprisonment." This also in spite of the fact that the European countries from which the penal laws currently in force in Africa were adopted "had amended their laws to introduce alternative means of dealing with offenders, such as corrective labor, community service, probation, parole, and conditional release."

From these brief excerpts, three preliminary conclusions should be obvious:

1. That despite their claims of acceptance of the rationality and need for such measures at international seminars, workshops, and related fora, most of the countries of the African region are not currently in any position to present recent experiential information on alternatives to imprisonment, because they have not yet enacted the relative enabling legislative measures.
2. That the substantive criminal and procedural laws in force in African countries today still bear the clear mark of their former colonial and neocolonial mentors: the criminal justice systems in these countries are still essentially nineteenth-century British, French, or Portuguese; the colonially inherited processing and sanctioning machinery has remained largely as it was, notwithstanding expedient amendments here and there without the benefits of hind-

sight nor the foresighted advantages derivable from social and scientific inquiry.

3. That the continuation or maintenance of this essentially procedure-dominated and prison-happy philosophy and practice is ironical, since it is in contradiction with the precolonial penal philosophy and practice of most African societies.

The next section of this chapter briefly outlines whatever alternatives to imprisonment do exist in the region and briefly highlights the bright prospects for—and fundamental obstacles to—the legislation and implementation of alternatives to imprisonment in African countries. The concluding section points out what should be the immediate action-oriented policy and research priorities of the African region on matters regarding alternatives to imprisonment.

Alternatives to Imprisonment in Africa

If alternatives to imprisonment are considered as sanctions (penal or otherwise) that exclude imprisonment, then it can be said that, in the region, formal legislation for such alternatives is rare, if it exists at all. Thus, whatever alternatives exist and are used at any one stage of the criminal justice process, they are either "tokens" or "illegalities," notwithstanding the findings of transnational researchers or experts about an alternative measure in a village or ward in any one said African country.

While it is difficult to back up this assertion with collated and published statistics or with the presentation of existing legislations (along with their hundreds of piecemeal amendments), available prisoner-statistics are indicative enough: Both prison admissions and convict populations are increasing considerably; the prison overpopulation rate ranges from about 30 percent to approximately 200 percent. In this respect it is also quite revealing that prison establishments in many of the countries are waxing stronger, with plans for the construction of more and/or "modern" prisons.

Again because of the dearth of collated and published statistics of crime and criminal justice operations, particularly judicial statistics, it is difficult to present, even minimally, precise information on the existing and employed "tokens" and "illegalities." (To highlight the problem of crime and criminal justice data, it is revealing that out of about fifty African countries, only five, twelve, and thirteen, respectively, responded to the 1976, 1982, and 1986 United Nations Surveys of Crime Trends, Operations of Criminal Justice Systems, and Crime Prevention Strategies, and then only with partially completed questionnaires.) Still, with available information, relevant literature, and impressionistic observations of realities, the existing and applied "token" and "illegal" alternatives to imprisonment can be outlined.

Alternatives to pretrial imprisonment include the following: bail (constrained by social/political status and economic means); diversion from the criminal justice system (dictated by bribery, social status, and personal relationships); personal reparation and/or social reconciliation/restoration (condoned, though not provided for, by the law); nolle prosequi (usually motivated by political considerations).

With regard to the trial and sentencing stages, some alternatives to imprisonment exist (by default rather than purposeful design) and are occasionally used; compounding of a variety of noncapital offenses (at the instance of the victim and, if after commencement of trial, with the permission of the trial court); fines (motivated by revenue generation and with imprisonment as the alternative in default); banning from a specified occupation or profession; compulsory labor; caning/corporal punishment; binding over for a specified period, as a sort of unsupervised probation; compensation or restitution (but usually in addition to imprisonment or fine, if at all).

For imprisoned offenders, alternatives to continued detention include the following: earned remission of one-quarter of the prison term (consequent upon good behavior by the prisoner); individual pardon and general amnesty (by the head of state and usually occasioned or determined by political considerations).

The African region constitutes a "nonstarter" in the matter of alternatives to imprisonment. Historically speaking, this situation is ironic and, at the same time, regrettable, for, from among all the regions of the world, it is precisely the African region that has the brightest prospects for the effective and efficient application of these measures:

1. There is an awareness of the patent failure and counterproductivity of imprisonment and prisons (in both developed and developing countries) for the majority of convicted offenders.
2. There are the ever-burdening infrastructural, monetary, and human costs of prisons and imprisonment, which many countries in the region cannot afford in the context of competing development demands on their meager resources.
3. There is the sociocultural disposition, and the research-proven, obvious preference of the majority of the population, for alternatives to imprisonment from which victims of crime could benefit and by which the harm or loss suffered be redressed or remedied.
4. There is the supporting fact that the dominant types of crimes and offenders belong to the category of street crimes and that there is no country in the region whose population of imprisoned dangerous offenders (e.g., murderers, armed robbers, violent rapists, and the like) is more than 10 percent of the total prison population.
5. There is the appreciation and supportive stance of highly placed governmental crime/delinquency prevention and control officials from all over the continent

for meaningful reform, particularly in the area of noninstitutional sanctions for certain categories of offenses and offenders.

6. There is adequate indigenous technical expertise in the region for advice, training, and research in all areas of crime/delinquency prevention and control. In fact, as a result of UNAFRI's "working visits" to about one-quarter of the countries in the region, about sixty well-trained, qualified, and experienced experts have been identified and documented.

With such possibilities, what then has been responsible for the situation under discussion? What are the operative fundamental obstacles?

- A lack of the necessary tradition of allowing social science knowledge and research to guide governmental social policy in this particular field, perhaps because of the colonially inherited law-and-order approach to crime prevention and control.
- The probable unwillingness and/or inertia of the relative authorities to carry out a comprehensive exercise of reexamining (and perhaps overhauling) the inherited system, an exercise without which issues such as alternatives to imprisonment may not come up for legislation.
- The vested interests of the overly Westernized (by training, orientation, and practice) legal profession in the countries of the region.

The foregoing does not in any way suggest that governments in the region have not been considering and making efforts in the required direction. In actual fact, a good number of them have created law reform or review commissions; some others are planning to establish national institutes for crime prevention and control; still others have organized conferences, seminars, and workshops on the problem of prisons and how best to reduce prison overpopulation; almost every single one of them has, at one time or another, sponsored the training of officials at some overseas courses on noncustodial sanctions; and a few have even legislated provisions for probation, community labor, or something similar.

The problem is that the three obstacles highlighted are so fundamental that they adversely affect the prioritization of policy action and the required political will to do what really needs to be done. This is the reason why the suggestions contained in the concluding section of this report may not fall into the modal pattern of the other regional reports presented.

Suggestions for Policy, Action, and Research Priorities toward Legislation and Effective Use of Alternatives to Imprisonment in the African Region

To fully accept the rationale for alternatives to imprisonment, and make the consequent legal provisions for their effective and practical application, cannot be done in isolation or outside the context of the operative system as

Table 2.1 Possibilities of Noncustodial Handling of Offenders

	Institution	Alternatives to institutions
Pretrial (police/prosecutor)	Offense	Decriminalization Depenalization
	Arrest	Diversion programs, informal adjudicatory bodies and community courts, communal dispositions
		Police warning, summons, citation
Jail	Charged	Deferred or suspended prosecution
	Awaiting detention	Bail, release on recognizance, release on supervision, provisional liberty
Sentencing (courts)	Found guilty	Admonition, reprimands, public censure
		Restitution
		Status penalties, disqualification, and deprivation of certain rights
		Economic sanctions and monetary penalities: fine, day fine, confiscation, expropriation, etc.
		Social obligations to the victim (compensation)
		Conditional or absolute discharge or bonds, suspended sentence, conditional sentence, probation, judicial supervision
		Limitation of liberty
		Corrective or supervised labor
		Community attendance centers
		Periodic detention, semiliberty weekend imprisonment
		Special health treatment
Postjudicial (corrections and aftercare services)		Furlough
	Prison	License or recognizance
		Work, educational, and conditional release
		Partly suspended sentence
		Community programs
	Parole	Pardon, amnesty
	Final release	

Source: Adapted from *Sixth United Nations Congress on the Prevention of Crime and the Treatment of Offenders,* A/CONF. 87/7, 9 July 1980, p. 20.

a whole. Rather, for the African region, it must involve a fundamental change in the principles and policies that inform and underpin the continued inherited criminal codes and procedures. One option for such a change is an adaptation of a 1980 United Nations document reproduced as table 2.1.

The approach outlined in table 2.1 would be a more promising and viable alternative to the present situation of piecemeal, token amendments here and there, amendments that are usually substantially and/or procedurally out of context with the existing setup of the various criminal justice systems.

Without this kind of change, the situation will not alter. In fact, this is why, in spite of numerous national and international conferences and seminars on this and related issues (e.g., remedies for victims of crime), there have not been any concrete or observable results in the majority of the countries of the African region. It is also for this reason that the scores and scores of African criminal justice officials who have attended training courses on the matter in Europe and America are unable, on return to their home countries, to put into practice the acquired knowledge, because the enabling provisions either are not there or, if there, are not enabling enough.

In order to implement the required changes, there is need for concrete action on the part of the criminal justice authorities in the region. Perhaps a focused two-day seminar or "summit" for attorneys-general and/or ministers of justice of the various countries of the region may bring about the required concrete action to usher in the required change. The question of differences in cultural and religious traditions, values, and orientations can only be an excuse for inaction, for continuing with the existing inherited system. In the same way that certain common and agreed-upon principles inform United Nations guidelines (e.g., on the treatment of prisoners or on victims of crime), so can certain common and agreed-upon principles inform this much-required fundamental change.

For example, decriminalization (of certain innocuous offenses carried over from colonial times and still punishable in the operative codes); criminalization (of certain emergent development-sabotaging, economic crimes or destructive drug-related offenses); reweighing (of penal sanctions relative to their contemporary social injuries); detechnicalization (of procedures in the administration of criminal justice for a variety of minor or nonserious offenses); victim-centeredness (in line with the region's traditions and in substantial negation of the existing criminal-centered tradition); democratization (of criminal justice administration for a variety of minor offenses, particularly at the grassroots level); promotion of noncustodial sanctions (at both the pretrial and the sentencing stages for nonserious offenders); and so on. The point is that these principles can accommodate a variety of cultural and religious differences existing in the region.

It does not require the expertise of a criminology "guru" or the status of a UN regional crime prevention institute to forecast that, unless the required fundamental change takes place and noncustodial measures are legislated and effectively used in the region, many African countries will not only continue to suffer the avoidable monetary and human burdens of the existing system, but, sooner rather than later, they will definitely also be confronted with spates of serious and destructive prison unrest and riots, as was the case in North America in the 1970s and more recently in a European country.

With regard to research, due to the stage of development of the countries of the African region, this "luxury" should be limited to the field of criminal justice policy and administration. At present, research on alternatives to imprisonment in the region should be action oriented, problem solving, country focused, and experimental, monitoring and evaluative with regard to isolated and scattered efforts being carried out all over the continent in this field. Such types of research should serve to convince "unbelieving and doubting" criminal justice authorities to correct errors of conception and to promote wider acceptance and implementation at the most crucial level (i.e., at the national level).

It is indeed fortunate that UNAFRI has been established and is being operationalized, though of course its long-term effectiveness will depend upon the payment of the assessed financial contributions from the Member States. In addition to the main components of its statutory mandates and the overall objective of its UNDP-funded 1990–1993 program of activities, the institute is required and expected to encourage innovative approaches that draw on African traditional, precolonial values and practices in the area of justice administration and penal sanctioning. It is toward this latter end that UNAFRI intends to pursue the reasoned policy, action, and research priorities outlined in this concluding section.

Notes

1. This report was prepared when the United Nations African Institute for the Prevention of Crime and the Treatment of Offenders (UNAFRI) Secretariat was still in the process of being established; therefore, no field survey was carried out. For this reason, it does not necessarily reflect the position in every (or any particular) African country. Rather, it is a "brief" on the subject by the director of UNAFRI at the instance of UNICRI, whose responsibility it was to cover the African region.

2. Inaugural seminar on "Crime Prevention and Criminal Justice in the Context of Development." Preparatory phase and temporary seating of UNAFRI at the United Nations Economic Commission for Africa, Addis Ababa, Ethiopia, June 1987.

3

Personal Reparations in Africa: Nigeria and Gambia

Adedokun A. Adeyemi

The Need for Alternatives to Imprisonment

In virtually all parts of Africa the phenomenon of prison overcrowding has grown to be a baneful reality and, thus, a source of worry. The reason for worry is the evident inadequacy of imprisonment to cope with the crime problem. Imprisonment has continued to augment, increasing financial burdens on the already deteriorating economies of these countries. Furthermore, in Africa, imprisonment imprints "on the ex-prisoner and his family social stigma, the closure of avenues to employment, rental accommodation, marriage for him and his children, and other forms of social ostracism."[1] Consequently, African countries have been giving serious thought to alternatives to imprisonment, arguing that "the more traditionally accepted measures of restitution, compensation and fines be adopted as the main penal measures in place of imprisonment, particularly as the African cannot appreciate a treatment like imprisonment which, if it benefits at all, is benefitting only the government, in total disregard of the victim and the African need to maintain social equilibrium."[2]

It is, therefore, obvious that in addition to the apparent inefficacy of imprisonment as a deterrent and the increasing financial burden it is imposing on the African countries, there is also a growing resurgence in the African region of its recognition as a culturally aberrant and abhorrent disposition. Hence the compelling need to look for viable alternative measures.

The Range of Alternative Measures

The various African countries, in their efforts to promote alternatives to imprisonment, have adopted several measures designed to reduce the dependency of their penal systems on prisons and imprisonment.

Thus, at the pretrial stage, countries have adopted measures ranging from bail,[3] through warning and diversion from the criminal process,[4] to the compounding procedure,[5] which also involves diversion from the criminal process.

At the trial stage, bail is still a prominent measure for diverting from prison. The compounding procedure is also available up to the time of conviction but before the pronouncement of sentence.[6] Finally, some jurisdictions employ judicial visits to prisons for the review of prisoners on remand, as well as other categories of prisoners.[7] The courts can, furthermore, order the offenders to enter into recognizance, with or without sureties, to keep the peace, and so on.[8]

At the conviction and sentencing stages the courts can employ measures ranging from absolute and conditional discharge (as in Nigeria, Gambia, Sudan, and Ghana), to restitution,[9] fine,[10] compensation (available in, among others, Nigeria, Ghana, Gambia, Kenya, but not in, for example, Cameroon and Burundi), compulsory labor (Tanzania), restriction on the exercise of occupation, amnesty, pardon (Cameroon and Burundi), probation,[11] suspended sentence (Cameroon), and so on.

Personal Reparation: General Considerations

Personal reparation, principally in the form of compensation, has been chosen for study for several reasons. First, because it has always been a prominent feature of the African traditional criminal justice systems. Moreover, the Sixth and Seventh United Nations Congresses on the Prevention of Crime and the Treatment of Offenders enjoined that crime prevention and criminal justice be viewed within the context of the social, economic, cultural, and political systems of member states.[12] Second, because despite the restricted provisions for compensation in some countries (Nigeria, Gambia, Malawi, Tanzania, etc.) or their total absence in the formal criminal procedure in others (i.e., Cameroon and Burundi), the compounding sentiments are widely shared among the African peoples, often leading to wide-scale diversion from the formal, largely Western-oriented, criminal justice system.[13] Third, because there is very little, if any, quantitative information on this matter, nor are there published statistics on it in Africa.

The term *reparation* covers both compensation and damages. Reparation ensures that the offender does not enjoy the fruits of his or her crime; it also provides a form of remedy aimed at restoring, as much as is financially possible, both the offender and the victim to the *status quo ante crimen*.[14] Personal reparation, therefore, refers to both compensation and damages, and it also includes costs. However, for the criminal justice system, these mean mainly costs and compensation, with the former hardly ever used, except in the case of victims of frivolous and vexatious charges—when they are not, in fact, an alternative to imprisonment. Consequently, for purposes of this study, the alternative measure we are concerned with is that of compensation, inasmuch as the term *damages* relates to civil proceedings.

Compensation is, by custom, a measure known to, and accepted in, virtually all African countries in the region.[15] Some countries have abolished the application of unwritten customs in their criminal justice administration (e.g., Nigeria[16] and almost all the francophone countries). Others allow customary law to operate side by side with their written (received) criminal law (e.g., Gambia).[17] For the former countries, specific provisions for compensation have had to be included in the penal codes and the criminal procedure, as is the case with Nigeria.[18] Such provisions are also available in Ghana, Gambia, Kenya, Tanzania,[19] Malawi, among others. Where there are no provisions, as in Cameroon and Burundi, the courts will not countenance compensation as a measure. In those countries where the operation of traditional criminal justice systems has not been altered, as is the case in Gambia, native or customary courts apply this measure as a legal remedy. It must be emphasized that the courts in such countries do not operate outside the criminal justice system and merely within custom; they operate within a system based on custom, in the same way as the courts that operate on the statutory provisions, even though statutory provisions are based on custom.

It therefore becomes clear that the emergence of compensation in Africa was not a result of its being designed as an alternative to imprisonment, inasmuch as it predated imprisonment in the region.[20] Rather, it is simply one of the measures provided for in the respective criminal justice systems. In this sense, compensation is as much an alternative measure to imprisonment as it is to either the death penalty or fines. In some countries—for example, Nigeria—the authorities, at the turn of the century, had to canvass imprisonment as a "desirable" alternative to fines, restitution, and compensation.[21] Courts in Africa have steadily sought to rely more heavily on imprisonment as a penal sanction. Yet some countries sought to introduce alternatives, such as compulsory labor (Tanzania),[22] and restricted exercise of occupation, amnesty, pardon, and so on (Cameroon and Burundi).[23] Noninstitutional measures like fines, probation, and discharge have been specifically introduced as part of a comprehensive penal package in some countries, with those measures being as much alternatives to imprisonment as imprisonment and the death penalty are alternatives to them. In fact, in many instances, fines and imprisonment are used complementarily, not as mutually exclusive.[24] An alternative to imprisonment, *stricto sensu*, should be employed only to the exclusion of imprisonment. It is in this respect that the Gambian and Nigerian courts have really treated compensation as an alternative to imprisonment, because they have hardly ever ordered compensation plus imprisonment. Rather, whenever compensation was combined with another measure, it was always with a fine and/or restitution.[25] This seems to be reminiscent of the idea of compensatory fines.[26] Historically speaking, the Nigerian courts saw fines as the elementary linkage to compensation.[27] Occasionally, however, the Gambian courts, in some exceptional cases of assault causing bodily harm, ordered imprisonment plus compensation, just as they did with caning and compensation. Still, these were cases involving needless and callous brutality on the part of the offender toward a victim who, victimologically speaking, can be regarded as innocent. However, such cases are rare in the sentencing practice of the Gambian courts.

The Legal Framework for Compensation in Africa

As in the case of francophone African countries (such as Burundi and Cameroon), in the Portuguese-speaking countries (Angola and Mozambique) and Somalia (which operates an Italian-based system), compensation is not provided for in their formal criminal justice systems. Similarly, some of the English-speaking countries, like the ten Southern States of Nigeria, have no real provisions for compensation as a sentence that can be regarded as an alternative to imprisonment. Provisions have been made for compensation in two situations. The first relates to cases of stealing or receiving stolen goods, where the evidence is insufficient to support the charge but sufficient to indicate the wrongful transfer of property; the court may order restitution of the property plus damages not exceeding twenty Nairs (approximately U.S. \$2.60).[28] The second concerns cases in which the court does not convict but decides on absolute or conditional discharge, or probation; it may also order the payment of damages (compensation) up to twenty Nairs.[29] The provisions governing these situations[30] came into operation in 1945, the year in which the original compensation provision—in the then Nigerian Criminal Code[31]—was repealed.[32]

On the other hand, quite a number of African countries, particularly the anglophone ones, have specific compensation provisions in their laws. Examples are found in the laws of the eleven Northern States of Nigeria (including the Federal Capital Territory of Abuja)[33] and those of Kenya,[34] Tanzania,[35] Uganda,[36] Gambia,[37] etc. The Northern Nigerian Penal Code provides for compensation to be awardable on conviction for any offense, without limit as to its quantum.[38] However, the Gambian provision is limited as to the amount awardable[39]; whilst the Northern Nigerian provision, for instance, is limited by the requirement that it is awardable only where the court imposes a fine[40]—"an almost total frustration of the good sense of section 78 both in logic and practice. Why should compensation only be available if the offender is fined? . . . there is no reason at all why compensation should only be relevant as a measure in addition to a fine rather than . . . to any other sentence."[41] The Gambian and Tanzanian provisions provide compensation where, in the opinion of the court, compensation is recoverable by civil suit.[42]

It is within these broad frameworks that African countries apply compensation in their sentencing practices within their formal criminal justice systems. However, there is some indication that those magistrates trained in Western jurisprudence have not applied these provisions satisfactorily. The situation has been complicated further by the confusion in some of the provisions, as is the case in Northern Nigeria,[43] or by the unnecessary limitation of compensation only to cases in which a fine is imposed (e.g., Northern Nigeria,[44] Kenya[45]).

Judicial Use of Compensation: Case Studies

Considerable difficulties were encountered in data collection. For a start, judicial statistics are extremely hard to come by in many African countries. Even in countries in which they are available, they are seldom published. Furthermore, unpublished statistics rarely contain data on compensation. This is due in part to the fact that compensation is, in practice, always ordered in combination with another measure, like restitution, a fine, or, in rare cases, imprisonment and corporal punishment. Moreover, the lack of reliable statistics on compensation is also due to its enormous dark figure, which, in turn, derives from the fact that both the formal and the informal criminal justice systems of a number of African countries provide for compounding procedures. The parties can compound an offense outside the formal system, in which case it will never be reported or recorded in judicial statistics. A reported offense can be compounded at any stage up to the conclusion of the trial, but before conviction and sentence, except that, once trial has commenced in the court, the offense can be compounded only with the authorization of the trial court.[46] The magnitude of the dark figure will be appreciated the more when one realizes the range of the offenses compoundable by law, namely, causing hurt, assault and use of criminal force, mischief resulting in injury, loss or damage to a private person, criminal trespass, house trespass, criminal breach of contract of service, adultery (including one resulting in pregnancy), enticing or taking away or detaining with a criminal intent a married woman, defamation, criminal intimidation, insult intended to provoke a breach of the peace, grievous hurt, hurt by act endangering life or safety or by a dangerous weapon, unlawful detention, burglary and housebreaking, and so on.[47] Outside the ambit of legal provisions, abundant evidence has been found in the various countries that homicide, rape, and defilement are also being compounded. Kenyatta for the Kikuyu,[48] Roscoe for the Baganda,[49] Haydon for the Buganda,[50] Clifford for Zambia,[51] and so forth, and, more recently, Adeyemi for Nigeria,[52] have reported on sentiments regarding this practice.

The present research discovered that an overwhelming number of cases are settled by the parties through the compounding procedure and are never brought to the attention of the authorities. In other words, these cases are diverted from the criminal process: approximately 20 percent of unintentional homicide, 60 percent of theft (these cases also involve restitution), 40 percent of rape and defilement, 67 percent of assaults, and so forth. In 1988, 72 percent of adultery cases in Nigeria (North and South) were settled by the compounding procedure without the invocation of the criminal process.

However, when judicial compounding was examined, the situation drastically changed. The total number of cases compounded in the courts in Nigeria oscillated between 8 percent[53] and 12 percent.[54] Of course, the compounding settlements always involved the payment of costs and other expenses, as well as compensation, in addition to restitution in appropriate circumstances.

Comparative Judicial Use of Compensation in Nigeria

An analysis of the available national data on the judicial sentencing practices in Nigeria over the last thirty years (1959–1988) shows the application of the various penal measures, as follows:

1.	Death penalty	0.43%
2.	Imprisonment	44.76%
3.	Fine	46.83%
4.	Corporal punishment	2.21%
5.	Binding over	5.86%
6.	Probation	nil
7.	Restitution	nil
8.	Compensation	nil

Investigation into the "nil" returns for probation, restitution, and compensation confirmed "nil" return for probation; but for restitution and compensation it was discovered that restitution had been ordered largely in addition to fines and imprisonment. Compensation, instead, was given largely in addition to restitution and fines. Further investigation, thereafter, revealed the use of compensation by the magistrate courts (in the Northern States) in over 20 percent of the cases. The Northern States area courts (Kano, Kaduna, Sokoto, Borno, and Bauch) use it in about 40 percent of the cases in combination with restitution (over 25 percent) and fines (over 70 percent). Altogether, five thousand cases decided in 1988 were sampled, and five hundred cases were further subsampled to enable a more complete study of compensation in combination with fines and restitution. These five hundred cases were taken from the courts' record books. The original five thousand cases were derived from the courts' monthly returns.

Comparative Judicial Use of Compensation in Gambia

Due to the lack of judicial statistics, the study had to rely on the monthly returns from the magistrate courts obtained from the Office of the Master of the Supreme Court, and those from the district courts obtained from the commissioner's office in Banjul. Five hundred cases were studied from the magistrate courts' 1988 returns, and five hundred from the district courts' returns for the same year.

The analyses of the data from the sampled cases revealed the following:

MAGISTRATES COURTS (1988)[55]

1.	Imprisonment	31.0%
2.	Fine	46.5%
3.	Corporal punishment	1.2%
4.	Binding over	4.3%
5.	Probation	nil
6.	Restitution	22.0%
7.	Compensation	5.0%

DISTRICT COURTS (1988)[56]

1.	Imprisonment	nil
2.	Fine	67.0%
3.	Corporal punishment	nil
4.	Binding over	nil
5.	Probation	nil
6.	Restitution	47.0%
7.	Compensation	45.0%

In both countries, the amount of compensation awarded has been relatively modest. In Nigeria, this is due to the fact that compensation can be awarded only when a fine is ordered, that is to say, compensation is awardable only in addition to a fine. In Gambia, it is limited, instead, to a maximum of £100. In terms of offenses, it was mainly applied for stealing, assault, adultery, abduction, occasioning bodily harm, willful damage to property, receiving stolen property, and other compoundable offenses listed earlier.

Both Gambia and Nigeria enforce compensation in a similar manner to fines, particularly in terms of imposing imprisonment in default of payment of compensation. In general it would appear that courts consider failure to pay compensation more aggravating than failure to pay a fine. For instance, the proportionate imprisonment term to be served in default of payment of compensation was usually proportionately higher than the term to be served for nonpayment of fine, pro rata. Table 3.1 illustrates this point.

Another phenomenon encountered was that while the amount of

Table 3.1

No.	Type of order	Amount of currency units	Term of imprisonment ordered in default of payment
1(a)	fine	500	9 months
(b)	compensation	150	3 months
2(a)	fine	350	6 months
(b)	compensation	150	6 months
3(a)	fine	500	12 months
(b)	compensation	200	12 months

Table 3.2

	Offense	Amount of compensation in currency units	Term of imprisonment ordered in default of payment
1.	Assault occasioning bodily harm	500	6 months
2.	Assaulting police officer	500	24 months

compensation ordered by the court appeared to be based on the "market value" of the need for the compensation, the term of imprisonment for default appeared to rest on the nature of the offense. The sentences listed in table 3.2 illustrate this point.

Perspectives and Prospects of Compensation in Africa

As observed earlier, the existing compensation provisions in Africa have not been institutionally resolved for effective application by the courts. A traditionally "compensatory continent" has now adopted provisions that are not totally supported by the institutions. For instance, the Western criminal justice systems received in virtually all sub-Saharan African countries operate on the underlying assumption that a crime is a dispute between the state and the criminal rather than between the criminal, on the one hand, and the state and the victim, on the other. Hence, the penal systems in most African countries have operated mainly on the theoretical assumptions of deterrence, reformation, elimination, and incapacitation.[57] With the exception of the few instances of compounding[58] and amicable settlements,[59] conciliation, restitution, and compensation were hardly compatible with the tenets of the "received" Western philosophy.[60] Hence the marked differences in the degrees of acceptability and utilization of compensation by both the Western type of courts and the native courts. The latter utilize compensation three times as much as the former do. But then, the jurisdiction of the native courts in criminal cases is severely limited. The paradoxical situation African criminal justice systems have been facing is the relatively low number of cases in which compensation is judicially ordered, in a cultural environment that regards compensation as an integral part of its dispute settlement mechanism.[61] This has been amply confirmed by the extent of public utilization of the pretrial compounding procedure and, indeed, by its utilization during the trial process. The multiple contributory factors to the observed paradox range from grudging or confusing legislation,[62] through the inadequate philosophical base of the "received" criminal justice system[63] and the Westernized training of the personnel of the formal "received" criminal justice system, to the severe limitations imposed upon the jurisdictions of the customary or native courts when trying criminal cases.[64] Some of the native courts in certain countries are compelled by law to apply only the provisions of the Western-originating penal codes.[65] If these institutional problems can be removed, it will be possible for the African courts, backed by the sentiments of age-long tradition in this regard, to apply compensation more freely and frequently than they are doing at present.

These problems, and their resultant practices, have become most unacceptable in certain African countries, on the ground that Africans can no longer afford to run criminal justice systems that have very few provisions for victim remedy. Consequently, steps are being taken to ensure that the criminal justice system is fundamentally overhauled to ensure a balanced system, whereby the courts will be obliged to take into full consideration the interests of the victim, those of the society, and those of the offender, with a view to maintaining social cohesion. Nigeria is, for example, currently preparing comprehensive legislation on victim remedy, which will embrace the conceptual need to reconcile the parties, the need to ensure restitution of wrongfully acquired property, and the need to compensate a victim for the loss, injury, or damage that she or he may have suffered in consequence of the offense.[66]

The Nigerian exercise is based on the realization that the Westernized approach of deterrence, incapacitation, elimination, and rehabilitation leads to unnecessary reliance on imprisonment. When it is realized that people who are sent to terms of imprisonment in default of payment of fines can be as much as 16 percent of the total prison population, then the excessive reliance of African courts upon imprisonment becomes evident. Furthermore, such increasing use of imprisonment at the sentencing stage, coupled with greater readiness to use it for offenders on remand, led to an increase in prison overcrowding. For a number of years now, African countries have been experiencing overcrowding rates ranging from 20 or 25 percent to over 60 percent.[67] Hence the need to break away from the prison-centered philosophy and to explore the traditionally more meaningful compensation and conciliation system. It is to this end that the draft legislation in, for example, Nigeria insists upon the enforcement of fines and compensation as damage in civil cases, that is, by writs of attachment and sequestration, rather than by continuing the present practice of imprisonment in default of payment of fines or compensation.

It is apparent that the compensation provisions and practices, as they stand today in Africa, are grossly inadequate. It is necessary to renovate the structures for amicable settlement of disputes and the compounding procedure. Further, it is necessary to enact full-scale provisions on compensation, which will take into account the need to satisfy the victim of the injury, the loss or damage he or she suffered in consequence of the offense, as well as the means of the offender and the interests of the society. Compensation should be applied in combination with, or in substitution for, any other sanction. However, doubts have been raised in some jurisdictions as to whether it is desirable to combine compensation with fines, in view of the poor financial situation of the citizens at large in Africa.[68] Accordingly, suggestions have been made for payment of compensation in installments[69] as well as for the need for a state compensation scheme, which should be funded through state earnings from fines, confiscations, and forfeitures ordered by criminal courts.[70] These are meant to enable payment of compensation to deserving victims, despite the overwhelming poverty in Africa. It is felt that the state should not be called upon to bear the cost of defraying compensation from its own meager resources. Furthermore, it is suggested that an impecunious offender, for whom the state has to pay, should be made either to pay back the state in installments or, as determined by the court, to carry out community service for a commensurate period. Under no circumstances should imprisonment be applied as an alternative for failure to pay compensation. It is believed that the creation and implementation of such a compensatory system would greatly contribute to the reduction of the prison population.

Lastly, it is pertinent to observe that this study has revealed the appalling situation regarding criminal justice data in general and, in particular, judicial statistics, which are lacking in most African countries. This makes the implementation of the resolutions on the development of criminal justice information and statistical systems[71] ever more compelling.

Notes

1. Second Seminar for Heads of Penitentiary Administration in African Countries, Report, Harare, Zimbabwe, 29 February–5 March 1988 (hereinafter referred to as "The Harare Report"), p. 2.

2. Ibid., p. 2.

3. The system of bail is available in practically all African countries.

4. This system is usually available to the police and is known as "police caution." The police are empowered to use it in trivial cases and for traffic violations. Also, the police are now known to employ the system in cases of domestic crimes (including assaults), and where the complainant has indicated a desire that the case should not be taken to court.

5. This procedure is contained in the criminal procedure of various African countries (Nigeria and Sudan, among others). In it, the victim and the offender agree on an amount to be paid in compensation; the acceptance of such payment precludes further right to invoke the criminal process.

6. See, for example, 1963 Laws of Northern Nigeria, Northern Nigerian Criminal Procedure Code, chap. 30, section 339.

7. Nigeria now employs this procedure of review of remand cases in loco (that is, the proceedings are actually conducted in prison by the state's chief judge), and prisoners remanded for such offenses as wandering, affray, and other trivial offenses are usually released. In addition, prisoners who have been remanded for six months or more, for minor offenses, are usually considered for release. Such is also the case with prisoners in poor health, debtor prisoners, etc.

8. See, for example, the provisions of criminal procedure in Nigeria, Gambia, Sudan, Ghana, Kenya, Tanzania, Uganda, Zambia, and Malawi.

9. Applied in most African countries.

10. A fine is the most frequently employed measure in Africa.

11. Probation is available in virtually all jurisdictions, although in some countries (e.g., Nigeria) it is usually not applied to adult offenders.

12. United Nations, "Caracas Declaration," *Sixth United Nations Congress on the Prevention of Crime and the Treatment of Offenders* (A/CONF.87/14/Rev. 1), 1980, para. 2; "Milan Plan of Action," *Seventh United Nations Congress on the Prevention of Crime and the Treatment of Offenders,* (A/CONF.121/22/Rev. 1), 1985, para. 4.

13. The author has found these sentiments to be present in Nigeria, Senegal, Gambia, Zimbabwe, Kenya, and even Ethiopia. See also T. O. Elias, "Traditional Forms of Public Participation in Social Defence," *International Review of Criminal Policy,* no. 27 (1969), p. 20. See also the earlier report by Schapera, *Handbook of Tswana Law and Custom,* p. 259, where he reported that Tswana awards most, if not all, the fine "as compensation to the victim." Both reports are indicative of the widespread sentiments regarding the settling of matters through payment of compensation, whether these go to court or not.

14. See "Report of the Commission on the Review of Administration of Criminal Justice in Ogun State," Nigeria, June 1981, in particular paragraph 3:11.3.1, p. 43.

15. See A. A. Adeyemi, "Criminology in Contemporary Africa," *Nigerian Journal of Criminology*, vol. 2, no. 1, pp. 1–29.

16. Constitution of the Federal Republic of Nigeria, 1989, section 35(11).

17. Constitution of the Republic of Gambia, 1970, section 20, does not contain the sort of exclusionary provision contained in section 35(11) of the Nigerian Constitution and, therefore, does not exclude the unwritten customary law of Gambia.

18. The Southern Nigerian provisions, which are contained in 255–61 and 435(2) of the Criminal Procedure Act, chap. 43 of the 1958 Law of the Federation, are not applicable when sentences are imposed. The Northern Nigerian provisions, which are sentencing measures proper, are contained in section 365 of the Criminal Procedure Code, chap. 30 of the 1963 Laws of Northern Nigeria, and section 78 of the Penal Code, chap. 89 of the 1963 Law of Northern Nigeria.

19. Tanzanian Criminal Procedure Code, section 176.

20. James S. Read, "Kenya, Tanzania and Uganda," in A. Milner, ed. *African Penal Systems* (London: Routledge and Keegan Paul, 1969), chap. 4, p. 103 William Clifford, "Zambia," chap. 9, pp. 241–242.

21. Lord Lugard, *Political Memoranda, 1913–1918*, Memo 3, para. 23; Memo 8, para. 54.

22. Section 87 of the Tanganyika Prisons Ordinance, 1933.

23. Cameroon Penal Code, 1975, sections 36, 73, 66, etc.

24. For example, Northern Nigerian Criminal Procedure Code, chap. 30, section 365. But see the strictures of the East African Courts on the operation of similar provisions in cases like *Mehar Singh v. R* (1951) 6 U.L.R. 265; and *Ahamed Mohamoud v. R* (1959) E.A. 1087.

25. In fact, the Northern Nigerian courts have ruled that the imposition of a fine is a precondition to an order of compensation. See *Jahilei and Anor v. Zaria N.A.* (1963) N.N.L.R. 82.

26. For example, Criminal Procedure Code, Laws of Zambia, chap. 7, section 164; Criminal Procedure Code, Laws of Kenya, chap. 75, section 175; and the Nigerian Native Courts Ordinance of 1933, section 17—see now the Anambra and Imo States Customary Courts Law (No. 2), 1966, section 30, etc.

27. See the reaction of the Nigerian native courts, which, in reaction to Lord Lugard's advice to his advisers that native courts should always add "punishment" to their orders of restitution, etc., reacted by imposing fines. See A. A. Adeyemi, "Criminology," p. 21.

28. Section 261 of the Northern Nigerian Criminal Procedure Act, chap. 43.

29. Section 435(1) of the Northern Nigerian Criminal Procedure Act, chap. 43.

30. Sections 261 and 435(1) of the Northern Nigerian Criminal Procedure Act, chap. 43.

31. Criminal Code, chap. 21 of the 1923 Laws of Nigeria, section 18(13).

32. Section 3 of the Criminal Code (Amendment) Act, 1945.

33. See section 78 of the Northern Nigerian Penal Code, chap. 89, and section 365 of the Northern Nigerian Criminal Procedure Code, chap. 30.

34. The Nigerian Section 78, ibid., was, in fact, borrowed back from the Kenyan provision (Criminal Procedure Code, section 176), which had originally borrowed from the repealed section 18(13) of the Northern Nigerian Criminal Code.

35. Northern Nigerian Criminal Procedure Code, section 134.
36. Northern Nigerian Criminal Procedure Code, section 177.
37. Criminal Procedure Code, chap. 39 of the 1965 Laws of Gambia, section 145.
38. Ibid., chap. 89, section 78. Compare the Kenyan provision. The Northern Nigerian provision was, however, later limited to the quantum of the amount the court can award in civil cases.
39. Section 145(1)—the limit is a maximum of £100, and the compensation is for the material loss or personal injury suffered as a consequence of the offense. Compare this provision with that in section 176 of the Tanzanian Criminal Procedure Code in this regard.
40. Section 365 of chap. 30, ibid.
41. J. Read, "Kenya, Tanzania, and Uganda," in A. Milner, ed., *The African*, p. 120.
42. Gambian Criminal Procedure Code, section 145(1); Tanzanian Criminal Procedure Code, section 176.
43. See provisions in section 78 of chap. 89, and section 365 of chap. 30.
44. Section 365 of chap. 30.
45. Section 175 of the Criminal Procedure Code.
46. See, for example, section 339 of the Nigerian Criminal Procedure Code, chap. 30.
47. See Appendix C of the Northern Nigerian Criminal Procedure Code, chap. 30, with additions from Gambia.
48. J. Kenyatta, *Facing Mount Kenya*, 1938, chap. 9.
49. Roscoe, *The Baganda*, 1911, p. 264.
50. Haydon, *Law and Justice in Buganda*, 1960, p. 296.
51. W. Clifford, "Zambia," in Milner, *African Penal Systems*, pp. 241–42.
52. A. Adeyemi, *Towards Victim Remedy in Criminal Justice Administration in Nigeria*, 1989.
53. See Milner, *African Penal Systems*, tables 7 and 8 (1962–1963 period), pp. 280 and 281.
54. The author's study for 1988 revealed this for all the courts in the five Northern States considered, namely, Sokoto, Kaduna, Kano, Bornu, and Bauchi.
55. Both restitution and compensation were either combined with each other and/or with fine, or with imprisonment. Hence the fact that each reflects respectively high percentages individually.
56. Restitution and compensation were combined with each other and/or with fine.
57. See Read, "Kenya," pp. 114, 154.
58. See, for example, Northern Nigerian Criminal Procedure Code, section 339, chap. 30.
59. See, for example, the old Eastern Nigerian Customary Courts (No. 2) Law, 1966, section 30.
60. Adeyemi, *Towards Victim Remedy.*
61. A. Milner, "Sentencing Patterns in Nigeria," in Milner, *African Penal Systems*, p. 269.
62. The various provisions like the Southern Nigerian provisions—sections 261

and 435(1) of chap. 43, and those of Northern Nigeria, Gambia, Tanzania, Kenya, Uganda, etc.

63. Read, "Kenya," *African Penal Systems*, pp. 114, 154.

64. See, for example, the provisions of the Ogun State of Nigeria's Customary Courts Law, No. 53, 1980.

65. Recall the implications of section 35(11) of the Nigerian Constitution, 1989. All customary/area court laws in Nigeria enjoin those courts to apply the penal codes.

66. Adeyemi, *Towards Victim Remedy*.

67. The issue of prison overcrowding in African countries was extensively dealt with at the Regional Seminar. See n. 1.

68. Adeyemi, *Towards Victim Remedy*.

69. Ibid.

70. These points are contained in the communique adopted by the National Conference on Criminal Justice: Restitution, Compensation and Remedies for Victims of Crimes, held in Abuja, Nigeria, 28–30 June 1989.

71. United Nations, Sixth United Nations Congress, Resolution 2, "Development of Crime and Justice Statistics"; Seventh United Nations Congress, Resolution 9, "Development of Crime and Criminal Justice Information and Statistical Systems."

Part II
Arab Countries

4

Alternatives to Imprisonment in Arab Countries

Ridha Mezghani

This chapter presents the findings of a survey on alternatives to imprisonment conducted by the Arab Security Studies and Training Center in a number of Arab countries.[1] The examination of responses to the questionnaire and provisions of penal codes in Arab countries reveals that imprisonment is still—as in many countries of the world—given precedence over other sanctions. Capital punishment is also provided for as a major sanction in almost all Arab penal systems, but it is only applied as a last resort for more serious crimes. Fines are usually applied as a supplementary sanction to imprisonment, but in some cases, such as minor offenses or acts of a financial nature of limited impact (e.g., tax evasion), they may stand alone.

In addition to the three major sanctions, there are some supplementary ones. These usually are: deprivation from certain rights, removal of professional status, dismissal from public office, closing of public stores, probation, or confiscation (Kuwait, Bahrain, Algeria, and Tunisia). Another sanction of a similar nature is deportation, which is characteristic, mainly, of the Arab Gulf states, due to the presence of a large expatriate labor force. Some Arab countries (Algeria and Tunisia) apply other supplementary sanctions, such as publicizing the verdict in order to expose the offender to public shame, especially for economic crimes.

It is worth mentioning that juveniles (up to a certain age) are generally subject to certain measures, and penal sanctions are not applied. These measures include, for example, castigation (Kuwait, the Emirates, etc.) or handing them over to their parents (Algeria and Tunisia). Though such measures can be considered as alternatives to imprisonment, in a wider sense they are usually associated either with incarceration or with fines for less serious offenses. Therefore, despite a noted trend toward their relative expansion, the application of alternatives in Arab countries is still limited.

Chapter 4

Expansion Trends in the Use of Noncustodial Sanctions

Information on the orientation of present criminal policies in Arab countries toward expansion in the application of noncustodial sanctions and reduction in the use of imprisonment indicates that there is, indeed, a general trend toward such an expansion, especially with respect to minor offenses (Iraq, Democratic Republic of Yemen, and Algeria). This trend is particularly evident in sanctions for misdemeanors and violations of financial laws, including those related to customs, taxes, and money exchange. However, this trend is mainly theoretical. Noncustodial sanctions are included only in the draft bills and are not provided for in the laws in force (Iraq). The officials who provided information were probably led by philosophical considerations; they expressed their support of the alternatives but did not mention whether they are actually applied in the legal systems (Kuwait, Bahrain, and Qatar), except for certain forms of alternatives, such as security measures (the Emirates) and suspended sentence and conditional release (Tunisia and Egypt). In short, the trend toward expansion in the application of alternatives to imprisonment is evident in the criminal policy orientation in a number of Arab countries, but it has not yet been legislated. Imprisonment still dominates the penal systems of these countries.

Although complete statistics are not available, such dominance is evidenced in data provided by some Arab countries. For example, data for 1987 from the Ministry of Social Affairs and Labor in Kuwait show that imprisonment is still the main sanction and, in terms of frequency of application, fines rank next. Statistics provided by the Ministry of the Interior of Qatar, Department of Prison Police, on sentenced offenders in 1982, 1984, and 1986 reveal that imprisonment is much more widely used than noncustodial sanctions. The total number of prison sentences during the above-mentioned period is 689, whereas the total number of noncustodial sentences is 32 (less than 5 percent).

Responses to the question on whether there have been any changes in the use of noncustodial sentences since 1980 indicated that no change has taken place in Qatar, Yemen, Algeria, and Iraq. On the other hand, Kuwait, the Emirates, Bahrain, and Tunisia reported new noncustodial sanctions. Sudan was the only country that reported the removal of noncustodial sanctions that existed before 1980.

Kuwait, Qatar, Bahrain, and Yemen reported, without giving explanations, that there are no current discussions or plans to extend or limit the use of noncustodial sanctions. Other countries expressed a trend to extend the use of alternatives and introduce new ones. Iraq indicated that its penal code provides for reconciliation and pardon by the victim in the case of offenses of minor criminal significance.

All these responses, though inaccurate, reflect a general trend to expand the application of alternatives. Yet, as noted before, this trend is only favored in theory, since it is not accompanied by concrete steps.

Reasons for the Use of Noncustodial Sentences in Arab Countries

Avoidance of Negative Effects of Being in Prison

There is consensus in Arab countries about the negative effects of imprisonment and, consequently, on the need to apply other sanctions to reform offenders. However, consensus is based more on philosophical considerations than on the sentencing process in practice. In spite of its negative effects, imprisonment is still the dominant form of punishment.

Assistance in Meeting the Needs of the Offender, the Family, and Society

Although not elaborated, the goal of helping to meet the needs of the offender, the family, and the society implicitly indicates the importance of the individualization of punishment, according to which the judge takes into consideration the personal and family circumstances of the offender, on the one hand, and the protection of the community, on the other.

Avoidance of Removing the Offender From Society

The desire to avoid removing the offender from society indicates an overall acceptance of the criticism against the isolating function of imprisonment. Instead of reintegrating the offender, it removes him from society. It is believed that alternatives can avoid such a negative effect and at the same time reform the offender.

The Application of Alternatives Does Not Result in a General Increase in Crime

The view that using alternatives does not result in an increase in crime was mentioned in responses from most Arab countries. The short history of alternative sanctions does not allow for clear evidence of their impact on crime rates. The Emirates, for example, indicated that no specific studies have been conducted on this matter.

Reduction of Prison Population

Two main factors are identified regarding reduction of the prison population. The first regards the restricted use of prison—only as a last resort. The second concerns the effects of reducing the prison population, thus enabling the application of adequate correctional programs that cannot be carried out in a densely populated prison. Some experts call for the application of "Malthus theory" on prisons.

Economic Reasons

The economic cost factor is given significant consideration in the promotion and selection of alternatives. Many Arab countries may find too expensive the application of new alternative sanctions, in particular those requiring sophisticated methods, techniques, and structures and highly specialized personnel. Yet, other alternatives may reduce the financial burden resulting from prison building and maintenance costs.

Noncustodial Sanctions in Arab Countries

Alternatives applied in Arab countries fall into the following categories.

Liberty-restrictive Alternatives

Conditional or Suspended Sentence with Supervision. Generally speaking, all Arab countries either apply this disposition for all crimes, or restrict it to felonies (the Emirates) or to offenders with no prior criminal record, provided the minimum term for the committed felony is less than two years' imprisonment (Tunisia). The suspension period ranges from three years (Qatar) to five years (Tunisia). In Arab penal systems, completion of the suspension period is considered as if the sentence had not been originally imposed at all—unlike some other jurisdictions, which consider the sentence term had been served. The trend in Arab countries appears to consist in avoiding imprisonment of first-time offenders and of those with the likelihood of good-conduct performance.

Conviction but Sentence Deferred for a Specified Period. The measure of conviction with a deferred sentence, which is also called "suspension of announcing the sentence," is applied in some Arab countries (Kuwait and Sudan), while it is restricted to juveniles in the Emirates, Tunisia, and Iraq.

Probation. In some countries, probation is applied only after the sentence has been announced and is usually associated with suspended sentence; in others it is associated with the deference of sentence for a specified period (Sudan and Kuwait). Costs involved have confined this measure to juveniles only (the Emirates, Tunisia, and Iraq).

Local Banishment. Local banishment is provided for in the general law and in special acts on drug abuse, in the Emirates. Tunisia applies it as a supplementary sanction for certain crimes. Qatar and Algeria indicated that they also apply local banishment, but they did not provide detailed information.

Deprivation of Certain Rights

Restriction of the Right to Travel and Residence Right. There is an increasing tendency in Arab countries to use restriction of the right to travel, which involves the withdrawal of passport. This measure is taken against persons who are suspected of behaving in a way that may mar the image of the country if they are allowed to travel abroad. Thus, they are compelled to live in their home states. Limitation of freedom of movement may also take the form of forbidding alcohol and drug addicts from entering certain places (the Emirates). Deportation is also applied either as an independent punitive measure or as a supplementary sanction against non-native residents.

Suspension of Driving License or Other Licenses. The suspension of licenses is also applied in all Arab countries, particularly in cases of traffic violations and the violation of firearms regulations. In the first case, the withdrawal of license is for a specific period, depending on the degree of seriousness of the violation. The withdrawal of license can be an independent or a supplementary sanction. In the second case, the license for carrying firearms, without which the offense could not have occurred, is withdrawn when it appears that its holder has misused it.

Removal of Professional Status. The removal of professional status (e.g., the disbarring of a lawyer) is usually applied either to supplement a penal sanction or as an independent punishment, depending on the degree of seriousness of the offense (Tunisia). It is also associated with offenses that involve abuse of profession (such as embezzlement by a cashier or moral offenses committed by persons who have been assigned to supervise others). Interdiction of occupation, in this case, is imperative to prevent the offender from committing the same offense again.

Moral and Community-based Alternatives

Reprimand and Warning. Kuwait, Qatar, and Algeria have indicated the use of reprimand and warning. The Emirates and Tunisia limit it to juveniles, particularly in respect to minor offenses.

Public Shaming or Admonition. Two countries (Sudan and Algeria) indicated that they apply the measure of public shaming or admonition, but they did not give details on the specific manner of application. The Emirates apply it as an alternative to imprisonment in the case of juveniles and for drug crimes. In Tunisia, it takes the form of announcing the verdict and is considered a supplementary sanction.

Finding of Guilt But No Sentence Imposed

Kuwait, the Emirates, Sudan, and Tunisia apply the measure of finding of guilt but no imposition of sentence to juveniles only, while Qatar, Bahrain, Iraq, Yemen, and Algeria do not apply it at all. This measure is applied in almost all Arab countries (except Qatar, Bahrain, and Yemen), provided that no other crime is committed over a determined subsequent period of time.

Treatment in a Community Program

Treatment in a community program is applied in the Emirates as an alternative to imprisonment for drug addiction. In Bahrain, treatment in a therapeutic institution is restricted to certain crimes. Democratic Yemen also reported the presence of such a measure. In Tunisia and Algeria, the application of this measure is limited to juveniles. The limited application of this measure in Arab countries is due to the relatively low convictions for drug abuse, on the one hand, and the high costs it involves, on the other.

Community Service

Community service takes the form of compulsory labor in three countries (the Emirates, Sudan, and Tunisia), but only for minor offenses and under certain conditions, in the Emirates, and in the form of correctional labor, in Tunisia. The low attention given to this measure can be attributed to the slow pace in developing the penal system in Arab countries. Traditional punishment is still given precedence over correction, which is primarily geared toward the common well-being and the compensation of damage.

Alternatives of a Financial or Physical Nature

Fines. Fines are applied as an alternative to imprisonment in almost all Arab countries. The reason for this is that costs of application are low, and, besides, fines provide the state treasury with financial resources. It is noted, however, that Arab countries apply fines without regard to the financial status of the offender. As a consequence, fines may deter the impecunious but not the well-to-do perpetrator.

Responses indicated that fines are applied as an independent sanction in most Arab countries for certain crimes (e.g., Kuwait and Algeria) or as a supplementary sanction (e.g., Yemen). In all Arab countries except Yemen, fine default can lead to a prison sentence. There are specific provisions for commuting fines into prison terms (for example, a day in prison equals ten riyals in Qatar; half a dinar, in Iraq; three dinars, in Tunisia; etc.). Most legislations define a maximum period of imprisonment for fine default (e.g., six months, in Qatar; half the maximum period of imprisonment envisaged for the offense, in Iraq). For fine default, the Emirates apply a sentence of obligation to work in a governmental institution for a certain period of time. Iraq, following the critique of applying imprisonment for fine default, has abandoned the commutation rule. According to Tunisian law, imprisonment in such case is regarded not as a substitute for a fine but rather as a means to enforce its payment, since the sentenced person remains indebted for the amount of the fine and is relieved of the debt only in case of payment or negative prescription; special or general pardon produces the same effect.

Generally speaking, Arab legislations regard imprisonment as an effective means to enforce fines. In practice, commuting a fine to a prison sentence is exceptional.

Confiscation of Property and Funds. Confiscation is restricted to private property, whereas in some Arab countries (e.g., the Emirates) confiscation of public property is constitutionally ruled out. This measure is particularly applied for drug crimes (Qatar). In some countries (Tunisia) it can be used as a supplementary sanction to imprisonment or fines.

Indemnity. All Arab countries except Kuwait, Iraq, and Bahrain apply this measure. However, in Tunisia it can also be applied as a supplementary sanction, but not as an alternative.

Restitution. Except for Kuwait, Bahrain, Iraq, Yemen, and Algeria, restitution is applied either as an independent sanction (Qatar and Sudan) or as a supplementary sanction (Tunisia and the Emirates).

Other Alternatives

Deportation is applied in the Emirates. Flogging can be administered to all offenders, in Sudan, but only to adolescents, in Qatar.

Summarizing, it can be noted that, apart from fines and forms of suspended sentence, other alternatives are rarely applied to adult offenders. They are more often applied as supplementary sanctions with imprisonment or fines, particularly for economic offenses (e.g., tax and customs violations).

Alternative Measures Regarding Juveniles

Although such measures are known to be present also in other countries of the region, Kuwait, the Emirates, Tunisia, and Algeria explicitly reported

75

committal to special institutions and/or handing the juvenile over to the parents. Flogging is applied in the Emirates, Bahrain, and Sudan. The Emirates made reference to a sanction consisting in committal to certain duties but did not provide details.

Offenses and Offenders Eligible for Noncustodial Sanctions

The trend to apply noncustodial sanctions is traditionally motivated by a desire to safeguard minor and accidental offenders against the bad effects of prison, which sometimes outweigh the benefit of a correctional program. This is particularly true in the case of offenders serving short-term sentences. Therefore, there is a general tendency in Arab countries to apply noncustodial sanctions for minor offenses, first-time offenders, and juveniles.

All Arab countries favor the application of alternative sanctions for minor offenses in general, including traffic violations, juvenile crimes, and crimes against the family (the Emirates, Sudan, Qatar, and Tunisia). This also applies to unintentional crimes resulting from negligence or indiscipline taken into consideration by modern penal systems (for example, issuing uncovered checks or violation of environmental protection rules). Thus, there is no need to add more financial burdens on the community by incarcerating the offender. Instead, a new sanction is established that makes the offender responsible for providing remedy for the damage (Tunisia). Similarly, Algeria applies alternatives for violations of financial laws.

According to some Arab legislations, sentencing to a noncustodial sanction is left to the discretion of the judge, taking into account the defendant's conduct, past record, and age, the circumstances surrounding the commitment of the crime, the seriousness of the offense, and the judge's conviction that the defendant will not abscond (e.g., Kuwait). For the same reasons, Iraq, Tunisia, the Emirates, and Sudan favor the application of alternatives to first-time offenders. In addition, this would avoid the negative effects of the custodial sanction, especially since a short-term sentence precludes the application of an adequate program of rehabilitation. Of course, it is also limited to minor offenses.

Besides the reasons mentioned above, alternatives are more concerned with reintegration than with punishment, bearing in mind the educational and psychological effects of correction, especially for juveniles, first-timers, or accidental offenders, as indicated in replies received from Qatar, Bahrain, Sudan, and Tunisia. This is also true of economic crimes. In addition, sentencing to alternatives, in some cases, rests on simplified procedure and often achieves reconciliation, thus relieving the burden of both the state and the sentenced person (Algeria and Tunisia).

Offenses and Offenders Exempt from Noncustodial Sanctions

Generally speaking, Arab countries do not favor the application of alternative sanctions for serious crimes—that is, crimes related to internal or external security of the state, crimes infringing upon the higher interests of the community and undermining its foundations and values, and crimes threatening the economic, social, or moral stability of the state (Kuwait, the Emirates, Yemen, and Tunisia). In Qatar and Kuwait, drug crimes are also exempt from noncustodial sanction. Other serious offenses exempted are premeditated murder, forcible robbery, aggravated assault, other intentional crimes, and crimes committed by recidivists (e.g., Iraq).

In short, according to Arab legal systems, alternatives should not be applied for serious offenses. Instead, society's security and stability make it imperative that serious offenders be sentenced to imprisonment.

Significant Factors in Sentencing to Noncustodial Sanctions

Examination of the survey data revealed a number of factors that a judge takes into consideration when sentencing to noncustodial sanction.

Age is given prominence in all Arab legislations, especially as regards juveniles, young adults, and the elderly.

The seriousness of the offense plays a significant role in sentencing. Misdemeanors (Kuwait), less serious crimes for which the death penalty is not prescribed (Qatar), unintentional crimes (Iraq), or minor offenses in general (Yemen) are usually considered for noncustodial sanctions.

The absence of a prior criminal record has a positive impact in sentencing to noncustodial sanctions (Kuwait). Iraqi response substantiates the same point in the following manner: "If the offender has previously committed a crime and was not reformed by imprisonment, how could he be reformed by an alternative sanction?" In general, judges in most Arab countries differentiate between first-time offenders and recidivists. It is in the first case that the judge more often chooses to sentence the offender to an alternative sanction.

The offender's family situation is also taken into consideration in the sentencing process. This factor is related to one of the objectives of alternatives, which consists in avoiding the separation of the offender from his family as a result of imprisonment. This is particularly the case with the offender who is the only supporter of the family (Iraq) and when imprisonment may lead to the deterioration of family ties (Tunisia).

The offender's sex was mentioned by the Emirates, Qatar, Bahrain, and Tunisia without elaborating on it. Iraq, Sudan, and Algeria pointed out that the alternative measures are more often applied to females, especially when the offender is a child-rearing mother (Algeria). In addition to the aforementioned factors, a number of other considerations were noted by the various responses.

Thus, Kuwait specifically referred to the offender's past behavior and general conduct and the circumstances surrounding the crime. The Emirates highlighted the importance of the judge's conviction of the offender's remorse and repentance, that imprisonment will not rehabilitate, and that the offender should be treated as a patient in need of psychological therapy rather than as a criminal. Special regard is paid to the offender's professional status, such as students (the Emirates), and highly respected professionals, such as professors and businessmen (Iraq), as well as whether the grieved party foregoes the right to a civil suit (Tunisia).

Conclusions

The development of punishment from revenge to reform led Arab countries to the application of prison sanctions on the belief that prison provides for rehabilitation and preserves the offender's identity and dignity. The reluctance to use capital punishment and hard-labor sanctions also accentuated the application of prison sanctions. In addition, fines, which are considered the most frequent alternative to incarceration and a major sanction in all Arab countries, are, due to default, often replaced by prison terms because the offenders are too poor to pay. In some cases a fine is not applied, on the grounds that it has limited deterrent effects on well-to-do offenders.

The economic situation in most Arab countries limits the use of alternative sanctions, especially those requiring high-cost organization and technology. As a result, correctional programs are placed below educational, health, and other services in the priority scale. Public opinion is also not particularly enthusiastic about bearing the costs of correctional programs, mainly in societies lacking in adequate schools and hospital equipment.

The slow progress in applying alternatives can also be attributed to reservations toward applying modern, untried measures. Some argue that even if such measures were successful in other countries, this does not necessarily mean that they are appropriate for Arab societies.

The limited use of alternative sanctions in Arab countries explains the lack of precise up-to-date statistics or references on prisons and noncustodial sanctions. This situation prompted the Arab Security Studies and Training Center to carry out this survey.

The use of noncustodial sanctions in Arab countries is, generally speaking, rare. On the other hand, the application of conventional prison sanctions is still dominant in Arab penal systems. However, a trend toward expansion of noncustodial sanctions is evident, and many Arab countries are considering the enactment of legislative acts facilitating the application of alternatives in the future.

Note

1. Fourteen public entities from eleven countries responded to the questionnaire:

- Kingdom of Saudi Arabia, Ministry of Justice
- Kuwait, Ministry of the Interior and Ministry of Social Affairs and Labor
- United Arab Emirates, Ministry of the Interior and Ministry of Labor and Social Affairs
- Qatar, Ministry of the Interior and Ministry of Labor and Social Affairs
- Bahrain, Ministry of Labor and Social Affairs
- Iraq, Ministry of the Interior and Ministry of Justice
- Democratic Republic of Yemen, Ministry of the Interior
- Sudan, Ministry of the Interior and Judicial Board
- Tunisia, Ministry of the Interior and Ministry of Justice
- Algeria, Ministry of the Interior
- Morocco, Ministry of Crafts and Social Affairs

In addition, the following countries sent information not related to the questionnaire:

- Oman, including articles from the Omani Penal Code concerning alternatives to imprisonment
- People's Democratic Republic of Yemen, on the reintegration of prisoners in the community
- Iraq, provisions from the Iraqi Bill on Reform of the Legal System, and Penal Law provisions on alternatives to imprisonment
- Qatar, reply from the permanent mission to the United Nations on alternatives to imprisonment and measures for social resettlement of prisoners
- Bahrain, same as Qatar
- Egypt, same as Qatar
- Embassy of Lebanon in Vienna, same as Qatar

5

Diyya Legislation in Islamic Shari'a and Its Application in the Kingdom of Saudi Arabia

Mohamed Faleh Al-Sagheer

Definition, Objectives, and Characteristics of Punishment in Islamic Shari'a

There are several definitions of punishment in Islamic Shari'a according to the different Mazaheb (schools of thought) of Islam. These, however, can be summarized by defining punishment as a retribution inflicted upon the offender as a result of his disobedience of the orders of the legislator, or his commission of prohibited actions or sins. It can also be defined as a retribution for the benefit of the community against those who disobey the orders of the legislator.

The primary goal of Islamic Shari'a is to achieve justice and mercy. God says: "We sent thee [the Prophet] not, . . . but as a Mercy for all creatures." Thus, the objectives of punishment in Islamic Shari'a are to establish justice and spread an atmosphere of mercy, security, and harmony among people in the Moslem community. They are also aimed at protecting virtuous morality from profanation for the good of both the individual and society.

Penalties in Islamic Shari'a are basically derived from the Holy Quran, Sunna (legally binding precedents based on the Prophet's sayings, doings, or tacit approval), and the independent judgments of Moslem jurisprudents.

According to Islamic Shari'a, punishment has two main functions:

- *Deterrence*. Punishment should deter the offender from committing further crimes. To function as a deterrent, it should inflict enough pain to cause the offender to desist from offending again.
- *Protection of the community and reforming the offender*. One of the primary functions of punishment in Islamic Shari'a is to protect society from the harmful effects of criminal behavior. This is achieved by both deterring the criminal and reforming him.

The most important characteristics of punishment in Islamic Shari'a are the following:

- It should be derived from, or based on, sources of Islamic Shari'a.
- It should be appropriate to the type of crime committed. God says: "And if ye do catch them out, catch them out no worse than they catch you out: but if ye show patience, that is indeed the best [course] for those who are patient."
- Only the offender is held responsible for his actions. God says: "Every soul draws the meed of its acts on none but itself: no bearer of burdens can bear the burden of another."
- All people are equal before the law; Islam does not differentiate between people in punishment. That is why intercession is ultimately prohibited, especially in cases where a crime punishable by Hudud (penalties mentioned in the Quran) is committed.
- It should be decided by a judge, otherwise it is considered illegal and cannot be implemented.

Types of Punishment in Islamic Shari'a

According to Islam, there are two major types of punishment:

1. Punishment in the Hereafter
2. Punishment in this world

The latter type of punishment can be divided into three main categories:

a. Divine and discretionary punishment, the former being that which is determined by God and is not subject to discussion, while the latter concerns penalties that are left to the discretion of the judge under certain conditions.
b. Original and nonoriginal punishment, the former consisting in that which is provided for by law, while the latter includes alternative, incidental, and supplementary sanctions. Alternative sanctions are those that replace, in certain cases, original ones. An example of this is Diyya, which is applied instead of retaliation if the offender is pardoned by the victim's blood heirs. Incidental sanctions are those that are associated with original punishment and do not need to be imposed by the judge. Supplementary sanctions are imposed in addition to an original punishment.
c. Corporal and physical punishment, the former being that which affects the offender's body or liberty or morale, while the latter affects the offender's financial resources by reducing them, such as through Diyya and confiscation. Physical punishment may be subject to Hudud or left to the discretion of the judge.

Felonies in Islamic Shari'a—Concept and Types

Since Diyya legislation and its application is closely related to felonies, it is necessary to discuss the concept and types of felonies in Islamic Shari'a. A felony is defined as an assault against a human being punishable by retaliation, physical compensation, or atonement. Felonies fall into two major categories: those against human life and those against the person.

Felonies against human life include the following:

a. *Premeditated murder.* This type of murder is committed willfully against a human being protected by law. There are three conditions underlying such a felony:

- The victim must be a living human being protected by law.
- The murder must be the result of the action of the murderer.
- The murderer must have intended to cause death.

According to Islam, the taking of another man's life without a just cause is completely prohibited and considered one of the greatest of all sins. God says: "Nor take life—which God has made sacred—except for just cause," and "Take not life, which God has made sacred, except by way of justice and law: thus doth He command you, that you may learn wisdom," and "If a man kills a Believer intentionally, his recompense is Hell, to abide therein [forever]: and the wrath and the curse of God are upon him, and a dreadful penalty is prepared for him." There are also many other sayings of the Prophet in this respect.

The punishment for premeditated murder in Islamic Shari'a is, under certain conditions, retaliation, or Diyya where retaliation is not used. This is indicated in the following verses of the Quran:

> We ordained therein for them: "Life for life, eye for eye, nose for nose, ear for ear, tooth for tooth, and wounds equal for equal."

> Ye who believe the law of equality is prescribed to you in cases of murder: the free for the free, the slave for the slave, the woman for the woman. But if any remission is made by the brother of the slain, then grant any reasonable demand and compensate him with handsome gratitude.

> In the Law of Equality there is [saving of] Life to you, O Ye men of understanding; that Ye may restrain Yourselves.

The rationale behind the retaliation penalty is obvious in the last verse, namely, to deter others from committing similar crimes, thereby saving the lives of other people. Thus, the retaliation penalty spreads security, prevents bloodshed, and preserves lives. It also eliminates grudges from the hearts of the slain person's relatives and protects society from corrupt people.

b. *Quasi-intentional murder.* This covers the case where the offender has intended to cause a certain degree of harm to the slain person, but not to actually kill him. An example of this is when someone strikes another with a whip or a small stick with no intention to kill him, but, as a result of the assault, the victim dies. There are three main conditions underlying this felony:

- The offender's action must cause the death of a human being.
- The offender must have committed this action with an aggressive intention.
- There must be a causal link between the offender's action and the death of the slain person in terms of which this action is the direct cause of death.

The following penalties are applied against the quasi-intentional murderer:

- Heavy Diyya is to be paid by the Aaqela (the offender's blood relatives).
- Atonement is to be paid from the offender's own resources.
- The offender is held responsible for the crime, since he carried it out intentionally.

c. *Unintentional manslaughter.* This refers to the situation where the offender has killed a person protected by law but did not intend to kill him. This felony is conditional on the following:

- There was an action conducive to a person's death.
- The action was the result of a mistake by the offender.
- There is a causal link between the offender's mistake and the result of the action.

According to Islamic Shari'a, unintentional manslaughter is divided into two types:

- A mistake in intention, as in the case of shooting an arrow at a person thought to be unprotected by law, but it later appears that he was so protected.
- A mistake in action, as in the case of shooting an arrow at a hunted animal but the arrow hits a person protected by law.

Murder committed by a child or an insane person is considered a form of manslaughter from the viewpoint of Moslem jurisprudence. Punishment for manslaughter consists of

- lighter Diyya to be paid by the offender's Aaqela; and
- atonement to be paid from the offender's own resources, as in the case of quasi-intentional murder.

Felonies Against the Person

Felonies against the person are any serious harms inflicted upon a human body that do not cause death. Felonies of this type include the following:

- Cutting off parts of the human body such as fingers, nose, and so on.
- Damaging the functioning of organs of the human body without removing them, such as causing loss of hearing or sight
- Causing head and face wounds
- Causing wounds to other parts of the body

As in the case of felonies against human life, these felonies may also be either intentional, quasi-intentional, or unintentional.

a. *Intentional felony against the person*. This refers to an action by the offender undertaken with the intention of inflicting harm on the body of another person, affecting its safety. Punishment for such an action is retaliation or Diyya. The verses quoted in relation to intentional murder also apply in this case.

b. *Quasi-intentional felony against the person*. This is the case where the offender intended to commit a certain action, but the result was different from that anticipated. An example of this is where a man slaps another on the face, and, as a result, the second man loses an eye. Punishment for such felonies is also Diyya.

c. *Unintentional felony against the person*. This refers to the situation in which the offender intended to carry out a lawful act, but it resulted in a felony against a person protected by law. An example of this is when a man throws a stone out of the window to get rid of it, but it hits a passerby. Punishment for such a felony is also Diyya.

The Application of Retaliation in Felonies against the Person

As already mentioned, one of the punishments for an intentional felony against the person is retaliation. But there are specific rules applied to each of the four felonies against the human body. In the first type (amputation), complete equality is observed: an eyelid for an eyelid, a tongue for a tongue, a finger for a finger, and so on. This type of retaliation is conditional upon three factors:

1. There is no prejudice involved, since prejudice means injustice.
2. There is similarity in description and position (for instance, a right hand should not be taken for a left hand, and vice versa).
3. There is equality in health and condition: A sound hand should not be taken for a paralyzed one.

In the other three previously mentioned felonies against the human body, retaliation is generally replaced by Diyya.

The Concept and Legality of Diyya

Definition and Legality of Diyya in Islamic Shari'a

There are several definitions of Diyya, but it is best defined as money paid to a harmed person or his heir in compensation for a felony committed against him.

The legality of Diyya is derived from the Holy Quran, Sunna, and Consensus (of Moslem jurisprudents), which are the three main foundations of Islamic jurisprudence. God says:

> Never should a Believer kill a Believer: but [if it so happens] by mistake [compensation is due]; if one [so] kills a Believer, it is ordained that he should free a believing slave, and pay compensation to the deceased's family, unless they remit it freely. If the deceased belonged to a people at war with you, and he was a Believer, the freeing of a believing slave [is enough].

Thus, Diyya is provided for in the Quran in certain cases, although it does not provide any detailed information on this institution; this may be found in Sunna. Diyya also reflects wisdom. As mentioned earlier, Diyya replaces retaliation in some cases of quasi-intentional and unintentional felonies against the human body. In such cases, it is applied both to compensate the harmed person or his heirs and to deter the offender. As a result, security is ensured, and grudges and evil are eliminated from the society.

The Effects of Diyya and the Rationale behind Its Application

In the pre-Islam age, the members of the family of a murdered person believed that it was their duty to take revenge. Women urged the men to carry out a vendetta when someone in the family was murdered and reproached those who agreed to reconciliation. On the other hand, there were people who tended to reconcile their differences on the basis of a certain amount of money determined by a middleman in accordance with the social position of the victim and his tribe. The money was usually paid by either the head of the tribe, the offender himself, or all of the members of the tribe. But there were no precise rules regulating such practice. When Islam appeared, this practice was organized into a precise system that applies to all people without differentiation. Many verses in the Quran and sayings from Sunna deal with the regulation and elaboration of Diyya.

As noted earlier, Diyya replaces retaliation if the victim's blood relatives waive their right of retaliation. This creates an atmosphere of mercy and harmony among people. It also means that only the harmed person or his blood relatives have the right to decide on the matter. In addition, Diyya makes the offender aware of the harm he has caused and encourages other people to remit retaliation. This limits the damages resulting from retaliation, reduces crime, and spreads a positive, pacific atmosphere in the society.

Is Diyya a Punishment or a Form of Compensation?

Moslem jurisprudents hold the following three differing opinions in this connection:

1. *Diyya is a punishment.* Advocates of this opinion argue that Diyya in respect of manslaughter is an original punishment and not an alternative sanction. The reason for this is that Diyya is linked to the offender's responsibility for his action and not to the right of its beneficiaries to claim it, although they virtually have the right to remit it later. God has commanded that the intentional murderer be punished by retaliation in this world and by torture in the Hereafter. But in the case of manslaughter, the offender is punished by atonement and Diyya. Thus, Diyya is intended as a punishment for the offender, to reprimand him for his action.

2. *Diyya is a form of physical compensation.* Another argument is that Diyya is a form of legal compensation for harm inflicted upon a human being. The fact that Diyya is regulated by special rules, different from other rules relating to damages, lies in the nature of the human being who, unlike other damaged items, cannot be repaired by money. The purpose of the regulation of Diyya was to prevent the overestimation of claims, as occurred in the pre-Islam age. The proponents of this argument indicate the following supporting evidence:

- Diyya is not affected by the status within the community of either the offender or the harmed person.
- It is not intended as revenge.
- It involves some rules that are incompatible with punishment.
- It is paid, in the case of manslaughter, by the offender's blood relatives, who were not involved in the offender's action and should not therefore be punished.

3. *Diyya is both a punishment and a form of compensation.* According to the advocates of this opinion, which is shared by the author of this report, Diyya is a punishment since it is intended to reprimand and deter the offender, while at the same time being a financial compensation, in the sense that it is paid to the harmed person in compensation for the harm inflicted upon him by the offender. God commanded that the killer by mistake be punished by atonement and Diyya, but did not link atonement with punishment, or Diyya with compensation. Thus, retribution is a combination, although Diyya tends to stand alone as compensation, since it is paid to the harmed person's relatives and not to the state treasury.

Conditions for the Application of Diyya

The following are the most important conditions for the application of Diyya:

- The offender's action is illegal and conducive in itself to injury.
- There is a causal link between the action and the resulting injury, or between the offender's behavior and the consequence of his action.
- The injury is to all or part of the body of a human being (damages caused to a car, for instance, are not punishable by Diyya).
- The harmed person is protected by law.
- The injury inflicted on the body of the harmed person is irremediable.
- The injury is caused by someone other than the harmed person himself.

In order for Diyya to be applied, the offender must first be proved guilty. According to Moslem jurisprudence, felonies and murders may be proved only in three ways:

- admission, which implies the offender's recognition of the rights of others;
- attestation, which involves asking someone to swear that he is telling the truth in relation to a certain matter; or
- Qasama (or compurgation).

The first and second methods are adopted when the murderer is known. Where, however, he has not been identified, the murder is proved by so-called Qasama (or compurgation). According to Qasama, the blood relatives of the victim accuse one person or a number of persons of having committed the murder. The accused swears (or swear) fifty times by conclusive oaths that he (or they) neither committed the murder nor know the identity of the murderer. If the perpetrator of manslaughter is identified in this way, he is punishable by Diyya, but if the offender committed murder, he is punishable by retaliation.

Cases in Which Diyya Is Applied

Premeditated Murder

As noted earlier, Diyya is applied against the murderer if retaliation is dropped. The following are the cases in which retaliation is dropped:

- The death of the murderer—in this case Diyya is paid from the murderer's estate
- Remission of retaliation
- Reconciliation between the victim's blood heirs and the murderer
- Inequality between the murderer and the victim in terms of religion and liberty

- Where there is a direct blood relationship between the victim and the murderer (e.g., where a parent kills his or her child; in the case of parenticide, retaliation is, however, applied)
- Where there is a relative of the murderer among the victim's heirs, such as a child or grandchild

Diyya in the case of premeditated murder should fulfill the following conditions:

- It should be paid from the murderer's resources and not from those of his blood relatives;
- It should be paid immediately and not delayed or paid in installments, unless the victim's blood relatives so agree; and
- It should be increased.

Quasi-intentional Murder

As is the case with intentional murder, quasi-intentional murder is punishable by increased Diyya, but it should be paid from the resources of the murderer's Aaqela (blood relatives), and it may be delayed.

Unintentional Manslaughter

Diyya is applied against the perpetrator of unintentional manslaughter, whether it resulted from a mistake in intention or in action. Basically, Diyya should be paid from the offender's own funds. God says: "Every soul draws the meed of its acts on none but itself: No bearer of burdens can bear the burden of another."

However, Islam, from its comprehensive view of life and man, has made the offender's Aaqela responsible for the payment of Diyya for manslaughter. Diyya in this case is reduced and can be paid in installments over a period of three years. But the offender should pay atonement from his own funds to the deceased's blood heirs. Atonement involves the freeing of a believing slave (at the time of the Prophet), or fasting for two months, or feeding sixty poor people.

Actions Similar to Unintentional Manslaughter. There are certain actions that are undertaken unintentionally and cause death, although not by way of direct mistake. Many Moslem jurisprudents associate such actions with unintentional manslaughter, since they are subject to the same punishment, namely, Diyya and atonement. There are two types of such actions:

1. Manslaughter by direct causation, such as the case where a sleeping person rolls over onto another person, causing the second person's death.

2. Manslaughter by indirect causation, when, for example, a man digs a hole in a road and does not warn passersby of the danger of falling into it at night. As a result, a man falls into the hole and dies.

Felony by Indirect Causation. This includes felonies that are committed not directly but through indirect causation. This means that the action has caused the damage not by itself but through a medium. An example of this is perjury leading to the death of an innocent person accused of murder.

According to most Moslem jurisprudents, the perpetrator of felonies, whether by direct or by indirect causation, is responsible for his action. If the killing has been carried out on purpose, the perpetrator should be punished by retaliation. But if the killing has taken place by mistake, Diyya is applied. However, some Moslem jurisprudents are of the opinion that the murderer by indirect causation should be punished by a heavier Diyya rather than retaliation, on the basis of the principle of equality in action. Diyya in this case should be paid from the murderer's own funds.

The same division of felonies into intentional, quasi-intentional, and unintentional applies also to felonies of direct and indirect causation. Thus, Diyya is applied according to the type of felony; if the felony is committed intentionally and retaliation is dropped, Diyya for intentional felony is applied. If the felony of direct or indirect causation is committed quasi-intentionally, or unintentionally, corresponding Diyyas are applied.

Diyya Rules and Amounts

Basically, it is the offender who should pay Diyya, whether the action was committed on purpose or by mistake. However, there are cases in which Diyya is paid by his Aaqela or from the state treasury.

Diyya Paid by the Offender

The offender should pay Diyya in the following cases:

- If retaliation is not possible in relation to a premeditated felony
- If reconciliation is reached between the blood heirs and the offender
- If the offender admits that he committed the crime by mistake or quasi-intentionally
- If the amount of Diyya is less than one-third of the Diyya of the person harmed
- If the felony is committed by mistake, and the offender has no Aaqela, or his Aaqela are poor, or they paid only a part of the Diyya, being unable to pay the full amount

Chapter 5

Diyya Paid by Aaqela

According to some Moslem jurisprudents, the offender is included among the members of Aaqela and should contribute in paying the Diyya. The rule that Diyya for unintentional and quasi-intentional felonies should by paid by Aaqela is taken from Sunna. Diyya should be paid by Aaqela in the following cases:

- Unintentional felony, since the offender has an excuse and the Diyya is too high for him to pay alone
- Quasi-intentional murder, since it also involves a mistake by the offender, as he did not intend to kill
- Intentional murder committed by a child or an insane person, since their actions are not punishable by retaliation and their intention is defective
- Diyya in respect of an embryo that died as a result of its mother's death, since its death was not intended

There are no definite rules for dividing Diyya among the members of Aaqela, but, as a general rule, they are not obliged to pay more than their means permit. The amount of Diyya is determined according to the degree of the relationship with the offender; parents pay first, then brothers and their families, then uncles and their families, and so on.

The rationale behind Aaqela paying Diyya can be found in the following:

- The payment of Diyya by the offender's Aaqela achieves justice and equality between him and the members of his Aaqela.
- As noted previously, Diyya is paid by Aaqela only in cases of unintentional and quasi-intentional felonies. This means that the crime has resulted, presumably, from neglect or reckless behavior. This can be blamed on the offender's close relatives, since they are responsible for his disorientation and ill-education and must therefore pay for their error or omissions.
- It is the duty of the offender's close relatives to help him when he needs their assistance.

Diyya Paid from the State Treasury

Diyya is paid from the state treasury if

- the offender has no Aaqela, provided that he is a Moslem and the crime was committed unintentionally or quasi-intentionally;
- the offender has not been identified;
- the felony was caused unintentionally or quasi-intentionally by people with vested authority, such as a judge; or
- the felony resulted from a mistake by an authorized doctor.

Amount of Diyya and Methods of Payment

Diyya is paid to the harmed person (if he is still alive) or his blood heirs or the state treasury. Originally it was paid in camels, and today the sum is estimated accordingly.

1. *Diyya for human life.*
   a. *Moslem male.* Diyya for a Moslem male is equivalent to one hundred camels and is paid from the offender's own resources if the murder was committed on purpose. Diyya may be reduced or increased according to the type of felony; if the felony was committed intentionally or quasi-intentionally, Diyya is increased, but if it is committed by mistake, Diyya is reduced.
   b. *Moslem woman.* Diyya for a Moslem woman is half of that for a Moslem man.
   c. *Embryo.* Diyya for an embryo depends on the type of crime committed against its mother.
   d. *Non-Moslems.* Diyya for a non-Moslem man is half of that for a Moslem man. Diyya for a non-Moslem woman is half of that of a non-Moslem man. Diyya for non-Moslems in respect of bodily injuries is equal to that for Moslems.
2. *Diyya for parts of the human body.*
   a. In respect of organs or limbs consisting of two parts, such as arms, legs, lips, and so on, Diyya for one part (for instance, one arm) is half of the full Diyya (i.e., fifty camels or their equivalent value). Diyya for both parts together is equivalent to one hundred camels.
   b. In respect of single organs, such as nose and tongue, the full amount of Diyya is paid.
   c. With organs or parts consisting of more than two components, such as eyelids, fingers, teeth, and so on, Diyya is paid in full.
3. *Diyya for loss of function of organs.* Full Diyya is paid for loss of functions of reason, smell, sight, hearing, speech, intercourse, and touch.
4. *Diyya for bodily injuries.* Diyya for bodily injuries, in general, is estimated according to specific rules provided for in Islamic juridical texts.

Many guidelines have been issued in the Kingdom of Saudi Arabia on the application of Diyya. An example of these is the guideline that the offender's Aaqela should pay the Diyya awarded in cases of quasi-intentional and unintentional felonies. Another guideline estimates Diyya in terms of a certain amount of money calculated in the local currency.

Part III
Asia and the
Pacific Region

6

An Overview of
Alternatives to Imprisonment
in Asia and the
Pacific Region

H. Sugihara, K. Horiuchi, N. Nishimura,
A. Yamaguchi, S. Sato, I. Nishimura,
Y. Nagashima, M. Nishikawa, and F. Saito

More than twenty countries are included in Asia and the Pacific region, excluding Arab countries. There are marked differences in terms of the political situation, economic level, social structure, and culture of the countries in the region. This chapter on alternatives to imprisonment in the region includes eleven countries and one territory: China, Fiji, India, Indonesia, Japan, Korea, Papua New Guinea, the Philippines, Singapore, Sri Lanka, Thailand, and Hong Kong. Although these were selected because substantial data was available, it is believed that they are representative of the entire region. United Nations documents and relevant data available at the United Nations Asian and Far East Institute for the Prevention of Crime and the Treatment of Offenders (UNAFEI), as well as information provided by criminal justice agencies, was supplemented with current information collected by UNAFEI staff dispatched to several target countries. The research entails a review of all alternative measures to imprisonment at all stages of criminal proceedings, including investigation, prosecution, adjudication, and disposition follow-up.

The overview consists of two parts: a general overview and country reviews. The general overview presents a brief summary, while more detailed information is available in the country reviews. The reason for the emphasis on country reviews lies in UNAFEI's integrated approach to criminal justice administration. Precise understanding of each alternative measure to imprisonment can be achieved only through an understanding of the entire criminal justice administration in each country.

General Overview

This overview is based on information provided in country reviews. All the existing alternative measures revealed in this chapter are listed in table 6.1.

95

Table 6.1

Country	Pretrial stage	Adjudication stage	Follow-up stage of disposition
China	Exemption from prosecution Guarantor and surveillance	Fine Control Suspended execution of sentence	Parole
Fiji	Restitution Suspension of prosecution Bail	Fine Probation Suspended sentence Binding over Absolute and conditional discharge Compensation order Reconciliation Disqualification Community work order	Compulsory supervision order Extramural punishment Remission of sentence Conditional pardon
India	Bail	Fine Suspended sentence Probation	Remission Furlough/leave Pardon
Indonesia	Bail/personal guarantee	Fine Probation/suspended execution of sentence	Conditional discharge/parole Prerelease treatment Work release Furlough Remission/pardon
Japan	Suspension of prosecution Bail	Fine Suspended execution of sentence Probation	Parole
Korea	Admonition by the police Suspension of prosecution Bail	Fine Suspension of sentence Suspended execution of sentence Probation	Work release Furlough Parole Pardon

Papua New Guinea	Village court Bail	Fine Suspension of sentence/ suspended execution of sentence Good-behavior bond Probation	Parole Release on license
The Philippines	Village court	Fine Probation	Open institution Parole Remission Pardon
Singapore	Bail	Fine Probation	Day release scheme Suspension/release of sentence
Sri Lanka	Bail	Fine Conditional sentence Suspended sentence Probation Community service order	Home leave Work release Parole/release on license Remission Amnesty
Thailand	Bail	Fine Suspended sentence/suspended execution of sentence Probation	Parole/remission Public work allowance Penal settlement Pardon
Hong Kong	Bail/provisional release	Fine Suspension of sentence Probation Community service order	Release under supervision/parole Prerelease employment scheme

As can be noted in table 6.1, there is much variety in the terminology used in the region for alternative measures to imprisonment. A term to express a type of alternative measure in one country may well refer to a totally different type of measure in another country. For example, *parole* means the conditional release of a prisoner in most of the countries but is utilized for furlough or leave in India. At the same time, the terms for similar measures differ from one country to another. For example, conditional release—called "parole" in most of the countries—is named "release on license" in Sri Lanka. Another point that should be noted is that the same measure varies from country to country in the details of legal framework, the organization responsible for its implementation, as well as the extent of its use. To better understand the situation of alternatives to imprisonment in the region, it is necessary to refer to the country reviews.

Crime Trends and Policies for Alternatives to Imprisonment

Recently most of the countries in the region have experienced an increase in crime. This is largely attributed to an increase of the young population, in India; to the explosive development of the economy, in Korea; to an increase of migrating population from rural areas to large cities, in the Philippines; to a large number of illegal immigrants, in Hong Kong; and so on. Coupled with other factors, the increase in crimes and offenders has caused serious prison overcrowding in some countries. Other countries, where prisons have not been faced with a serious overcrowding problem, are searching for more humane and more effective treatment measures for offenders' reintegration into the society. Under these circumstances, most of the countries in the region are developing or expanding alternative measures to imprisonment at all levels of criminal justice administration.

Alternatives to Imprisonment at the Pretrial Stage

Most of the countries in the region have some kind of measures at the police stage to divert minor offenders from formal criminal procedures by giving them only warnings or admonitions, but these kind of measures are not analyzed in this report, since they are not considered alternative measures to imprisonment.

For offenders who have committed rather serious offenses, there are some significant measures at the pretrial stages to divert them from formal criminal proceedings. One such measure is nonprosecution or suspended prosecution in China, Fiji, Japan, and Korea. Under this program, a public prosecutor has discretionary power not to prosecute an offender, even if the prosecutor has enough evidence of guilt, taking all the circumstances of the offense and the offender into account. In Fiji, nonprosecution is often accompanied by a system of compensation; that is, if restitution is made by the offender to the victim, no prosecution is initiated.

Another measure is the village court system in the Philippines and Papua New Guinea. Community members elect their leaders to be village court magistrates who have judicial powers to settle some kinds of criminal cases, and thus avoid lengthy and expensive trials. Since most of the sanctions imposed at village courts are community-based, like compensation orders, the village court system results in sparing some offenders from imprisonment.

Bail is the most common alternative to the detention of an offender under investigation or under trial. It exists in all countries in the region without exception. However, the extent of its use in actual practice may vary from one country to another, although no statistical data was available in most countries.

Since most of the offenders in the region come from a low economic status and are unable to pay bail, some countries have special programs that allow the offender under trial to be released. China, Indonesia, the Philippines, and Thailand have systems of release on recognizance or on personal guarantee; under these programs an offender awaiting trial may be released on his recognizance or on his personal guarantor's appearance in court. Thailand also has special programs to provide offenders with financial aid for release on bail.

Noncustodial Sanctions in Sentencing

All countries in the region have noncustodial alternative sanctions to imprisonment.

Fines, which are the most traditional alternative sanction to imprisonment, can be found in all the countries selected for this overview, but with some diversities in the use of fines in sentencing. One of the major obstacles to the use of fines is that most of the offenders in the region are too poor to pay a fine. However, no country was found to have introduced a day-fine system, and in most of the countries those offenders who fail to pay fines are imprisoned. Detailed analysis regarding fines is not included in the country reviews.

The most common noncustodial sanctions are suspended sentence and suspended execution of sentence, either of which is found in almost all the countries in the region. Under this program the pronouncement of sentence or the execution of sentence is suspended; however, if the offender commits a new offense, the sentence is pronounced or executed. Fiji has a special measure of binding over whereby, after conviction, an offender is released and enters a bond for a few years. The offender is required to keep good behavior, and if the offender fails, he must pay a sum of money.

Probation, which is often accompanied by suspended sentence or suspended execution of sentence, is also found in most of the countries. An offender placed on probation usually is supervised by a probation officer or other authorities. Since probation was introduced very recently in most of the countries, for example, in 1976 in the Philippines, 1979 in Thailand, 1985 in Papua New Guinea, and 1989 in Korea, it is still in a developing stage.

Probation supervision is carried out by a probation officer in most of the countries; in China, it is carried out instead by a community unit, and in Indonesia, by a public prosecutor. Most of the countries are faced with a shortage of qualified probation officers to expand the probation system. To assist professional probation officers, volunteer citizens are utilized to supervise and help probationers in Japan, Singapore, and Thailand.

The community service order is not widely utilized in the region. Only three countries, Fiji, Sri Lanka, and Hong Kong, have introduced it recently, and it is still in the experimental stage.

A few countries implement other noncustodial sanctions. Fiji, for example, has a wide variety of noncustodial sanctions, including compensation orders, reconciliation, and disqualification in addition to probation, suspended sentence, binding over, and community work orders.

Follow-up Stages of Dispositions

Two major measures are found in the region as alternatives to imprisonment for offenders serving their sentences in prison: remission and parole. Remission reduces the term of imprisonment mainly on the basis of good behavior in prison. Parole is the conditional release of a prisoner after he has served part of the sentence; he is usually supervised by a parole officer during the rest of the sentenced term.

Remission plays a major role in India and Singapore, as does parole in China, Japan, Korea, Papua New Guinea, Thailand, and Hong Kong. Other countries, such as Fiji, Indonesia, the Philippines, and Sri Lanka, have both remission and parole.

The day-release scheme in Singapore and the prerelease employment scheme in Hong Kong are special programs to utilize halfway houses to bridge the gap between the prison and the free society. Under both programs, before complete release from prison, a prisoner is required to reside in a hostel or halfway house and to work outside.

In some countries, pardon or amnesty seems to be widely utilized for reducing imprisonment, but statistical data was not available to confirm this for most countries.

COUNTRY REVIEWS

People's Republic of China

Crime Trends and Policy for Alternatives to Imprisonment

Efforts to set up a modern criminal justice system in China started soon after the establishment of the People's Republic of China in 1949. The efforts, however, were obstructed during the ten years of the Cultural Revolution, mid 1960 to 1970s. It was not until 1977 that the Criminal Law and the Criminal Procedure Law were enacted. The court system and the public prosecution system were reorganized in 1980. Thus, the criminal justice administration in China is now in its nascent stage. Limited information available on the actual practice of criminal justice administration made it somewhat difficult to analyze the situation of alternatives to imprisonment in China.

Pretrial Stage

Exemption from Prosecution. Public prosecutors are given the discretionary power to grant exemption from prosecution even if there is sufficient evidence to prove the guilt of the offender. Article 101 of the Criminal Procedure Law of China provides: "In cases where, according to the provisions of the Criminal Law, it is not necessary to impose a sentence of criminal punishment, or an exemption from criminal punishment may be granted, a people's procuratorate may grant exemption from prosecution."

In order to prevent the abuse of this discretionary power, several safeguards have been established. For example, section 2 of article 102 provides: "When a people's procuratorate decides to exempt from prosecution a case that a public security organ [police] has transferred for prosecution, it shall deliver the document of exemption from the prosecution to the public security organ. When the public security organ considers that a decision to exempt from prosecution is erroneous, it may demand reconsideration, and if its opinion is not accepted, it may request review by the people's procuratorate at the next level up." Section 3 of the same article provides: "When there is a decision to exempt from prosecution a case in which there is a victim, the people's procuratorate shall deliver the document of decision to exempt from prosecution to the victim. If the victim does not agree, he may, within seven days after receipt, petition the people's procuratorate. The people's procuratorate shall inform the victim of the result of its reexamination."

In China, the system of exemption from prosecution is generally considered to be a useful measure not only to reduce the excessive burden of the court and other penal institutions but also to release minor offenders from formal criminal procedure at an early stage, thus encouraging their resocialization.

Guarantor and Surveillance. The systems of guarantor and surveillance are implemented as alternatives to detention of a defendant awaiting or undergoing trial.

Article 38 of the Criminal Procedure Law of China stipulates:

> The people's courts, the people's procuratorates, and the public security organs, according to the circumstances of the case, may summon a defendant for detention, allow him to obtain a guarantor and await trial out of custody, or allow him to live at home under surveillance. A defendant who lives at home under surveillance may not leave the designated area. Surveillance of his home is to be carried out by the local public security station or by the people's commune or the defendant's unit entrusted with the task. In cases where the defendant is allowed to obtain a guarantor and await trial out of custody or to live at home under surveillance, when changes in the circumstances develop, these measures shall be revoked or altered.

Adjudication Stage

Control. Control is one of the five types of principal punishments stipulated in Criminal Law and is the least severe. It is a criminal penalty imposed on minor offenders by the people's courts and executed by the public security organ (police). Control is, to some extent, similar to probation in other countries, but it is a final disposition without the possibility of future revocation. The term of control cannot be less than three months or more than two years.

Article 34 of the Criminal Law stipulates that an offender who is sentenced to control must abide by the following rules during the term in which control is being implemented:

a. Abide by laws and decrees, submit to the supervision of the masses, and actively participate in productive labor or work.
b. Report regularly on his or her own activities to the organ executing the control.
c. Report to, and obtain approval from, the organ executing the control for a change in residence or departure from the area. An offender who is sentenced to control shall, while engaged in labor, receive equal pay for equal work.

Control is applied mainly to the minor crimes of theft, fraud, forcible seizure, disturbance of the social order, hooliganism, posing as state personnel to cheat and bluff, gambling, luring women into prostitution or sheltering them in prostitution, abuse or abandonment of family members, and so on.

It is claimed that control, as a measure of community-based corrections, is proving its effectiveness in corrections and rehabilitation of offenders in China.

Suspended Execution of Sentence. According to article 67 of the Criminal Law, suspension of sentence may be pronounced for an offender who has been sentenced to criminal detention or to fixed-term imprisonment for not more than three years, according to the circumstances of his or her crime and his or her demonstration of repentance, and where it is considered that applying a suspended sentence will not, in fact, result in further harm to society.

Article 70 of the Criminal Law provides: "An offender for whom a suspension of sentence has been pronounced is to be turned over by the public security organ [police] to his or her unit or to a basic-level organization for observation during the probation period for suspension, and, if he or she commits no further crime, upon the expiration of the probation period for suspension the punishment originally decided is not to be executed."

As is indicated in the above-mentioned provision, the public security organ, during the period of suspension of sentence, utilizes the mass organizations of the community to help watch the offender's daily behavior and to lead him or her to become a law-abiding citizen.

It seems that in China the number of revocations of suspension of sentence due to the committal of a new crime is very small and that this type of community-based treatment has been proving very successful.

Follow-up Stage of Dispositions

Parole. An offender sentenced to fixed-term imprisonment of which not less than half has been executed, or an offender sentenced to life imprisonment of which not less than ten years has actually been executed, may be granted parole if he or she demonstrates true repentance and will not cause further harm to society. If special circumstances exist, the above restrictions relating to the term executed need not be imposed (article 73 of the Criminal Law). When prisons or reform-through-labor organs find that parole should be granted according to law, they submit a written opinion to the people's court for consideration and parole order (article 162 of the Criminal Procedure Law). Supervision of the parolee is also executed by the public security organ. If he or she does not commit further crime, the punishment to which he or she was originally sentenced is to be considered as having been completely executed; if he or she commits any further crime, the parole is to be revoked (article 75 of the Criminal Law).

During the period of parole supervision, the public security organ also utilizes the mass organization of the community to watch the offender's daily behavior and to help his or her resocialization. It appears that the parole supervision is successful and that the rate of revocation is low.

Fiji

Crime Trends and Policy for Alternatives to Imprisonment

Over a seven-year period (1980–86) the total number of recorded crimes in Fiji has consistently edged upward. In 1986, 15,648 crimes were reported to the police (table 6.2).

Although recent data on convictions are unavailable, figures for 1979 indicate there was a total of 3,820 convictions, excluding traffic offenses, of which 848 resulted in imprisonment, 1,910 were fined, 207 were bound over, 52 received probation as well as suspended sentences, and 751 were disposed of through other sanctions.

While Fiji experienced prison overcrowding problems in 1979, the situation has eased considerably, with 913 inmates incarcerated in 1986 in correctional facilities having the capacity to hold more than 1,000. Another reason cited for the recent absence of prison overcrowding is the expansion of noncustodial sanctions.

Evidently, the Fiji laws provide a wide range of sentencing options as alternatives to imprisonment. In the past, however, there was a tendency to underutilize such options. Quite recently, the community work order program was implemented, complementing the existing noninstitutional measures, which is in line with the current trend toward promoting community-based treatment programs for the rehabilitation of offenders.

Pretrial Stage

Restitution or Compensation. A system of compensation (restitution) for property stolen or property damaged exists and often has priority over the prosecution of the case. If restitution is made, there is often no prosecution.

Suspension of Prosecution. The Director of Public Prosecutions (DPP) in his or her discretion may decide not to institute proceedings although there may be *prima facie* evidence of guilt. Section 71 (1) of the Criminal Procedure Code allows the DPP to enter a *nolle prosequi* in any criminal case at any stage but before verdict or judgment. When this happens the result is discharge of the accused and not acquittal, hence there is always a possibility that the accused may be charged once more on the same basis. However, in practice the nolle prosequi means the end of the case.

Table 6.2 Number of Major Crimes Recorded in the Police Stations

Type of crime		Total for calendar year						
		1980	1981	1982	1983	1984	1985	1986
Intentional homicide		15	23	22	23	23	24	19
Nonintentional homicide								
Assault:	Major assaults only	166	169	165	196	221	254	247
	Including minor assaults	2,146	2,216	2,280	2,011	2,462	2,329	2,265
Rape		36	48	46	34	38	34	53
Robbery		128	119	158	186	229	250	310
Theft:	Major thefts only	1,505	1,366	1,766	2,007	2,073	2,269	2,992
	Including minor thefts	4,739	4,598	4,728	4,724	5,192	5,213	5,508
	Fraud	273	355	440	441	427	157	443
	Embezzlement	172	208	107	285	176	127	171
Drug-related crimes:								
	Simple possession	7	4	5	9	23	21	86
	All other drug offenses		17		17	15	6	23
Bribery and/or corruption		12	17	16	1	1	6	10
Total number of recorded crimes		12,479	12,399	12,829	13,808	14,313	14,168	15,648

Source: The Third UN Survey.

Chapter 6

Bail. Section 26 of the Criminal Procedure Code, chapter 21, gives senior police officers the power to release accused persons on bail, with or without sureties, with the obligation to appear before a magistrate's court at a stipulated time—unless the offense appears to the officer to be a serious one. If it is not serious, the accused persons are entitled to bail.

Similarly, section 108 of the Criminal Procedure Code provides:

(1)...Where any person, other than a person accused of murder or treason, is arrested or detained without warrant by a police officer or appears or is brought before a court and is prepared at any time while in the custody of such officer or at any stage of the proceedings before such court to give bail, such person may in the discretion of the officer or court be admitted to bail with or without a surety or sureties and, in the case of a court, subject to such conditions and limitations as the court may think it fit to impose.

(2) The amount of bail shall be fixed with due regard to the circumstances of the case and shall not be excessive.

In practice in Fiji, bail is granted in all except the most serious cases or in cases where the accused has frequently been in breach of bail conditions.

It should be noted here that absconding while on bail has caused an increase in the number of cases pending trial in the Fiji courts, because it sometimes takes months for the police to trace defendants who have absconded.

Adjudication Stage

Probation. As stipulated in the Probation of Offenders Act, a court may order an offender to probation for a period of not less than one year and not more than three years.

The probation service is guided by the Probation Offenders Act, chapter 22, which stipulates that the probation officer must assist, befriend, and guide the probationer, and the probationer, in turn, is required to comply with the instructions of the supervising officer. If an offender breaches any of the conditions of the order, the order is revoked, the offender is taken to court, and the original sentence is reactivated.

In 1983 the number of probationers was 175, representing a decline of 17 percent on the previous year's probationers. Although an increase in probationers was recorded from 1981 to 1982, the overall probation population over time appears to be declining. In view of the rising crime rate in the country and the high occupancy rate in prison, probation could be utilized as an inexpensive and effective alternative to imprisonment.

Suspended Sentence. Suspended sentences are intended to give an offender an incentive to avoid trouble by fixing an imprisonment term that could become operational on his or her committing a further imprisonable offense. In Fiji, there appears to be no clear-cut policy in the use of suspended sentences. There is a widely held view that the suspended sentence is a soft option.

Section 28 A of the Penal Code makes provision for suspended sentence, which gives the courts the power to suspend a term of imprisonment. The legislation imposes no restrictions on the factors that the court must consider in deciding whether suspension is appropriate. However, a suspended sentence can be considered by the court only where a sentence of imprisonment is for a term of not more than two years. The court may order that the sentence shall not take effect unless during the period specified in the order the offender commits another offense punishable with imprisonment (section 28 A [1]).

Where the offender commits an offense punishable with imprisonment during the operational period, (a) the court may order that the suspended sentence may take effect with the original term unaltered, or (b) it may substitute a lesser term, and (c) it may also vary the original order by extending the operational period, which, however, may not extend beyond three years from the variation date (section 28 B). The court is under obligation to state its reasons if it does not invoke the original term.

A probation order cannot be made where a court has passed a suspended sentence in respect of another offense that the court has dealt with (section 28 A [2]).

Binding Over. In Fiji the measure of binding over is found in sections 35 and 36 of the Penal Code and also in sections 33 to 36 of the Criminal Procedure Code. The term *binding over* refers to two quite different provisions:

a. A person may be bound over on bond and required to keep the peace and demonstrate good behavior; if that person fails to do so, he or she will be required to pay a sum of money. This measure may be applied even in cases where there is no conviction.
b. Following a conviction a person may be bound over to come up for judgment when called upon, usually subject to some specific condition. If the offender is called upon, he or she may be sentenced for the original offense.

The power to bind over an offender to keep the peace and be of good behavior is found in section 35 of the Penal Code. Instead of, or in addition to, imposing a punishment, the court may, except where the offense is punishable by death, require the offender to enter into a recognizance with or without sureties. The amount and the time required for the offender to keep the peace and be of good behavior is fixed by the court, but the time must not exceed a period of two years.

The power to bind over a person to come up for judgment is found in section 36 of the Penal Code. Where a person is convicted of an offense (not punishable with death), and if it appears to the court that the circumstances are such that it is expedient to release the offender on probation, the court may, instead of sentencing the offender at once to a punishment, order that he or she be released on entering into bond—with or without sureties—for a period not exceeding two years. In the meantime he or she is to keep the peace and be of good behavior and to comply with such conditions as the court may impose (section 36 [1]). If the offender fails to observe any of the conditions of recognizance, he or she may be apprehended on a warrant, and the court can either remand the offender in custody or admit him or her to bail until sentencing occurs. The conditions for binding over are usually given in general terms. Magistrates have found this provision useful where neighbors or relatives are involved, and the power conferred by section 35 (2) is helpful as it allows a complaint and/or an acquitted defendant to be bound over.

Discharge—Absolute and Conditional. An order discharging a person absolutely or conditionally is, in the words of section 38 of the Penal Code, appropriate where a court is of the opinion that it is inexpedient to inflict punishment and that a probation order is not appropriate. The court may, with or without proceeding to conviction, make an order discharging the offender absolutely, or if the court thinks fit, discharge him or her subject to conditions. The court's power to make and enforce an order as to restoration, restitution, or compensation is not affected by the fact that the offender was discharged without conviction (section 38 [4]).

An absolute discharge is used where the court, having found the offender guilty of the offense, considers that no further action is required on its part beyond the finding of guilt.

An order for conditional discharge imposes the condition that the offender commit no further offense during a period of twelve months from the date of the order. The court may impose other conditions, such as the payment of costs or compensation, the restitution of goods, or the payment of money in lieu of goods (section 38 [1]).

An order for conditional discharge differs from a probation order in that it involves no supervision of the offender. The one condition that always applies is that the offender must not commit another offense.

A conditional discharge is sometimes used by the court as an alternative to probation in situations where the offender has indicated the wish to return to the outlying islands where there is no resident probation officer available, or where the court takes an individualized approach toward the offender but considers that supervision by a probation officer is either unnecessary or inappropriate. In other cases it is being used where a minor offense is committed under aggravated circumstances but with the presence of substantial mitigating factors.

Conditional and absolute discharges are more widely used by the courts than probation, suspended sentence, or binding over.

Compensation to Victims. Section 161 of the Criminal Procedure Code authorizes a restoration order of property to the rightful owner without prejudice to any civil proceedings. Provision is also made for the utilization of the property or the proceeds thereof toward the satisfaction of costs or compensation. Under section 159 A, any money found on the thief or a receiver may be paid to the innocent purchaser after restitution of the stolen property to the rightful owner.

Section 158 (2) confers a very wide discretion to the court. It reads as follows: "Any person who is convicted of an offense may be ordered to pay compensation to any person injured by, or who suffers damage to his property or loss as a result of, such offense, and such compensation may be either in addition to, or in substitution for, any punishment or other sentence."

During 1979 a total of 328 compensation orders were passed:

Offenses against authority	14
Offenses against morality	3
Offenses against person	123
Offenses against property	188
Total	328

Reconciliation. In section 160 of Criminal Procedure Code (as amended), reconciliation is permissible at the discretion of the court for only four offenses. These are criminal trespass, common assault, assault causing actual bodily harm, and damaging or destroying property. The discretion of the court in the promotion of reconciliation in these four offenses is again limited to cases that are substantially of a personal or private nature and that are not aggravated. Reconciliation is normally effected on terms of payment of compensation or on other terms approved by the court. Thereafter the proceedings are either stayed or terminated.

In addition, there have been different traditional models of dispute settlement outside the magistrate courts. "Soro" and "bulubulu" traditionally have played, and indeed still play, important roles in ending disputes and burying grievance. Soro and bulubulu are the traditional presentation of the whale's tooth (taboo) to make amends for a misdeed. Once the whale's tooth is accepted by the wronged party, it is generally concluded that the wrong is forgiven, and the ceremony is rounded off by the drinking of yagona and the singing of songs. The reconciliation can be arranged directly between the parties concerned or through the intervention of a third party or a village chief.

Disqualification. Disqualification is a noncustodial sentence whereby an offender is temporarily or permanently disbarred from engaging in an activity, an occupation, or a profession. As far as traffic offenses are concerned, courts in Fiji are empowered only to disqualify an offender from obtaining or holding a driving license in respect to traffic offenses specified by the Traffic Act (chapter 152): for example, drunken driving or driving under the influence of liquor.

Community Work Order. The community work order is imposed as an alternative to imprisonment by the chief magistrate under a provision of the Penal Code. The offenders ordered to carry out community work are supervised by the welfare agencies, with the overall supervision of the scheme being in the hands of the Social Welfare Department.

In June 1983 a pilot community work order program became operational. Up to the end of 1983, twenty-four offenders had been sentenced to community work ranging from forty to three hundred hours' work. Of those sentenced to community work, only two failed to comply with the terms of their work orders.

Under the pilot work order program, immediate supervision is carried out by the Salvation Army, whose officer also interviews the offender to ascertain his or her suitability for a community work order. Before the offender is sentenced to a community work order, he or she must consent to such a sentence.

Follow-up Stage of Dispositions

Compulsory Supervision Order. Release by compulsory supervision order may be described as one of the two equivalents of overseas parole programs available in Fiji.

Section 65 of the Prisons Service Act provides that

1. the minister may at any time, in his discretion, direct that a prisoner shall be released on an order of compulsory supervision, for such period as the minister may think fit, and the commissioner shall forthwith comply with such directions;
2. where no order has been made under the provisions of subsection (1), the commissioner
   a. shall, in the case of a prisoner who, having being sentenced to

imprisonment on not less than two previous occasions, is serving a sentence of imprisonment for any period of three years or more; and

b. may, in the case of any other prisoner sentenced to imprisonment for any period of three years or more, where he considers it necessary or desirable to do so,

make an order providing for the compulsory supervision of the prisoner on his or her release for a period not exceeding one year.

Sections 66 and 67 of the Prisons Act deals with revocation or cancellation of an order as well as its effect. Any prisoner who, under a compulsory supervision order, has been convicted of an offense or has contravened or failed to comply with any of the terms or conditions of his or her order, may be subject to revocation of the order and the issuance of a certificate to that effect by the commissioner. If the offender is convicted of an offense or fails to comply with any term or condition of the order, he or she shall be guilty of an offense and liable to three months' imprisonment.

When a compulsory supervision order is revoked, the offender, after undergoing any other punishment to which he or she may have been sentenced for an offense in consequence of which the order was revoked, could serve a further term of imprisonment equal to that portion of sentence that remained unexpired at the time of his or her release under the compulsory supervision order.

The system of release under supervision, which was introduced into Fiji by Act. No. 20 of 1968 has proved effective and successful. As of 1 January 1982, a total of 92 persons were under compulsory supervision orders, representing a daily average for 1981 of 84 or an annual rate of 13.57 per one hundred thousand population. The return rate of persons to prison while under compulsory supervision orders is approximately 3 percent; this is not by any means considered excessive and, to some extent, indicates the success of this system of release.

In 1983, a total of 145 prisoners were released on this order, one hundred of whom were granted by the minister and forty-five by the commissioner. In 1986, among thirty-nine offenders who left the prison under this order, five failed to comply with the conditions and their orders were revoked.

Extramural Punishment. A prisoner is eligible for release to extramural punishment if his or her sentence does not exceed twelve months in the aggregate. Prisoners serving longer sentences become eligible when their earliest date of release with remission is no more than twelve months away and provided the prisoners may not be subject to the commissioner's compulsory supervision order when due for release. The criteria and procedures are stipulated in the Fiji Prisons Service Act, chapter 86.

A person released to extramural punishment and undertaking public work should be employed under the supervision of any person or authority appointed by the controller or a supervisor of prisons for a certain number of hours specified by the controller or supervisor of prisons, but not less than thirty hours per week.

According to the Prison Amendment Act, 1980, the expression *public work* includes undertaking work under the supervision of provincial council, city, town, or district council, local authority, or religious, charitable, or other body approved in writing by the minister.

Where the controller or the supervisor of prisons is satisfied that a person undergoing extramural punishment is unsuitable or unable to continue with extramural punishment, the supervisor may order his or her recall to prison.

Although different in its application to the system of release by compulsory supervision order, extramural punishment is the other form of release under supervision that is equivalent to parole. This system has also proved successful and plays a major role in the reduction of the prison population and in the creation of incentives for prisoners.

The daily average of prisoners undergoing extramural punishment was 293.5 in 1981 and increased to 364 in 1986. The total number of prisoners placed on extramural punishment during 1986 was 508, including eleven females. However, 95 prisoners absconded while they were out of prison.

Remission of Sentence. Remission is provided for in sections 63 and 64 of the Prisons Act.

Section 63 provides that

a. every convicted criminal prisoner under sentence of imprisonment for any period exceeding one calendar month, whether by one sentence or by cumulative sentences, and whether suffering extramural punishment or not, shall, after serving one month's imprisonment or extramural punishment, as the case may be, be eligible by diligence and good conduct, to a remission of one-third of his or her total sentence of imprisonment, provided that the remission so earned shall not reduce the period of imprisonment or extramural punishment to less than one month;
b. on the recommendation of the commissioner, the minister may grant such further remission as he or she shall determine on special grounds, such as exceptional merit or permanent ill health;
c. for the purpose of giving effect to subsection (1), each convicted criminal prisoner, on admission, shall be credited with the full amount of remission that he or she could earn and shall forfeit such portions of such remission as a punishment for idleness, lack of diligence, or any other offense against prison discipline as the commissioner or the supervisor shall determine.

In the event of a prisoner being punished by the loss of remission, the number of days lost will be added to the date of release with remission, and the necessary alteration will be made to all relevant records, registers, and warrants.

Conditional Pardon. The Fiji Constitution, which is presently suspended, states:

> The Governor-General may, in Her Majesty's name and on Her Majesty's behalf—
> a. grant to any person convicted of any offense under the law of Fiji a pardon, either free or subject to lawful conditions;
> b. grant to any person a respite, either indefinite or for a specified period, of the execution of any punishment imposed on that person for such an offense;
> c. substitute a less severe form of punishment for any punishment imposed on any person for such an offense; or
> d. remit the whole or part of any punishment imposed on any person for such an offense or of any penalty or forfeiture otherwise due to the Crown on account of such an offense.

In the event of the governor-general exercising any of his or her powers as outlined above, where any conditions are imposed they are usually in the same form as those applied to persons released on a compulsory supervision order. The governor-general's powers may be extended to both fixed and indeterminate sentences.

India

Crime Trends and Policy for Alternatives to Imprisonment

The number of reported offenses envisaged in the Indian Penal Code (IPC) has shown an increase during the decade 1976–86 (table 6.3). Criminal offenses numbered 1,093,897 in 1976 and topped 1,383,177 in 1986, an increase of 26.4 percent. In particular, the most serious crimes against persons increased, as seen by the rise in rape (90.8 percent), murder (63.4 percent), culpable homicide (38.6 percent), and kidnapping (28.7 percent). Conversely, some types of property offenses, such as criminal breach of trust, burglary, and theft, declined significantly. Such an increase of crimes was attributable to an increase of the young population. Quite a number of people have been arrested each year. The total number of persons arrested amounted to 2,007,530 in 1982. The highest number of arrests (570,378) were for riots, comprising 28.4 percent of total arrests (table 6.4). As a result, a total of 2,334,028 persons were under custody or on bail during the

Table 6.3   Incidence of Crime; Volume of Crime per Lack of Population and Percentage (Variation during 1986 over 1976 over quinquennial average of 1981 to 1985 and over 1985)

VARIATION DURING 1986 OVER 1976 OVER QUINQUENNIAL AVERAGE OF 1981 TO 1985 AND OVER 1985

Sl. No.	Crime Head	1976	1981	1982	1983	1984	1985	Quinquennial average of 1981 to 1985 (Q.A.)	1986	Percentage variation in 1986 (+increase, -decrease)		
										over 1976	over QA	over 1985
1	Murder	16673 (03)	22727 (03)	23339 (03)	25112 (04)	25250 (03)	25279 (03)	24341	27238 (04)	+ 63	+ 12	+ 08
2	Culpable homicide not amounting to murder	2584 (00)	3272 (01)	3427 (01)	3793 (01)	3555 (01)	3231 (00)	3456	3582 (01)	+ 39	+ 04	+ 11
3	Kidnapping and Abduction	11250 (02)	13839 (02)	13340 (02)	13842 (02)	13646 (02)	14923 (02)	13917	14477 (02)	+ 29	+ 04	- 03
4	Rape	3893 (01)	5409 (01)	5427 (01)	6019 (01)	6203 (01)	6326 (01)	5877	7429 (01)	+ 91	+ 26	+ 17
5	Dacoity	10910 (02)	14626 (02)	12700 (02)	12382 (02)	10202 (01)	9458 (01)	11874	9005 (01)	- 18	- 24	- 05
6	Robbery	17974 (03)	22996 (03)	21938 (03)	21310 (03)	21634 (03)	21045 (03)	21785	21547 (03)	+ 20	- 01	+ 02
7	Burglary	168655 (28)	157540 (23)	142726 (20)	139103 (19)	126031 (17)	122950 (16)	137670	122302 (16)	- 28	- 11	- 01
8	Thefts	365138 (60)	422059 (61)	375240 (53)	353536 (49)	322300 (44)	324367 (43)	359500	314781 (41)	- 14	- 12	- 03
9	Riots	63675 (10)	110361 (16)	106511 (15)	108101 (15)	89546 (12)	86043 (12)	100112	82474 (11)	+ 30	- 18	- 04
10	Criminal Breach of Trust	23656 (04)	20579 (03)	18259 (03)	18514 (03)	14537 (02)	14613 (02)	17300	15859 (02)	- 33	- 08	+ 09
11	Cheating	19588 (03)	17761 (03)	17471 (03)	19767 (03)	16935 (02)	19530 (03)	18294	20595 (03)	+ 05	+ 13	+ 06
12	Counterfeiting	887 (00)	1004 (00)	939 (00)	809 (00)	1149 (00)	1326 (00)	1046	1530 (00)	+ 73	+ 46	+ 15
13	Other IPC Crime	389014 (63)	573584 (83)	612586 (87)	627578 (87)	667739 (91)	697031 (93)	635703	742358 (97)	+ 91	+ 17	+ 07
	Total Cognizable Crime	1093897 (178)	1385757 (201)	1353903 (192)	1349866 (187)	1318727 (179)	1346122 (179)	1350875	1383177 (181)	+ 26	+ 02	+ 03

Source: Crime in India, 1982.

Notes: Figures from 1984 to 1986 are based on quarterly crime reviews and are provisional.

Figures in parentheses show rate of crimes per one lack of population.

114

Table 6.4 Persons Arrested under Indian Penal Code Crime Heads

Sl. No.	Crime Head	Persons Arrested 1981	Persons Arrested 1982	% variation in 1982 over 1981	% to total persons arrested during 1982
1	Murder	56,060	56,421	+ 01	03
2	Culpable homicide not amounting to murder	6,337	7,086	+ 12	00
3	Rape	7,407	7,442	+ 01	00
4	Kidnapping and Abduction	17,468	17,389	- 01	01
5	Dacoity	54,053	47,651	- 12	02
6	Robbery	28,169	26,843	- 05	01
7	Burglary	105,629	102,256	- 03	05
8	Thefts	252,738	234,787	- 07	12
9	Riots	573,186	570,378	- 01	28
10	Criminal Breach of Trust	16,946	16,686	- 02	01
11	Cheating	14,988	15,138	+ 01	01
12	Counterfeiting	545	750	+ 38	neg.
13	Miscellaneous	879,562	904,703	+ 03	45
	Total Cognizable Crime	2,013,088	2,007,530	+ 00	100

Source: Crime in India, 1982.
Note: Neg. = Negligible, i.e., less than 0.05.

115

Table 6.5   Disposal of Persons Arrested under Indian Penal Code Crime under Investigation by Police during 1982

Sl. No.	Crime Heads	Total persons in custody or on bail (A)[a]	persons in custody or on bail at the end of the year	Persons in whose cases charge-sheets were laid during the year		
1	Murder	70,677	14,801	52.563	21	74
2	Culpable homicide not amounting to murder	8,868	1,871	6,373	21	72
3	Rape	9,579	2,208	6,685	23	70
4	Kidnapping and Abduction	22,128	5,172	13,903	23	63
5	Dacoity	66,455	17,662	35,846	27	54
6	Robbery	32,011	5,121	22,446	16	70
7	Burglary	115,878	14,248	88,770	12	77
8	Thefts	268,459	33,961	195,933	13	73
9	Riots	690,137	128,143	503,026	19	73
10	Criminal Breach of Trust	24,997	7,887	14,268	32	57
11	Cheating	21,399	6,071	13,161	28	62
12	Counterfeiting	1,129	430	436	38	39
13	Total Cognizable Crime	2,334,028	341,622	1.794.469	15	77

Source: Crime in India, 1982.

[a] Including persons under arrest carried over from previous year.

investigation stage in 1982. Charge sheets were handed down for 76.9 percent of those persons, and 14.6 percent remained under custody or on bail at the end of the year pending completion of investigation. The remaining 8.5 percent were released by the police or the courts before trial (table 6.5).

During the same year, a total of 2,304,389 cases were under trial, including cases pending from the previous year (table 6.6). Out of those cases, 5.6 percent were compounded or withdrawn, and 24.0 percent of trials were completed, while 70.4 percent were still pending at the end of the year (table 6.7).

The percentage of convictions for trial cases was 51.9. The highest percentage was found in theft (59.6 percent), followed by burglary (53.7 percent), and the lowest was for kidnapping (33.4 percent).

On 30 June 1986, there were 1,054 correctional institutions in India, with a total capacity of 183,616. The number of offenders incarcerated was 165,930, including 105,832 remand prisoners under trial (63.8 percent). This means that India is not faced with prison overcrowding, in general, but prisons in large cities are often overcrowded, mainly due to the large population of prisoners on remand.

Long before the country's independence, the Indian Jail Committee, 1919–20, declared that the purpose of imprisonment should be rehabilitation of the offender and that individualized treatment programs in cooperation with resources outside prisons should be encouraged. At present, India adheres to that principle and encourages alternative measures to imprisonment and community support.

Pretrial Stage

Bail. Bail is a sum of money demanded by a court, paid by or for a person accused of wrongdoing, as security that he or she will appear for trial, until which time he or she is allowed freedom. Bail can be allowed in both pretrial and trial stages.

Offenses are classified into two categories: bailable and nonbailable. In bailable offenses, bail can be granted either by the police officer or by the court. In the case of nonbailable offenses, powers of granting bail are exercised only by the court.

In practice, bail is granted in all nonbailable offenses except in cases where there appear reasonable grounds for believing that the offender has been guilty of an offense punishable with death or imprisonment for life (section 437 of the Code of Criminal Procedure).

Table 6.6 Disposal of Cases under Indian Penal Code by Courts during 1982

Sl. No. Crime Head	Total No. of cases for trial during the year[a]	No. of cases compounded or withdrawn during the year	No. of cases in which trials were completed during the year	No. of cases ended in conviction during the year	No. of cases pending trial at the end of the year
1 Murder	50,149	327	14,085	6,335	35,737
2 Culpable homicide not amounting to murder	7,816	76	2,115	924	5,625
3 Rape	11,759	83	3,164	1,164	8,512
4 Kidnapping and Abduction	23,644	321	5,503	1,840	17,820
5 Dacoity	34,141	112	7,433	3,577	26,596
6 Robbery	61,627	1,706	11,922	5,413	47,999
7 Burglary	175,835	5,004	43,079	23,134	127,752
8 Thefts	418,717	15,186	104,303	62,199	299,228
9 Riots	258,228	15,531	44,290	16,212	198,407
10 Criminal Breach of Trust	47,105	932	8,037	3,861	38,136
11 Cheating	34,884	1,357	6,299	2,977	27,228
12 Counterfeiting	501	14	113	47	374
13 Other IPC Offences	1,179,983	88,907	301,711	159,007	789,365
TOTAL COGNIZABLE CRIME	2,304,389	129,556	552,054	286,690	1,622,779

Source: Crime in India, 1982.
[a] Including cases carried over from the previous year.

Table 6.7 Percentage of Disposal of Cases under Indian Penal Code by the Courts during 1982

Sl. No.	Crime Head	% cases compounded or withdrawn to total cases for trial	% cases in which trials were completed to total cases for trial	% cases pending trial at the end of the year to total cases for trial	% cases ended in conviction to total cases for which trials were completed
1	Murder	01	28	71	45
2	Culpable homicide not amounting to murder	01	27	72	44
3	Rape	01	27	72	37
4	Kidnapping and Abduction	01	23	75	33
5	Dacoity	00	22	78	48
6	Robbery	03	19	78	45
7	Burglary	03	25	73	54
8	Thefts	04	25	72	60
9	Riots	06	17	77	37
10	Criminal Breach of Trust	02	17	81	48
11	Cheating	04	18	78	47
12	Counterfeiting	03	23	75	42
13	Other IPC Offenses	08	26	67	53
	TOTAL COGNIZABLE CRIME	06	24	70	52

Source: Crime in India, 1982.

Adjudication Stage

Suspended Sentence and Probation. The suspension of sentence and release of offenders on probation has been accepted as the most constructive alternative to imprisonment in India. Section 360 of the Code of Criminal Procedure, 1973, lays down that

> when any person not under twenty-one years of age is convicted of an offence punishable with fine only or with imprisonment for a term of seven years or less, or when any person under twenty-one years of age or any woman is convicted of an offence not punishable with death or imprisonment for life, and no previous conviction is proved against the offender, if it appears to the Court before which he is convicted, regard being made to the age, character or antecedents of the offender, and to the circumstances in which the offence was committed, that it is expedient that the offender should be released on probation of good conduct, the Court may, instead of sentencing him at once to any punishment, direct that he be released on his entering into a bond, with or without sureties, to appear and receive sentence when called upon during such period (not exceeding three years) as the Court may direct and in the meantime to keep the peace and be of good behavior.

The substantive law provisions regarding probation are supplemented by a special law, the Probation of Offenders Act, 1958. Under the act, the courts have been empowered to release on probation, in all applicable cases, an offender found guilty of having committed an offense not punishable with death or life imprisonment. Where the sentence is up to seven years' imprisonment, the court should first consider the desirability of release on probation. The court, while releasing the offender, may pass a supervision order directing that the offender remain under the supervision of a probation officer for not less than a year and may impose certain conditions regarding residence, abstention from intoxicants, and so on. If the offender has failed to observe any of the conditions, the court may sentence him or her for the original offense. Rules on probation in various states provide for the establishment of probation hostels to accommodate eligible probationers. However, these facilities in most states are inadequate and need further extension.

In India, about thirteen thousand persons are sentenced to imprisonment every year for a period not exceeding six months, and about twelve thousand more for a period not exceeding one year. Thus, about twenty-five thousand prisoners can easily be released on probation on good conduct and placed under the supervision of probation officers. At present, there are eight hundred probation officers in the country. Duties of probation officers include

a. to make initial inquiries regarding the home, social conditions, conduct, character, and health of the offenders under supervision;
b. to visit offenders in their homes and places of employment and submit monthly reports; and
c. to advise, guide, and assist the offenders and to find employment for them.

Follow-up Stage of Dispositions

Remission. Remission is the concession granted to prisoners as a reward for good behavior in prison; nonetheless, it is not a right.

The state government reserves the right to withdraw concession of remission. Remission of sentences is provided under section 59 (5) of the Prisoners Act.

Remission is generally of three types: ordinary remission, special remission, and state government remission. Ordinary remission is granted generally at the rate of four days per month for good behavior and discipline and five days per month for satisfactorily performing the allotted work in accordance with the prescribed standard. Besides, the superintendent and inspector general of prisons may each grant special remission to any prisoner, not exceeding 30 days a year, while the state government may grant such remission for 120 days a year. Normally, the total period of remission should not exceed one-third of the sentence.

Parole/Furlough/Leave. Parole in an international sense means premature release, but in India it means a short, midimprisonment release. Parole, being synonymous with furlough, ordinary leave, and emergency leave, is generally used in India for the award of temporary release for a short duration for providing an opportunity for some selected prisoners to be with their relatives. Different concepts, such as parole, furlough, ticket of leave, emergency leave, and home leave, are used in different states to denote grant of leave or emergency release of a prisoner from prison.

Furlough. A prisoner who is sentenced to imprisonment for more than one year and less than five years can be released on furlough after completion of one year of imprisonment. If the individual is convicted for more than five years, he or she may be released on furlough after completion of two years. Furlough is given to those who show good behavior in prison. Furlough of two weeks can be given at any time. After a lapse of one year, he or she may be given the second furlough. The inspector general of prisons grants furloughs. Amount of remission earned, conduct, educational attainment, family ties, *inter alia*, are some of the considerations taken into account for furlough. Before the prisoner is released on furlough, the superintendent of police is consulted, who suggests the conditions to be imposed. The prisoner, before going on furlough, signs the forms imposing conditions. For breach of these conditions, he or she is punished with a cut of remission, warning, withholding interviews, and so forth. Furlough is counted toward the sentence imposed.

Emergency Leave. Emergency leave can be given in cases of serious illness or death of a close relative of the prisoner. The inspector general of prisons is empowered to release prisoners on emergency leave. In one year, the maximum period for release is fifteen days, and this period will not count as a part of the sentence.

Ordinary Leave. This type of leave is given on the recommendation of the inspector general of prisons for foreseeable needs like cultivation, harvesting, partition of property, arrangement or conduct of the marriage of children, and so on.

Pardon. Article 72 of the Constitution empowers the president to grant pardons to any person in certain cases. Article 161 of the Constitution specifies the power of the governor of a state to grant pardons to any person convicted of any offense against any law relating to a matter that is under the jurisdiction of the executive power of the state.

Republic of Indonesia

Crime Trends and Policy for Alternatives to Imprisonment

Indonesia experienced a serious increase of crimes from the mid 1970s to the early 1980s. Since 1982, however, crimes have declined dramatically (table 6.8). The reason for this decrease seems to be attributed to the enhanced law enforcement policy of the government. President Suharto stressed the importance of crime prevention at the armed forces board meeting in Jakarta, 13 March 1982, stating, "The recent criminal incidents must be tackled radically. It is hoped that the security apparatus, especially the police with the help and cooperation of the armed forces and other security apparatus, can take steps and find an operational pattern of the most effective prevention and eradication of crime."

In 1985, a total of 313,798 crimes and offenses (minor crimes, in Indonesia, including traffic violations) were reported to the police—a relatively low incidence of crimes, at only 190 per 100,000 population (table 6.9). Among the reported crimes and offenses, excluding traffic violations, burglary was the most reported (61,195), followed by assault and aggravated assault (30,812) and theft (10,854).

In the same year (1985), 96,869 crimes, or 53.8 percent of reported crimes, were cleared by the police. Rape (68.4 percent), assault (68.0 percent), and murder (63.1 percent) were cleared at high rates, but robbery (33.7 percent) and burglary (37.3 percent) were cleared at low rates. As a result, 60,191 persons were referred to public prosecutors in 1985 (table 6.10).

Table 6.8 Number of Crimes and Offenses Reported, by Type, 1980–1985

TYPE OF CRIME AND OFFENSE	YEAR					
	1980	1981	1982	1983	1984	1985
Crime						
Political	1	4	4	1	33	8
Against Head of State		1	19	2		
Against public order	1.231	1.959	1.702	1.094	926	805
Arson	246	299	389	300	305	317
Fire	2.114	2.997	3.941	3.234	2.816	3.510
Bribery	16	28	97	118	122	151
To receive bribery	59	525	136	195	147	128
Money counterfeiting	67	130	153	147	268	317
Seals, documents and trade marks forgery	414	461	562	629	722	601
Adultery	45	142	128	152	477	365
Sex	1.682	2.147	1.842	2.261	2.114	1.923
Rape	1.695	2.176	1.731	1.945	2.009	1.728
Gambling	1.803	1.972	1.327	1.889	2.092	2.420
Kidnapping	162	283	170	348	265	256
Murder	1.210	1.616	1.547	1.769	1.457	1.549
Aggravated assault	12.444	15.264	14.466	14.173	13.379	12.414
Assault	11.704	16.524	18.553	19.169	18.662	18.398
Burglary	79.748	98.199	84.552	78.670	50.964	61.195
Theft	9.372	11.738	16.480	13.516	26.884	10.854
Robbery	9.117	17.048	16.303	12.637	7.380	6.181
Blackmail	1.956	2.259	2.459	2.896	2.202	1.389
Embezzlement	5.363	6.973	7.053	7.775	7.010	6.273
Swindle	10.540	13.592	13.995	15.215	14.910	13.617
Destruction	3.690	4.855	5.330	5.593	4.960	4.552
Fence	972	1.414	553	1.340	964	683
Others	20.189	26.908	30.083	31.033	28.186	29.937
Economic	309	641	193	783	539	399
TOTAL OF CRIMES	176,149	230.155	223.768	216.884	189.793	179.970
Offense						
Against Penal Code	1.470	1.117	1.310	1.323	3.936	3.076
Traffic violation	146.483	92.764	115.285	69.571	71.310	129.480
Economic violation	300	298	5.774	462	536	1.272
TOTAL OF OFFENSES	148.253	94.179	122.369	71.356	75.782	133.828
TOTAL OF CRIMES AND OFFENSES	324.402	324.334	346.137	288.240	265.575	313.798

Source: Crime statistics, data from police force, 1985, Indonesia.

In 1986, the district courts in Indonesia dealt with 58,603 criminal defendants, of which 2,013 (or 3.4 percent) were acquitted and the rest (56,645) were convicted. Among the convicted, the overwhelming majority of 45,883 (81 percent) were sentenced to imprisonment (table 6.11).

Due to the decrease of reported crimes, the prison population in

Table 6.9   Number of Crimes and Offenses Reported and Cleared and Clearance Rate by Type, 1985

TYPE OF CRIME AND OFFENSE	Reported	Cleared	Clearence (%)
Crime			
Political	8	6	75
Against Head of State			
Against public order	805	378	47
Arson	317	193	61
Fire	3,510	2,349	67
Bribery	151	74	49
To receive bribery	128	111	87
Money counterfeiting	317	130	41
Seals, documents and trade marks forgery	601	385	64
Adultery	365	251	69
Sex	1,923	1,280	67
Rape	1,728	1,182	68
Gambling	2,420	2,098	87
Kidnapping	256	114	45
Murder	1,549	978	63
Aggravated assault	12,414	8,077	65
Assault	18,398	12,510	68
Burglary	61,195	22,815	37
Theft	10,854	5,225	48
Robbery	6,181	2,086	34
Blackmail	1,389	782	56
Embezzlement	6,273	3,556	57
Swindle	13,617	6,858	50
Destruction	4,552	2,502	55
Fence	683	740	100
Others	29,937	22,070	74
Economic	399	119	30
TOTAL OF CRIMES	179.970	96,869	54
Offense			
Against Penal Code	3.076	2,916	95
Traffic violation	129,480	120,358	93
Economic violation	1,272	1,184	93
TOTAL OF OFFENSES	133,828	124,458	93
TOTAL OF CRIMES AND OFFENSES	313,798	221,327	71

Source: Crime statistics, data from police force, 1985, Indonesia.

Table 6.10 Number of Suspected Persons in Crime Cases and Delivered to Prosecutor, by Sex and Regional Police Force, 1985

Polda Regional Police Force	Number of suspected persons in crime			Number of persons delivered to Prosecutor		
	L/M	P/F	L+P/M+F	L/M	P/F	L+P/M+F
I. Aceh	2,381	44	2,425	1,196	16	1,212
II. Sumatera Utara	44,440	793	45,233	22,260	485	22,275
III. Sumatera Barat	2,149	59	2,208	850	23	873
IV. Riau	1,869	77	1,946	769	6	775
V. Sumatera Bagian Selatan	8,444	182	8,626	6,160	93	6,253
VI. Metro Jaya	14,238	233	14,471	5,812	77	5,889
VII. Jawa Barat	5,157	62	5,219	2,163	6	2,169
VIII. Jawa Tengah	8,959	442	9,401	5,818	208	6,026
IX. Jawa Timur	11,501	185	11,686	6,921	92	7,013
X. Kalimatan Barat	1,572	35	1,607	328	11	339
XI. Kalimatan Selatan Tengah	3,584	30	3,614	2,290	9	2,299
XII. Kalimatan Timur	3,339	93	3,432	1,018	31	1,049
XIII. Nusa Tenggara	3,258	88	3,346	1,555	35	1,590
XIV. Sulawesi Selatan Tenggara	...	...	...	...	...	...
XV. Sulawesi Utara Tengah	11,384	308	11,692	1,470	27	1,497
XVI. Maluku	1,283	123	1,406	138	15	153
XVII. Irian Jaya	1,709	43	1,752	299	10	309
Indonesia	125 267	2,797	128,064	59,047	1,144	60,191

Source: Crime statistics, data from police force, 1985, Indonesia.

125

Table 6.11 Number of Defendants in Crime Cases Brought into Civil Court,
by Type of Verdict

Type of Verdict	Year				
	1982	1983	1984	1985	1986
death/lifelong sentence	4	5	13	6	8
imprisonment	45,061	42,596	38,602	44,743	45,883
custody	280	275	322	98	34
conditional sentence/probation	7,883	8,003	9,062	10,265	9,055
fine	1,502	1,660	1,292	1,135	1,530
additional	-	-	-	-	-
returned to parents/ family	126	152	117	120	116
trusted to Government care	32	33	39	71	19
free from accusation	3,653	2,729	1,995	2,165	2,013
unknown	-	-	-	-	-
Total:	58,541	55,453	51,442	58,603	58,658

Source: Crime statistics, data from police force, 1986, Indonesia.

Indonesia has dropped in recent years. In 1981, 33,148 convicted prisoners were incarcerated by the end of the year, but the number fell to 19,570 by the end of 1985 (table 6.12). In addition to convicted prisoners, it is reported that approximately fifteen thousand remand prisoners are incarcerated in detention houses throughout the country. There are 132 prisons, with capacity for 43,000, and 293 detention houses, with capacity for 26,500. Therefore, Indonesia does not face a serious problem of overcrowding.

Remission (pardon) is utilized widely to reduce the prison population. However, other alternative measures to imprisonment are not developed in pretrial, trial, or postrial stages of criminal justice administration in Indonesia.

Pretrial Stage: Bail/Personal Guarantee

According to the Code of Criminal Procedure (C.C.P., law 8, 1981), the police are authorized to make an arrest (article 16, C.C.P.), and the police, the public prosecutor, and the judge at a court session are all authorized to order a detention (article 20, C.C.P.). At the request of the suspect or defendant, they can allow a suspension of detention with or without money or personal guarantee on the basis of set conditions (article 31, C.C.P.).

In practice, the suspension of detention on bail rarely occurs in Indonesia at the investigation, prosecution, or trial stages. One of the reasons is that most offenders come from the low-income bracket. Offenders from the middle-income bracket usually do not post bail but use personal guarantee by friends or relatives who hold important or influential positions. Those offenders who come from the high-income bracket always request the suspension of detention on bail, but the court usually turns down the request. The rejection is made mostly not on a legal basis, but to eliminate possible public suspicion that there is collusion between the court and the defendant, since most of the public do not know the criminal law procedures allowing suspension of detention. The last reason is that the strictly limited detention time set by the law to guarantee a speedy trial sometimes makes the court find no urgent reason to grant bail.

Adjudication Stage: Suspended Execution of Sentence/Probation

The Penal Code of Indonesia stipulates that when a judge passes a sentence of imprisonment of at most one year, short imprisonment, or a fine, the judge may give the order of probation (suspension of execution of sentence; article 14 [1]). The maximum probation period is three years (article 14b [1]). With a probation order, the judge may, in addition to the general order not to commit a punishable act, fix a special condition to compensate for damages caused by the offense (article 14c [1]). The probation order, however, should not be issued unless the judge is convinced that adequate supervision can be exercised regarding the fulfillment of conditions (article 14a [4]). Under the Penal Code, a probation supervision of an offender is carried out by a public prosecutor, not by a probation officer (extrainstitutional officer; article 14d [1]). In practice, however, the prosecutor usually does not exercise the supervision himself or herself but often asks the police or other local agencies to supervise the probationer, and sometimes no supervi-

Table 6.12   Number of Inmates in Prison by Regional Prison Institutes at End of Year, 1981–1986

Regional Prison Institute	Year					
	1981	1982	1983	1984	1985	1986
1. Dareah Istimewa Aceh	...	453	628	732	840	571
2. Sumatera Utara	2,670	2,019	2,015	3,547	2,782	1.715
3. Sumatera Barat	1,466	555	603	576	748	464
4. Riau	...	734	507	601	871	470
5. Jambi						262
6. Sumatera Selayan	2,413	1,656	1,640	2,314	2.553	1,020
7. Bengkulu						280
8. Lampung	...	806	1,208	1.151	1,067	706
9. DKI Jakarta	4,049	2,223	2,658	3,555	2,480	2,154
10. Jawa Barat	2,738	2,084	2,224	2,223	2,395	1,638
11. Jawa Tengah						1 386
12. DI Yogukarta	5,079	4,541	3,556	2,827	3,336	166
13. Jawa Timiur	7,602	6,339	5,283	4,469	4,227	3 218
14. Bali						306
15. Nusa Tenggara Barat	2,104	605	806	903	901	333
16. N.T.T./Timor Timur	...	1,045	989	1,181	1,173	751
17. Kalimatan Barat	...	528	626	457	463	450
18. Kalimatan Tengah						167
19. Kalimatan Selatan	1,158	622	838	909	993	427
20. Kalimatan Timur	...	418	424	450	509	485
21. Sulawesi Utara						565
22. Sulawesi Tengah	819	908	753	846	899	205
23. Sulawesi Selatan						993
24. Sulawesi Tenggara	2,309	1,732	2,003	2,144	2,070	163
25. Maluku	345	288	272	365	402	160
26. Irian Jaya	396	234	292	335	418	470
Indonesia	33,148	27,790	27,325	29,495	29,127	19,570

Source: Crime statistics, data from police force, 1985, Indonesia.

sion is carried out. Under the same law, assistance can be provided to the probationer by the Extrainstitutional Treatment Office. The sentencing judge can, if he or she deems it necessary, ask the Extrainstitutional Treatment Office or other agencies to provide help and assistance to the probationer in fulfilling the special conditions (article 14d [2]). However, such a request for assistance is not issued often, because of the shortage of probation officers.

If a probationer, during the probation period, is found guilty of a punishable act and is sentenced, or breaches any of the special conditions, the execution of the original sentence may be ordered, or the probationer may be admonished by the judge who has issued the probation order (article 14f [1]).

The number of probation orders has increased in recent years. According to the statistics on judgment at the first instance in the district courts throughout the country, probation orders increased from 7,883 in 1982 to 9,055 in 1986 (table 6.11).

Under the Department of Corrections, Ministry of Justice, there were forty-two extrainstitutional treatment offices (probation offices), with fifty probation officers and twenty-five administration staff, throughout the country in 1988. Since the supervision of probationers is carried out by the public prosecutors, the role of the probation officers is limited to providing assistance to probationers. Accordingly, probation officers in Indonesia are oriented to social work. The required qualification is a degree from a social work school or the Correctional Science Academy. Some volunteers are also working as probation officers.

Follow-up Stage of Dispositions

Conditional Release/Parole. The person sentenced to imprisonment can be released on parole after serving two-thirds of his or her imprisonment term and at least nine months of imprisonment (article 15 [1], Penal Code). This means that parole is granted only to offenders sentenced to more than one year's imprisonment. Parole is not considered a prisoner's right. The period of parole is the remaining term of his or her sentence plus one year (article 15 [3], Penal Code). The decision of parole is made by the minister of justice after the hearing of the Central Parole Board (article 16 [1], Penal Code). In reality, the screening process starts in prison. After the examination of an inmate, the head of the prison submits an application for parole to the Ministry of Justice. The application for parole is required to include the following references:

a. The fact that the inmate has served two-thirds of his or her sentence and nine months of imprisonment
b. The fact that the inmate has shown good conduct in the prison

c. Case history
d. Information on the offender's behavior in court when interrogated
e. Confirmation by the public prosecution that the offender is not under investigation for other criminal charges
f. Opinion on his or her parole release from the head of the village he or she is going to return to
g. Opinion of the victim's relatives, in murder cases
h. Opinion of the offender's family
i. Detailed information on the offense

The application is examined by the members of the Central Parole Board in the Ministry of Justice. The board consists of ten persons, and its function is to give advice or suggestions to the Directorate General of Corrections. Finally, the decision of parole is made by the Directorate General of Corrections in the name of the minister of justice.

Certain conditions are imposed on a person released on parole:

a. Not to commit punishable acts nor misbehave (the general condition provided by article 15a [1] of the Penal Code)
b. To report once a month to the public prosecutor's office in charge of the area where the parolee is going to reside
c. To give previous notice to the public prosecutor and the probation office when changing residence

Some other special conditions are sometimes fixed for the purpose of providing help and assistance to the parolee.

The supervision of, and assistance to, a parolee is carried out in the same way as in probation. Under the Penal Code, every parolee is supervised by the public prosecutor, but assistance and help to the parolee can be provided by the probation office or other agencies only when special supervision is requested (article 15a [2] and [3]).

Parole may be revoked if a parolee, during parole period, breaches parole conditions (article 15b [1]). The public prosecutor can detain a parolee at most sixty days when there is a reasonable suspicion that the parolee has breached his or her parole conditions (article 16 [3] [4]). The decision of parole revocation is made by the minister of justice on the advice from the public prosecutor after the hearing of the Central Parole Board (article 16 [1]).

In practice, a small number of prisoners are released on parole. In 1978, 230 prisoners were released on parole from among approximately 38,000 inmates (including unconvicted prisoners); no recent data is available. One of the reasons for the limited use of parole release is that in many cases the requirements for parole application cannot be fully completed. In particular, it is pointed out that the attitude of victims, village heads, and

Table 6.13 Number of Prisoners at the End of August and Number of Prisoners Obtaining Remission on Indonesia's Independence Anniversary, by Age, Type of Remission, and Regional Prison Institute, 1986

Regional prison institute	Total prisoners at the end of August 1986	Prisoners obtaining remission					
		Adults, Part	Adults, Total	Youth and children, Part	Youth and children, Total	Total, Part	Total, Total
1. Dareah Istimewa Aceh	620	416	72	...	...	416	72
2. Suatera Utara	2,125	1,692	358	424	134	2,116	492
3. Sumatera Barat	451	326	62	59	33	385	95
4. Riau	798	543	138	136	25	679	163
5. Jambi	481	201	44	...	...	201	44
6. Sumatera Selayan	1,370	1 043	209	156	199	1,199	408
7. Bengkulu	188	123	16	...	...	123	16
8. Lampung	716	419	71	135	146	554	217
9. DKI Jakarta	1,959	1,205	427	...	...	1,205	427
10. Jawa Barat	1,868	1,467	307	16	13	1,483	320
11. Jawa Tengah	1,871	1,360	364	16	16	1,376	380
12. DI Yogukarta	235	134	49	...	...	134	49
13. Jawa Timur	3,449	2,618	579	9	16	2,627	595
14. Bali	369	218	41	1	10	219	51
15. Nusa Tenggara Barat	689	279	65	...	...	279	65
16. N.T.T./Timor Timur	1,180	828	69	4	-	832	69
17. Kalimatan Barat	427	295	56	...	...	295	56
18. Kalimatan Tengah	195	123	18	...	...	123	18
19. Kalimatan Selatan	544	400	72	...	...	400	72
20. Kalimatan Timur	327	231	76	...	...	231	76
21. Sulawesi Utara	545	387	65	...	...	387	65
22. Sulawesi Tengah	238	179	24	...	...	179	24
23. Sulawesi Selatan	1,481	1,240	150	10	5	1,250	155
24. Sulawesi Tenggara	140	114	15	...	...	114	15
25. Maluku	254	226	18	...	...	226	18
26. Irian Jaya	315	251	39	18	40	269	79
Indonesia	22,835	16,318	3,404	984	637	17,302	4,041

Source: Crime Statistics, data from police force, 1985, Indonesia.

offenders' families are usually not favorable to the parole release. The public is not appreciative of the parole system, and the community sometimes does not want to accept an ex-offender.

Prerelease Treatment. Prerelease treatment is a long leave of a prisoner given by the Directorate General of Corrections. It is granted as a prerogative and a substitute for parole for those prisoners who do not qualify for parole. Its duration does not exceed six months, and only inmates sentenced to more than one year's imprisonment are eligible.

Work Release. The work-release program allows prisoners in minimum security prisons to work outside during the day. They can earn a living, for example, as barbers, join a private enterprise, fill jobs as factory hands, or even work for government agencies (i.e., as drivers).

Furlough. Furlough is a short leave of forty-eight hours for qualified prisoners. It is granted normally for such purposes as taking part in yearly religious festivals and joining the family on other occasions.

Remission. Remission is a kind of pardon to reduce imprisonment terms, given by the president each year on 17 August, Independence Day of Indonesia. It is given to good-conduct prisoners but not to recidivists. The length of the reduced term ranges from one to six months. Remission is widely utilized each year. At the end of August 1986, there were 22,835 prisoners in prisons, of whom the majority (17,302) received partial reduction of their imprisonment term and 4,041 received total reduction (table 6.13).

Japan

Crime Trends and Policy for Alternatives to Imprisonment

Japan has not experienced a serious increase in crime over the last three decades. As figure 6.1 shows, the number of reported Penal Code offenses, excluding traffic accidents, peaked in 1948, then showed a decline until the middle of the 1970s, and since then has gradually increased. Recent increase in reported crime is caused mainly by an increase in petty theft, such as shoplifting and bicycle theft. The most serious crimes, such as murder and robbery, have demonstrated a decreasing trend in recent years (table 6.14). In 1987, a total of 2,132,592 offenses were reported to the police (table 6.15). Among them, larceny was the most prevalent offense, comprising 64 percent, followed by traffic professional negligence offenses, which accounted for 26 percent. These two categories accounted for 90.0 percent of the total.

Figure 6.1: Trends in the Number of Penal Code Offenses Reported and Offenders Cleared, 1946–1987

1. Penal Code offenses reported

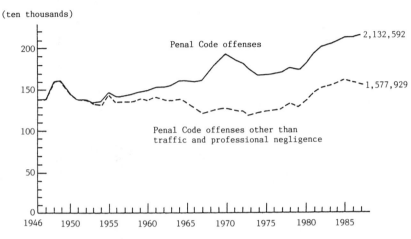

2. Penal Code Offenders Cleared

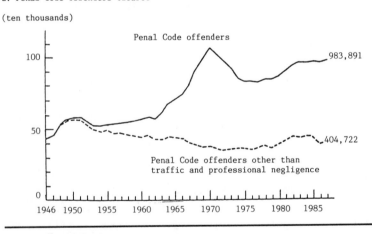

Source: National Police Agency.

If traffic professional negligence is excluded, larceny represents the overwhelming majority (86.5 percent), followed by fraud (4.4 percent) and embezzlement (2.7 percent).

One of the major reasons for a low crime rate in Japan may be a high clearance rate. In 1987, some 73.5 percent of all the reported Penal Code offenses were cleared by the police (table 6.15). In particular, the clearance

Table 6.14 Number of Reported Heinous Offenses and Offenders Cleared by the Police, 1983–1987

Category	Homicide		Robbery		Robbery resulting in death		Robbery resulting in bodily injury		Robbery and rape	
	Number	Index	Number	Index	Number	Index	Number	Index	Number	Index
Offenses										
1983	1,745	100	2,317	100	65	100	815	100	111	100
1984	1,762	101	2,188	94	61	94	780	96	99	89
1985	1,780	102	1,815	78	67	103	743	91	92	83
1986	1,676	96	1,949	84	68	105	834	102	92	83
1987	1,584	91	1,874	81	61	94	803	99	73	66
Offenders										
1983	1,789	100	2,069	100	69	100	993	100	56	100
1984	1,788	100	2,031	98	68	99	945	95	54	96
1985	1,833	102	1,777	86	64	93	881	89	56	100
1986	1,692	95	1,842	89	72	104	940	95	53	95
1987	1,651	92	1,707	83	65	94	880	89	49	88

Source: National Police Agency, Japan.

rate was extremely high for the most serious offenses; for example, 98.0 percent of the reported homicides, 78.2 percent of robberies, and 87.4 percent of rapes. Larceny or theft is rather difficult to clear, but 60.2 percent of the larcenies were cleared. Alternative measures to imprisonment fall in a small range, and existing measures are limited to bail and suspended

Table 6.15   Number of Penal Code Offenses Reported to and Cleared by the Police and the Number of Offenders Cleared, 1987

Offense	Number of offenses reported	Number of offenses cleared	Number of offenders cleared	Clearance rate	Difference from the previous year Number of offenses reported	Number of offenders cleared
Total	2,132,592	1,566,713	983,891	73.5	8353(0.4)	15,919(1.6)
Homicide	1,584	1,552	1,651	98.0	* 92(5.5)	* 41(2.4)
Robbery	1,874	1,465	1,707	78,2	* 75(3.8)	*135(7.3)
Bodily injury	21,046	19,585	27,463	93.1	* 125(0.6)	* 917(3.2)
Assault	9,970	9,292	12,146	93.2	*838(7.8)	*1,616(11.7)
Intimidation	1,106	1,065	1,108	96.3	49(4.6)	169(18.0)
Extortion	11,855	9,951	11,196	83.9	* 1,049(8.1)	* 1,105(9.0)
Unlawful assembly with weapons	102	103	842	101.0	10(10.9)	14(1.7)
Larceny	1,364,796	821,831	261,934	60.2	* 10,300(0.7)	1,401(0.5)
Fraud	69,844	67,784	13,566	97.1	5,056(7.8)	187(1.4)
Embezzlement	42,580	42,451	43,594	99.7	5,144(13.7)	6,105(16.3)
Breach of trust	87	87	105	100.0	* 6(6.5)	* 12(10.3)
Purchase, etc of stolen property	2,074	2,072	1,916	99.9	* 28(1.3)	115(6.4)
Rape	1,823	1,593	1,608	87.4	73(4.2)	31(2.0)
Indecent assault	2,404	1,824	1,046	75.9	113(4.9)	* 59(5.3)
Public indecency	983	957	910	97.4	* 90(8.4)	* 41(4.3)
Distribution of obscene literature, etc.	1,202	1,202	1,105	100.0	* 161(11.8)	23(2.1)
Arson	1,814	1,589	836	87.6	38(2.1)	* 60(6.7)
Fire caused by negligence	933	717	687	76.8	* 169(15.3)	* 164(19.3)
Bribery	328	329	487	100.3	* 14(4.1)	51(11.7)
Kidnapping	106	103	84	97.2	* 7(6.2)	* 1(1.2)
Obstruction of the performance of an official duty	1,209	1,209	1,048	100.0	*92(7.1)	* 72(6.4)
House-breaking	11,776	5,149	3,310	43.7	* 788(6.3)	114(3.6)
Destruction of property	11,976	3,903	2,758	32.6	937(8.5)	* 44(1.6)
Forgery and counterfeiting	11,899	11,813	1,574	99.3	* 1,187(9.1)	* 149(8.6)
Gambling	2,122	2,127	8,990	100.2	383(22.0)	1,309(17.0)
Violent acts	75	70	148	93.3	19(33.9)	36(32.1)
Traffic professional negligence	554,663	554,663	579,169	100.0	11,802(2.2)	11,058(1.9)
Others	2,361	2,227	2,903	94.3	* 250(9.6)	* 278(8.7)

Source: National Police Agency, Japan.
Notes: Clearance rate = (number of offenses cleared / number offenses reported) × 100. Some clearance rates may exceed 100.0% as offenses reported prior to but cleared during 1986 are counted.
Figures in parentheses show the percentage of increase of decrease.
*Indicates a decrease.

Table 6.16 Average Daily Population of Penal Institutions, 1945, 1950, 1975, 1985–1987

Type of prisoner	1945	1950	1975	1985	1986	1987
Convicted prisoners	48,977	85,254	37,850	45,805	46,107	46,076
Prisoners sentenced to death	...	76	41	26	25	27
Unconvicted prisoners: Total	4,553	17,259	7,606	9,268	9,058	8,944
Accused	4,074	15,295	7,203	9,042	8,868	8,770
Suspect	479	1,963	402	226	190	174
Confinement in a workhouse	127	581	183	155	148	150
Arrestee by warrant	-	-	3	2	2	6
kanchi confinement (during trial, as disciplinary punishment, etc.)	-	-	-	-	-	-
Temporary detention for protective reasons	-	-	7	7	6	6
Total	53,656	103,170	45,690	55,263	55,348	55,210

Source: Annual Statistics on Prison Administration and Annual Statistics on Corrections, Japan.
Notes: "Average daily population" means total number of persons detained for every 24 hours throughout the year divided by total days in the year.
The number 4,074 for unconvicted prisoners in 1945 includes prisoners finally sentenced to death.

Figure 6.2: Trend in the Number of Newly Admitted Prisoners, 1945–1987

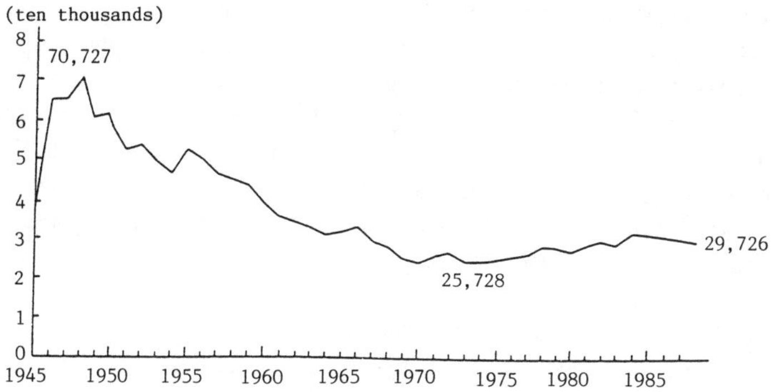

Source: Annual Statistics on Prison Administration and Annual Statistics on Corrections

prosecution at the pretrial stage, suspended execution of sentence and probation as noncustodial sanctions in sentencing, and parole at the postsentencing stage. However, each of these measures is utilized to a maximum extent. The maximum use of alternatives to imprisonment and the low incidence of crimes kept the prison population at a minimum. In 1987, the average daily population of convicted prisoners serving imprisonment sentences was 46,076, representing a rate of 37.9 per 100,000 population (table 6.16 and figure 6.2)

Pretrial Stage

Suspended Prosecution. In Japan a public prosecutor has wide discretionary power to suspend prosecution even if he or she has enough evidence to secure the conviction of a case. The public prosecutor's office is composed of the Supreme Public Prosecutor's Office, eight high public prosecutor's offices, fifty district public prosecutor's offices, and 575 local public prosecutor's offices. Each office corresponds to the respective court structure. There are approximately eleven hundred public prosecutors, nine hundred assistant public prosecutors, and ten thousand public prosecutor assistant officers throughout Japan. The qualification for the appointment to public prosecutor is equal to that for a judge, and they receive equal salaries according to the length of the term of office. Although every public prosecutor is appointed by the minister of justice when he or she is recruited from among the lawyers, the minister has no power to direct an individual public prosecutor as to how to dispose of a specific case.

Japan does not have the system of private prosecution, and there is no system of preliminary hearings conducted by judges. The prosecutor has the exclusive power to decide whether to institute prosecution or not. Though the police have primary responsibility for criminal investigation, the public prosecutor is also authorized to investigate criminal cases. When the police complete investigation, the case is referred to the public prosecutor. Then the prosecutor in charge of the case may either instruct the police to conduct further investigation or may investigate the case himself or herself until he or she obtains enough evidence to decide whether or not to prosecute. In such cases as corruption, economic crimes, and tax evasion, the public prosecutor often initiates and conducts investigation without the assistance of the police.

The dispositions of nonprosecution include nonprosecution based on insufficiency of evidence and suspension of prosecution. Suspension of prosecution is based on a rehabilitation-oriented idea, to give an offender the opportunity to become a responsible member of the society without being labeled "criminal." Therefore, even when there is sufficient evidence to secure conviction, the public prosecutor has the discretion not to prosecute, taking all the circumstances of a case into consideration. Article 248 of the Code of Criminal Procedure provides that if, after considering the character, age, and situation of the offender, the gravity of the offense, the circumstances under which the offense was committed, and the conditions subsequent to the commission of the offense, prosecution is deemed unnecessary, prosecution need not be instituted.

When the prosecution is suspended, an offender is immediately discharged from criminal procedure. He or she is not supervised by any authority, but under the Law for Aftercare of Discharged Offenders he or she can voluntarily apply to a probation office for some material aid or for accommodation at a halfway house.

A large number of prosecutions are suspended each year. In 1987, a total of 356,283 cases, including 80,093 nontraffic cases and 276,190 traffic cases, were suspended from prosecution (table 6.17). Even for serious offenses such as robbery and homicide, it is not rare for prosecution to be suspended. For instance, in 1987, prosecution of fifty-three robbery cases was suspended, representing 5.4 percent of all the robberies that could be prosecuted. The percentage of suspended prosecution differs according to types of offenses. While it was as high as 44.5 percent for larceny, it was quite low (only 5.4 percent) for violations of the Stimulant Drugs Control Law.

Public prosecutors often suspend prosecution of cases where the suspect is a first-time offender or where there are some other mitigating factors, if the suspect remedies the damage and the prosecutor finds that the victim's feelings are remedied. Though plea bargaining is not permissible in

Table 6.17   Number of Suspects Disposed of by the Public Prosecutor's Office, by Offense, 1987

| Offense | Total | Prosecution | | Nonprosecution | | Referral to family court |
		Formal trial	Summary Proceedings	Suspension of prosecution	Other	
Total	2,647,253	125,421	1,617,087	356,283	51,622	496,840
Penal Code offenses	933,272	79,730	297,674	266,535	42,135	247,198
Homicide	2,868	1,060	-	57	1,667	84
Robbery	1,753	872	-	53	240	588
Bodily injury	30,566	4,856	11,003	3,639	751	10,317
Assault	7,824	390	3,707	2,043	82	1,602
Extortion	11,454	3,743	-	1,375	426	5,910
Larceny	205,107	37,513	-	30,067	2,853	134,674
Fraud	17,573	10,095	-	4,237	2,429	812
Embezzlement	26,613	1,323	91	4,159	475	20,565
Rape	1,902	803	-	161	360	578
Indecent assault	1,314	437	-	76	399	402
Public indecency	910	38	640	155	6	71
Distribution of obscene literature, etc,	1,066	528	335	165	23	15
Arson	1,080	580	2	118	246	134
Bribery	682	460	57	107	58	-
Gambling	7,473	1,723	3,061	2,446	81	162
Violent acts	5,688	1,039	1,471	567	140	2,471
Traffic professional negligence	584,905	9,825	272,593	211,839	27,315	63,333
Others	24,494	4,445	4,714	5,271	4,584	5,480
Special Law offenses	1,713,981	45,691	1,319,413	89,748	9,487	249,642
Firearms and swords	4,839	1,482	1,768	927	223	439
Stimulant drugs	27,273	22,858	-	1,302	1,547	1,566
Road-traffic violations	1,578,642	10,725	1,271,595	64,351	5,587	226,384
Other	103,227	10,626	46,050	23,168	2,130	21,253

Source: Annual Statistics Report of Prosecution, Japan.

Japan, the suspect's confession is one of the most important conditions for suspension of prosecution.

The system of suspended prosecution not only contributes to reduce the burden on the courts but also functions as an actual alternative to imprisonment.

There are two kinds of safeguards against abuse of the above-mentioned discretionary power of public prosecutors; one is the examination by inquest of prosecution, and the other is private prosecution for specific crimes committed by government officials.

The law on inquest of prosecution was established in 1948. There are about two hundred inquests of prosecution all over Japan, each of which is an independent committee consisting of eleven lay people as juries chosen by lot from among the citizens. When a public prosecutor does not prosecute a case, the offended party or complainant may apply to the inquest of prosecution for reexamination of the case. The inquest may also conduct the examination *ex officio* if the majority members so decide.

The inquest of prosecution has the authority to evaluate whether the decision of nonprosecution by a public prosecutor was proper or not. The results of examination are reported to the chief prosecutor of the district public prosecutor's office to which the case belongs. Depending upon the contents of the notification, the chief prosecutor orders a more experienced public prosecutor to conduct a reinvestigation of the case. The law gives the notification by the inquest of prosecution only an advisory effect, so even if the decision is made by the inquest of prosecution calling for prosecution, it does not bind a public prosecutor. However, once such a decision by the inquest is made, it actually has a considerable impact on a public prosecutor, which leads to a thorough reinvestigation of the case and a careful reexamination of the initial disposition not to prosecute.

The other safeguard is one specially designed against nonprosecution of specific crimes of abuse of authority by civil servants or of violence and cruelty by law enforcement officers, under articles 193 to 196 of the Penal Code and under article 45 of the Subversive Activities Prevention Law. If the public prosecutor declines to prosecute the suspect of these crimes, any person who has lodged a complaint to a public prosecutor or a judicial police officer may apply to the court to have the case committed for trial. This is called "analogical institution of prosecution through judicial action." If the application is granted, then one of the practicing lawyers is appointed by the court, and he is to exercise the functions of a public prosecutor.

Bail. Prosecution includes two types of prosecution. One is for formal trial, the other is for summary procedure of trial. A summary court, on a public prosecutor's request, imposes a fine of not more than 200,000 yen or a minor fine by a summary court order prior to public trial proceedings. This summary order is issued by the judge based upon the evidence referred to him from the public prosecutor together with the information charging the offense and a written consent of the defendant to the effect that he wishes to be tried through the summary procedure without appearing in open trial and that he has no objection against the imposition of the penalty requested by the prosecutor. Under this summary procedure, almost 95 percent of all cases dealt with in the courts of first instance, including the district courts, were disposed of in recent years.

Suspects prosecuted in a formal trial are rather few in number, but since they have committed serious offenses, most of them are detained during the prosecution phase. The court can release them on bail during the trial. According to articles 88 and 89 of the Code of Criminal Procedure, when the accused under detention, his defense counsel, or some of his family members request his release on bail, the court must allow it except in the following cases:

1. Where the accused is charged with an offense punishable with the death penalty or imprisonment for life or for a minimum period of more than one year
2. Where the accused was previously convicted of an offense punishable with the death penalty or imprisonment for life or for a maximum period of more than ten years
3. Where the accused has habitually committed an offense punishable with imprisonment for a maximum period of three years or more
4. Where there is reasonable ground to suspect that the accused may injure the body or damage the property of the injured party or some other person who is considered to possess necessary information for trial, or a relative, or may commit a threatening act toward the injured party or witnesses
5. Where the name or dwelling of the accused is unknown

The court may also, if it deems proper, grant release on bail *ex-officio* (Code of Criminal Procedure, article 90).

Bail money is fixed at an amount sufficient to insure the presence of the accused, taking into consideration the nature and circumstances of the offense, the weight of evidence against the offender, and his or her character and financial conditions (Code of Criminal Procedure, article 93). At the district courts throughout the country in 1986, a total of 63,204 defendants were finally adjudicated in formal trials (table 6.18). Among the total defendants adjudicated, the majority, 45,913 persons (72.6 percent), were under detention when prosecuted, while 10,964 defendants (23.9 percent) were released on bail by the court after their prosecution. The situation was almost the same in the summary courts, but a smaller number of defendants were granted bail than in the district courts. In the same year, a total of 15,398 defendants were finally adjudicated in formal procedures of the summary courts (table 6.18). Among the total defendants adjudicated, 12,979 persons (84.3 percent) were prosecuted under detention, and a small portion of them, 1,359 defendants (10.5 percent), were released on bail.

The amount of bail money fixed by the court is usually high. In 1986, bail money for the majority (67.1 percent) of the defendants released on bail was between one and three million yen (table 6.19). The amount of bail money fixed by the courts has gradually increased in recent years.

Table 6.18 Number of the Accused Detained Pending Trial in Courts of First Instance, 1984–1986

Court/Year	Number adjudicated (A)	Number detained (B)	Length of detention			Number released on bail (C)	B/A (%)	C/B (%)
			1 month or less	3 months or less	Over 3 months			
District courts								
1984	66,311	49,400	11,829	28,609	8,962	13,438	74.5	27.2
		(100.0)	(23.9)	(57.9)	(18.1)			
1985	65,553	48,190	10,616	28,380	9,194	11,980	73.5	24.9
		(100.0)	(22.0)	(58.9)	(19.1)			
1986	63,204	45,913	9,697	27,560	8,656	10,964	72.6	23.9
		(100.0)	(21.1)	(60.0)	(18.9)			
Summary courts								
1984	16,198	13,816	3,480	9,339	997	1,685	85.3	12.2
		(100.0)	(25.2)	(67.6)	(7.2)			
1985	15,54	13,438	3,058	9,276	1,104	1,609	86.5	12.0
		(100.0)	(22.8)	(69.0)	(8.2)			
1986	15,398	12,979	2,805	9,188	986	1,359	84.3	10.5
		(100.0)	(21.6)	(70.8)	(7.6)			

Source: Annual Report of Judicial Statistics, Japan.

Notes: Adult criminal cases under Juvenile Law adjudicated in family courts are not included.
Figures in parentheses show percentages.

Table 6.19   Amount of Bail Money in Courts of First Instance, 1984–1986

	Total number of decisions to	Amount of bail money				
Year	release on bail	3,000,000 yen or more	1,000,000 yen or more	700,000 yen or more	500,000 yen or more	Less than 500,000 yen
1984	15,298	631	8,889	3,590	1,737	451
	(100.0)	(4.1)	(58.1)	(23.5)	(11.4)	(2.9)
1985	13,754	567	8,497	2,945	1,388	357
	(100.0)	(4.1)	(61.8)	(21.4)	(10.1)	(2.6)
1986	12,430	717	8,337	2,201	914	261
	(100.0)	(5.8)	(67.1)	(17.7)	(7.4)	(2.1)

Source: Annual Report of Judicial Statistics, Japan.
Notes: Adult criminal cases under Juvenile Law adjudicated in family courts are not included.
Figures in parentheses show percentages.

Adjudication Stage

Probation and Suspended Execution of Sentence. As principal punishments, the Penal Code provides the death penalty, imprisonment with or without labor for life or for a determined term, fine, penal detention, and minor fine (Penal Code, article 9). Alternative measures are available to imprisonment and to fine, namely, the execution of sentence can be suspended for imprisonment of a determined term and for a fine. There are two types of suspended execution of sentence; one is accompanied by probationary supervision, and the other is without supervision (table 6.20). Only the suspension of execution of sentence with probationary supervision is called "probation" in Japan. Suspended execution of sentence was introduced in 1905, and probation was established by expanding the system of suspended execution of sentence in 1954.

Article 25 of the Penal Code provides the requirements for suspended execution of sentence and for probation as follows:

a. The sentence is imprisonment of three years or less or a fine of two hundred thousand yen or less,

b. the offender has not been sentenced to imprisonment for the last five years, and

c. the offender, even if he or she has been previously granted suspension of execution of the sentence, is sentenced to imprisonment for one year or less, and there are extenuating circumstances especially favorable to him. However, this cannot be applied to an offender who has been previously placed under suspended sentence with probationary supervision.

*For more detailed information, see "Adult Probation in Japan," chapter 7 of this volume.

Table 6.20   Principal Punishment and Alternative Measures in Japan

Principle punishment	Alternative measures
Death	
Imprisonment with labor	
for life	
for determined term ⟶	Suspended execution of sentence
	with probationary supervision
Imprisonment without labor	without supervision
for life	
for determined term ⟶	
Fine ⟶	
Penal detention	
Minor fine	

Source: The Penal Code, articles 9 and 25, Japan.

Requirement (c) indicates different legal statuses for offenders under probation and those under suspended execution of sentence without supervision. An offender under suspended execution of sentence without supervision may have suspension of execution of sentence imposed when he or she commits a new offense. But an offender under probation has no opportunity for receiving suspended execution of sentence if he or she commits an offense punishable by imprisonment.

A probation order is mandatory when the new sentence is to be suspended again regarding an offense that took place during the period of previous suspension unaccompanied by a probation order. In other cases of suspended sentence, probation is discretionary by the court (Penal Code, article 25-2).

All the requirements in the law refer only to the gravity of sentence and criminal record, having no reference to type of offense. Accordingly, even an offender who has committed an offense of a serious nature, such as murder or robbery, may be placed under suspended execution of sentence or probation if special circumstances justify it.

The term of probation, as well as of suspended execution of sentence, is fixed by the court for a specific period between one and five years (Penal Code, article 25).

Revocation of probation or of suspended execution of sentence is mandatory when an offender during the period of such suspension is sentenced to actual imprisonment for another offense (Penal Code, article 26-1). However, revocation is in the discretion of the court when a fine is imposed (Penal Code, article 26-2). And probation may be revoked at the court's discretion when a probationer fails to observe any of the conditions imposed and the circumstances are seriously unfavorable to him or her (Penal Code, article 26-2-[2]). If probation or suspension of execution of sentence is revoked, the offender has to serve the sentence originally imposed.

When a period of probation or suspension of execution of sentence elapses without revocation, the sentence loses its effect (Penal Code, article 27).

A huge number of offenders are adjudicated by the criminal courts every year. In 1987, the total number of persons finally adjudicated by all the criminal courts, including summary procedures, throughout the country amounted to 1,741,044 (table 6.21). Most of them (94.3 percent) were sentenced to fines by the summary courts. A relatively small number, 68,178 (3.9 percent), were sentenced to imprisonment with labor, and only 5,240 (0.3 percent) were sentenced to imprisonment without labor.

These figures included a number of offenders whose execution of sentence was suspended. According to the statistics of prosecution offices, in 1987, execution of sentence was suspended for a total of 42,473 offenders,

Table 6.21   Number of Persons Finally Adjudicated, 1983–1987

Category	1983	1984	1985	1986	1987
Guilty					
Death	1	3	2	-	7
Life imprisonment with labor	36	43	38	41	56
Imprisonment with labor	72,265	73,941	72,238	69,803	68,178
Imprisonment without labor	4,977	4,947	5,088	5,197	5,240
Fine	2,272,970	2,374,394	2,383,868	2,260,791	1,642,969
Penal detention	41	41	77	122	127
Minor fine	25,418	29,138	29,505	27,004	22,508
Acquittal	165	121	117	115	93
Others	2,929	3,336	2,788	2,006	1,866
Total	2,378,802	2,485,964	2,493,721	2,365,079	1,741,044

Source: Annual Statistics Report of Prosecution, Japan.
Note: Others include dismissal of prosecution, acquittal on procedural grounds, etc.

including those placed under probationary supervision. Execution of sentence was suspended for 37,576 (55.1 percent) of those sentenced to imprisonment with labor and for 4,890 (93.6 percent) of those sentenced to imprisonment without labor. But the sentence was suspended for only 7 fine cases among a total of 1,642,969. This indicates that, in sentencing practice, suspended execution of sentence, including probation order, is used mainly for imprisonment both with and without labor and that suspension of execution is usually granted for sentences to imprisonment without labor.

Not all the offenders whose execution of sentence was suspended are placed under probationary supervision. A total of 6,438 offenders were placed on probationary supervision when their execution of sentence was suspended in 1987 (table 6.22). This number represented only 15.2 percent of the total 42,473 offenders ordered to suspension of execution of sentence. In detail, 1,307 offenders were ordered probation mandatorily because they committed offenses during their previous suspended execution of sentence without supervision, while the rest of 5,131 were placed on probation by the discretion of the courts. The number of probationers placed on discretionary probation represented a small percentage (12.5) of all the offenders who might have been given a probation order with suspended execution of sentence. This may imply that judges are somewhat careful in ordering probation at their discretion.

The conditions imposed on an adult probationer are regulated in a less restrictive manner by article 5 of the Law for Probationary Supervision of Persons under Suspension of Execution of Sentence as follows:

    a. to report specific place of residence to the probation office immediately after the probation order is rendered;

Table 6.22   Number of the Convicted Granted Suspended Execution of Sentence, by Type of Suspension, 1983–1987

Type of suspension	1983	1984	1985	1986	1987
First suspension (A)	43,826	44,172	43,179	41,887	41,166
First suspension with probation (B)	6,128	6,183	5,773	5,113	5,131
	{4}	{3}	{4}	(-)	{2}
B/A (%)	14.0	14.0	13.4	12.2	12.5
Second suspension with probation	1,583	1,464	1,363	1,268	1,307
	{1}	{2}	(-)	(-)	{1}
Total	45,409	45,636	44,542	43,155	42,473

Source: Annual Statistics Report of Prosecution, Japan.
Notes: Above figures include suspension of execution of sentence with or without labor and fines.
Probation includes protective measures (Hodoshobun) under the Antiprostitution Law, and the figures in parentheses show actual numbers for these.

Table 6.23   Number of Probationers and Parolees under Supervision at the End of 1988

Category	Number	Percent
Total	83,388	100.0
Adult		
Probationer	18,447	22.2
Parolee	8,185	9.8
Juvenile		
Probationer	50,363	60.4
Parolee	6,393	7.7

Source: Annual Statistics Report on Rehabilitation of Offenders, Japan.

b. to keep good conduct; and
c. to give the probation office previous notice regarding change of residence or the making of a journey that exceeds one month.

These conditions are imposed on every adult probationer and explained to him or her in the court and in the probation office. Neither the court nor the probation office has the authority to impose any additional conditions on adult probationers.

Supervision of adult probationers is conducted by the probation offices independently of the courts. There are a total of fifty probation offices under the Ministry of Justice. In addition to adult probationers, the probation offices supervise juvenile probationers and adult and juvenile parolees. The daily average population of all the offenders under supervision amounts to more than eighty thousand, including about eighteen thousand adult probationers (table 6.23). Supervision of probationers and parolees is carried out by a small number (less than one thousand) of professional probation officers with the assistance of a large number (forty-eight thousand) of volunteer probation officers. To make good use of the limited number of supervisors, especially professional probation officers, the probation offices have made every effort to improve the effective supervision of offenders, by, for example, opening local and day offices and developing differential supervision schemes.

Follow-up Stage of Prisoners

Parole. Parole is the sole alternative measure to imprisonment applicable for a prisoner serving a sentence in prison. Selected prisoners are released on parole by parole boards and are supervised by probation officers during their parole periods.

Conditional release of prisoners was introduced a hundred years ago (in 1882), but before 1949, prisoners were released by the decision of the minister of justice, and after release they were under police surveillance and did not receive aftercare services from any government authority. It was the Offenders Rehabilitation Law of 1949 that established a screening system of prisoners for parole by parole boards and supervision of parolees by probation officers.

Article 28 of the Penal Code regulates two requirements for parole as follows:

a. that the prisoner has served one-third of his or her fixed sentence or ten years of a life sentence, and
b. that he or she proves genuinely reformed.

Since requirements in the parole law do not specify type of offense, even an offender who has committed a serious offense has a chance to be released on parole.

The period of parole supervision is for the remaining term of the sentence, except for "life-termers," where the period of parole is for the rest of his or her life unless pardon is awarded. Early discharge from supervision is available only for those under indeterminate sentence. Indeterminate sentence is applicable only in juvenile cases where an offender has committed an offense punishable by imprisonment of more than three years, had it been committed by an adult. In other words, a sentence of that nature is rendered only for juveniles committing a very serious offense. In 1988 only 95 persons (0.9 percent) of a total of 16,890 prisoners who were released on parole were serving indeterminate sentences. Thus, for most of the cases, parole is granted to a prisoner serving an imprisonment sentence with a determinate term.

According to article 29 of the Penal Code, parole may be revoked in the following cases:

a. When the parolee commits a new crime while he or she is on parole and is sentenced to a fine or heavier punishment
b. When a fine or a graver punishment is imposed for another crime committed prior to parole
c. When punishment is to be executed with respect to another crime for which a fine or heavier punishment was imposed prior to parole
d. When a parolee fails to observe any of the established conditions for parole

A regional parole board has the authority to examine and make a decision on parole release and on parole revocation. The regional parole boards are administered under the Rehabilitation Bureau of the Ministry of Justice and located in eight cities where the high courts are located. The boards consist of three to twelve commissioners who are full-time officials selected mainly from directors of probation offices, superintendents of correctional institutions, public prosecutors, and so forth. Parole investigation officers are attached to the parole boards. Their main duties are to collect information on inmates and submit social reports to the boards for parole hearings, not including supervision of parolees after their release. They have the same qualifications, training, and official status as probation officers. The law requires them to have certain degrees of competence in the areas of medical science, sociology, psychology, education, and/or other disciplines relevant to the treatment of offenders.

As a part of the preparole investigation, inquiry into conditions at the place the inmate is expected to return to upon release is initiated as soon as he is committed to a prison. For this purpose, the prison sends the probation office a classification summary giving the offender's case history. It includes information about his physical and psychological traits, employment plan, and name and address of the family. Usually a probation officer entrusts the duty of such inquiry to a volunteer probation officer who lives near the family of the inmate. The volunteer is supposed to visit immediately the prospective home of the inmate and to find out if his return to the place is feasible. If there exist any negative factors, the volunteer worker tries to overcome these in cooperation with the family. Efforts toward such adjustment are made continuously until the date of release. When the offender has no family to live with after release, similar efforts are directed toward finding an appropriate relative, employer, friend, or rehabilitation aid hostel. On the other hand, the regional parole board sends the parole investigation officer periodically to the institution to make preparations for the parole release by personal interview with the offender and make contacts with staff of the institution for arrangements of the release. In Japan a prisoner has no right to file an application for parole. It is only the superintendent of the prison who submits an application for parole to the parole board. In doing so, due consideration is given to the progress the inmate has achieved in the institution. Incidentally, the parole board is empowered to initiate parole examination in its own right, even when the application is not filed on the part of the institution. In practice, however, this is rarely the case.

The parole board, on receipt of the application, sends a board member to the institution to have the inmate in question interviewed. Later, three members of the board examine the case on the panel and evaluate as to whether the individual really meets the requirements for parole on the basis of the interview and the various information gathered.

When the panel of three board members finds not only that an inmate is formally eligible for parole in the light of the requirements but also that parole will better serve the goal of correctional efforts, it determines a definite date of parole, the place where the parolee should return to, and conditions that he should abide by during the period of supervision.

Table 6.24   Number of Applications for Parole from Prison Received and Disposed
Of, 1983–1987

Disposition	1983	1984	1985	1986	1987
Number of applications received	19,566	20,385	20,314	20,138	19,621
Number of applications disposed of Approval	17,292	18,897	18,194	18,270	17,823
Rejection	897	790	894	942	974
Rejection rate	4.9	4.0	4.7	4.9	5.2

Source: Annual Statistics on Rehabilitation of Offenders, Japan.
Note: Rejection rate = (Rejection / (Approval + Rejection)) × 100.

The following general conditions, as provided for by the law, are automatically imposed:

a. To live at the specified residence and to engage in a lawful occupation
b. To keep good conduct
c. To discontinue criminogenic companionship
d. To request approval for change of residence or any long journey

In addition to the general conditions, the parolee is also required to abide by special conditions that the parole board sets forth as a guide toward a law-abiding life. Special conditions vary widely, as they are designed to meet the individual needs of each parolee. Those in frequent use are restriction of alcoholic beverages, regular contact with the volunteer probation officer, and support of the family. Failure to comply with a special condition can be a cause of reincarceration exactly in the same way as a violation of a general condition may result in revocation of parole.

In recent years approximately 18,000 prisoners were annually released on parole. In 1987, the regional parole boards received a total of 19,621 parole applications from prisons, granted parole for 17,823 cases, and rejected parole for 974 cases (table 6.24). In the same year (1987) 17,603 prisoners were actually released on parole, while an additional 13,413 prisoners were released on the expiration of their imprisonment sentence. This means that more than one-half, 56.8 percent, of prisoners were released on parole before expiration of their sentences. It should be noted here that parole is not applied for a short-term prisoner serving a sentence of six months or less, since the term is too short for parole examination and parole supervision.

By law, a prisoner can be released on parole after he or she has served one-third of his or her sentence. But, in practice, most parolees are released after they have served more than 70 percent of their sentence terms (table

6.25). Since the duration of parole supervision corresponds to the remaining term of sentence, and parole is granted after a prisoner has served most of his or her sentence, the duration of parole supervision is usually very short (table 6.26). In 1987, more than 40 percent of parolees had short-term parole, three months or less, while less than 10 percent had been on parole for more than one year.

After being released from prison, a parolee is supervised and given assistance by a probation officer and a volunteer probation officer. The method and intensity of the supervision is basically the same as that for a probationer,* but there is one particular in the supervision of parolees that must be mentioned: over one-fifth of the parolees from prisons are accommodated at the rehabilitation aid hostels, owing to the lack of an adequate place to live in.

In this sense, the rehabilitation aid hostels serve as an important social institution for the administration of the parole system. At present, there are one hundred rehabilitation aid hostels (halfway houses) run by private associations. Under the Law for Aftercare of Discharged Offenders of 1950, these hostels are licensed and supervised by the minister of justice. They accommodate those probationers and parolees who voluntarily seek shelter aid and are referred by probation offices. The total capacity of the halfway houses is twenty-four hundred, and the capacity of each facility ranges from ten to eighty. While it is the general rule that the resident goes out every day to work, some halfway houses have their own workshops to provide jobs for persons who are unfit for outside employment. About 50 percent of the total expenses of halfway houses are borne by the national government, and the remainder must be either raised by the organizations themselves or covered by contributions from outsiders.

Table 6.25 Executed Term of Determinate Sentence Parolees Served Prior to Release, by type of Offender, 1987

Type of Offender	Total	Executed Rate of Sentence				
		Under 60%	Under 70%	Under 80%	Under 90%	90% and over
non-recidivist	100.0 (10,985)	2.3	29.5	40.8	20.6	6.7
recidivist	100.0 (6,723)	0.1	1.0	9.1	53.5	36.3

Source: Annual Statistics of Rehabilitation of Offenders, Japan.
Note: Figures in parentheses show actual numbers.

*For detailed information, refer to the section on probation and suspended execution of sentence in this report and to "Adult Probation in Japan," chapter 7 of this volume.

Table 6.26 Percentage of Newly Received Probationers and Parolees, by Duration of Probation, 1987

Duration	Adult parolees	Adult Probationers
1 month or less	2.3	-
2 months or less	21.4	-
3 months or less	18.4	-
6 months or less	31.6	-
1 year or less	20.4	0.0
2 years or less	4.5	2.3
3 years or less	1.0	51.0
4 years or less	0.2	35.0
5 years or less	0.1	11.7
Over 5 years	0.0	-
Life	0.2	-
Total	100.0	100.0
	(17,603)	(6,477)

Source: Annual Statistics on Rehabilitation of Offenders, Japan.
Note: Figures in parentheses show actual numbers.

Table 6.27 Termination of Adult Probation and Adult Parole, by Type of Reason, 1988

Reasons of termination	Adult Probation	Adult Parolees
Expiration of term	4,864 (69.5)	15,607 (90.4)
under discharged supervision	1,350	
Revocation	2,015 (28.8)	1,489 (8.6)
for offenses	1,881	54
for violation of conditions	134	1,435
Others	120 (1.7)	166 (1.0)
Total	6,999 (100.0)	17,262 (100.0)

Source: Annual Statistics Report, Report on Rehabilitation of Offenders, Japan.
Note: Figures in parentheses show percentages.

A special halfway house program was launched in 1979 at selected rehabilitation aid hostels for parolees serving sentences of eight years or more. Parolees who consent to participate in this project are accommodated for the initial three months after release and given intensive individual as well as group counseling in addition to assistance and guidance regarding ordinary social life, from which they have been secluded for many years.

In 1988, a total of 17,262 parolees terminated their parole periods (table 6.27). From among them, 15,607 (90.4 percent) completed their parole supervision without parole revocation; parole was revoked for only 1,489 (8.6 percent). The low rate of revocation indicates the success of the administration of the parole system in general.

Republic of Korea

Crime Trends and Policy for Alternatives to Imprisonment

In general, crimes reported to the police in Korea have increased in recent years, with some exceptions, such as assault, bribery, and corruption. Due to the rapid development of the economy, some economic offenses, like fraud and embezzlement, have increased (table 6.28). The same trend is observed in the number of offenders brought into the criminal justice system as suspects or arrestees (table 6.29).

In spite of the recent increase of reported crimes, the number of persons prosecuted has not shown a similar increase, which means that public prosecutors in Korea have preferred not to prosecute (table 6.30). The prison population has also not increased. Notably, although the number of those taken into preventive detention increased from 1982 to 1986, the number of those sentenced to imprisonment decreased over the same period (table 6.31).

In Korea, alternative measures or community-based treatment programs are now being expanded. Probation for adult offenders was initiated on 1 July 1989, and subsequently the number of prisoners who enjoy furlough has increased. The ratio of those who are released on parole is also increasing.

Pretrial Stage

Admonition by the Police. Admonition by the police is linked to the discretionary power entrusted to the directors of police stations. As for very minor offenses punishable by fines (of less than ten thousand won) or by short detention (of less than one month), the director of the police station can divert the offender from criminal justice procedures. Supervision is not

Table 6.28 Number of Crimes Recorded in the Criminal (Police) Statistics

Type of crime	Total for calendar year						
	1980	1981	1982	1983	1984	1985	1986
Homicide	527	568	498	493	551	541	565
Assault	11,183	12,128	11,051	9 904	8,862	7,666	7,007
Rape	3 003	3,446	4,164	3 973	4,051	4,188	3,909
Robbery	2,684	2,680	2,720	2 887	3,007	3,288	2,983
Theft	91,492	105,675	112,428	119 359	106,731	103,006	100,562
Fraud	42,408	58,015	56,221	65 962	58,870	56,423	54,538
Embezzlement	13,522	17,645	17,968	17 207	18,615	20,085	18,676
Kidnapping	152	145	157	316	233	278	235
Drug-related crimes	375	445	392	489	311	371	523
Bribery and/or corruption	680	658	919	725	422	254	287
others	454,684	430,545	448,665	575 624	583,055	598,677	629,433
Total number of recorded crimes	620,710	631,950	655.183	786,939	784,708	794,777	818 718

Source: The Third UN Survey, Republic of Korea.

154

Table 6.29 Total of All Offenders Brought into Formal Contact with the Criminal Justice System, First Recorded as Suspected, Arrested, or Otherwise Classified

All Offenders by type of crime	1980	1981	1982	1983	1984	1985	1986
				Total number of persons for the year			
Homicide	568	576	547	546	547	573	599
Assault	12127	12804	12328	10566	9293	8172	7767
Rape	4022	5011	6004	5758	5831	5795	5158
Robbery	3529	3728	3895	3891	3908	4308	4185
Theft	54061	66032	75693	68909	61126	60349	61463
Fraud	39053	53000	55013	57205	59229	54143	51282
Embezzlement	12970	16549	17341	17163	88135	17443	17406
Kidnapping	184	218	204	402	316	404	349
Drug-related crimes	512	635	485	525	486	519	547
Bribery and/or corruption	922	995	1310	1109	706	461	473
others (specify)	521974	504657	548088	642837	657738	670331	700967
Grand total number of persons arrested	649922	664205	720908	808911	817315	822498	850196

Source: The Third UN Survey, Republic of Korea.

Table 6.30 Number of Persons Prosecuted

Adults by type of crime	1980	1981	1982	1983	1984	1985	1986
Homicide	471	550	505	495	572	584	545
Assault	8,888	9,996	9,398	8,187	7,425	6,611	6,374
Rape	3,338	3,606	4,252	4,026	4,340	4,334	4,036
Robbery	1,565	1,708	1,832	1,851	1,987	1,285	2,243
Theft	36,136	38,730	41,576	37,901	35,902	36,593	36,401
Fraud	62,346	15,134	79,720	77,665	89,754	83,340	77,904
Embezzlement	15,450	20,055	1,453	20,424	23,921	23,533	23,648
Kidnapping	354	324	379	472	382	441	436
Drug-related crimes	181	189	240	481	312	474	272
Bribery and/or corruption	401	509	352	398	187	144	159
others (specify)							
Grand total number of adult males prosecuted	420,087	404,663	375,156	393,456	406 702	397,485	442,260

Source: The Third UN Survey, Republic of Korea.

Table 6.31   Persons Incarcerated

Category of incarceration	1982	Total for the calendar year 1984	1986
Awaiting trial or adjudication	19,623	20,030	21,903
Sentenced	29,820	27,320	25,691
Otherwise adjudicated			
Preventive detention	1,481	3,069	4,863
For nonpayment of penal fine	360	342	276
Civil law incarceration			
Other			
Total	51,284	50,761	52,733

Source: The Third UN Survey, Republic of Korea.

provided for those released. Admonition is not provided for in the law, but it is admitted by the public prosecutor general, who is responsible for the investigation and disposition of offenses and offenders in general.

Suspension of Prosecution by the Public Prosecutor. The public prosecutor in Korea monopolizes the authority of prosecution and, at the same time, can suspend prosecution even if there is enough evidence to prosecute the case, taking all the circumstances of the offense and the offender into account.

Article 247 (1) of the Penal Procedure Code states, ''The public prosecutor can suspend prosecution taking the factors described in article 51 of the Penal Code into consideration.'' And article 51 of the Penal Procedure Code states, ''In determining the sentence, the following factors should be taken into account: (1) age, character, mental faculty, and circumstances of the offender, (2) relationship with the victim, (3) motive, means, and results of the offense.''

During the term of suspension, the offenders are not under the supervision of authority, but they may request aid such as lodging, vocational training, and job referral from the official rehabilitation program. There is no provision about the term of suspension. Though this disposition does not have the binding power not to forego prosecution of the same case later, it is quite exceptional for the public prosecutor to prosecute such cases.

There is no limitation concerning the types of offenses to be suspended. Generally, prosecution was suspended for 13.9 percent of offenders in 1986. Among theft offenders, the suspension rate was as high as 37.3 percent.

Bail. Offenders can be released on bail after they are prosecuted. Article 95 of the Penal Procedure Code states:

The Court should release the defendants on bail upon request, unless

- death penalty, life imprisonment, or imprisonment for ten years or more are possible for their alleged offense,
- the alleged offense is a habitual offense,
- the defendants have destroyed evidence, or there is reasonable ground to suspect that they may destroy evidence,
- the defendants have escaped, or there is reasonable ground to suspect that they may escape,
- the addresses of the defendants are not clear.

Article 98 (2) of the same code says: ''The Court should not determine the amount of bail money exceeding the limit the offender can afford.''

In 1986, 86,631 were formally prosecuted while in detention. From among these, 6,019 (6.9 percent) were released on bail.

Adjudication Stage

Suspension of Sentence. To avoid offenders having the stigma of conviction, the Penal Code provides the court with the discretionary authority to suspend sentence for those offenders who show sincere repentance. Sentence can be suspended for those cases for which the court deems it appropriate to give a sentence of imprisonment for one year or less or a sentence of a fine, and when the offender shows sincere repentance (article 59 of the Penal Code).

When the offender whose sentence was suspended passes two years without being prosecuted or sentenced for committing another offense, the prosecution is automatically dismissed. When the offender commits another crime, he or she will be sentenced for both the original and the new offense.

During the term of suspension, the offenders are not under the supervision of authority, but they too may request aid from the official rehabilitation program.

In 1986, 4,180 prosecuted cases were dismissed, and most of them were cases that were dismissed after two years of suspension.

Suspended Execution of Sentence. In order to give the offender a last chance to rehabilitate, the Penal Code provides the court with the discretionary authority to suspend the execution of sentence. The execution of sentence can be suspended for those cases in which the court sentences to imprisonment for three years or less and believes that it is appropriate to suspend the execution (article 62 of the Penal Code).

The court decides the term of suspension (between one and five years). When the offender completes his or her term without committing another offense, the sentence itself becomes invalid. When the offender is sentenced to imprisonment, the suspension of the execution of the original sentence will be revoked—that is, the two sentences are executed consecutively. During the term of suspension, the offenders are not under the supervision of authority but may request aid from the official scheme of rehabilitation.

In 1986, 47,840 cases received suspension of the execution of sentence. To expand the possibility of suspension of the execution of sentence, a new category, suspension of the execution of sentence with probationary supervision, was introduced on 1 July 1989; to date, detailed information is not available on this category.

Follow-up Stage

Work Release for Vocational Training. In 1984, the work release of prisoners for vocational training was started. In this program, a selected group of well-behaved inmates are trained in the vocational training institutes installed in civilian factories located near the correctional institutions. There inmates receive technical training for eight hours a day under conditions similar to those for civilian trainees, without wearing prison uniforms.

Furlough. Furlough is granted to eligible prisoners. Though the Correction Administrative Law does not say anything about furlough, it is awarded by the prison warden according to an administrative standard. The requirements for granting it are these:

a. As regards prisoners, furlough is limited to
  • those who have shown sincere repentance and have done well in prison, and
  • those who have served for one year or more, and at least half of their sentences.
b. The main reasons for permitting furlough are these:
  • Death or critical condition of their lineal ancestors or descendants
  • Marriage of their lineal descendants
  • Sixtieth birthdays of their parents or when their son joins the army
  • Serious damage to their property
c. Other requirements:
  • The number of furloughs is limited to one per year and a maximum of three per term of imprisonment.
  • The total length of furlough cannot exceed three weeks.

When a prisoner is permitted to go on furlough, he or she can do so without prison guards but is under the obligation to return to the institution by the designated time.

Over the last years, there has been no problem in regard to furlough, and this scheme seems to be well accepted by the public. In 1986, 455 prisoners were released on furlough, and the number is increasing year by year.

Parole. Parole is granted by the minister of justice. The requirements to grant it are stipulated in the Penal Code as follows (article 72):

- Having shown sincere repentance and having done well in prison.
- Having served more than ten years (for a sentence of life imprisonment), or having served one-third or more of the sentence

Prisoners on life imprisonment who have been granted parole and have not violated parole conditions for ten years are considered to have served the entire sentence. The same applies to offenders on parole for the remaining term of the original imprisonment. If the parolee has violated conditions, parole may be revoked.

During the parole term, the parolees are supervised by probation officers. This supervision system was introduced on 1 July 1989. Parolees may request aid such as lodging, vocational training, and job referrals from the official rehabilitation program. In 1986, 7,690 inmates were released on parole. That was about 29.6 percent of total prisoners released from prison. The number and the ratio of those who are released on parole are increasing.

Pardon. Pardon is granted by the president (Constitution, article 79). There are four types of pardon: namely, general pardon, which is granted with respect to crimes or types thereof; special pardon, which is granted with respect to specific persons; reduction of punishment, which is granted with respect to crimes or types of punishment; and restoration, which has the effect of restoring the capacity that the offender was deprived of by the sentence.

Papua New Guinea

Crime Trends and Policy for Alternatives to Imprisonment

In Papua New Guinea, there were 22,908 reported crimes in 1987, and there was an overall clearance rate of 51.7 (table 6.32). In absolute numbers, theft and property crimes approximated nearly half of all reported crimes.

The Papua New Guinea court system processed around 38,358 cases in 1987, of which 65 percent resulted in convictions, 17 percent were dismissed, 9 percent were withdrawn, and the remaining 9 percent were struck out (table 6.33).

Although the prison population has been falling over the six-year period (1982–88), Papua New Guinea still has a large number of prisoners, compared with its total population of 3.426 million (1986). In 1988, 7,705 remand prisoners and 8,916 convicts were admitted to prisons, making a total of 16,621, resulting in 485 prisoners per 100,000 population (table 6.34). As of 1988, Papua New Guinea was operating nineteen open corrective institutions and one maximum security institution, with a combined capacity of 5,550 inmates (table 6.35); there appears to be a problem with prison overcrowding at this time.

To solve overcrowding in prisons and further more effective rehabilitation programs for offenders, Papua New Guinea, at present, is in a process of creating alternative measures to imprisonment. Probation was introduced

Table 6.32 Summary of Annual Crime Statistics for the Period 1/1/87 to 12/31/87

Type of Offense	Crime Statistics		Arrest Statistics	
	Reported/ Recorded	Detected/ Cleared	Cleared Up	Rate/100,000
Against the person	3,831	2,107	55.00	110.24
Sexual offenses	1,935	550	28.42	55.58
Property Breakings	3,756	788	21.10	108.94
Theft without violation of premises	6,428	3,815	59.39	176.08
Motor vehicle theft	494	226	46.74	14.21
Offenses involving fraud	506	317	67.40	14.33
Drug offenses	58	59	100.00	1.56
Arson	332	94	23.31	9.55
Malicious damage and injury to property	1,752	823	46.97	50.41
Offenses against public Order and justice	1,653	1,141	59.02	47.56
Other coded offenses	2,139	1,929	90.18	61.91
Total	22,908	11,951	51.73	650.5

Source: Report of the Royal Papua, New Guinea, Constabulary.

Table 6.33 Summary of Court Results, 1987

Total	38,358
Convictions	24,918
Withdrawals	3,581
Dismissals	6,473
Struck Out	3,388

Source: Report of the Royal Papua, New Guinea, Constabulary.

Table 6.34   Number of Persons Incarcerated, 1982–1988

	Total	Remand Prisoners	Convicted Prisoners
1982	21,453	9,329	12,124
1983	19,362	8,787	10,576
1984	18,362	8,923	9,439
1985	16,975	8,924	8,051
1986	14,998	7,956	7,042
1987	14,846	7,747	7,099
1988	16,621	7,705	8,916

Source: Report of the Department of Corrections Institution Services, Papua, New Guinea.

Table 6.35   Authorized Capacity of the Twenty Open Correctional Institutions and One Maximum Security Institution

1.	Baisu	500 to 800
2.	Bomana	300 to 500
3.	Buimo	300 to 500
4.	Kerevat	300 to 500
5.	Boram	300
6.	Beon	300
7.	Bihute	300
8.	Barawagi	300
9.	Kuveria	300
10.	Bui Iebi	300
11.	Biru	200
12.	Gili Gili	200
13.	Kavieng	200
14.	Lekimata	200
15.	Wabag	200
16.	Daru	100
17.	Tari	100
18.	Ningurum	100
19.	Laiagam	100
20.	Kerima	closed
21.	Maximum Security Institution	50
	Total	5,550

Source: Report of the Department of Correction Institution Services, Papua, New Guinea.

in 1985 and was planned to spread all over the country by the end of 1990. The Department of Correctional Services has proposed various community-based programs, including weekend imprisonment, home leave, release of prisoners on license, and voluntary supervision, programs that will be implemented as soon as the Parliament passes relevant legislation.

Pretrial Stage

Village Courts. The village courts system was established some years ago in a few provinces in the country, and it is moving slowly into other provinces and districts. This is a community-based court system, and it has worked well in some provinces. The community members themselves elect their leaders to be village court magistrates, who have judicial powers like those of the magistrates. Most of the prescribed offenses in the Village Courts Act relate to the community and customary laws. When a village clerk receives a complaint from someone, he or she writes out a summons paper and passes it on to the offender. After the hearing is completed the village court magistrate will hand down his or her decision based on community-based programs. Most of the time the magistrates order compensation for the complaint. Examples of compensation conditions are as follows:

a. To complete a certain number of hours of community service work
b. Monetary compensation to the state for damages incurred
c. Monetary compensation to the complainant or victim
d. To work a certain number of hours for the complainant as retribution for the offense

The community at large does not want to see people in the community go before the district court and end up in corrective institutional services.

Bail—Release on Recognizance. Papua New Guinea provides for a bail system whereby a person taken into custody prior to his or her trial can be released on bail if specified conditions, designed for securing his or her appearance at court, are met. While in police custody, the prisoner is allowed to pledge bail and thereupon be released. The prisoners who are not eligible for police bail are those who have been charged for indictable offenses (serious offenses).

Adjudication Stage

Suspended Sentence/Suspended Execution of Sentence. The judge of the National Court or a magistrate of the district court can use the discretionary power under the National or District Court Act to suspend sentence or suspend execution of the sentence.

Good Behavior Bond. The National Court is a high court, and it hears and adjudicates cases regarding indictable offenses. When the judge finds the offender guilty, he or she may impose imprisonment or a fine or authorize a good-behavior bond. The district courts are run by the magistrates, and they deal with minor cases (summary offenses). These courts can also sentence to short-term imprisonment, a fine, or a good-behavior bond.

Probation. In 1985 Papua New Guinea's Department of Justice established the probation service, and by 1990 all provinces in the country were to have probation officers. The programs have so far been successful, and the national government is being requested to allocate more funds in order to spread out and speed up the application of these programs.

Follow-up Stage of Dispositions

Parole. Parole, which is the conditional release of an offender from a penal or correctional institution after a portion of the sentence has been served, is granted to a prisoner who is sentenced to an indeterminate sentence. An application for parole is considered by the Board of Parole.

The criteria for parole are as follows:

a. That the inmate maintains a record of progress in prison
b. That there is a reasonable probability that he or she will live and remain at liberty without violating the law
c. That release on parole is not incompatible with the welfare of society

Release on License or Recognizance. The minister of justice can release any prisoner on license; however, at present there is no proper scheme or method for selecting prisoners for this scheme.

Republic of the Philippines

Crime Trends and Policy for Alternatives to Imprisonment

Crimes reported to the police in the Philippines maintained a continuous upward trend since the mid 1970s, but the increase slowed down in recent years. In 1987, a total of 183,355 crimes were reported, including 117,847 index crimes, which consist of murder, homicide, physical injuries, robbery, rape, and theft (figure 6.3). Nationwide index crimes per one hundred thousand population did not show an increase except in 1987, but the index crime rate in Metro Manila showed a continuous increase in recent years (figure 6.4), which was attributed to an increase of young population migrating from rural areas to Manila.

Due to the increase of crime volume in the country, criminal cases pending in the courts increased substantially, from 302,978 in 1976 to 471,244 in 1982. The government made various efforts to reduce the courts' work load. The village court system was encouraged, and a number of new judges were recruited. As a result, the situation somewhat improved, and the pending cases in the courts had been reduced to about 270,000 in 1987.

There are three different levels of confinement facilities for offenders in the Philippines. Sixty-five city jails and 1,450 municipal jails managed by the Integrated National Police accommodate remand prisoners and those convicted to imprisonment for six months or less. In 1988, the total population of these jails was 15,147, of which only 1,528 (10 percent) were

Figure 6.3: Nationwide Crime Volume

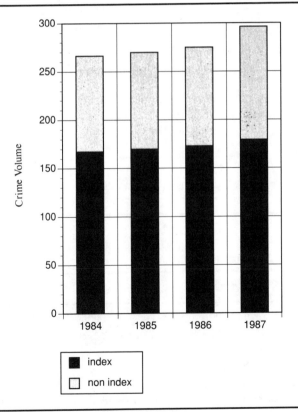

sentenced prisoners, while the majority (13,619 or 90 percent) were remand prisoners awaiting trial or pending dispositions (table 6.36). Seventy-two provincial jails administered by the provincial governors hosted those with sentences from six months and a day to three years. Although no detailed data are available, a total yearly average of about 10,000 prisoners are estimated to be in jail. Seven national prisons under the director of prisons in the central government accommodate those convicted to more than three

Figure 6.4: Metro Manila and Nationwide Total Index Crime Rates

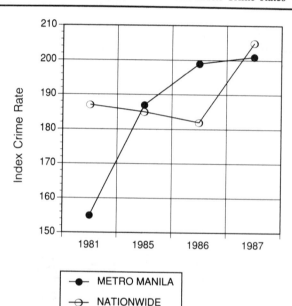

Table 6.36   Jail Population Nationwide

YEAR	SENTENCED	DETAINED	TOTAL
1984	2,668	11,064	13,752
1985	2,471	12,340	14,811
1986	1,631	13,803	15,434
1987	1,775	13,238	15,013
1988	1,528	13,619	15,147

Source: Position Paper for The Republic of the Philippines/Eighth United Nations Regional Preparatory Meeting on Crime Prevention and the Treatment of Offenders for Asia and the Pacific.

years' imprisonment. The population of prisoners in national prisons in 1988 was 12,591 (table 6.37).

In total, there are approximately fifteen thousand remand prisoners and twenty-four thousand convicted prisoners in the Philippines. While the number of convicted prisoners, both in local jails and in national prisons, has decreased, the number of remand prisoners in city and municipal jails is still increasing (tables 6.36 and 6.37). The increase of remand prisoners has brought about overcrowding and difficulties for prison administrations in some city jails. The criminal justice system in the Philippines is pursuing alternatives to imprisonment by utilizing the village courts in the court system as well as probation and parole in corrections.

Pretrial Stage

Village Court: Barangay/Lupong Tagapayapa. Under the Philippine criminal justice system, petty crimes punishable with a fine of not more than two hundred pesos or imprisonment for thirty days or less are no longer lodged formally for adjudication by the courts. Instead, the Lupong Tagapayapa (village courts) were established in 1979 by Presidential Decree No. 1508 to settle these cases and avoid lengthy and expensive trials. In the Philippines, the involvement of the community as the fifth component of the criminal justice system (law enforcement, prosecution, courts, corrections, and community; known as the "five pillars") attests to its important and indispensable role in crime prevention and control. The primary community organization is the Barangay, which is the smallest political unit of the society. As a political unit, the Barangay exercises acts of government through its council officers headed by the Barangay captain, who is elected by all voters in the locality. A significant innovation was introduced into the Barangay system in 1978 when the government officially recognized the time-

Table 6.37   Bureau of Prisons Population and Percentage of Recidivism

YEAR	POPULATION	NUMBER OF RECIDIVISTS	PERCENTAGE OF RECIDIVISTS PER YEAR
1984	14,099	195	.014
1985	13,412	79	.006
1986	12,714	459	.036
1987	12,243	84	.068
1988	12,591	92	.007

Source: Position Paper for The Republic of the Philippines/Eighth United Nations Regional Preparatory Meeting on Crime Prevention and the Treatment of Offenders for Asia and the Pacific.

honored tradition of settling disputes among Barangay members at the Barangay level without recourse to the courts.

The Lupong Tagapayapa was mandated in each Barangay to be composed of between ten and twenty respected members of the community who are appointed by the captain for a term of two years. This group thoroughly investigates all disputes within its jurisdiction, and a conciliation panel composed of three group members is constituted if the dispute is not immediately mediated. An important feature of this system of justice is that no complaint, petition, or legal action that falls within the competence of the Barangay groups can be filed in the court unless it can be certified that the dispute was brought before the Barangay and that an acceptable settlement could not be reached at that level.

The success of this form of community-based justice can be seen from the fact that, since the implementation of the Lupong Tagapayapa, more than 570,000 disputes have been settled by the village courts, where more than 280,000 petty crime offenders have been spared from serving prison sentences (table 6.38).

Bail/Release on Recognizance. The Philippines provides for a bail system under which a person taken into custody prior to his or trial should be released on bail on specified conditions designed for securing his or her appearance at court. Within the context of the country's criminal justice system, all offenders except for those guilty of capital offenses are entitled to bail.

In the Philippines, many inmates confined in city and municipal jails

Table 6.38   Cases Brought to Village Courts, 1980–1987

YEAR	TOTAL NO. OF DISPUTES SUBMITTED	SETTLED DISPUTES	FORWARDED TO COURTS	PENDING DISPUTES
1980	39,645	32,888	1,987	4,770
1981	66,542	58,964	4,113	3,465
1982	73,211	64,675	4,822	3,714
1983	76,538	73,204	5,447	2,870
1984	63,359	56,834	4,141	2,384
1985	81,613	75,280	4,649	3,777
1986	106,197	94,139	7,464	4,594
1987	128,901	113,649	9,323	1,766
Total	636,006	569,633	41,946	27,340

Source: The Third UN Survey, The Philippines.

are prisoners awaiting or undergoing trial. Some of them are confined because they pose grave risks to society, but a larger group are detained simply because they cannot afford bail. More than 75 percent of all criminal defendants in the Philippines belong to the lower socioeconomic strata and have limited financial resources. The resultant high rate of detention is said to be the major cause of overcrowding in jails.

While the right to bail is available to all offenders, it is only affordable by few. Thus, to reduce the number of detained prisoners other than through bail, release on recognizance or into the custody of social services (in the case of indigent offenders) or parents (in the case of juvenile delinquents) are measures that are commonly practiced. A number of laws have been enacted that allow the release of offenders in the following circumstances:

a. Persons charged with violations that carry a penalty not higher than imprisonment for one to six months and/or a fine of two thousand pesos or both
b. Offenders who have undergone preventive imprisonment during their trial (these are allowed full-time credit)
c. Offenders who have undergone preventive imprisonment equal to or more than the maximum prison sentence that could be imposed

Under this system, a person charged with violations of municipal or city ordinances and criminal offenses that carry a penalty of not more than imprisonment of one month and one day to six months and/or a fine of two thousand pesos are released when it is established by the court, or a relative authority, that he or she is unable to post the required cash or bail bond. The offender is placed in custody and is subject to the authority of a responsible citizen in the community who is willing to accept such a responsibility. It is reported that these measures have reduced to some extent the number of people detained in jails.

Adjudication Stage

Probation/Suspended Execution of the Sentence. Probation is used in the Philippines as one of the most important and promising alternatives to imprisonment.

In the Philippines, probation for juvenile offenders was introduced in 1924, and its use has been gradually expanded. In addition, emphasis on community-based programs for the rehabilitation of offenders led to the adoption of an adult probation system. The promulgation of Presidential Decree No. 968 in 1976 (the Adult Probation Law of 1976) provided for the use of probation as an alternative to imprisonment. The Adult Probation Law of 1976 was put into force on 3 January 1978. According to the law, the court may, after it has convicted and sentenced a defendant, suspend the

Table 6.39   Persons Placed on Probation, 1978–1987

1978	3,199
1979	5,336
1980	5,577
1981	6,629
1982	7,883
1983	7,469
1984	7,627
1985	7,728
1986	6,985
1987	5,476
Total	63,909

Source: The Third UN Survey, The Philippines.

execution of the sentence and place him or her on probation for such period, and under such terms and conditions, as it may deem proper.

A probation order is made generally for an offender with no previous conviction and after he/she is sentenced to an imprisonment of less than six years. Those offenders who have committed offenses against the state are excluded from probation. The term of probation cannot exceed six years. For the first year of its operation, 3,349 persons were placed on probation to be supervised by about 450 probation officers. Since then, probation was expanded; more than 5,000 offenders were placed on probation annually, and 26,366 probationers were under supervision at the end of 1987. The Probation Administration Office of the Department of Justice is responsible for the administration of probation services.

Under the central office in Manila and fourteen regional offices, there are a total of 158 city and provincial probation offices throughout the country. In 1988, 904 probation officers were engaged in presentence investigation and the supervision of probationers. The adult probation system in the Philippines mobilizes volunteers to assist probation officers in the supervision of probationers.

A probationer must report to a probation officer at least once a month. The probation officer sometimes visits a probationer's home or workplace. If the probationer breaches his or her conditions or commits another offense, his or her probation order may be revoked by the court. Conversely, when he or she keeps good conduct and further supervision is unnecessary, the court can make the decision of early termination based on the recommendation of the probation officer. The revocation rate of probation orders has been stable and as small as 1.3 percent in recent years.

Since its implementation, this noninstitutional measure has proven effective in the rehabilitation of certain types of offenders, reduced the overcrowding problem, and saved the government substantial sums of money that would have been allotted for institutionalized care.

For the last ten years, an accumulated saving of 430 million pesos has already been realized from the difference of the probation administration's yearly appropriations and the cost of maintaining the probationers if they are in jail or prison.

A total of 6,158 probationers have paid some 2.9 million pesos out of a total of 3.4 million pesos of civil liabilities to their victims. While this is only 8.5 victim compensation performance, it is definitely better than having no payment at all if the probationers were in jail or prison. Due to the beneficial results of the probation system, a study is now under way to increase its probationer clientele by including first offenders whose sentences exceed six years.

Follow-up Stage of Dispositions

Open Institution. Open institutions, which may be characterized by the absence of walls and other physical measures of precaution against escape, have been developed in the Philippines.

In the Philippines, Iwahig, Davao, and Sablayan Penal Colonies are independent open institutions established on a permanent basis. In addition, there are several penal farms attached to prisons, including San Ramon (Zambonga) and New Bilibid (Muntinlupa). Relieving overcrowding in prisons and exploiting the vast natural resources of the multi-island republic appear to have been the main forces leading to the creation of the penal colonies. More recently, the rehabilitative potential of open treatment for convicted persons has come to the attention of the public and administrators. At Iwahig Penal Colony, colonists can call their families at government expense to live in the colonists' village, and they can cultivate a piece of land and raise poultry and livestock for their personal use. They may earn extra money in their spare time in addition to the prescribed remuneration. Offenders released from the colony may be allotted a piece of land in the vicinity to settle on permanently. Open prison programs in this country are generally considered to be successful, since notable improvements are observed in the health, work habits, and general conduct of the inmates. A low recommitment rate among prisoners released from open prisons is also reported.

Parole. Parole, which is the conditional release of an offender from a penal or correctional institution after he or she has served a part of the sentence, has been adopted in the Philippines since 1933 as a major form of extramural treatment following incarceration.

As a rule, a prisoner with no pending criminal case is eligible for parole on or before the expiration date of his or her minimum sentence. A parole does not pardon the prisoner; he or she still remains in legal custody. It suspends the execution of the penalty and temporarily releases the convict from imprisonment on conditions that he or she is at liberty to reject. He or she is still under the supervision of the parole board and subject to be remanded to prison if he or she fails to perform, or violates, the conditions of the parole. The Board of Pardons and Parole attached to the Department of Justice has the authority to make parole decisions. Parole supervision is carried out by judges of district courts, but there is a proposition to switch it over to probation officers.

The number of prisoners released on parole decreased around 1982 but increased to 2,185 in 1985. Approximately 15,000 parolees were under supervision in recent years.

Remission, Good-time Allowance, or Mandatory Release. Under remission, good-time allowance, or mandatory release, prisoners are automatically released from prison when they have served their term of sentence minus a specified amount of time credited for good behavior. Remission is different from parole in that it is mechanically granted if prisoners meet the requirements. Although released automatically, prisoners may be returned to prison to serve the remaining term of their sentence if they violate any release conditions. The major justification for this form of release is that it provides prisoners with an incentive to keep good behavior and contribute to prison discipline.

In the Philippines, good-conduct time allowance is applied to all prisoners who have fully observed the rules and have not been subject to disciplinary measures. A prisoner who has been classified as a penal colonist or trustee is given a five-day additional allowance for every month of service. A prisoner may be classified as a colonist or trustee after serving one-fifth of his or her maximum sentence, or seventeen years in the case of life-timers.

Pardon. Pardon has long been in existence as a device for tempering justice with mercy and for righting the wrongs done in the course of justice. Cases for pardon include prisoners who are afflicted by serious diseases, old age, or physical invalidity.

For five years (1983 to 1987), a total of 338 inmates in the national prisons were granted pardon by the president through the Board of Pardons and Parole.

Republic of Singapore

Crime Trends and Policy for Alternatives to Imprisonment

In Singapore, the number of major crimes reported to the police increased over the period from 1980 to 1986 (table 6.40). It escalated in 1981 and again in 1985, and reached 53,756 in 1986, a 163.4 percent increase from 1980. The number of persons arrested climbed to 20,393 in 1981 and advanced again after a decline in 1982, totaling 19,204 in 1986 (table 6.41). Although the number of arrested persons increased, the number of prosecutions did not show a significant increase. In 1986, 8,459 persons (less than half of the arrested) were prosecuted (table 6.42).

The number of convictions also decreased, from 5,341 in 1980 to 4,340 in 1986 (table 6.43). The ratio of convictions to prosecutions in a year also decreased, from 66 percent in 1980 to 51 percent in 1986 (tables 6.42 and 6.43).

In spite of the decrease of total convictions, there was a striking increase in prison population. Prison population at year's end jumped from 2,522 in 1982 to 4,140 in 1986 (table 6.44). This may suggest that judges in Singapore have preferred to use imprisonment more or that they have chosen longer terms of imprisonment. Singapore, however, is not facing prison overcrowding, since Singapore prisons have sufficient capacity (table 6.45) and the proportion of remand prisoners is not large.

Alternative measures to imprisonment are being utilized to some extent in Singapore. Among others, probation is expected to play a significant role in dealing with convicted offenders. In practice, however, the courts tend to be hesitant to place adult offenders above the age of twenty-one years on probation.

Pretrial Stage

Bail. In Singapore, all offenses are classified as either bailable or nonbailable under the Criminal Procedure Code. A bailable offense is an offense for which bail can be asked for as a right, and the court has no discretion, when releasing the offender on bail, to impose any conditions or bond.

A nonbailable offense is one in which the offender is not entitled to bail as a right. In the case of nonbailable offenses, the court or police officer may grant bail on discretion in all cases except where there are reasonable grounds for believing that the offender is guilty of an offense punishable with death or imprisonment for life. The rationale here is that the severity of the possible sentence is sufficient to cause the offender to abscond, yet even here there is discretion to grant bail if the offender is under sixteen years of age, a woman, or sick or infirm.

Table 6.40 Number of Crimes Recorded in the Criminal (Police) Statistics

Type of crime	Total for calendar year						
	1980	1981	1982	1983	1984	1985	1986
Intentional homicide	64	53	43	61	69	70	71
non-intentional homicide	1						
assault: maior assaults only	491	672	626	662	1,115	1,011	1,105
including minor assaults	N.A.	N.A.	N.A.	N.A.	N.A.	N.A.	N.A.
Rape	68	93	78	82	105	85	111
Robbery	1,264	1,392	1,286	1,472	1,620	1,628	1,676
theft: major theft	4,881	5,195	5,568	7 160	7,465	7,722	6,506
minor theft	13,813	16,847	16,629	16,895	18,371	19,629	21,649
Fraud	1,172	1,375	1,751	1,675	1,847	1,975	2,278
Embezzlement	298	392	399	383	375	473	487
Kidnapping	11	29	20	27	27	28	38
Drug-related crimes: simple possession	3,731	4,352	3,944	4,045	881	789	760
All other drug offenses					2,850	3,289	3,545
Bribery and/or corruption	N.A.	N.A.	N.A.	N.A.	N.A.	N.A.	N.A.
other	7,099	12,671	12,611	11,864	13,230	13,463	15,530
Total	32,893	43,071	42,955	44,326	47,955	50,162	53,756

Source: Records of the Criminal Investigation Department and Central Narcotics Bureau of Singapore.

Table 6.41 Total of All Offenders Brought into Formal Contact with the Criminal Justice System First Recorded as Suspected, Arrested, or Otherwise Classified

All offenders by type of crime	Total number of persons for the year						
	1980	1981	1982	1983	1984	1985	1986
Intentional homicide	77	125	169	69	60	100	86
Nonintentional homicide							
Assault	306	370	360	351	433	422	450
Rape	34	41	48	49	71	71	77
Robbery	514	534	415	393	432	444	416
Theft	4 052	4 458	4 213	4 319	5 230	6 271	6 284
Fraud	407	358	376	376	406	476	487
Embezzlement	135	156	152	161	155	175	178
Kidnapping		10	10	11	16	11	10
Drug-related crimes:							
Simple possession	3 731	4 352	3 944	4 045	881	789	760
All other drug offenses					2 850	3 289	3 545
Bribery and/or corruption	N.A.	N.A.	N.A.	N.A.	N.A.	N.A.	N.A
Others (specify). Other seizable offenses	4 471	9 989	6 852	7 509	8 115	7 607	6 911
Grand total	13 727	20 393	16 539	17 283	18 649	19 655	19 204

Source: Records of the Criminal Investigation Department and Central Narcotics Bureau of Singapore.

175

Table 6.42   Number of Persons Prosecuted

Total of offenders by type of crime	Total number of persons for the year						
	1980	1981	1982	1983	1984	1985	1986
Intentional homicide	32	46	39	50	59	78	58
Non-intentional homicide							
Assault	191	236	234	203	266	220	251
Rape	13	25	33	23	25	35	26
Robbery	418	451	344	331	383	388	357
Theft	3,443	3,658	3,062	3,201	3,670	3,975	4,105
Fraud	285	230	255	267	223	259	287
Embezzlement	107	111	109	135	99	96	91
Kidnapping		6	5	10	5	6	10
Drug-related crime: Simple possession	748	563	413	340	414	446	428
All other drug offenses	719	859	792	465	646	1,070	976
Bribery and/or corruption	N.A.	N.A.	N.A.	N.A.	N.A.	N.A.	N.A.
Others (specify). Other seizable offenses	2,121	2,234	2,124	2,377	2,045	1,997	1,870
Grand total	8,077	8,419	7,410	7,402	7,835	8,570	8,459

Source: Records of the Criminal Investigation Department and Central Narcotics Bureau of Singapore.

Table 6.43 Number of Persons Convicted in the Criminal Courts

Total of all offenders by type of crime	Total number of persons for the year						
	1980	1981	1982	1983	1984	1985	1986
Intentional homicide	3	1	9	12	5	7	1
Nonintentional homicide							
Assault	125	103	101	94	150	127	104
Rape		2	2	1	10	1	6
Robbery	249	214	150	95	124	163	130
Theft	2,910	2,731	2,879	2,204	2,802	2,627	2,508
Fraud	192	145	129	127	129	173	144
Embezzlement	72	68	69	80	64	55	38
Kidnapping				6			
Drug-related crimes:							
Simple possession	N.A.	N.A.	N.A.	N.A.	N.A.	N.A.	N.A.
All other drug offenses	N.A.	N.A.	N.A.	N.A.	N.A.	N.A.	N.A.
Bribery and/or corruption	N.A.	N.A.	N.A.	N.A.	N.A.	N.A.	N.A.
Others (specify): Other seizable Offenses	1,790	1,710	964	1,686	1,590	1,580	1,415
total	5,341	4,974	4,303	4,305	4,874	4,733	4,346

Source: Records of the Criminal Investigation Department and Central Narcotics Bureau of Singapore.

Table 6.44   Persons Incarcerated

Category of incarceration	Total for the calendar year		
	1982	1984	1986
Awaiting trial or adjudication	190	250	395
Sentenced	2,332	3,077	3,745
Otherwise adjudicated	N.A.	N.A.	N.A.
Preventive detention	N.A.	N.A.	N.A.
For nonpayment of penal fine	N.A.	N.A.	N.A.
Civil law incarceration	N.A.	N.A.	N.A.
Other	N.A.	N.A.	N.A.
Total	2,522	3,327	4,140

Source: The Third UN Survey, Singapore.

Article 350 (1) of the Criminal Procedure Code states that when any person other than a person accused of a bailable offense is arrested or detained without warrant by a police officer or appears or is brought before a court and is prepared at any time while in the custody of the officer or at any stage of the proceeding before the court to give bail, that person shall be released on bail by any police officer in such cases as are specified in orders issued by the commissioner of police or by that court.

Article 351 (1) of the Criminal Procedure Code states that when any person accused of any nonbailable offense is arrested or detained without warrant by a police officer or appears or is brought before a court, he or she may be released on bail by any police officer not below the rank of sergeant or by that court, but he shall not be so released if there appear to be reasonable grounds for believing that he has been guilty of an offense punishable with death or imprisonment for life.

Adjudication Stage

Police Supervision. Police supervision is utilized as an alternative to imprisonment. Under article 11, 14 of the Criminal Procedure code, when a person, having been convicted (whether in Singapore or elsewhere) of an offense punishable with imprisonment for a term of two years or upward, is convicted of any other offense also punishable with imprisonment for a term of two years or upward, the court may, in addition to any other punishment to which it may sentence him direct that he shall be subject to the supervision of the police for a period of not more than three years, commencing immediately after the expiration of the sentence passed on him for the last offense.

Every person directed to be subject to the supervision of the police who is at large in Singapore shall personally present himself and report the place of his residence to the officer in charge of the police division in which that residence is situated, and whenever that person changes such residence, he shall personally present himself and report such change of residence to the officer in charge of that police division.

Probation. Section 5 of the Probation of Offenders Act provides that if a court, by or before which a person is convicted of an offense for which no sentence is fixed by law, is of the opinion that, having regard to the circumstances, including the nature of the offense and the character of

Table 6.45   Resources of Penal and Correctional Institutions: Number of Prisons (penal and correctional institutions) for Adults

Rated capacity of institutions	Number of prisons as December 31		
	1982	1984	1986
Very small institutions, less than 100 persons			
Small institutions, 100-499 persons	6	6	6
Medium sized institutions, 500-999 persons	2	2	2
Large institutions, 1,000 persons or more	1	1	1
Total number of spaces ("beds") available			

Source: The Third UN Survey, Singapore.

offender, it is expedient to do so, the court may, instead of sentencing him, make a probation order, that is to say, an order requiring him to be under the supervision of a probation officer or volunteer probation officer for a period to be specified of not less than one year or more than three years.

The Probation Officers Act also provides for the appointment of a chief probation officer and volunteer probation officers.

The Probation of Offenders Rules, 1976, regulate the duties and responsibilities of the chief probation officer, the Probation Committee, and its two case committees, namely the Adult and Juvenile Probation Committees. It also lays down the duties and responsibilities of the probation officer in relation to preparation of presentence reports, supervision of offenders, and maintenance of case records. The Probation of Offenders Act provides a constructive form of corrective treatment outside the institutional setting. It could apply to any offense except for crimes like murder or treason, where the sentence is fixed by law. The act permits the release of an offender to the supervision and personal care of a probation officer for a specified period ranging from one to three years.

There are no conditions with regard to the offender's age or sex or the number of times he or she may be placed on probation. However, the court invariably exercises a certain degree of selectiveness when considering probations. For this, the courts rely on the probation officers for probation or presentence reports on the offender. A probation order imposes certain conditions that must be observed by the probationer. Failure to comply with any of the conditions specified in the probation order constitutes a breach of the order, and the probationer is brought back to the court to receive sentence on the offense for which he or she was placed on probation.

Follow-up Stage of Dispositions

Day-Release Program. In 1981, the day-release program commenced as the last stage of imprisonment for criminal law detainees, invoked under an executive order. This is based on the principle of a halfway house to bridge the gap between a strictly controlled regime in prison and liberty.

Under the program, the detainees leave the camp during the day to work with an outside employer, where they are paid normal wages, and return to camp at the end of the day. It enables the detainee to gradually adjust to free society, to earn normal wages, and thus resume some of the obligations of a free person, such as those to his family, and to assume a role in the economic life.

It helps the person build up self-respect while providing a critical test of readiness to rejoin society as a useful and law-abiding citizen. Although it lasts a year, at the end of the first three months, and subject to good behavior, the detainee is permitted to go on home leave during weekends.

Any breach of discipline at the workplace or of conditions attached to weekend leave would immediately invoke measures to have the detainee removed from the program and recalled to prison to serve out the rest of his or her detention order, which is subject to annual reviews. Absconders are dealt with in court. Upon successful completion of the program, the detainee returns to society as a free person but has to undergo a one-year mandatory police supervision.

Suspension, Remission, and Commutation of Sentence

According to article 236 of the Criminal Procedure Code, when any person has been sentenced to punishment for an offense, the president, acting in accordance with the provisions of section 8 of the Republic of Singapore Independence Act, 1965, may at any time, without conditions or upon any conditions that the person sentenced accepts, suspend the execution of the person's sentence or remit the whole, or any part, of the punishment to which he or she has been sentenced.

Whenever an application is made to the president for the suspension or remission of a sentence, the president requires the presiding judge of the court before or by which the conviction was passed to state an opinion as to whether the application should be granted or refused.

If any condition on which a sentence has been suspended or remitted is, in the opinion of the president, not fulfilled, the president may cancel the suspension or remission, and thereupon the person in whose favor the sentence has been suspended or remitted may, if at large, be arrested by any police officer without warrant and remanded to undergo the unexpired portion of the sentence.

Democratic Socialist Republic of Sri Lanka

Crime Trends and Policy for Alternatives to Imprisonment

According to the Third U.N. Survey, the total reported crimes in Sri Lanka increased from 58,777 to 61,391 over a six-year period (1980–86; table 6.46). In particular, intentional homicide increased from 1,227 to 2,069, and fraud jumped from 1,218 to 3,510. Drug-related offenses also increased in 1986, while theft is an exception, in that it decreased in recent years.

Although no nationwide statistical data are available on arrests, prosecutions, and convictions, a survey conducted by the police in Colombo in June 1986 indicated that suspects were arrested for 70 percent of the reported crimes, 50 or 60 percent of those suspects were prosecuted, and subsequently 20 to 25 percent of those were found guilty.

Sri Lanka is not faced with a serious problem of overcrowding in prisons. The average daily population in prisons, however, has slightly increased, due to the gradual increase of remand prisoners (table 6.47).

Table 6.46   Number of Crimes Recorded in the Criminal (Police) Statistics

Crime	Total for calendar year						
	1980	1981	1982	1983	1984	1985	1986
Intentional Homicide	1227	1344	1501	1862	1883	2069	2069
Nonintentional homicide							
Assault: Major assaults only	9703	9643	6363	10654	11316	10625	11010
Including minor assaults	25360	25026	19886	23202	23276	23573	20762
Rape	229	262	267	241	277	294	274
Robbery	5058	4533	4505	5138	5156	6345	5319
Theft: Major thefts only	31464	32398	3282	26053	25411	22150	28451
Including minor thefts	64190	64145	28520	46262	50047	36680	40440
Fraud	1218	1396	1464	3273	4250	4209	3510
Embezzlement							
Kidnapping	312	267	308	250	290	309	356
Drug-related crimes: Simple possession	6211	6263	5229	4736	6894	6681	8378
All other drug offenses	1		4	2	8	12	31
Bribery and/or corruption	408	373	289	240	227	210	267
Other (specify)							
Riots	103	321	89	1586	108	129	112
Counterfeiting currency	17	11	20	12	2	54	74
Offenses against the State	1	10			16	8	5
Offensive weapons	31	40	17	30	1	7	15
Total number of recorded crimes	28777	60390	56084	64421	59182	58392	61391

Source: Police Headquarters, Colombo 01, Sri Lanka.
Note: Figures include "attempts to commit."

Table 6.47   Daily Average of Convicted and Unconvicted Prisoners, 1976–1985

YEAR	DAILY AVERAGE OF CONVICTED	DAILY AVERAGE OF REMANDEES	TOTAL	RATIO OF DAILY AVERAGE CONVICTED	REMANDEES	TOTAL	PERCENTAGE OF REMANDEES
1976	5,732	4,903	10,635	1	0.9	1.9	46.0
1977	5,161	4,732	9,993	1	0.9	1.9	48.0
1978	4,907	4,529	9,436	1	0.9	1.9	48.0
1979	5,179	6,204	11,383	1	1.2	2.2	54.0
1980	4,777	6,005	10,782	1	1.3	2.3	56.0
1981	4,211	5,991	10,202	1	1.4	2.4	59.0
1982	3,843	5,720	9,563	1	1.5	2.5	60.0
1983	3,909	7,311	11,220	1	1.9	2.9	65.0
1984	4,252	7,441	11,693	1	1.7	2.7	64.0
1985	4,690	6,472	11,162	1	1.4	2.4	58.0

Source: Department of Prisons, Sri Lanka.

Also, it is pointed out that more than 50 percent of convicted prisoners serve short-term imprisonment of less than six months.

Various alternatives to imprisonment have been implemented at all levels of criminal justice administration. Bail is utilized in order to reduce the number of remand prisoners. At the trial stage, conditional sentences, suspended sentences, probation, and community service orders are implemented. However, probation is not yet fully and actively utilized, because of the shortage of specialized probation officers. Community service orders are now implemented on an experimental basis, because of insufficient social resources. At the posttrial stage, home leave, work release, release on license, remission, and amnesty are implemented in order to reduce the prison population and at the same time to improve the quality and effectiveness of correctional services.

Pretrial Stage: Bail

According to sections 402 to 408 of the Code of Criminal Procedure of 1979, "bail" in Sri Lanka can be defined as "the release or setting at liberty of a person arrested, either on his own recognizance or upon others who become sureties for his appearance to the court on a future date."

The nature and circumstances of offense are considered when bail is granted. If the accused has a long criminal history, the grant of bail may be less justified. On the other hand, young persons or those who have no previous convictions may have a better chance to be released on bail. No statistical information is available, but bail is highly utilized.

Adjudication Stage

Conditional Sentence. The general policy of criminal justice in Sri Lanka is that, if possible, first-time offenders not be sent to prison. Section 306 of the Code of Criminal Procedure Act of 1979 states:

> Where any person is charged before the Magistrate's Court with an offence punishable by such court, and the court thinks that the charge is proved, but is of opinion that, having regard to the character, anteced-ents, age, health, or mental condition of the person charged, or to the trivial nature of the offence, or to the extenuating circumstances under which the offence was committed, it is inexpedient to inflict any punishment, or . . . [is of the opinion] that it is expedient to discharge the offender conditionally . . . the court may, without proceeding to conviction, either:
>
> a. order such offender to be discharged after such admonition as to the court shall seem fit; or

b. discharge the offender conditionally on his entering into a recognizance, with or without sureties, to be of good behavior, and to appear for conviction and sentence when called on at any time during such period, not exceeding three years, as may be specified in the order of the court.

When the person has been convicted on indictment of any offense punishable with imprisonment, the court also may, in lieu of imposing a sentence of imprisonment, make an order discharging the offender conditionally.

In the application of the above-mentioned sanctions, the court may, in addition, order the offender to pay

a. compensation, and/or
b. state cost, in an amount not exceeding 1,500 rupees, as the court thinks fit.

In actual practice, the application of conditional sentence is not as frequent as expected.

Suspended Sentence. Suspended sentence of imprisonment was introduced into the law in 1972. Section 303 of the Code of Criminal Procedure Act states:

A court which imposes a sentence of imprisonment on an offender for a term not exceeding two years for an offence may order that the sentence shall not take effect unless, during a period specified in the order being not less than five years from the date of the order, such offender commits another offence punishable with imprisonment.

In case the sentence to be imposed is less than six months, and the offender has no previous experience of imprisonment, the court shall suspend sentence, unless

a. the offense involved the use or threat of violence, or the use or possession of a firearm or an explosive weapon;
b. the offender was subject to a suspended sentence at the time when the offense was committed; or
c. the court is of the opinion that a suspension of sentence would be inappropriate in the circumstances of the case.

On imposing the suspended sentence, the court shall explain to the offender in ordinary language his or her liability if he or she commits an offense during the suspension period. If the offender does not commit a subsequent offense during the operational period, which was specified by the order of the court, the conviction and the suspended sentence imposed on the offender shall be deemed, for all purposes, never to have been entered or imposed.

Probation. The statutory provision available for the probation order under section 3 of the Probation Ordinance of 1944 states:

> Where any person is convicted by any court of any offence committed in a proclaimed judicial division and punishable by that court and if it appears to court having regard to all the circumstances of the case including the nature of the offence and the age, sex and condition of the offender that it is expedient that the offender should be released on probation, the court may make a Probation Order in respect of the offender in lieu of sentencing him to any other punishment which the court may have power to impose.

According to the law, the court shall, before making the probation order, consider all such information relating to the character, antecedents, and environmental and mental or physical condition of the offender. No probation order shall be made by a court unless

a. the court has in simple language communicated to the offender the proposed order and the conditions to be included therein, and explained that if he or she fails to observe any such conditions or commits another offense, he or she will be liable to be sentenced for the original offense; and,
b. the offender has given his or her written consent to the making of the order and agreed to observe the conditions thereof.

Table 6.48   Number of New Probation Orders from 1975 to 1985

Year	Male	Female	Total
1975	1,241	278	1,519
1976	1,365	268	1,633
1977	1,023	188	1,211
1978	1,228	219	1,447
1979	858	199	1,057
1980	569	126	695
1981	856	150	1,006
1982	727	150	877
1983	723	176	899
1984	722	211	933
1985	580	150	730

Source: Probation and Child Care Department, Sri Lanka.

Legally, the length of probation can be from one to three years; in practice, it is usually for two years.

The number of probation cases has been gradually decreasing in Sri Lanka (table 6.48). This is due to the fact that judges are hesitant to utilize the probation order because of the insufficient number of probation officers in each community.

Probation officers are not attached to the court or the correction agencies, but they are stationed in the Probation and Child Care Services Office, which is under the control of the Probation and Child Care Department of the Ministry of Social Services. The 114 probation officers, who are also in charge of childcare services in the community, are almost fully occupied with juvenile cases and do not have enough time to deal with adult probationers. It is therefore expected that, in order to fully utilize the probation order, the number of probation officers will be increased.

Community Service Order. The community service order was first introduced in Sri Lanka by Administration of Justice Law No. 44 of 1973 and was continued in section 18 of the code of Criminal Procedure Act of 1979. According to the law, "The Court may in lieu of imposing a sentence of imprisonment on conviction of an accused person or in lieu of imposing a sentence of imprisonment of an accused person in default of payment of a fine enter an order hereinafter referred to as a 'community service order', directing the accused person to perform stipulated service at a named place in a State or State-sponsored project, if regulations have been made by the Minister for carrying out such an order."

The order is for a period of less than one year if made by a magistrate, or less than three years if made by a High Court judge. The failure to comply with an order may result in its cancellation and the imposition of a term of imprisonment.

The use of the community service order is now in an experimental stage. The community service order is expected to be an innovative and imaginative approach to community-based corrections. To date, however, the order is not fully utilized in Sri Lanka and can be made only for those offenders who live in places where the community service program exists. Due to the fact that social resources are not always available or prepared and that the supervisory agencies do not necessarily exist, it is difficult to guarantee the full and appropriate implementation of community service orders.

Follow-up Stage of Dispositions

According to section 94 of the Prison Ordinance of 1877, which was revised in 1956, "The Minister may from time to time make all such rules, not inconsistent with this Ordinance or any other written law relating to prisons, as may be necessary for the administration of the prisons in Ceylon and for carrying out or giving effect to the provisions and principles of this Ordinance.'' On the basis of this provision, various innovative measures of correctional treatment have been introduced and actually carried out in prisons in Sri Lanka, in order to facilitate the rehabilitation of offenders.

Home Leave. On the basis of the administrative regulations concerned, the home leave program is defined as follows: ''A scheme under which certain categories of prisoners are permitted to visit their homes unescorted for a maximum period of seven days at a time, once in six months.'' The privilege of home leave for long-term prisoners, for up to a period of seven days at a time, was introduced in Sri Lanka in 1974.

In practice, the home leave program is applied to those prisoners who maintain good behavior and show rehabilitative improvement in prison. This program has been fairly as well as actively implemented in order to maintain good relations between inmates and their families. About one hundred prisoners are tentatively released on the home leave program each year, and very few prisoners violate the law (table 6.49).

Work Release. According to the administrative regulations concerned, the work-release program is defined as ''a scheme under which selected prisoners are allowed to get themselves employed in the open community unescorted during day and return to a prison for the night.''

The work-release program may be applied to those prisoners who have

Table 6.49   Number of Home Leave Cases from 1977 to 1986

Year	Home Leave Cases	Cases Who Violated Law
1977	133	0
1978	155	0
1979	93	1
1980	94	0
1981	84	1
1982	52	0
1983	82	0
1984	105	0
1985	115	0
1986	108	0

Source: Department of Prisons, Sri Lanka.

successfully completed part of their prison term (two years or more) and who have yet a remainder of two years' or less imprisonment. Among these prisoners, some are selected for the program when and where the resources for implementation are available. This program was inaugurated in May 1974. Under this program, prisoners for whom suitable employment can be found in the community are sent to work either from a prison or from a work-release center, where they return in the evening, and they are therefore technically still in custody. The prisoners receive normal wages, which they can send to their families or which they can collect on their discharge. In the process the prisoner gets accustomed to conditions and regulations prevailing in the workplace.

Prison welfare officers occasionally visit the workplaces to meet employers to monitor the progress of the inmate. If the work and conduct are unsatisfactory, the inmate can be withdrawn from the program. Work release is applied to about one hundred prisoners each year (table 6.50).

Release on License or Parole. What is commonly known as "parole" is referred to as "release on license" in Sri Lanka. According to the administrative regulations concerned, the release on license is defined as "a scheme under which certain categories of prisoners are conditionally released from prison prematurely under the supervision of prison welfare officers."

The release on license scheme was first introduced in 1969 for the benefit of long-term prisoners. It has proved to be a success because of the

Table 6.50 Number of Work-Release Cases from 1977 to 1986

Year	No. of Cases Engaged on Work Release	No. of Cases Found Unsuitable
1977	141	2
1978	77	17
1979	123	18
1980	114	24
1981	86	10
1982	66	6
1983	106	16
1984	104	15
1985	112	13
1986	121	12

Source: Department of Prisons, Sri Lanka.

low rate of violations, and at present the scheme is applicable to all prisoners who meet the following conditions:

a. those who were sentenced to four years or more and have completed half of their sentence; or
b. those who have served in prison for more than six years; or
c. those who have served in prison for five years and then served at least one year in an open institution.

According to the present regulations, therefore, those prisoners whose sentences of imprisonment are less than four years cannot be eligible for release on license. Selection of inmates and recommendation for release on license is made by the warden of the prison. A social report comprising the antecedents of the offender, some details of the offense, vocational and other training he or she had in prison, information regarding his or her prospects for employment, and a plan for his or her rehabilitation in the community is prepared by prison welfare officers and submitted to the License Board.

The examination and final decision concerning this program is made by the License Board, which is composed of nine members appointed by the minister of justice. At every License Board hearing, the offender is present, and if for any reason he or she is not granted release on license, the offender is informed of the facts so that he or she can act accordingly and request another hearing. Those who are released prematurely on this program should keep communications with, and be supervised by, prison welfare officers.

The selection and examination of prisoners for release on license are very carefully made. Thus a quite limited number of prisoners, fewer than fifty, are released on license each year (table 6.51).

Table 6.51   Number of Prisoners Released on License from 1977 to 1986

Year	No. of Cases Released on Parole
1977	78
1978	74
1979	53
1980	27
1981	32
1982	27
1983	51
1984	37
1985	25
1986	27

Source: Department of Prisons, Sri Lanka.

Remission. Subsection 2 of section 94 of the Prison Ordinance states:

In particular and without prejudice to the generality of the foregoing powers, the Minister may make rules for all or any of the following purposes or matters:

> j. rewards for good conduct and the remission of sentences to be allowed to prisoners for industry and good conduct, and the conditions in which such remission may be allowed.

On the basis of this regulation, "one-third remission" is commonly and widely implemented in prisons in Sri Lanka. Actual length of sentence is reduced by one-third as long as good conduct and industrious attitudes are maintained.

Amnesty. Amnesty is given, in the name of the president, to convicted offenders on special occasions, such as Independence Day and Wesak Full Moon Day. Amnesty can reduce or nullify the sentence.

Kingdom of Thailand

Crime Trends and Policy for Alternatives to Imprisonment

In 1986, a total of 563,824 crimes were reported to the Thailand police, an amount that has not changed in recent years (table 6.52). Although there are no nationwide statistical data available on clearance rates, the Bangkok Metropolitan Police in 1983 solved 54.7 percent of reported murders, 53.1 percent of gang robberies and robberies, and 51.0 percent of larcenies, which shows some improvement from 1976 (table 6.53). In 1986, the Public Prosecutor's Office prosecuted 462,000 cases from among the 478,000 cases brought to the office.

Table 6.52   Criminal Cases Throughout the Country, 1982 to 1986

Year	Crime Rate
1982	564,115
1983	545,777
1984	545,061
1985	592,828
1986	563,824

Source: Research and Planning Division, Police Department, Ministry of the Interior, Thailand.

Table 6.53   Volumes of Crimes Against Persons, Crimes Against Property, and Sex Crimes in Bangkok and Thonburi, 1976–1983

Offenses	1976 Known	1976 Arrests	1977 Known	1977 Arrests	1978 Known	1978 Arrests	1979 Known	1979 Arrests	1980 Known	1980 Arrests	1981 Known	1981 Arrests	1982 Known	1982 Arrests	1983 Known	1983 Arrests
Murder	467	165	434	179	447	205	506	240	531	251	602	279	501	259	450	246
Manslaughter	32	18	24	20	32	17	26	11	31	19	29	17	15	11	16	10
Attempted Murder	467	234	339	160	332	159	409	213	404	201	375	162	322	134	351	156
Assault	1790	1291	1549	970	1336	925	1519	1057	1491	1066	1660	1191	1667	1220	2072	1594
Gang Robbery	412	202	302	203	319	173	432	243	385	247	291	181	251	172	254	165
Robbery	720	261	649	278	625	300	75	481	872	414	632	405	678	300	760	373
Pickpocketing	409	279	470	340	456	363	527	447	493	400	403	300	452	310	445	336
Larceny	8184	2966	6600	2550	6450	2505	6350	3081	7132	3575	7913	3717	7341	3671	7126	3634
Fraud	761	595	625	475	500	443	736	521	923	623	975	644	1157	730	1215	747
Forcible Rape and Murder	0	0	3	2	3	0	0	0	1	0	4	2	6	3	2	1
Forcible Rape	264	196	284	226	247	191	257	191	201	210	220	176	203	144	233	103

Source: National Police Department, Department of Corrections, Thailand.

Table 6.54   Staff and Prison Population, 1977–1986

Year	Total Number of Correctional Staff	Total Number of Prison Officers	Average Number of Inmates in Custody	Ratio of Officer to Inmates
1977	7 268	6 957	66 788	1:10
1978	7 366	7 055	69 797	1:10
1979	7 457	7 130	68 329	1:10
1980	7 751	7 415	75 496	1:10
1981	8 120	7 784	73 464	1:09
1982	8 270	7 934	71 387	1:09
1983	8 467	8 130	80 463	1:10
1984	8 633	8 290	85 208	1:10
1985	8 805	8 456	89 053	1:11
1986	8 931	8 582	92 841	1:11

Source: Department of Corrections, Thailand.

At the end of 1987, there were approximately 95,990 prisoners in custody, a 30 percent increase over the inmate population of 1977 (table 6.54). While the prison population has increased to 95,990, the total capacity of prisons is only about 50,000, a condition resulting in administrative problems, including shortage of funds and staff and prison overcrowding. Faced with these realities, the criminal justice administrators are considering innovative schemes to solve the problem of overcrowding and improve the humanitarian treatment measures for offenders. Since the problem of overcrowding results mainly from the use of imprisonment as the principal penal sanction, an attempt was made to reduce prison entries with the application of the probation system introduced in 1979.

Pretrial Stage: Bail or Provisional Release

The alleged offender or the accused may be provisionally released, without bail or with bail, with or without security (sections 106–119, Criminal Procedure Code). The application for provisional release may be filed by the alleged offender or the accused or any interested person to the appropriate authority as follows:

1. Where the alleged offender is kept in custody and has not yet been charged in court, the application is to be made to the inquiry official or the public prosecutor, as the case may be.
2. Where the alleged offender is detained under a warrant of detention of a court but has not yet been charged, the application is to be made to the court.
3. Where the alleged offender has been charged in court, the application is to be made to the court that tries the case.

Provisional release may be granted without bail only in cases relating to offenses punishable with maximum imprisonment of less than one year. Otherwise, it will be granted with bail, with or without security as the appropriate authority or the court considers suitable.

Where the alleged offender or the accused is to be provisionally released without bail, he or she must make, before being released, an oath or affirmation that he or she shall appear as requested or according to the summons. Where the offender is to be provisionally released with bail either with or without security, the applicant or the surety must sign the bail bond before the release takes place. The bail bond contains conditions that the alleged offender or the accused or the bailer shall comply with the appointment or the summons of the official or the court granting the provisional release, and a specified sum of money is to be paid in case of a breach of the bail bond.

Where provisional release is granted with bail and security, the security required must be furnished by the applicant before the release takes place. There are three kinds of security, namely:

a. A deposit in cash
b. A deposit in other valuable securities
c. A person standing as surety by declaring his or her valuable securities

A bail program has been implemented to provide indigent defendants with surety for the exchange of liberty during the trial, particularly during presentence investigation granted probation.

Criteria for consideration of the accused or defendant eligible for the bail bond include such factors as that (1) the defendant must have a fixed place of residence, and (2) the evidence in the preliminary investigation for probation shows that he or she is likely to appear before the court whenever he or she is called upon to do so.

Financing of the program is supported by the Foundation for the Rehabilitation of and Aftercare Services for the Offenders (FRASO). FRASO has allocated 420,000 baht, or 15,550 dollars, for implementing the program. However, the budget is too small to manage the program at full scale. In considering the amount of bail bond, the court takes into account the seriousness of charges as the significant determinant. From 1984 to 1986, fifty-one defendants obtained the benefit of the bail program.

Adjudication Stage

Suspended Sentence and Suspended Execution of Sentence. The court may suspend the sentence or, after the determination of punishment, may suspend the execution of the sentence, and release the offender, with or without imposing control conditions (section 56 of the Penal Code), which must not exceed five years.

In the case of noncompliance with the imposed conditions, the court may admonish the offender, determine the punishment, or inflict the suspended punishment.

Probation. Initiated in Bangkok with 41 officials and 320 supervision cases in 1979 as the result of the Probation Procedure Act, probation service has been extended to fourteen provinces with 238 officials and 9,402 supervision cases in 1986. The rate of increase in work loads is high, but it is relatively low in comparison with the potential number of cases in which probation could be applied.

Statistical analysis shows that there were 80,986 cases brought to the metropolitan courts in 1983. Although judges may request presentence investigation reports for the purpose of granting probation, the courts, in fact, ordered only 1,640 presentence investigation reports (2 percent) and granted probation in 3,686 cases (4.6 percent). Two years later, in 1985, the courts in the metropolis ordered presentence investigation reports for 2,229 defendants (2.1 percent) and granted probation to 3,976 offenders (3.8 percent) from a total of 110,844 cases. The situation in the regions is similar to that of the metropolis. Only 568 cases (1.7 percent) out of 21,028 defendants were ordered for presentence investigation, while 764 cases (3.4 percent) were granted probation. Supervision begins after the offenders have been placed under probation, and probation officers are assigned to supervise the offenders under the conditions imposed by the court. The probationers must report periodically to the probation officers. The probation officers must also visit probationers' homes or places of work at least once a month to check on their conduct. The probation officers will make efforts to provide counseling and render material assistance to probationers in the form of jobs, relief, and vocational guidance. A probationer may apply for investment funds, employment guarantees, and lunch allowances from the FRASO of the Ministry of Justice.

In case of a violation of the conditions for probation or commission of a new offense, a probation report must be submitted to the court immediately for further consideration. The court may issue a summons or arrest warrant for the probationer for reprimand, or send him or her to prison. However, if the probationer meets the necessary conditions and completes the probation period, a final report is submitted to the court, resulting in the closure of the case.

At present, the Ministry of Justice has one Central Probation Office in Bangkok and twenty-two provincial probation offices in rural areas. The Ministry plans to increase the number of probation offices until there is one in each province throughout the country.

As the purpose of probation is to reform and correct offenders through reintegrative methods in the community, it is impossible to achieve the goal without cooperation and aid from the community. The administrators of probation services are developing strategies to enhance public awareness of the system and gain more support. The implementation of the volunteer probation officer program seems not only to correspond to this philosophy but also to reduce the expenditures in dealing with offenders. The volunteer program is fostered by the government and the National Economic and Social Development Board. In compliance with national policies, the Ministry of Justice has set down a concrete plan to expand programs in all provinces where probation services operate.

In 1989 there were 2,073 volunteers working in close cooperation with professional officers in twenty-two provinces. By 1991, if the plan worked out according to schedule, there should have been 10,739 volunteers providing services to probationers. There was a noticeable increase in public participation, demanding a systematic monitoring.

Follow-up Stage of Dispositions

Parole and Remission. The parole system, as applied in Thai correctional work, is regarded as an incentive to good conduct and rehabilitation of prisoners. It is also a reward granted to a prisoner, permitting him or her to leave prison provisionally before the termination of his or her sentence and resume normal life with his or her family. The Department of Corrections may grant parole to a prisoner who fulfills certain conditions. For example, a prisoner with a term of imprisonment for ten years who has a family (e.g., a spouse and children), has served a certain part of the term, and has maintained good conduct, and for whom the local official certifies that he or she will not disturb the peace in community, may be granted parole.

The parolee is required to observe and follow parole conditions strictly. If any of the conditions fixed for release on parole are violated, the parolee will be returned to prison immediately to serve the remaining term of imprisonment. A parolee who maintains good behavior and strictly observes the conditions of parole will be allowed to live in freedom until his or her term of imprisonment expires. However, effectiveness of parole administered in Thai correctional institutions is hindered by the shortage of parole officers.

The Penitentiary Act of 1936, as amended by the act of 1977 and its Ministerial Regulations, authorizes the Department of Corrections to grant parole and release a prisoner from the prison in which he or she has served a part of his or her term of imprisonment according to his or her status: namely, good, very good, or excellent. The terms under which a prisoner may be granted parole are as follows;

1. An excellent-class prisoner shall become parole eligible when one-third of the term of imprisonment remains to be served;
2. a very-good-class prisoner shall become parole eligible when one-fourth of the term of imprisonment remains to be served; and
3. a good-class prisoner shall become parole eligible when one-fifth of the term of imprisonment remains to be served.

The process starts from the consideration of a local review committee, which consists of a prison warden and other prison officers. The committee then makes a recommendation to the Parole Board. The board, which consists of seven high-ranking officials, including the deputy director-general of the Department of Corrections acting as chair, reviews recommendations of the local review committee, including the prisoner's domestic background or criminal record, circumstances of the offense, conduct during his or her stay in prison, postrelease plans, and some other information, so as to make sure that parole will successfully help the prisoner to return to society. The final decision to grant parole depends largely on the director-general of the Department of Corrections. A prisoner granted parole is conditionally released from a prison and placed under the supervision of a parole officer who also belongs to the Department of Corrections.

Apart from parole, a prisoner may be granted remission of part of the sentence on the grounds of industrious and good conduct, as follows:

1. An excellent-class prisoner may be granted remission of five days per month;
2. a very-good-class prisoner may be granted remission of four days per month; and
3. a good-class prisoner may be granted remission of three days per month.

Only a prisoner with a definite term of sentence who has served a sentence for more than six months is eligible for remission.

The Sentence Board, consisting of representatives from the Department of Corrections, the Police Department, the Public Prosecution Department, the Social Welfare Department, and a psychiatrist from the Public Health Department, has the authority to grant remission. Such a decision is final.

Upon release, prisoners are subject to supervision by a parole officer for the remaining period of their original sentence. If they do not comply with the supervision, or if they commit another crime, they must return to prison for the remaining period. Thousands of prisoners benefit from the good-behavior allowance system. It has also been used to mitigate the destructive impact of imprisonment in an overcrowded prison.

The Corrections Department trains volunteer professional officers to assist parole officers to cope with the lack of parole officers. By 1985, 8,139 volunteers, 7,492 of which were in provinces, had been trained. The volunteer has to pass through the screening and training processes before taking the responsibility of supervision over prisoners being conditionally released on parole or receiving sentence remission either by public work allowances or by good-behavior allowances. Each volunteer takes care of approximately ten conditionally released prisoners. Volunteers work, with no salary, under the supervision of, and in coordination with, full-time aftercare (parole) officers. The Department of Corrections selects volunteers from respected persons in the local community. The volunteers quickly earn the conditionally released prisoners' trust, and their close relationship provides them a good opportunity to play a significant role in helping the prisoners readjust to the society.

Public Work Allowance. The Department of Corrections is able to lawfully employ prisoners for public work outside prison. This program provides an employment opportunity for prisoners and utilizes prison labor for the public interest. The prisoners who are assigned to work in public work projects get paid not over 80 percent of the net profit. The officers who supervise the project would get 10 percent, and the remaining 10 percent would be put in the investment fund of the prison for public work projects. The other benefit earned by the assigned prisoner is sentence remission by one day for his or her one day working outside.

Penal Settlement. At present, there is one penal settlement in Thailand. The program provides an opportunity for a prereleased prisoner to readjust to the community. Prisoners who are qualified for program participation have to serve their sentences in prison for not less than one-fourth of their term, with the remaining term being not less than two years, and also have good behavior and good performance in prison. The penal settlement selection committee would consider all applications, with preference for those who have previous experience in farming and do not have land of their own. The participant prisoners would each get eight acres of land at a penal settlement site. They are allowed to have their families stay with them. All products of their farming belong to them. They have to build their own houses and are able to stay for life. When a prisoner dies, the land may be transferred to his or her successor.

Pardon. Pardon is the main countermeasure against prison overcrowding in Thailand. There are two forms of pardon: individual pardon and collective pardon. However, the one that is used as the main countermeasure is collective pardon. It is occasionally granted to all convicted prisoners on special days or during important national events. Under the Royal Pardon Decree, convicted prisoners are entitled to either a certain amount of sentence remission or unconditional release, depending on the details of their conditions (table 6.55).

Table 6.55   Number of Pardons Granted, 1977–1987

Year	Unconditional Release	Sentence Remission	Occasions
1977	13,359	22,319	Royal Marriage of H.R.H. Crown Prince
1977	17,595	23,010	His Majesty the King's Birthday
1979	12,033	32,158	Royal Ordination of H.R.H. Crown Prince
1980	16,174	29,661	Her Majesty the Queen's Birthday
1982	18,438	36,188	Rattanakosin Bicentennial Celebration
1987	36,397	46,701	His Majesty the King's Birthday

Source: Department of Corrections, Thailand.

Hong Kong

Crime Trends and Policy for Alternatives to Imprisonment

Crimes in Hong Kong showed a rapid increase from 1978 to 1982 due to a large number of illegal immigrants from China, who were mainly young people and one of the major sources of crime. The Hong Kong government enforced a strict control policy against illegal immigration beginning in 1982, and the increase in crimes abated. As a result, the number of reported crimes each year since 1983 stabilized between 81,100 and 87,000, registering 81,411 in 1986. The crimes reported in 1986 included 67 intentional homicides, 4,622 assaults, 5,372 robberies, 32,750 thefts, and others. Narcotic drug offenses, however, including manufacturing, trafficking, and possession of drugs, accounted for 4,118 (a remarkable increase). In 1986, a total of 38,978 crimes were cleared by the police; this number represented 47.9 percent of all reported crimes. Intentional homicides were cleared with the highest rate (73.1 percent), while robberies sustained the lowest clearance rate (21.6 percent).

A total of 37,363 persons were prosecuted in 1986; these persons had committed 46.5 percent of all offenses cleared. Of those prosecuted, 47.9 percent were detained in custody. The length of pretrial detention was relatively short, with an average of 20.4 days for magistrates court remand, 46.1 days for district court remand, and 79 days for trial court remand. Hong Kong is not faced with a problem of prison overcrowding.

The Correctional Service Department operated over twenty institutions in 1986, including thirteen prisons, two drug addiction treatment centers, three training centers for young offenders between fourteen and twenty years of age, one detention center for young and young adult offenders between fourteen and twenty-four years of age, one psychiatric center, three halfway houses, and an escort unit. While the total capacity of inmates in these institutions was 8,876 with 6,368 staff, the average daily population in 1986 was 8,106.

The criminal justice system in Hong Kong provides the courts with a wide variety of sentencing options, especially in dealing with young offenders. Under the Prisons Ordinance, anyone over fourteen years of age can be incarcerated. An adult offender over twenty years old can be detained in an institution, including a prison, a detention center, or a psychiatric center. Under the Training Centres Ordinance, a person under twenty years old can be detained for a minimum period of six months to a maximum of three years. According to the Detention Centre Ordinance, a person aged between fourteen and twenty-four years sentenced to the detention center can be detained for a minimum period of one month to a maximum period of twelve months.

In Hong Kong the noninstitutional treatment measures have been recognized not only to be effective in their own way of treating a given age and type of offender but also to be very humanitarian and very economically efficient when compared with other treatment measures. Along these lines, a release under supervision program (parole) and a prerelease employment program were introduced in 1988 to facilitate reintegration of prisoners into society.

Pretrial Stage: Bail

An offender can be released on bail after being prosecuted, according to article 12A of the Criminal Procedure Ordinance, chapter 221, provided that "the court or a judge may at any time, on the application of any accused person, order such person, whether he has been committed for trial or not, to be admitted to bail, and the recognizance of bail may, if the order so directs, be taken before any magistrate or justice of the peace or before the Commissioner of Correctional Services. No magistrate or justice of the peace, however, shall admit any person to bail for treason or murder, nor shall such person be admitted to bail except by order of a judge."

Adjudication Stage

Suspension of Sentence. The Criminal Procedure Ordinance provides the court with the discretionary power to permit conditional release of offenders.

Article 107 of the ordinance provides:

> Where any person has been convicted or indicted of an offense punishable by imprisonment, and the court is of the opinion that, after taking into consideration the character, antecedents, age, health, or

mental condition of the person charged, the serious nature of the offense, or the extenuating circumstances under which the offense was committed, it is inexpedient to inflict punishment or any other than nominal punishment, the court may, in lieu of imposing a sentence of imprisonment, make an order discharging the offender conditionally on his recognizance, with or without sureties, requiring the person to demonstrate good behaviour and to appear for sentencing when called on at any time during such period, not exceeding 3 years, as may be specified in the order.

Probation. In Hong Kong, probation is a formal and legal procedure that places an offender under the supervision and administration of the Social Welfare Department. Probation applies to offenders of all ages. It allows offenders to remain in the community under the supervision of a probation officer and subject to prescribed rules set by courts for a period of one to three years. If the probationer has relapsed into crime or failed to comply with any requirement of the probation order, the probation officer has to report it to the court for further deliberation.

During 1985 and 1986, the total number of cases where probation was granted amounted to 1,384, of which 462 were completed satisfactorily, while in 167, failure to comply with the requirements of the probation order resulted in subsequent committal to prison.

Community Service Order. Under the Community Service Order Ordinance, courts may order offenders over fourteen years of age who are convicted of an offense punishable by imprisonment to perform unpaid work for the community for a number of hours not exceeding 240 in a period of twelve months.

A two-year pilot scheme on community service orders was implemented beginning 1 January 1987 in three magistrates. Offenders subject to a community service order are supervised by probation officers who provide them with counseling and guidance and arrange work for them. While offenses punishable with imprisonment cover a wide spectrum from the serious to the relatively minor, serious offenses like manslaughter, rape, arson, serious injury, and major drug offenses are regarded as unsuitable for community service orders. In January and February of 1987, courts ordered twelve community service orders ranging from 80 to 240 hours, the norm being 120 hours.

Follow-up Stage of Dispositions

Release under Supervision. Release under supervision is similar to the parole system. Before 1987, the program had been applied only to young offenders, but the Prisoners Ordinance of 1987 was expanded by the

Legislative Council on 14 October 1987 to provide aftercare supervision to adult prisoners with strong motivation and with a high likelihood to reform.

Under the program, any prisoner who has served not less than one-half, or twenty months, of a sentence of three years or more, could be released on application. If release is granted by the Supervision Board under the Department of Correctional Services, supervision could last the full length of the remainder of the sentence. During the period of release, the offender is placed under the supervision of the aftercare officer of correctional services.

Prerelease Employment. The prerelease employment program was introduced in 1988 to facilitate reintegration of prisoners into society. The program is open by application to any prisoner serving a sentence of imprisonment of two years or more and within six months of completing the sentence. If so recommended by the Release under Supervision Board, he or she could be placed under supervision for the remainder of the sentence, up to six months. He or she would be required to reside in a hostel provided for the purpose during this period and to remain employed. A prisoner who breaches his or her supervision order is liable to be recalled.

7

Adult Probation in Japan

Masakazu Nishikawa

Adult probation in Japan has evolved over thirty-five years and presently plays an important role in criminal justice administration. It entails some unique features in the philosophy, legal framework, and actual practice of sentencing and supervision of offenders, which can be summarized as follows:

- Adult probation is considered as one of the many components that constitute a broader concept of offender rehabilitation services, the others including adult parole, juvenile probation and parole, and aftercare for ex-offenders. In terms of this concept, the idea of reintegrating offenders into the community is emphasized in the administration of all these components, including adult probation.
- Adult probation accompanied by supervision is one type of suspended execution of sentence and coexists with another type of suspended execution of sentence without probationary supervision. Both types are utilized to the maximum extent as alternatives to imprisonment in actual sentencing practice, but since probation is a more severe form of punishment than other types of suspended sentence, probation orders are limited to a smaller percentage of offenders.
- Supervision includes both functions of controlling offenders to prevent their committing further offenses and assisting them in their social reintegration. Emphasis is also placed on providing the offenders with assistance.
- A large number of citizens and organizations volunteer to act as volunteer probation officers and halfway houses and are thus involved in the supervision of probationers. Their activities are highly appreciated, not only as a result of their contribution to cost-effectiveness, but also because of the contribution they make to the success in supervising offenders effectively.

This chapter intends to shed some light on these features of adult probation in Japan.

Historical Background

Adult probation was established in Japan in 1954 by the expansion of an already existing program of suspended execution of sentence. However, its introduction owed much to the prior development of aftercare services for offenders, juvenile probation, and parole.

In the period from the seventeenth century to the middle of the nineteenth century, criminal justice in Japan was administered by the principle of feudalism. The country was divided into almost three hundred autonomous territories controlled by feudal lords. Tokugawa Shogunate was the most powerful and the leader of the feudal lords. The functions of police and court were not separated but exercised by a single agent of Tokugawa Shogunate or any of the other local feudal lords. There were no prisons, since the principal forms of punishment were death, exile, tattooing, and caning. The rules and practices of criminal justice varied from one territory to another.

After the Meiji Restoration in 1868, the Meiji government placed a disproportionately high priority on the establishment of a uniform criminal justice system in order to gain acceptance by the international community following the inequitable treaties concluded by Tokugawa Shogunate with certain other states just before the Restoration. These treaties included a clause admitting the consular court of the party countries, thus recognizing the extraterritoriality of their nationals, on the ground that the legal and court systems in Japan were not sufficiently developed to safeguard their nationals' rights. The discriminatory nature of the treaties caused much anger among the Japanese people, the Samurai in particular, and led to the overthrow of the Tokugawa Shogunate regime. The modernization of the criminal justice system thus became a matter of the utmost urgency for the Meiji government in order that they might amend these treaties.

The government had to create an entirely new system, comprising laws and institutions such as police forces, courts, and prisons, and find the personnel to staff them. Experts in criminal justice were invited, and ideas, laws, and regulations were imported from developed countries. During these developing stages, the international cooperation that had just begun, mainly among European countries, in the late nineteenth century was helpful to the development of the criminal justice system in Japan. Soon after the establishment of the International Penitentiary Committee in 1872, the government of Japan sent a report on prison reforms to the first chairman of the committee, C. E. Wines, in 1880. Following the fourth congress at St. Petersburg in Russia in 1890, Japan continuously sent its delegations to the congresses of the committee.

It was not long after the Restoration that the criminal justice system was established. In 1882, the first Penal Code (1880) and the Code of

Criminal Instruction (1880) (the Code of Criminal Procedure) came into effect.

The court system and prison system had already been organized, and the first Prison Rules were also enacted in 1882. The Penal Code provided for various types of imprisonment as one of the principal categories of punishment and included conditional release of prisoners before the expiration of their sentences. Released prisoners were placed under the surveillance of the police but did not receive assistance from any governmental authorities.

Under these circumstances, efforts to give ex-prisoners some help toward their reintegration into society were initiated by private citizens. In one case, rejection by the family and members of the community drove a discharged prisoner to commit suicide. A philanthropist who was moved by this incident established a fund and pioneered a private aftercare hostel in 1889 to give shelter, employment, and guidance to discharged offenders who had no home to return to. His project gave rise to a number of similar attempts by other volunteers and religious organizations, and the hostels founded in this way were the precursors of the halfway houses or rehabilitation aid hostels of the present time.

The criminal justice system established around 1882 did not function well in the early stages. The acquittal rate in the courts was very high, and prisons were seriously overcrowded. In 1882, the prison population was around thirty-two thousand but increased to sixty-five thousand within three years. There were many difficulties, not only in the administration of prisons but also in the apportionment of government budgets. In fact, the budget for prisons exceeded the total budget for the armed forces at that time. To reduce the burden on the prisons, the nonprosecution program was introduced into the prosecution system, whereby the prosecutor was given the discretionary power to resist initiating prosecution for minor offenses even where he had enough evidence to obtain convictions in court. The nonprosecution program was not permitted by the laws of that time but was widely exercised in practice. Later, firmly established in both law and practice, the system of suspended prosecution continued and is still used up to the present day.

The Constitution of the Empire of Japan came into force in 1890. In the same year, the Code of Criminal Instruction was amended and renamed "the Code of Criminal Procedure," and the Court Organization Law and new Prison Rules were enacted. In 1899, the long-standing aspiration of the Meiji government to abolish the jurisdiction of the consular courts was finally fulfilled, and the treaties were amended accordingly.

After the initial goal of modernizing the criminal justice system was achieved, efforts at improving the system did not stop. The program of suspended execution of sentence was introduced by the Law for the Suspension of Execution of Sentence in 1905. Under this law, those defendants sentenced to less than one year's imprisonment had the chance of receiving a suspended execution but were not placed under any supervision. The Penal Code of 1880 was superseded by the Penal Code of 1907, which has been retained to the present day, although it has undergone revisions. In 1908, when the new Penal Code came into force, a new Prison Code also became effective, and it too has been retained up to the present time. The new Penal Code adopted the parole system and incorporated the suspended execution of sentence in relation to terms of imprisonment of two years or less. However, supervision or assistance was not carried out by the government authorities in cases of either parole or suspended sentence but entrusted to the voluntary work of private citizens.

General pardons were promulgated on two occasions of bereavement of members of the Imperial Family, in 1912 and 1914. The two decrees resulted in the awarding of amnesty and commutation to a total of 36,731 prisoners. In order to accommodate the greater part of the prisoners who were thus to be suddenly released into the community, the government urgently pursued a policy of encouragement and support for the expansion of private aftercare facilities. The headquarters of a religious sect that had organized aftercare services issued a circular asking the subordinate temples to intervene and help those offenders who had returned home to improve their relationships with their families. In this way, private aftercare associations rapidly increased. They not only provided discharged offenders with accommodation but also gave counseling and assistance to those who returned home. This was an early prototype of the function now being assumed by volunteer probation officers, who will be described in greater detail elsewhere.

The use of suspended execution of sentence has gradually been expanded since its introduction in 1905. In 1924, the Code of Criminal Procedure formally authorized the system of suspended prosecution, which, as mentioned above, had been developed in 1885 as an informal device for diverting offenders who had committed minor offenses from the criminal justice system. Since a large number of the offenders to be disposed of along the lines of these programs were in acute need of help, the voluntary aftercare services came to embrace such offenders as well.

In 1939, the Rehabilitation Services Law was enacted. It provided the basic framework for two sets of voluntary bodies, namely, the rehabilitation workers (precursors of the volunteer probation officers) and the rehabilitation service associations (predecessors of rehabilitation aid hostels, which will be referred to later). The law also required the government to supervise and support these bodies, and this system survived until 1950, when the Voluntary Probation Officers Law and the Law for Aftercare of Discharged Offenders came into force.

In 1922, the First Juvenile Law was enforced, introducing probation and parole accompanied by supervision into the juvenile justice system much earlier than their introduction into criminal justice for adults. The law defined juveniles as youths under the age of eighteen (presently, under twenty) and provided for them lesser penalties, indeterminate sentences, and the prohibition of detention in lieu of unpaid fines as applied to adults. The law also established the Juvenile Tribunal as a decision-making and supervisory agency and the reform school as a correctional institution.

The Juvenile Tribunal, an administrative agency, carried out both decision-making and supervisory functions and handled juvenile delinquents who were not prosecuted in the criminal courts. Having received a wide discretion, this quasi-judicial agency was able to act upon the needs of individual cases with great flexibility. It had at its disposal nine kinds of disposition, ranging from simple admonition to commitment to reform school and including probationary supervision. Since it was vested with the power to alter treatment from one type to another, as required by the particular case, the tribunal could release a reform school inmate conditionally or send a probationer to reform school or to a hostel. Probationary supervision in the field and in the hostel was carried out by the probation officers attached to the tribunal. The staff of the tribunal consisted of referees, clerks, and regular and voluntary probation officers. As time went on, the shortage of regular staff was supplemented by an increasing number of volunteers. Due to a lack of financial resources, however, it was not until 1943 that the law was enforced throughout the country.

After World War II, under the new Constitution of 1946, a number of vital changes were brought about in the criminal justice administration. A new Code of Criminal Procedure was enacted in 1949, changing the style of procedure from an inquisitorial one to an accusatorial one. Much more attention was paid to due process and the protection of the rights of citizens, while juvenile justice, corrective measures, and rehabilitation services for offenders also underwent drastic reorganization.

As a result of the enactment of a new Juvenile Law and the Offenders Rehabilitation Law in 1949, the Juvenile Tribunal was abolished, and its functions were taken over by three new organizations: the Family Court, the Juvenile Parole Board, and the Juvenile Probation Office. The Juvenile Probation Office was charged with the supervision of juvenile probationers and parolees from prison or training school.

For adult offenders, parole supervision was introduced by the Offenders Rehabilitation Law. The Adult Parole Board and the Adult Probation Office were established as the agencies responsible for screening inmates for parole and for supervising parolees. The adult parole system made a particularly significant contribution between 1949 and 1953 to the administration of corrective measures when prisons were under pressure from the tremendous population growth.

In order to ensure effective probation and parole services, the law required the regularly employed probation officers, as the mainstay of the system, to have sufficient expertise in the behavioral sciences. The Voluntary Probation Officers Law of 1950 recognized voluntary workers who had been engaged in juvenile and adult rehabilitation services as juvenile or adult volunteer probation officers, respectively, and gave them official duties in a position subsidiary to the professional probation officers.

Both the adult aftercare hostels and the private juvenile institutions, which had functioned as a combination of probation hostels and reform schools since the prewar period, were screened in light of new provisions of the Law for Aftercare of Discharged Offenders of 1950 and subjected to the control and supervision of the government to ensure standardized treatment and facilities.

Law reforms were pursued continuously in the ensuing years to extend further the community-based treatment of offenders in the country. The Parole Board, the Probation Office, and the volunteer probation officers for juvenile and young offenders were integrated with their respective adult counterparts in 1952 by means of an amendment to the applicable laws. Thus the basic structure of the present noncustodial correction and aftercare services was established, and the adult probation system was finally implemented.

Adult probation was introduced as a result of revisions in the Penal Code in 1953 and 1954. Probationary supervision became applicable to an offender placed under suspended execution of sentence, while suspended execution of sentence including probation was simultaneously expanded to imprisonment of up to three years. The Law for Probationary Supervision of Persons under Suspension of Execution of Sentence was enacted, and probation of adult offenders came into practice in 1954.

Basic Legal Framework

Probation for an adult offender in Japan is not an independent punishment but is used as a complementary measure to the suspension of execution of sentence. The principal punishments provided by the Penal Code are the death penalty, imprisonment with or without labor for life or for a fixed term, fine, penal detention, and minor fine (Penal Code, article 9). Alternatives to imprisonment and to fine are available. The execution of sentence can be suspended in relation to imprisonment for a fixed term and fine. There are two types of suspended execution of sentence, one accompanied by probationary supervision, and the other not (table 7.1). Only the suspension of execution of sentence with probationary supervision is called "probation" in Japan, and it takes the form of an additional order when the execution of sentence is suspended. Article 25 of the Penal Code provides the requirements for suspended execution of sentence and for probation as follows:

a. The prison sentence should be of three years or less, while the fine should be of two hundred thousand yen or less.
b. The offender must not have been sentenced to imprisonment within the last five years.
c. The offender, even if he or she has been previously granted suspension of execution of the sentence, is sentenced to imprisonment for one year or less, and there are extenuating circumstances especially favorable to him or her. This cannot, however, be applied to an offender who has previously been placed under suspended sentence with probationary supervision.

Requirement (c) indicates the different legal status attaching to offenders under probation and those granted suspended execution of sentence without supervision. An offender under suspended execution of sentence without supervision may have suspension of execution of sentence imposed when he or she commits a new offense, whereas an offender under probation has no

Table 7.1 Principal Punishment and Alternative Measures in Japan

Principal punishment	Alternative measures
Death	
Imprisonment with labor	
for life	
for determined term ⟶	Suspended execution of sentence
	with probationary supervision
Imprisonment without labor	without supervision
for life	
for determined term ⟶	
Fine ⟶	
Penal detention	
Minor fine	

Source: The Penal Code, articles 9 and 25, Japan.

opportunity for receiving suspended execution of sentence if he or she commits an offense punishable by imprisonment. It is clear that probation is considered to be a more serious punishment than suspended execution of sentence without supervision but, obviously, less severe than actual imprisonment. An offender may be placed on probation as well has have to pay a fine, but in practice probation is very rarely used with fines. Hence, the ascending order of severity of punishment is fine, suspended execution of sentence without supervision, probation, and actual imprisonment.

Probation is mandatory when the sentence is to be suspended in relation to an offense that took place during the period of previous suspension unaccompanied by a probation order. In other cases of suspended sentence, probation is at the discretion of the court (Penal Code, article 25-2). The legal requirements refer only to the gravity of the sentence and criminal record, making no reference to the type of offense. Accordingly, even an offender who has committed an offense of a serious nature, such as murder or robbery, may be placed on probation if special circumstances justify it.

The terms of probation and suspended execution of sentence are fixed by the court and may vary from one to five years (Penal Code, article 25).

An offender under probation may be provisionally discharged from supervision by a disposition of the administrative authority (Penal Code, article 25-2) that is specified as the regional parole board by another law. When an offender is provisionally discharged from supervision, supervision is suspended, although the offender is not discharged from suspended execution of sentence itself. However, provisional discharge does have an advantage, since the offender has a chance of receiving suspended execution of sentence again if he or she commits a further offense punishable by imprisonment.

Revocation of probation or of suspended execution of sentence is mandatory when an offender is sentenced to actual imprisonment for another offense during the period of such suspension (Penal Code, article 26-1). However, revocation is at the discretion of the court when a fine is imposed (Penal Code, article 26-2), and probation may be revoked at the court's discretion when a probationer fails to observe any of the conditions imposed and the circumstances are seriously unfavorable to him or her (Penal Code, article 26-2-[2]). If probation or suspension of execution of sentence is revoked, the offender has to serve the sentence originally imposed.

When a period of probation or suspension of execution of sentence elapses without revocation, the sentence is no longer applicable (Penal Code, article 27). Supervision of probationers is carried out by the probation offices under the Ministry of Justice. The principles and procedures of supervision are regulated by the Law for Probationary Supervision of Persons under Suspension of Execution of Sentence (1954). The Offender

Rehabilitation Law (1949) provides for the organization of the probation offices and the regional parole boards, which have the authority to provisionally discharge probationers from supervision.

The wide use of volunteer workers and private organizations in supervising and assisting offenders under probation and parole is the most unique feature of the administration of noncustodial corrections in Japan. The authorized volunteer workers are called "volunteer probation officers" (VPOs) and the requirements concerning their qualifications, recruitment, duties, and other relevant matters are prescribed in the Voluntary Probation Officers Law (1950). The Law for Aftercare of Discharged Offenders (1950) regulates the management of halfway houses (rehabilitation aid hostels), which are run by private organizations authorized to accommodate discharged offenders, probationers, and parolees on behalf of the state.

Decisions on Probation

Courts

All courts in Japan are part of a national judicial system. There are five types of courts: the Supreme Court, high courts, district courts, family courts, and summary courts. Since district courts and family courts are at the same level, there are four levels of courts, with the Supreme Court at the top.

Summary courts are the lowest courts, numbering 453 in 1988. A single judge presides over cases involving minor criminal matters. A summary court may not, in principle, impose either imprisonment or capital punishment. However, for offenses proscribed by law, such as housebreaking, habitual gambling, theft, embezzlement, conversion of lost articles, and accepting or buying stolen property, a summary court may impose a prison sentence not exceeding three years.

District courts are ranked above summary courts. There were fifty district courts and 242 branches in 1988. District courts have general jurisdiction over all cases in the first instance. While a single judge presides over minor cases, more serious cases punishable by death or imprisonment for a minimum term of not less than one year are heard by a collegiate body comprised of three judges.

Family courts deal with family disputes as well as with cases related to juvenile delinquency (persons under twenty years of age) and offenses harmful to the welfare of juveniles. There are fifty family courts and 338 branches and local offices.

High courts are courts of appeal against decisions taken by district, family, or summary courts in ordinary criminal cases. All appellate cases are heard by a collegiate body of three judges.

The Supreme Court is the highest court. It will normally hear a Jokoku (appeal) from a high court on the following grounds: (a) a violation of the Constitution or an error in constitutional interpretation, or (b) adjudication contrary to precedents of the Supreme Court or a high court. The Supreme Court may also hear the Jokoku of any case that it considers to involve an important point of statutory interpretation.

Judges

Assistant judges are all appointed by the Cabinet from among those who have passed the National Law Examination, completed two years of training in the Legal Training and Research Institute, and passed the institute's final qualifying examination. The Cabinet appoints these judges from a list of persons nominated by the Supreme Court. To become a full-fledged judge, it is necessary for a candidate to have practical experience of at least ten years as an assistant judge, a public prosecutor, a practicing lawyer, or a professor of law or to have equivalent related experience.

The Constitution of Japan provides that "all judges shall be independent in the exercise of their conscience and shall be bound only by this Constitution and the laws" (article 76 [3]). Supervision of judicial administration is exercised exclusively by the Supreme Court and the inferior courts. To ensure the smooth running of the judicial administration, the General Secretariat of the Supreme Court was established, under an order of the Judicial Assembly of the Supreme Court, as a department separate from the Ministry of Justice, dealing with matters concerning budget, personnel, and other miscellaneous services.

Decision-making Process of Sentencing

Presentencing investigation is not available in the criminal courts. No probation officer is attached to the criminal courts, and probation officers in probation offices are not under a duty to make presentence investigations in court. The structure of the criminal procedure is not inquisitorial but accusatorial. The prosecution and defense contend with each other, presenting evidence favorable to their positions, and the court acts as a referee. The information on which sentencing is based is limited to evidence presented by the prosecution and the defense. The shortage of information necessary for sentencing, especially that relating to the offender's personality and living conditions, has been pointed out by some judges.

Laws provide for a wide range of punishments in relation to each offense. For example, a homicide is punishable by death or by imprisonment with labor for life or for not less than three years. In cases of fraud or theft, imprisonment with labor for not more than ten years is provided. In the final stage of a trial, a public prosecutor recommends an appropriate sentence for a case. This recommendation can be an important reference for sentencing, but it only refers to the type of punishment and its term or amount, usually not mentioning whether suspended execution of sentence should be imposed or whether a probation order is necessary. The decision as to whether a sentence including an order of suspended execution of sentence or a probation order is appropriate lies with the sentencing court.

Once the offender has been found guilty, there are three considerations to be examined before a probation order can be issued. Theoretically, the first question concerns the type of principal punishment to be imposed, the length of the term of imprisonment, or the amount of the fine. The second, if relevant, is whether the execution of the sentence should be suspended or not. In the actual process of decision making, however, it is common that the second question, the execution of the sentence, is decided first and then the term of imprisonment is determined. Lastly, if the execution of the sentence is to be suspended, and if probation is discretionary, the decision must be made as to whether probation should be ordered or not.

It is generally understood that two major factors, namely, the gravity of the offense committed by the offender and the possibility that he or she will commit further offenses in the future, determine a sentence. The recidivism factor influences the necessity of supervision and care to prevent future recidivism. In theory, the gravity of the offense determines the type of punishment, such as death, imprisonment with labor, imprisonment without labor, or fine, and its term or degree. In the next phase, once the type of punishment and its degree have been decided, the probability of recidivism plays an important role in determining whether the execution of sentence is to be suspended and whether a probation order is to be imposed. If the offender is found to show little danger of committing crimes in the future, the execution of the punishment will be suspended. In the last phase, the necessity of supervision and care is a major factor in deciding whether a probation order is to be imposed, while the capacity of the relevant supervisory agency may also be taken into consideration. However, in reality this sequence of decision-making phases for sentencing is not observed, for two reasons.

First, the varying severity of the three punishment measures relating to imprisonment, that is, actual imprisonment, probation, and suspended execution of sentence without supervision, are keenly recognized by judges. Most judges share the view that the different types of measures adopted in sentencing, including alternative measures, must reflect the seriousness of the offense. When both probation and suspended execution are considered possible, each phase in the decision-making process, from the choice of punishment to the final choice of probation, is made with regard to the gravity of the offense.

Second, the determination of the major factors (i.e., the gravity of the offense and the possibility of recidivism) is made through a process of evaluating facts pertaining to the crime and the offender as revealed through the fact-finding court procedure. Thus, the determination is largely dependent upon the accuracy and amount of information presented. Sometimes the information obtained is limited, making it difficult to assess the factors fully. This is particularly true in terms of predicting future recidivism of the offender, and this fact is sometimes ignored by judges in sentencing. When this occurs, the gravity of the offense becomes the sole factor in the determination of the final sentence.

Probation Orders among Court Decisions

Since a large number of criminal cases are diverted from the formal procedure of trial through nonprosecution and through summary trial procedure, some explanation of the program of suspended prosecution and summary trial procedure is necessary before analyzing the outcome court decisions.

One important feature of prosecution in Japan is that a public prosecutor has wide discretionary power to suspend prosecution even if he has enough evidence to secure a conviction in a case. Article 248 of the Code of Criminal Procedure provides that if, after considering the character, age, and situation of the offender, the gravity of the offense, the circumstances under which the offense was committed, and the conditions subsequent to the commission of the offense, prosecution is deemed unnecessary, prosecution need not be instituted.

Suspension of prosecution is based on the rehabilitation-oriented idea of prosecution in Japan, that is, to give an offender the opportunity to rehabilitate himself as a responsible member of society without becoming labeled as a criminal. A public prosecutor must always give adequate consideration to the possibility of suspension of prosecution, though the decision should reflect the gravity of the offense in question. A large number of prosecutions are suspended each year. For example, a total of 356,283 cases, including 80,093 cases of nonroad traffic offenses and 276,190 road traffic offenses, were suspended from prosecution in 1987 (table 7.2). Even for serious offenses such as robbery and homicide, it is not rare for prosecution to be suspended. For instance, in 1987 the prosecution of some fifty-three cases of robbery was suspended, representing 5.4 percent of all robberies that could have been prosecuted. The percentage of suspended prosecutions differs according to the type of offense. While it was as high as 44.5 percent for larcenies, it was only 5.4 percent for violations of the Stimulant Drugs Control Law.

Prosecution may be one of two types: for formal trial or for summary trial procedure. A summary court, on a public prosecutor's request, can impose a fine of not more than two hundred thousand yen or a minor fine by means of a summary court order prior to public trial proceedings.

A large number of cases are disposed of by means of imposing a fine, partly in order to avoid the adverse effects of short-term imprisonment. Around 95 percent of all defendants convicted by the court of first instance were sentenced to a fine, and most of these cases were disposed of through

Table 7.2   Number of Suspects Disposed of by the Public Prosecutor's Office, by Offense, 1987

Offense	Total	Prosecution Formal trial	Prosecution Summary Proceedings	Nonprosecution Suspension of prosecution	Other	Referral to family court
Total	2,647,253	125,421	1,617,087	356,283	51,622	496,840
Penal Code offenses	933,272	79,730	297,674	266,535	42,135	247,198
Homicide	2,868	1,060	-	57	1,667	84
Robbery	1,753	872	-	53	240	588
Bodily injury	30,566	4,856	11,003	3,639	751	10,317
Assault	7,824	390	3,707	2,043	82	1,602
Extortion	11,454	3,743	-	1,375	426	5,910
Larceny	205,107	37,513	-	30,067	2,853	134,674
Fraud	17,573	10,095	-	4,237	2,429	812
Embezzlement	26,613	1,323	91	4,159	475	20,565
Rape	1,902	803	-	161	360	578
Indecent assault	1,314	437	-	76	399	402
Public indecency	910	38	640	155	6	71
Distribution of obscene literature, etc,	1,066	528	335	165	23	15
Arson	1,080	580	2	118	246	134
Bribery	682	460	57	107	58	-
Gambling	7,473	1,723	3,061	2,446	81	162
Violent acts	5,688	1,039	1,471	567	140	2,471
Traffic professional negligence	584,905	9,825	272,593	211,839	27,315	63,333
Other	24,494	4,445	4,714	5,271	4,584	5,480
Special Law offenses	1,713,981	45,691	1,319,413	89,748	9,487	249,642
Firearms and swords	4,839	1,482	1,768	927	223	439
Stimulant drugs	27,273	22,858	-	1,302	1,547	1,566
Road-traffic violations	1,578,642	10,725	1,271,595	64,351	5,587	226,384
Other	103,227	10,626	46,050	23,168	2,130	21,253

Source: Annual Statistics Report of Prosecution, Japan.

Table 7.3 Number of Persons Finally Adjudicated, 1983–1987

Category	1983	1984	1985	1986	1987
Guilty					
Death	1	3	2	-	7
Life imprisonment with labor	36	43	38	41	56
Imprisonment with labor	72,265	73,941	72,238	69,803	68,178
Imprisonment without labor	4,977	4,947	5,088	5,197	5,24
Fine	2,272,970	2,374,394	2,383,868	2,260,791	1,642,969
Penal detention	41	41	77	122	127
Minor fine	25,418	29,138	29,505	27,004	22,508
Acquittal	165	121	117	115	93
Other	2,929	3,336	2,788	2,006	1,866
Total	2,378,802	2,485,964	2,493,721	2,365,079	1,741,044

Source: Annual Statistics Report of Prosecution, Japan.
Note: "Others" includes dismissal of prosecution, acquittal on procedural grounds, etc.

summary proceedings in the summary courts. The imposition of a fine through summary proceedings and discretionary prosecutions reduces the burden on the courts and contributes effectively toward the speedy disposal of more substantial criminal cases.

A huge number of offenders are adjudicated by the criminal courts every year. In 1987, the total number of persons adjudicated by all the criminal courts, including those subjected to summary procedures, throughout the country amounted to 1,741,044 (table 7.3). Most of them (94.3 percent) were sentenced to the payment of a fine. A relatively small number, 68,178 (3.9 percent), were sentenced to imprisonment with labor, and only 5,240 (0.3 percent) were sentenced to imprisonment without labor.

These figures included a number of offenders the execution of whose sentences were suspended. According to the statistics of prosecution offices, in 1987 execution of sentence was suspended for a total of 42,473 offenders, including those placed under probationary supervision. Execution of sentence was suspended for 37,576 offenders, more than a half (55.1 percent) of those sentenced to imprisonment with labor and for 4,890, or 93.6 percent, of those sentenced to imprisonment without labor. However, sentence was suspended in only 7 cases of fines out of a total of 1,642,969. This indicates that in sentencing practice, suspended execution of sentence including probation order is mainly used in relation to imprisonment both with and without labor and that suspension of execution is usually granted for sentences of imprisonment without labor.

Not all the offenders whose executions of sentence have been suspended are placed under probationary supervision: A total of 6,438 offenders were placed on probationary supervision when execution of their sentences was suspended in 1987 (table 7.4), and this represents only 15.2 percent of the total 42,473 offenders ordered to suspension of execution of sentence. More precisely, 1,307 offenders were placed on mandatory probation because they committed offenses during their previous suspended execution of sentence without supervision, while the remaining 5,131 were placed on probation at the discretion of the courts. The number of probationers placed on discretionary probation represents a small percentage (12.5) of all the offenders who might have had probation orders imposed with suspended execution of sentence. This may imply that judges are somewhat careful in ordering discretionary probation. In the Penal Code, the requirements for probation and for suspension of execution of sentence do not discriminate among types of offenses. In relation to which types of offenses are suspended execution of sentence or probation used widely?

Table 7.5 shows adjudications made in formal criminal procedures in all the district and family courts in 1986 according to the type of offense, and table 7.6 specifies prison sentences imposed, including suspended execution and probation. In reply to the question raised above, we can thus

Table 7.4 Number of the Convicted Granted Suspended Execution of Sentence, by Type of Suspension, 1983–1987

Type of suspension	1983	1984	1985	1986	1987
First suspension (A)	43,826	44,172	43,179	41,887	41,166
With probation (B)	6,128 [4]	6,183 [3]	5,773 [4]	5,113 [-]	5,131 [2]
B/A (%)	14.0	14.0	13.4	12.2	12.5
Second suspension	1,583	1,464	1,363	1,268	1,307
with probation	[1]	[2]	[-]	[-]	[1]
Total	45,409	45,636	44,542	43,155	42,473

Source: Annual Statistics Report of Prosecution, Japan.

Note: Figures include suspensions of execution of sentence with or without labor and fines.
Probation includes protective measures (Hodōshobun) under the Antiprostitution Law, and the figures in parentheses show actual numbers for these.

218

Table 7.5 Number of Persons Adjudicated by District/Family Courts, by Offense, 1986

Offense	Total (A)	Death	Life	Determinate term (B)	Guilty — Imprisonment — Suspended execution of sentence (C)	C/B%	Suspension with probation	Fine, minor fine	Not guilty (D)	D/A%	Other
Total	63,198	5	36	62,328	3,466	55.6	4,618	584	69	0.1	176
Penal Code offenses	34,673	5	36	34,365	19,152	55.7	2,293	123	51	0.1	93
Homicide	986	2	8	968	206	21.3	30	-	4	0.4	4
Robbery	690	3	28	655	91	13.9	41	-	1	0.1	3
Bodily injury	3,949	-	-	3,904	1,937	49.6	325	29	6	0.2	10
Extortion	2,718	-	-	2,714	1,401	51.6	245	-	2	0.1	2
Larceny	5,328	-	-	5,322	1,405	26.4	392	-	6	0.0	4
Fraud	4,249	-	-	4,234	1,775	41.9	306	-	6	0.1	9
Rape	703	-	-	702	236	33.6	74	-	1	0.1	-
Arson	409	-	-	408	141	34.6	43	-	1	0.2	-
Gambling	740	-	-	739	602	81.5	30	1	-	-	-
Violent acts	795	-	-	778	220	28.3	36	15	1	0.1	1
Professiona negligence	10,108	-	-	9,994	8,486	84.9	499	56	15	0.1	43
Others	3,998	-	-	3,947	2,652	67.2	272	22	12	0.3	-
Special Law offenses	28,525	-	-	27,963	15,508	55.5	2,325	461	18	0.1	83
Election Law offenses	657	-	-	629	621	98.7	-	13	-	-	15
Firearms and swords	810	-	-	807	196	24.3	32	1	1	0.1	1
Stimulant drugs	14,891	-	-	14,867	5896	39.7	1,371	-	9	0.1	15
Horse Race Law	209	-	-	209	167	79.9	13	-	1	-	-
Road-traffic violations	8,089	-	-	7,996	5,928	74.1	688	54	1	0.0	38
Other	3,869	-	-	3,455	2,7	78.1	221	393	7	0.2	14
	[439]			[252]	{192}	[76.2]	{24}	{185}	[2]	[0.5]	

Source: Annual Report of Judicial Statistics, Japan.

Note: Figures in parentheses show the number of adults whose criminal cases under Juvenile Law were adjudicated in family courts.

state that, first, suspended execution of sentence both with and without probation was utilized in relation to all types of offense, ranging from homicide to road traffic law violations. However, the extent of the use of these programs differed from one type of offense to another. Thus, the percentage of suspended executions of sentence including probation compared to the total number of prison sentences was as high or even higher than 70 percent in relation to gambling (81.5 percent), election offenses (98.7 percent), horse-racing offenses (79.9 percent), and road traffic law violations (74.1 percent), while it was low in relation to homicide (21.3

Table 7.6 Number of Persons Imprisoned by District/Family Courts, by Offense, 1986

Offense	Determinate term (A)	Suspended execution of sentence (B)	Suspension with probation (C)	B/A (%)	C/B (%)
Penal Code offenses	34,365	19,152	2,293	55.7	12.0
Homicide	968	206	30	21.3	14.6
Robbery	655	91	41	13.9	45.1
Bodily injury	3,904	1,937	325	49.6	16.8
Extortion	2,714	1,401	245	51.6	17.8
Larceny	5,322	1,405	392	26.4	27.9
Fraud	4,234	1,775	306	41.9	17.2
Rape	702	236	74	33.6	31.3
Arson	408	141	43	34.6	30.5
Gambling	739	602	30	81.5	5.0
Violent acts	778	220	36	28.3	16.4
Professional negligence	9,994	8,486	499	84.9	5.9
Others	3,947	2,652	272	67.2	10.3
Special Law offenses	27,963	15,508	2,325	55.5	15.0
Election Law offenses	629	621	-	98.7	-
Firearms and swords	807	196	32	24.3	16.3
Stimulant drugs	14,867	5,896	1,371	39.7	23.3
Horse Race Law	209	167	13	79.9	7.8
Road-traffic violations	7,996	5,928	688	74.1	11.6
Other	3,455	2,700	221	78.1	8.2
	{252}	{192}	{24}	{76.2}	{12.5}
Total	62,328	34,660	4,618	55.6	13.2

Source: Annual Report of Judicial Statistics, Japan.
Note: Figures in parentheses show the number of adults whose criminal cases under Juvenile Law were adjudicated in family courts.

percent), robbery (13.9 percent), larceny (26.4 percent), violent acts (28.3 percent), rape (33.6 percent), arson (34.6 percent), firearms (24.3 percent), and stimulant drug offenses (39.7 percent). It is clear that suspended execution of sentence is utilized much more widely for offenses of a less serious nature.

Second, although the percentage of probation orders was low in comparison to the total number of suspended executions of sentence (13.2 percent, on the average), the percentages differed among the types of offenses. While probation was used with suspension of execution of sentence for a considerable portion of cases of robbery (45.1 percent), larceny (27.9 percent), rape (31.3 percent), arson (30.5 percent), and stimulant drug offenses (23.3 percent), it was very rarely used in cases of gambling (5.0 percent), professional negligence (5.9 percent), and election law offenses (none). Thus, it is clear that when the execution of sentence is suspended for a serious offense, it is highly likely that suspension will be accompanied by a probation order.

Some Features of Offenders Placed on Probation

Most adult probationers are male and tend to be younger. According to the statistics provided by the probation offices, males made up 91.4 percent of all probationers newly received by the probation office in 1987, while females constituted only 8.6 percent (table 7.7). Since police statistics reveal that females formed 19.3 percent of all the Penal Code offenders detected by the police in the same year, a much smaller portion of female offenders than of male offenders were placed on probation.

Almost one-half (48.3 percent) of probationers in 1987 were aged between twenty and thirty years (table 7.7). In particular, 24.7 percent were adolescents between twenty and twenty-two years of age, the period commonly recognized as the most crime-prone.

A considerable portion of adult probationers in Japan are offenders who have committed offenses of a rather serious nature or those who have a high propensity for committing crimes again in the future. One of the reasons for this is, as mentioned before, that there exists another kind of suspended execution of sentence not accompanied by supervision. Probationers are inevitably selected from among those offenders who committed offenses of a more serious nature than offenders who were placed under suspended execution of sentence not accompanied by supervision. Another reason is that, as mentioned earlier, approximately 20 percent of probationers are placed under supervision because they committed offenses during the term of their previous suspended execution of sentence not accompanied by supervision. Obviously, they have a tendency toward the repetition of crimes.

The Rehabilitation Bureau of the Ministry of Justice reported that some 6.2 percent of adult probationers under supervision at the end of 1988 were members of criminal organizations (Boryokudan or Yakuza) and that 19.6 percent were found to have had experience in drug abuse.

Some of the offenders placed under probationary supervision have difficulty in discontinuing criminal activities or rehabilitating themselves in the community, and this is reflected in the terms of their supervision fixed by the courts. Although the court can determine a term of probationary supervision of any period between one and five years, in actual practice the courts tend to favor orders approaching the maximum, rather than the minimum, term. According to the statistics compiled by the probation offices, more than 97 percent of probationers placed under supervision in 1987 served terms of over three years, including 11.7 percent who received the full five-year term (table 7.8).

Table 7.7   Percentage of Newly Received Probationers, by Sex and Age Group, 1987

Sex/Age	Adult probationers
Sex	
Male	91.4
Female	8.6
Age[a]	
15 years and under	
16 - 17 years	1.9
18 - 19 years	
20 - 22 years	23.6
23 - 29 years	24.7
30 - 39 years	24.1
40 - 49 years	17.1
50 - 59 years	7.0
60 years and over	1.5
Total	100.0
	(6,477)[b]

Source: Annual Statistics on Rehabilitation of Offenders, Japan.
Notes: Age is at the time placed under probation.
Figures in parentheses show actual numbers.

Trend of Probation Orders in the Courts

The adult probation system in Japan was established in 1954 through the expansion of the system of suspended execution of sentence, which had already existed since 1905. Table 7.9 shows the trend in prison sentences, including their suspended execution both with and without probation, every five years from 1951 to 1986 and in 1987.

First, the total number of prison sentences, including those suspended,

Table 7.8 Percentage of Newly Received Probationers, by Duration of Probation, 1987

Duration	Adult probationers
1 year or less	0.0
2 years or less	2.3
3 years or less	51.0
4 years or less	35.0
5 years or less	11.7
Total	100.0
	{6,477}

Source: Annual Statistics on Rehabilitation of Offenders, Japan.
Note: Figure in parentheses shows actual numbers.

Table 7.9 Number of Persons Sentenced to Imprisonment and of Those Granted Suspended Execution of Sentences, 1951–1986, 1987

Year	Imprison-ment (A)	Suspended Execution (B)	without Probation	with Probation (C)	B/A (%)	C/B (%)
1951	118,229	54,272	-	-	45.9	-
1956	102,275	48,969	42,047	6,922	47.7	14.1
1961	83,249	43,142	35,075	8,067	51.8	18.7
1966	78,814	42,142	34,130	8,012	53.4	19.0
1971	69,467	40,361	33,910	6,451	58.1	16.0
1976	75,498	45,892	37,654	8,238	60.7	18.0
1981	76,219	44,269	36,052	8,217	58.0	18.6
1986	74,856	42,589	36,347	6,242	56.8	14.7
1987	73,183	42,062	35,609	6,453	57.4	15.3

Source: Annual Statistics Report of Prosecution and Annual Report of Judicial Statistics, Japan.
Note: Imprisonment includes both with labor and without labor, but does not include life sentences.

decreased drastically from 118,229 in 1951 to 78,814 in 1966, and since then it has stabilized at around 75,000 each year. Second, the percentage of suspended executions compared to the total number of prison sentences was already as high as 45.9 percent in 1951, when probationary supervision had not yet been introduced into the system of suspended execution of sentence. After the introduction of probation in 1954, the percentage of suspended executions including probation increased gradually to 58.1 percent, more than half, in 1971. Since then it has stabilized at that level. Third, during the early years of its introduction, the total number of probation orders, expressed as a percentage of all the suspended executions of sentence, increased from 14.1 percent in 1956 to 18.7 percent in 1961. Since then it has leveled off at around 18 percent, although a slight decrease has been observed in recent years.

These findings indicate that after the early years following the introduction of probation, the sentencing policy of the courts in relation to probation has not changed substantially.

There are a total of fifty district courts in Japan, and they play a major role in dealing with criminal cases. These courts are located in each of the forty-six prefectures and the four areas in Hokkaido Island. According to the prosecution offices' statistics, some disparity in the decisions rendered by these courts has been observed, but it is not serious enough to threaten the overall administration of the probation system. In 1987, the number of probation orders, expressed as a percentage of all the suspended executions of sentence imposed by all the criminal courts, was 15.2 percent on average, as previously mentioned. Percentages among prefectures ranged from 7.9 percent to 27.2 percent, but in all forty jurisdictions the percentages fell between 10 and 20 percent.

The main reason for the stability in court decisions on probation may be that in Japan the crime situation in general has not deteriorated greatly since the late 1950s, when the probation system was established. This favorable crime situation has not created critical needs to change the legal framework and sentencing policy in relation to probation.

The reason for its uniformity may lie with the administration of the courts. First, although an explicit sentencing guideline does not exist, judges have developed sentencing standards that are unwritten. The court also refers to recommendations of appropriate sentences made by public prosecutors, which are based upon criteria adopted by public prosecutor offices throughout Japan. Second, both the defendant and the public prosecutor may appeal to a high court on the ground that the original court handed down an improper sentence. Decisions rendered by high courts in such appeals play an important role in decreasing disparities in sentences. Third, the Japanese judiciary consists of career judges who have had more or less similar education, training, and experience.

Supervision of Probationers

Organization and Personnel

Probation Offices. Supervision of adult probationers is carried out by the probation offices. There are a total of fifty probation offices and three local branch offices, together with twenty-seven local subbranch offices, coming under the Rehabilitation Bureau of the Ministry of Justice. The activities of the probation offices are not limited to the supervision of adult probationers. The offices are also responsible for the supervision of juvenile probationers and both adult and juvenile parolees. Their main duties can be summarized as follows:

a. Supervision of probationers and parolees of all ages
b. Adjustment of inmate's family relationships and other social conditions prior to parole release from correctional institutions
c. Aftercare of offenders who have been discharged from prisons or detention houses without supervision
d. Investigation and application for pardons
e. Promotion of crime prevention activities in the community

All of these functions are carried out by probation officers in close collaboration with a number of volunteer workers and private organizations, including volunteer probation officers and halfway houses. The duty to promote and to supervise the activities of these voluntary workers and organizations is also the work of the probation officers. The probation officers form the basis of community corrective measures in Japan.

Regional Parole Boards. Although the prime function of a parole board is to make decisions concerning release on parole from training schools, prisons, or women's guidance homes and the revocation of parole, the regional parole board in Japan has the authority to discharge adult probationers provisionally from supervision.

The regional parole boards are located in eight cities where the high courts are found. The boards consist of three to twelve commissioners who are full-time officials selected mainly from directors of probation offices, superintendents of correctional institutions, public prosecutors, and so on. Parole investigation officers are attached to the parole boards, and they have the same qualifications, training, and official status as probation officers in probation offices, but their main duties are to collect information on inmates and submit social reports to the boards for parole hearings. The regional parole boards are also administered under the Rehabilitation Bureau of the Ministry of Justice.

Rehabilitation Bureau. The Rehabilitation Bureau is one of the seven major departments of the Ministry of Justice and is responsible for the overall administration of community-based correction and aftercare services in the country.

Probation officers. A total of 1,342 officials, including 900 probation officers, were working in fifty probation offices, eight regional parole boards, and the Rehabilitation Bureau of the Ministry of Justice in 1989. Some 822 probation officers were engaged mainly in the supervision of probationers and parolees.

Probation officers are full-time officials employed by the Ministry of Justice on the basis of a merit system. The law requires them to have certain levels of competence in the areas of medical science, sociology, psychology, education, and/or other disciplines relevant to the treatment of offenders. In practice, probation officers are recruited from the list of candidates who have passed the national civil service examination specializing in psychology, education, sociology, social work, law, or public administration.

Since staff training has vital importance in the rehabilitation services, the Rehabilitation Bureau places much emphasis on in-service training programs. At present the following five levels of training courses are regularly organized by the Research and Training Institute of the Ministry of Justice for probation officers.

- *Primary course.* This is an initial training course arranged every year for newly appointed probation officers. Being the longest course, it aims at giving basic knowledge in a wide range of subjects essential for the probation officer.
- *Secondary course.* Designed for probation officers who have been in the service for a few years, this course emphasizes practical aspects of the service, including legal aspects and procedures. It is conducted at the regional level in cooperation with the local training institute of the Ministry of Justice and the parole board.
- *Special course.* This course places much emphasis on the behavioral sciences, with a special view to enriching the body of knowledge and skills concerning treatment of offenders. Participants are probation officers with several years of experience in the service.
- *Senior course.* Probation officers who are expected to take supervisory positions are selected annually to participate. Procedures and legal aspects are given greater weight in the allocation of hours.
- *Supervisor course.* This course is organized for section supervisors, and the curriculum is centered around the philosophy and techniques of management.

In addition to the courses just described, top management seminars for probation office directors, conferences of supervisory personnel, and training sessions aimed at counseling and other treatment skill development of probation officers are organized from time to time.

Volunteer probation officers. Probation, parole, and other aftercare services for offenders in Japan are characterized by the extensive participation of volunteers. This was initiated in Japan more than three decades ago only because there had been a long history of public participation in the rehabilitation of offenders in the community.

When the present community-based correction system was organized after World War II, it was argued that probation and parole services should be established as a professional service. However, the new organization emerged in the form of a combined service of professional staff and volunteer workers. Although the shortage of funds at that time precluded volunteers from becoming professionalized, the main reason for keeping volunteers obviously lay in the fact that the faith of the authorities in the potential of volunteer workers was overwhelming.

Under these circumstances, the Volunteer Probation Officer Law came into effect in 1950, and the system of volunteer probation officers (VPOs) was established in its present form. By law, the fixed number of volunteer probation officers is 52,500, but there were 48,547 active members as of 1 July 1989. The most important role of volunteer probation officers is to supervise and assist the probationers and parolees assigned to them, but they also have other duties. They inquire into, and make adjustments to, the environment into which an inmate in a correctional institution is expected to return upon his or her release on parole, locate a probationer or parolee who has moved from another area and take over his or her supervisory casework, and conduct preliminary investigations in the case of candidates for pardons.

In the promotion of crime prevention, volunteers carry out many forms of activity pertaining to the concept of community organization. Among other things, they collaborate with public and private organizations in exploring and coordinating social resources in the community, spread the rehabilitative philosophy and efforts among individual neighbors or the public as a whole, and attempt to eradicate crime-precipitating conditions in cooperation with community residents.

Legally, volunteer probation officers are defined as nonpermanent officials of the national government and are entitled to the benefit of national compensation when they suffer any bodily injury in the performance of their duties. However, they are not paid any remuneration for their services, the government paying only the total expenses incurred by them in discharging their duties, or a part thereof. In practice, VPOs were reimbursed a certain amount of the following expenses in the fiscal year 1989: (a) a maximum of 4,270 yen per month for supervising a probationer or parolee; (b) 1,000 yen for a report on the investigation of environments and adjustments made thereto in respect of inmates soon to be paroled; and (c) 800 yen for a day's attendance at a training meeting. In the case of (b) and (c), mileage may be paid within the limits of an appropriated national fund when travel exceeds a

227

certain distance. Thus, there is no incentive for volunteer probation officers in terms of material benefit. As in any other field of volunteer work, what constantly motivates them is a sense of mission and gratification achieved through helping others. Of course, the social prestige attached to the volunteer's activity may act as an incentive. Manifest recognition of meritorious service, which is awarded regularly on formal occasions by the emperor or other authorities at different levels, has traditionally been a practical means of encouraging the voluntary services.

The qualifications required of a volunteer probation officer are stated in the Volunteer Probation Officer Law as follows:

- To have the confidence of, and be popular in, the community with respect to his or her character and conduct
- To have enthusiasm for the work and time for such work
- To have financial stability
- To be healthy and active

The term of service of a volunteer probation officer is two years, and it is renewable. This fixed term provides the opportunity to remove those who have proved to be unsuitable. In practice, most are reappointed repeatedly for a number of years, since volunteer work is such that, generally, a person has to work at it for more than two years to acquire the minimum knowledge and skill that the work requires.

To recruit volunteers, the directors of the fifty probation offices prepare a list of candidates on the basis of information gathered from various sources in the community. In effect, the list reflects to a great extent the opinion of representatives of the Volunteer Probation Officers' Association.

Further screening is done by an advisory committee that consists of representatives of the courts, the prosecution, the bar, correctional institutions, probation and parole services, and other public commissions, as well as learned citizens. The candidates who have passed the screening process are then appointed as volunteer probation officers by the minister of justice. The volunteers are each assigned, on the basis of their places of residence, to one of the 883 rehabilitation areas in the country, where they are supervised and guided by a professional probation officer in a probation office. The Volunteer Probation Officers' Association, with which every volunteer probation officer is affiliated, plays an important role in the maintenance of solidarity, development of ability, and coordination of efforts and resources. This association is a voluntary organization formed by VPOs.

According to the data in the Rehabilitation Bureau, some 20 percent of volunteer probation officers are female, and most fall into the older age group. In 1988, their average age was 61.2 years, and 61 percent of them were between 60 and 79 years of age (table 7.10). The probation offices always try to recruit younger people as volunteer probation officers, but they are confronted with some difficulties in finding younger candidates, since middle-aged people, who are the most appropriate for service as volunteer officers, are usually preoccupied with their own lives.

Their occupational backgrounds are extremely varied (table 7.11). The largest group (25.7 percent) is unemployed, mostly consisting of housewives and retired men, followed by those engaged in primary industries (18.4

Table 7.10   Volunteer Probation Officers by Age, 1988

Age	Number of VPOs	%
Under 40	624	1.3
40-49	4,093	8.4
50 -59	14,161	29.1
60 - 69	20,952	43.1
70 - 79	8,696	17.9
80 and over	78	0.2
Total	48,604	100.0

Source: Rehabilitation Bureau, Ministry of Justice, Japan.

Table 7.11   Volunteer Probation Officers by Occupation Groups, 1988

Occupation	Number of VPOs	%
Unemployed[a]	12,473	25.7
Fishing; farming	8,953	18.4
Religious people	5,849	12.0
Sales	4,855	10.0
Managers	3,926	8.1
Government officials	2,059	4.2
Company Employees	2,418	5.0
Manufacturing	1,906	3.9
Services	1,104	2.3
Teachers	815	1.7
Physicians; dentists	183	0.4
Social workers	1,065	2.2
Practicing attorneys	55	0.1
Others	2,943	6.1
Total	48,604	100.0

Source: Rehabilitation Bureau, Ministry of Japan, Japan.
*Includes retired persons and housewives.

percent) such as farming and fishing. The religious profession forms the third largest group (12 percent), still reflecting the tradition stemming from the early days of the rehabilitation services. A variety of people from almost all fields of society, such as government officials, company employees, manufacturers, shopkeepers, school teachers, medical doctors, social workers, and private lawyers, participate in the work of the volunteer probation officers. In order to help volunteer probation officers acquire the knowledge and skill required for their service, probation offices regularly organize various VPO training courses, including the ones for newly appointed VPOs, for VPOs who have served less than a year, and for those who have served two to four years, and courses focusing on the treatment of offenders with specific problems. Aside from these training courses formally organized by the probation agencies, each local association of volunteer probation officers holds case conferences and other study meetings from time to time, attended by a professional probation officer as a leader.

Rehabilitation Aid Hostels (Halfway Houses). At present, there are one hundred rehabilitation aid hostels (halfway houses) run by private associations in the country. Under the law for Aftercare of Discharged Offenders of 1950, these hostels are licensed and supervised by the minister of justice.

They accommodate those probationers and parolees who are referred to them by a probation office, as well as others who voluntarily seek shelter aid. The total capacity of the halfway houses is twenty-four hundred, and the capacity of each facility ranges from ten to eighty. The total number of employees is 475, with an average of 4 or 5 working in each facility. Of the 475 employees, some 327, or at least 1 in each house, are authorized by the minister of justice as being in charge of the treatment of offenders. Most of them have concurrently been appointed as volunteer probation officers. The others are assistant treatment workers, clerks, cooks, and helpers.

The major area of service of the halfway houses is to provide room and board and guidance for probationers, parolees, and other discharged offenders. It should be noted, however, that neither the court nor the probation agency has the authority to commit a probationer to a facility on a compulsory basis.

While it is the general rule that the resident goes out every day to work, some halfway houses have their own workshops to provide jobs for persons who are unfit for outside employment. One halfway house has purchased a vacuum wagon to be used by a group of residents who work for the city sewerage service, while another is attached to a psychiatric hospital and specializes in the accommodation of mentally disturbed ex-offenders.

About 50 percent of the total expenses of halfway houses are borne by the national government, and the remainder must be either raised by the organizations themselves or covered by contributions from outsiders.

Other Volunteer Organizations. In addition to the organizations mentioned previously, there are other private organizations that are not directly involved in the supervision of adult probationers but give much support to community correction measures in various ways.

The Big Brothers and Sisters (BBS) association is an organization of youths engaged in befriending delinquent youngsters and forestalling delinquency. The first BBS association was organized in Japan in 1947 by university students in Kyoto. The idea of the movement interested many young people in other districts and rapidly spread throughout the country within a few years.

At the present time, the number of members in Japan amounts to sixty-eight hundred. Anyone between seventeen and thirty years of age and capable of befriending minors with a proper understanding of their needs and problems may be admitted as a member, regardless of his or her educational and occupational background.

The members assist professional and volunteer probation officers in supervising and helping mainly juveniles under the care of the probation offices. The association is also interested in involving community residents in their efforts to eliminate environmental factors generating delinquency, and it often organizes recreational programs for children.

The Woman's Association for Rehabilitation Aid (WARA) is an autonomous voluntary association of women that assists public and voluntary organizations engaged in the prevention of crime or the rehabilitation of offenders. It is a body representing mothers and housewives in society who are concerned about crime, delinquency, and the welfare of offenders and their families. Any woman can become a member of the association, irrespective of her age, material status, or social class. Total membership throughout the country amounts to approximately 180,000.

The activities of the association include the provision of financial, material, and moral support to volunteer probation officers, rehabilitation aid hostels, and BBS groups, the encouragement of correctional institution inmates and their families, and the dissemination of rehabilitative ideas and information on efforts to the public.

Lastly, there are employers who take much interest in rehabilitating offenders and willingly employ and guide offenders who have been under probationary or parole supervision. Such employers are commonly called "cooperative employers," and probation offices have made a list of their names and are making further efforts to develop this form of assistance. At present, the number of cooperative employers throughout Japan amounts to three thousand.

Chapter 7

Conditions of Adult Probation

The conditions imposed on an adult probationer during his or her probationary period are regulated by article 5 of the Law for Probationary Supervision of Persons under Suspension of Execution of Sentence as follows:

- To report his or her specific place of residence to the probation office immediately after the probation order is made
- To maintain good conduct
- To give the probation office notice before changing residence or making a journey exceeding a month

These conditions are imposed on every adult probationer and explained to him or her in court and in the probation office. Neither the court nor the probation office has the authority to impose any additional conditions on adult probationers.

If the probationer violates any of the conditions, his or her probation may be revoked by the court, but only when "the circumstances are seriously unfavorable to him" (Penal Code, article 26-2-[2]). This means that only a serious breach of the conditions can lead to the revocation of probation. In practice, probation of an adult offender is rarely revoked as a result of a technical violation of the conditions. For instance, if a probationer changes residence without notifying the probation office, he or she violates one of the conditions, but probation will not be revoked unless he or she has committed a new offense during that absence from supervision.

The conditions imposed on adult probationers are less restrictive than those imposed on other offenders under the supervision of a probation officer. For example, in addition to the aforementioned conditions, others, such as engagement in a lawful occupation and a prohibition on frequenting criminogenic groups, are imposed on prison parolees by law, and the regional parole board has the authority to add special conditions, such as a restriction on the consumption of alcoholic beverages and the imposition of regular visits to the volunteer probation officer, according to the individual needs of each parolee. The violations of these parole conditions are dealt with more severely than are those for adult probationers.

The less restrictive nature of probation conditions for adults was the result of the view of the legislature in the 1950s that adult probationers' personal freedom should not be restricted to a great extent, since adults, in general, play a more important role in society and probationers have committed less serious offenses than parolees who have served actual imprisonment.

Supervision Process

Article 2 of the Law for Probationary Supervision of Persons under Suspension of Execution of Sentence regulates the principle of supervision of adult probationers, stating that "supervision shall be carried out by guiding and aiding the person and by leading and supervising him so that he observes the conditions provided for in article 5." It is clear that supervision of adult probationers includes functions of both helping offenders reintegrate into society and controlling them to prevent their committing further offenses. This principle is basically the same as in the supervision of other types of offenders in the community, such as adult parolees. However, since the conditions imposed on adult probationers are less restrictive than those of adult parolees, the function of assistance to offenders is emphasized more with the supervision of adult probationers than with the supervision of prison parolees.

Supervision is carried out through collaboration between professional and volunteer probation officers. Present routine processes of supervision may be briefly outlined as follows.

a. The offender who has been placed on probation is advised to report immediately to the probation office. At the office he or she is interviewed by the probation officer in charge of the area where the supervisee is going to reside. The officer explains to the probationer what probation is, including the conditions imposed and the possible provisional discharge from supervision. Since information necessary for the supervision has normally not yet been sent by the court to the officer, the probation officer uses the interview to try to understand the offender's personality and try to get information from him or her, such as his or her home address, job, personal history, family, lifestyle, and offenses committed.

b. Taking into consideration all the information obtained at the interview, together with the available data in case record, the probation officer assesses the individual's needs and problems requiring special attention or care and works out a treatment plan. He or she chooses one of the volunteer probation officers who lives close to the probationer and assigns the volunteer to supervise the probationer. In the final stage of the interview, the officer tells the probationer the name, address, and other pertinent information regarding the volunteer probation officer who has been assigned to him or her.

c. The probation officer makes a summary of the case record, indicates his or her view on the case, and sends a copy by mail to the volunteer.

d. Receiving the information from the probation officer, the assigned volunteer probation officer starts supervising the probationer. The volunteer keeps in touch with the client and his or her family by means of mutual visits and interviews, which generally take place twice a month or so, although the frequency and mode of contact vary as the case requires.

e. The volunteer submits a regular progress report on each offender to the probation office every month. In addition, he or she is supposed to make a phone call or send a written report to the professional officer whenever an unusual incident has taken place in relation to the offender.

f. When the probation officer thinks it necessary, judging from the report from the volunteer or information received from the police or the offender's family, he or she may take some action. Usually, the probation officer starts such action by interviewing the probationer. He or she may visit the offender personally or send a letter to the offender, suggesting that he or she come to the office.

g. After several months, or a few years, of supervision, the success or failure of the probationer becomes evident in some cases. If the success is clear, the probation officer institutes action for his or her provisional discharge from supervision. If the probationer has made a serious breach of conditions, the necessary steps are taken for the revocation of his or her probation. For the remainder, supervision continues until the termination of the probation period.

The professional probation officer and the volunteer probation officer play different roles in supervising a probationer. For the most part, routine supervision of a probationer is carried out by a volunteer probation officer under the direction of a professional probation officer. A probation officer is a case manager or supervisor of the work of the volunteer officer. There are some merits in being a volunteer officer supervising a probationer. First, the volunteer can keep in closer contact with a probationer and provide more intensive assistance than a professional officer. Volunteer probation officers usually have their homes in the neighborhood where probationers reside and are thus able to keep in touch with them more easily, visiting them on weekends or holidays or in the evening, thus not disturbing them during work or school hours. In other words, volunteer probation officers working in the local community can spare the offenders the mental burden and loss of time that might otherwise be incurred as a result of receiving supervision as probationers. Second, they are not official, but informal and less threatening, and thus fill the gap between officers and clients.

A professional officer gives directions to the volunteer officers under him or her and supervises their work. Some of the shortcomings of amateur or semiprofessional volunteer officers in dealing with offenders are made up for by professional officers.

One of the most important duties of a professional officer is to arrange a good match between a supervising volunteer officer and the case. There is as great a variety of volunteer officers in terms of age, experience, knowledge, skills, and personality as there is of probationers. A female probationer may be suited to a female volunteer, a traffic offender to a volunteer who has sufficient knowledge of safe driving, and a tough gangster to a reliable male volunteer.

A probationer who has personal problems or problems with his or her family may be assigned to a counseling-oriented volunteer officer who can understand social and emotional problems, while a probationer who has problems in employment is assigned to a service-oriented volunteer who can provide concrete advice to the client. In order to make a good match, probation officers must develop a heightened awareness of volunteer officers' strengths and weaknesses as well as probationers' needs.

Many incidents and problems emerge during the course of the supervision of a probationer, some more serious than others. When a volunteer officer is confronted by a problem, such as a probationer who refuses to visit the volunteer or a probationer who commits a minor offense and is arrested by the police, he or she sometimes does not know what to do or becomes discouraged and feels a sense of inadequacy. Another important task of the professional officer is to consult with the volunteer in trouble, to give suitable suggestions, and to encourage him or her.

When a very serious problem occurs that cannot be dealt with by a volunteer, a professional officer intervenes directly in the crisis. The professional officer inevitably requires a high degree of knowledge and skills to find solutions to problems that arise.

Material Aid to Probationers

Many offenders under probation or parole supervision face financial difficulties. To meet the needs of such offenders, the probation officer tries to encourage and assist them along the lines of social work principles so that they may tackle the personal problems underlying the hardship more effectively. The probation officer often has to help the offender to find a satisfying job or to improve the offender's relationship with his or her family.

On the other hand, the importance of material aid can never be overlooked when the offender is in acute financial difficulty. Under the Law for Aftercare of Discharged Offenders, a probation office can provide some kinds of material aid to the probationer or parolee if he or she applies for it. A total of 3,322 offenders under supervision, including 286 adult probationers, received material aid such as meals, clothes, costs of medical care, and travel fares from probation offices in 1988 (table 7.12). It is usually parolees, more than probationers, who need this kind of aid.

In addition, there are a number of offenders under supervision who have been rejected by their families and have no place to live. Halfway houses accommodate such offenders on the referral of the probation office. In 1988, a total of 6,466 probationers and parolees, including 387 adult probationers, were referred to halfway houses.

The Japan Rehabilitation Aid Association and various local organizations, such as volunteer probation officers associations and rehabilitation service promotion associations, set aside a special fund within their own

Table 7.12   Number of Probationers and Parolees Receiving Material Aid, 1988

Type of aid	Total offenders under supervision	Adults probationers
Meals	644	150
Clothes	738	29
Costs of medical care	19	1
Travel fares	314	99
Total	3,322	286

Source: Annual Statistics Report on Rehabilitation of Offenders for 1988, Japan.

budgets to disburse sums where necessary to supplement the limited national fund for aiding probationers and parolees.

Efforts for More Effective Supervision

Local Offices. Each probation office covers one of the prefectures, which vary in size and population. If a large prefecture has only a main probation office, and all probation officers are based at that office, this makes it very inconvenient for the probation officers and probationers or volunteers living in remote areas to visit each other, and this hampers the effective supervision of probationers. To enhance the contact between probation officers and probationers or volunteers, the Rehabilitation Bureau has made continuous efforts to open local probation offices in major cities remote from prefectural capitals in which the main offices are located. At present thirty such offices have been opened. The number of probation officers working at each local office ranges from one to fourteen. As a complement to main offices, these local offices have proved to be an effective means of providing volunteers with closer supervision and counseling and for facilitating direct probation-parole casework by the probation officers.

Day Offices. For the same purposes as underlie the opening of more local offices, it has become common practice for almost all probation officers of both main offices and local offices to visit the local community and receive during regular office hours in a room at the municipal office, town hall, or youth center at regular intervals. The frequency of the "day office" in the area ranges from once a week to once every two months, depending on local circumstances and the caseload of the area.

Activities of the probation officer at the day office include interviewing probationers and parolees, family counseling, case consultation with volunteers, consultation with school teachers and employers, home visits, liaison with community agencies, and the like.

Differential Supervision. The differential supervision system was introduced into the work of all probation offices in 1971. Under this system, based on a prediction table of recidivism, all probationers and parolees under supervision are classified into two groups, Group A requiring more intensive supervision and Group B representing no acute or serious problem.

Persons classified in Group A are placed under intensive supervision and given special attention by both professional and volunteer probation officers. According to the data of the Rehabilitation Bureau, at the end of 1988, 18.1 percent of adult probationers were classified in Group A and placed under intensive supervision, while 7.3 percent of adult parolees, 6.3 percent of juvenile probationers, and 32.2 percent of juvenile parolees were placed under intensive supervision. It is very interesting that the portion of those under intensive supervision is much larger among adult probationers and juvenile parolees than among adult parolees and juvenile probationers.

Group Work Programs. While the greatest part of supervision of offenders is carried out by the casework method on a one-officer-to-one-offender basis, probation offices have developed group work programs in addition to the traditional casework approach.

Present group work programs are mainly concerned with juvenile probationers who have been placed on probation as a result of violations of road traffic laws. The most typical one is the Short-term Probation for Juvenile Traffic Cases, introduced throughout the country in 1977. In this program the group work constitutes the major part of the treatment, supplemented by monthly written reports on the probationers, who are discharged from probation after three or four months, so long as they fulfill all the requirements. There has been an increasing number of attempts among the probation offices to provide group work sessions for adult probationers inclined to abuse harmful drugs. Such group work programs are still, however, sporadic, and may be said to be at the experimental stage.

Direct Supervision Units. In the supervision of probationers, professional probation officers act as coordinators, consultants, and supervisors for volunteer officers and sometimes intervene in crisis situations. They require advanced knowledge and skills that can be obtained only through experience in dealing with offenders. In order to provide them with the opportunity to obtain experience of supervising probationers directly, direct supervision units have been established in two probation offices, in Tokyo and Osaka, since 1974. Several probation officers, mainly younger ones, are allocated to one of the units and engage in direct supervision of the most difficult cases without the assistance of volunteer officers. At the same time, they conduct research projects and publish their results in order that other probation officers can share their experiences.

Outcome of Supervision. Although neither the court nor the director of the probation office can completely discharge an adult probationer from probation, the parole board has authority to discharge a probationer provisionally from supervision upon the request of the director of the probation office.

In recent years, probation offices throughout the country have adopted a positive policy toward the use of this program based on a philosophy that it is useless and often even detrimental to continue supervision until the period fixed by the court expires, disregarding the progress of the individual offender. Table 7.13 shows the total number of probationers and those provisionally discharged from probationary supervision at the end of every five years from 1955 to 1985 and in 1988. It is clear that the number of probationers discharged from supervision has increased since the 1970s and has recently reached more than 10 percent of the total number of probationers. On the other hand, in a "failure case" involving one who has committed an offense while on probation, the new charge is dealt with by the court, and the probationer may be committed to a correctional institution or given some other sentence, as the case requires. The original probation may be revoked or continued at the discretion of the court. In the meantime,

Table 7.13   Number of Adult Probationers and Number of Those under Provisional Discharge from Supervision at end of Year, 1955–1985 and 1988

Year	Total number under probation (A)	Under provisional discharge from supervision (B)	B/A (%)
1955	6,012	10	0,2
1960	22,483	339	1,5
1965	23,649	502	2,1
1970	22,233	813	3,7
1975	21,555	1,025	4,8
1980	23,368	2,220	9,5
1985	21,430	2,489	11,6
1988	18,447	1,926	10,4

Source: Annual Statistics Report on Rehabilitation of Offenders, Japan.

Table 7.14   Termination of Adult Probation and Adult Parole, by Type of
Reason, 1988

Reasons of termination	Adult probationers		Adult parolees	
Expiration of term	4,864	{69.5}	15,607	{90.4}
under discharged supervision	1,350			
Revocation	2,015	{28.8}	1,489	{8.6}
for offenses	1,881		54	
for violation of conditions	134		1,435	
Others	120	{1.7}	166	{1.0}
Total	6,999	{100.0}	17,262	{100.0}

Source: Annual Statistics Report on Rehabilitation of Offenders, Japan.
Note: Figures in parentheses show percentages.

action is taken in cases of technical or serious violation of conditions. The
director of the probation office files an application for revocation to the
criminal court through the public prosecutor. Such applications have recently
been encouraged among probation offices to maintain a healthy balance
between policies in relation to successful and unsuccessful cases.

Table 7.14 shows the number of adult probationers and adult parolees
in respect of whom supervision was terminated in 1988, according to the
type of reason. Probationary supervision was terminated for a total number
of 6,999 adult probationers. Among these, 69.5 percent completed their
probation without any revocation, including 1,350 probationers who received provisional discharge from supervision and then completed their
terms of suspended execution of sentence. Thus, nearly 70 percent of
probationers may be considered successful cases. However, for the remaining
28.8 percent, probation was revoked, mainly as a result of the committing of
a new offense during supervision. If these figures are compared with those
for prison parole cases, the percentage of revocation was much higher in
probation cases than in parole cases. Since there are no basic differences, in
method or intensiveness, between the supervision of probationers and the
supervision of parolees, except for small differences in the restrictiveness of
the conditions imposed, the reason for this may be found in the fact that
parole is more selectively applied to adult cases, thus excluding poor risks.
In addition, the period of parole is generally too limited to enable a clear
distinction between good and poor adjustment to be made at the time of
expiration. Conversely, the period of adult probation is far more extensive,
and the court, when it pronounces a suspended sentence, usually applies
probation as an additional measure more selectively to those offenders who
reveal greater criminal tendencies.

Chapter 7

Allocation of Resources to Probation Agencies

Work Force. A total of 18,477 adult probationers were under the supervision of probation officers at the end of 1988 (table 7.15). At the same time, an additional 8,185 adult parolees, 50,363 juvenile probationers, and 6,393 juvenile parolees were also under supervision, making a total of 83,388 offenders under supervision.

On the other hand, there were 856 probation officers and 48,604 volunteer probation officers registered in the same year. Among the 856 probation officers, some 623 were field probation officers, excluding those in administrative and supervising positions, such as directors and section chiefs. On average, one probation officer was supervising 134 offenders with the assistance of 78 volunteer officers, and each volunteer officer was dealing with two cases.

To evaluate this average caseload, some points should be noted. First, the 623 field probation officers included those officers who were totally or partially engaged in a variety of duties other than probation or parole supervision, such as voluntary aftercare of discharged offenders, liaison, and public education. Second, a probation officer is not engaged in presentence investigation in the courts, although he or she is engaged in a part of the preparole investigation process. With the assistance of a volunteer probation officer, he or she investigates a family, a relative, or an employer to whom an inmate in prison or in juvenile training school is going to return when parole is granted. The investigation starts immediately after the inmate is imprisoned and continues until his or her parole release. Every six months the probation officer makes a report and sends it to a regional parole board.

Table 7.15   Number of Probationers and Parolees under Supervision at end of 1988

Category	Number	Percent
Adult		
Probationer	18,447	22.2
Parolee	8,185	9.8
Juvenile		
Probationer	50,363	60.4
Parolee	6,393	7.7
Total	83,388	100.0

Source: Annual Statistics Report on Rehabilitation of Offenders, Japan.

The report provides important information for a parole decision to be made. A total of 45,922 such cases were in the hands of probation officers throughout the country at the end of 1988, an average of 74 cases per officer. This kind of work occupies a considerable amount of a probation officer's daily schedule.

Also the caseloads vary among the probation offices. Much larger caseloads are found in offices located in areas where the population has been increasing rapidly, such as the Kanagawa, Chiba, and Saitama prefectures near Tokyo. In such offices, one probation officer, with the assistance of more than 150 volunteer officers, may have a caseload of more than 250.

An ideal caseload depends on the individual probation officers and on the area they cover, but it is generally understood among the field probation officers that an ideal caseload is less than one hundred cases. The Rehabilitation Bureau has been making every effort to increase the number of field probation officers since the probation system began, and it succeeded in expanding the number of officers by 53, from 577 in 1979 to 630 in 1989, despite the general policy of the government that the total number of government officials should not be increased. However, the present caseload remains too large to assure a sufficient degree of coordinated work with volunteers to guarantee more effective supervision of offenders. Among the administrators and probation officers, the general opinion is that the total number of probation officers should be expanded to at least two times the present number.

Various efforts have been made to make good use of the limited work force in probation agencies. One example is the differential supervision program that was mentioned earlier. Another typical example is computerization of the work in probation offices. Computers are used not only in administrative work, like accounting, but also in case management and in the supervision process. Basic data on probationers and parolees under supervision are input to a computer and utilized as a data base for various purposes, such as statistical analysis and classification of offenders for differential supervision. At present, computers have been introduced into six major offices, in Tokyo, Yokohama, Osaka, Nagoya, Kobe, and Urawa, and will later be installed in more offices.

Budget for Community Corrections. Since supervision of adult probationers is one of the components of a broader system of offender rehabilitation services, it is impossible to specify the national budget for the adult probation system from among the total budget for the overall system. A rough estimate of the amount of national funds appropriated to probation and parole supervision and aftercare service in the fiscal year 1988 is shown in table 7.16. Approximately 12.125 million yen was spent for noncustodial correctional and aftercare services. Among the total budget items, about 64 percent was spent on office expenses, including salaries for officials, traveling expenses, and office supplies, 21 percent for expenses of volunteer probation officers, and 11 percent for accommodation of probationers and parolees at halfway houses.

The noncustodial correctional measures, including adult probation, operate under a more stringent budget than that for custodial measures. The total budget for custodial correction amounted to 137.047 million yen in the same fiscal year of 1988. Custodial correction in Japan consists of sixty-seven prisons, seven detention houses, fifty-four juvenile training schools, and fifty juvenile classification homes. All institutions are administered by the Correctional Bureau of the Ministry of Justice and accommodate a daily average of 59,284 inmates—54,344 prisoners in prisons and detention houses, 3,745 juvenile offenders in juvenile training schools (as at the end of March 1988), and 1,195 juvenile detainees awaiting trial in juvenile classification homes.

To sum up, the custodial correction system accommodated daily about 59,000 inmates with an annual budget of 137 billion yen, while the noncustodial corrections supervised about 83,000 offenders daily with an annual budget of 12 billion yen. Administrators of noncustodial corrective measures feel the present appropriation of funds is far from sufficient to ensure the effective treatment of offenders on probation and parole. The volunteer probation officers associations and other voluntary organizations also spend considerable amounts of money each year to supplement the

Table 7.16   Budget for Rehabilitation Services, 1988

Items	Amount of money (yen)	
Office expenses	7,738,475	63.8
Expenses of volunteer probation officers	2,579,705	21.3
Accommodation at halfway houses	1,349,092	11.1
Material aids	12,471	0.1
Clothes	3,859	
Travel fare	5,482	
Meals	2,023	
Medical care	1,107	
Other	446,216	3.7
Total	12,124,740	100.0

Source: Annual Report of the Ministry of Justice, 1988, Japan.
Note: Office expenses includes salaries, travel expenses, office supplies, and the like.

funds made available by the national government for training of volunteer probation officers, the upkeep of halfway houses, and providing aid to probationers and parolees, while they also spend funds for various kinds of other activities not directly connected with the supervision of offenders.

Coordination Between the Courts and the Probation Offices

The courts responsible for decisions on probation and the probation offices responsible for the supervision of probationers are independent organizations in Japan. There is no system of presentence investigation by probation officers in the criminal courts. Under these circumstances, special efforts are needed to promote mutual understanding between the courts and the probation offices, through exchange of information and views, to improve the implementation of adult probation. In particular, it is indispensable for judges in the criminal courts to understand the reality of the supervision of probationers, its effectiveness, and its limits.

In the interests of such mutual understanding between the courts and the probation offices, in every prefecture a district court and a probation office held regular conferences every year or every two years for some twenty-five years after the introduction of adult probation in 1954. These conferences were attended by judges and clerks from the court and by the directors, section chiefs, and field probation officers of the probation offices and were sometimes expanded to include some public prosecutors. Experiences and wishes were exchanged, and often probation decisions and the supervision of some special cases were analyzed from the different viewpoints of the two sides. Such conferences were held until the early 1980s, when most of the courts and probation offices thought that the aim of the conferences had been almost achieved, since adult probation was firmly established in the administration of both the courts and the probation offices after more than twenty-five years' practice, and the conferences were discontinued in most of the prefectures for some years. However, from the mid-1980s, a few years after the discontinuation of the conferences, a slight decrease was noticed in the number of probation decisions taken in the courts throughout the country. Administrators in the probation offices viewed this decrease in probation orders as the outcome of the break-off of the conferences between the probation office and the courts. They came to attach greater importance to the continuance of such conferences, and, as a result, most of the probation offices resumed their efforts to hold regular conferences with the courts on better administration of probation.

Evaluation of Adult Probation

Before evaluating the success of the administration of adult probation by criminal justice practitioners, scholars, and the general public, it is appropriate to recall its legal framework and actual practice described up to now.

As alternatives to imprisonment of three years or less, the law provides for two types of suspended execution of sentence, one without supervision, the other with supervision (i.e., probation). There is a clear difference in the legal status of offenders under these two types of suspended execution. While the offender under suspended execution of sentence without supervision has a chance of receiving another suspended execution of sentence if he or she commits a major offense, the offender under probation has no such chance. It is at the discretion of the court to choose between probation or suspended execution of sentence without supervision for those offenders who have not previously received suspended execution of sentence. But probation is compulsory when a suspended execution of sentence is ordered for an offender who committed an offense during his or her previous probation.

Under this legal system, the courts have followed a basic sentencing policy that minimizes the use of actual imprisonment through maximum use of alternative measures including probation. For many years, more than half of all prison sentences have been suspended with or without supervision each year. As a result, the prison population in Japan is extremely low, while the number of offenders who are placed on probation at the discretion of the court has stabilized at between five thousand and six thousand each year. The major reason for this may be that the court is reluctant to impose probation orders on nonserious offenders, since this precludes the chance of an alternative measure to imprisonment in the future. Other reasons may be that the courts take the capacity of supervising agencies into consideration when sentencing. On the other hand, approximately fifteen hundred offenders have been compulsorily placed on probation each year because they committed new offenses during their previous suspended execution of sentence. As a result, the number of offenders placed on probation each year has been very constant, at a relatively small level of between six thousand and eight thousand, but includes a large portion of offenders who are crime prone. The sentencing policy in the courts has been remarkably consistent since the introduction of adult probation in 1954, and there are no records of serious disparities in sentencing. Supervision of adult probationers is conducted by the probation offices independently of the courts. In addition to adult probationers, the probation offices supervise juvenile probationers and both adult and juvenile parolees. The daily average population of all offenders under supervision amounts to more than eighty thousand, including about eighteen thousand adult probationers. Supervision of probationers and parolees is carried out by a small number (less than one thousand) of professional probation officers with the assistance of a large number (forty-eight thousand) of volunteer probation officers. To make good use of the limited manpower, especially the shortage of professional probation officers, the probation offices have made every effort to improve the effective supervision of offenders, through, for example, the opening of local and day offices and differential supervision programs. In spite of the efforts to provide more effective supervision, the revocation rate of adult probation is still relatively high for the reasons mentioned above.

Since its establishment, the legal framework of adult probation has not been seriously challenged by criminal justice practitioners, scholars, or legislators. However, some aspects in the present framework have been pointed out as bottlenecks in the expansion of the use of probation. When the Legislative Council proposed a draft revised Penal Code to the minister of justice in 1974, it recommended some changes in the legal framework of probation. In the draft, to enable the unrestricted imposition of suspended execution of sentence to probationers, it recommended that the offender under probationary supervision should also have a chance of receiving another suspended execution of sentence in the future. If this change is introduced into practice, judges will be less reluctant to impose probation orders on offenders. But the draft is still under consideration by the Ministry for submission to the Diet. The feasibility of other types of alternatives to imprisonment, such as social service orders, is also being studied by some practitioners and scholars, but no conclusive decision has been reached. The reason for this is simply the fact that prisons are not overcrowded. Confronted by a lack of the information necessary for sentencing, some judges are demanding the introduction of presentence investigation by probation officers attached to the court. Such requests have also been voiced by some probation officers supervising probationers, but they still remain the exception to the rule.

The policy and practice of sentencing in the courts have enabled the maximum use of alternative measures to imprisonment, including probation, meriting high praise from practitioners and scholars of criminal justice for keeping the prison population at a minimum. The probation offices have enjoyed a stable inflow of probationers from the courts. A relatively small number of probation orders imposed by the courts has enabled the probation offices to concentrate their limited resources on those offenders most in need of control and assistance. The problem is whether the offenders who need supervision and care the most are actually selected for probation orders. Basically, the probation offices admit the inflow of some offenders whose rehabilitation is difficult and understand that the legal framework and the sentencing policy of maximizing the use of alternative measures force the courts to place these offenders on probation. Instead of excluding all the offenders with less possibility of rehabilitation, the probation supervisory agencies are demanding that the courts entertain the feasibility of future changes in their sentencing considerations to exclude a specific type of offender in respect of whom supervision is totally impossible. These would include offenders who have no residence but do not wish to live at halfway houses. For this purpose, some probation officers approve of the introduction of presentence investigation in the courts. Yet the majority of probation officers expect that mutual understanding will be improved through frequent exchanges of information between the courts and the probation offices.

The success in supervision of probationers by active participation of a large number of volunteer workers is fully appreciated by practitioners, scholars, legislators, and the general public. The high estimation of volunteers comes not only from their contribution to cost-effectiveness but also from the benefit of their supervision and assistance to offenders in the community. It is true that in the early stages of the probation system there were some fears or criticisms of the use of volunteers in supervising offenders, since they were considered mere amateurs. The probation offices have made continuous efforts to provide the volunteer workers with training and to exclude some volunteers who proved to be unqualified or too old to perform their duties. Presently, such fears and criticism seem to have subsided.

Both the probation offices and the courts share a common concern about the relatively high rate of revocation of probation, or recidivism among probationers. Although both of them basically admit that high recidivism rates are unavoidable under the present legal framework and sentencing policy, they recognize the necessity of some measures to minimize it. One of the countermeasures to be encouraged in the probation offices is the active use of revocation for violation of conditions before the probationer commits a new offense. Active revocation for technical violation of probation conditions does not reduce the revocation rate but contributes to the prevention of serious offenses that might be caused by probationers.

Lastly, it is worth presenting the public's evaluation of the courts and the volunteer probation officers, as revealed in the public opinion poll conducted in 1986 by the Prime Minister's Office and the Research and Training Institute of the Ministry of Justice. The survey consisted of various questions that were formulated to reveal people's attitudes toward crime and their evaluations of activities of criminal justice agencies, including the courts and probation offices. The target of the survey included three groups—ordinary citizens, prisoners, and members of prisoners' families—and all the samples were selected at random.

To evaluate penalties imposed by the courts, one of the questions in the survey asked, "Has assessment of the penalty been conducted appropriately?" The answers are shown in table 7.17. Although almost half of all the groups were unable to answer, the majority of those who gave decisive answers in all the groups sampled thought that penalties were appropriate. But the second largest percentage (18.7 percent) of ordinary citizens thought that penalties were too lenient, while the second largest portion of prisoners and their families thought, conversely, that penalties were too heavy. It is natural that prisoners and their families consider the penalties to be too heavy, but attention should be given to the responses of ordinary citizens who consider current penalties too lenient. Although the question of penalties did not directly touch upon probation and suspended sentences, the answers give some indication as to the general public's attitude toward the current sentencing practice of probation. Also, to evaluate the activities of volunteer probation officers, another question in the survey asked the respondents, "Do you think volunteer probation officers are useful for the rehabilitation of offenders?" Their answers are shown in table 7.18. Excluding a large portion in each group who could not give decisive answers, the

Table 7.17   Views on Assessment of Penalty in Trials (percent)
(Has assessment of penalty been conducted appropriately?)

Choices	Ordinary citizens	Prisoners	Family members of prisoners
Too heavy	1.0	22.4	11.8
Appropriate	28.0	27.6	28.1
Too lenient	18.7	1.1	3.3
Cannot give a decisive answer	34.6	39.5	25.7
Do not know	17.7	9.4	31.1
Total	100.0	100.0	100.0
	{2,392}	{2,648}	{727}

Sources: The Public Opinion Poll, Prime Minister's Office for Ordinary Citizens; Research Training Institute, Ministry of Justice, for Prisoners and Family Members of Prisoners, Japan.
Note: Figures in parentheses show actual numbers.

Table 7.18   Evaluation of the Activities of VPOs (percent)
Do you think volunteer probation officers are useful for the rehabilitation of offenders?

Answers	Ordinary citizens			Prisoners			Family members of prisoners		
	Total	Male	Female	Total	Male	Female	Total	Male	Female
Yes	40.3	43.3	38.0	42.1	42.8	27.9	62.0	72.8	57.8
No	7.1	9.2	5.4	12.6	12.6	11.7	1.4	2.4	1.0
Cannot give a decisive answer	26.2	26.1	26.3	25.9	25.9	26.1	10.6	9.7	10.9
Do not Know	26.4	21.5	30.3	19.4	18.7	34.2	26.0	15.0	30.3
Total	100.0	100.0	100.0	100.0	100.0	100.0	100.0	100.0	100.0
	[2,392]	[1,067]	[1,325]	[2,648]	[2,537]	[111]	[727]	[206]	[521]

Source: The Public Opinion Poll, Prime Minister's Office for Ordinary Citizens; Research and Training Institute, Ministry of Justice, for Prisoners and Family Members of Prisoners, Japan.
Note: Figures in parentheses show actual numbers.

overwhelming majority of those who responded did so positively, while very few gave negative responses. For example, among the group of ordinary citizens, although 58.6 percent were unable to answer, 40.3 percent responded "Yes" and only 7.1 percent responded negatively. The evaluation of volunteer probation officers was very high in all the groups and was particularly high (62.7 percent) among prisoners' families. While a prisoner serves his or her sentence in a prison, a volunteer probation officer usually helps the prisoner's family prepare for his or her return home. The high evaluation of volunteer probation officers among prisoners' families might be based on their own experiences of actual contact with such volunteers.

Conclusion

Although some minor problems can be found, adult probation in Japan has made considerable achievements in performing its various functions as an alternative measure to imprisonment. Furthermore, it has potential for further expansion in the future.

The success in probation, as well as the success in other areas of the criminal justice system in Japan, such as police, prosecution, courts, and prisons, owes much to the favorable crime situation experienced over the last three decades. But it is unrealistic to assume that Japan will automatically be spared from the general trend involving increases in crime that accompany societal development. Responding to the rapid changes in society, which is shifting toward an advanced stage of development, criminal justice in Japan, including adult probation, must be prepared to incorporate more effective crime prevention strategies for the future.

References

There are numerous publications in Japan on adult probation, but most of them are in Japanese. Only those available in English are listed here.

Correctional Bureau of the Ministry of Justice, *Correctional Institutions in Japan 1985*.
Japanese Code of Criminal Procedure, Law No. 131 of 1948.
Japanese Law for Aftercare of Discharged Offenders, Law No. 203 of 1950.
Japanese Law for Probationary Supervision of Persons under Suspension of Execution of Sentence, Law No. 54 of 1954.
Japanese Law for the Inquest of Prosecution, Law No. 147 of 1948.
Japanese Offenders Rehabilitation Law, Law No. 142 of 1949.
Japanese Penal Code, Law No. 45 of 1907.
Japanese Prison Law, Law No. 28 of 1908.
Japanese Volunteer Probation Officer Law, Law No. 204 of 1950.
Ministry of Justice, "Criminal Justice in Japan."

A. Nagashima, "Criminal Justice Administration in Japan in the Context of her Tradition and Culture," lecture paper for UNAFEI, 1989.

Rehabilitation Bureau of the Ministry of Justice, "Community-based Treatment of Offenders in Japan," 1985.

"Summary of the White Paper on Crime (1963–1988)." Research and Training Institute of the Ministry of Justice.

UNAFEI, "An Introduction to the Criminal Justice Legislation of Japan" (Tokyo, 1988).

Part IV
Australia

8

Alternatives to Imprisonment in Australia and New Zealand

Dennis Challinger

Australia

Each of Australia's six states and two territories has its own independent criminal justice system, and it is therefore impossible to speak confidently of an Australian position. There are pronounced differences with respect to criminal justice practices within these eight jurisdictions, although they all have common problems. Most notably, all jurisdictions have overcrowding problems in prisons, and most are suffering lengthy delays in the hearing of criminal cases in court.

Some jurisdictions are quicker than others to produce statistical summaries of their activities, which means that complete contemporary data for Australia as a whole are not available. However, the flavor of Australian sentencing can be obtained by consideration of the latest available statistics for the lower courts and superior courts in the largest state, New South Wales. These are set out in table 8.1.

Broadly speaking, over 80 percent of Australia's prisoners are sentenced in magistrates' courts, even though a fairly small percentage of all criminal cases heard in those courts actually result in prison sentences. The predominant use of fines for criminal offenses dealt with in lower courts of New South Wales is fairly typical of sentencing in lower courts throughout Australia. And the fairly restricted use of prison for serious criminal offenses heard in higher courts in South Australia is also consistent with Australia-wide practice.

Those statistics, however, do not reflect the number of Australian adults who are subject to some court order as a result of their offending. Table 8.2 provides statistics showing the distribution of such adults.

Table 8.1   Results of Court Hearings for Criminal Offenses in One Australian Jurisdiction, 1988

Result of Court Hearing	New South Wales Magistrates' Courts (N = 60,817*)	New South Wales Higher Courts (N = 5,089)
Not guilty	6.2%	15.3%
Case dismissed withdrawn, etc.	9.9	8.9
No conviction recorded	7.2	0.4
Rising of court	0.5	0.1
Fine	50.8	0.5
Recognisance	15.1	25.1
Community service order	3.0	7.5
Other	-	2.3
Prison	7.3	39.9
TOTAL:	100.0	100.0

Sources: Court Statistics, 1988 (1989), Bureau of Crime Statistics and Research, NSW Attorney-General's Department, Sydney; New South Wales Higher Criminal Court Statistics 1988 (1990), Bureau of Crime Statistics and Research, NSW Attorney General's Department, Sydney.
*Comprises general offenses, less serious offenses plus drug offenses.

New Zealand

The criminal law in New Zealand is legislated by the national Parliament and is administered by courts of general jurisdiction, that is, the Court of Appeal, the High Court, and district courts. The latter have a summary jurisdiction, but some district court judges are also warranted to preside over jury trials. The 1988 *Annual Report of the New Zealand Department of Justice* indicates that 546,066 summary cases (including traffic offenses) were heard in district courts over a twelve-month period, compared with 825 jury trials of individuals. The High Court heard 651 criminal trials in the same year.

    The results of criminal trials in 1987 were published by the New Zealand Department of Statistics and are summarized in table 8.3. When those statistics are compared with the Australian statistics for higher courts shown in table 8.1, they suggest a greater tendency to imprison. However, New Zealand, through its Criminal Justice Act of 1985, has adopted a philosophy that offending should, as much as possible, be dealt with in the community.

Table 8.2   Adult Offenders under Supervision and Detention Orders, Australia, 1987

	Number	Rate[a]
Non-custodial orders		
Probation	21,167	176.6
Community service orders	7,070	59.0
Other non-custodial orders[b]	2,179	18.2
Total non-custodial orders	30,416	
Total number of persons on non-custodial orders	28,238	235.5
Prison orders		
Remand in custody	1,574	13.1
Sentenced prisoners	10,517	87.7
Total persons in prison	12,113	101.0
Post-prison orders		
After-care probation	1,927	16.1
Pre-release orders	176	1.5
Parole/licence	4,907	40.9
Total post-prison orders	7,037	
Total numbers of persons on post-prison orders	7,028	58.6
Total Supervision and Detention Orders	49,566	
Total Persons[c]	46,907	391.3

Sources: Australian Community-Based Corrections 1987 and Australian Prisoners 1987.

Note: The data in this table relate to June 30, 1987.

[a] Rate per 100,000 adult population (i.e., 17 years and over).

[b] Includes presentence supervision fine option/default orders, attendance center orders, and supervised suspended prison sentences.

[c] Columns do not add to totals because of persons serving more than one type of order.

Table 8.3   Results of Criminal Trials, New Zealand, 1987

Result of Court Hearing	District Court (N = 894[a])	High Court (N = 1139[b])
Not guilty	16.2%	8.9%
No trial or no verdict taken	9.0%	6.1%
Convicted and discharged	0.3%	0.4%
Fine	11.9%	2.1%
Supervision or probation	3.2%	4.2%
Suspended sentence/periodic detention	21.8%	11.1%
Community care or community service	4.8%	2.9%
Prison (and corrective training)	32.8%	64.3%

Source: Justice Statistics 1987 (1989), New Zealand Department of Statistics, Wellington.
[a] Of 918 persons committed for trial, 24 were still awaiting trial. The relevant base is therefore 894.
[b] Of 1,161 persons committed for trial, 18 were still awaiting trial and 4 were found legally insane. The relevant base is therefore 1,139.

Pretrial Stage

Detention

Persons on remand comprise substantial and increasing numbers of prisoners in both Australia and New Zealand. In the latter country, about 11 percent of the prison population are neither convicted nor sentenced (and that figure is an increase from 9.8 percent in the National Prison Census of 1987).

In Australia, at 1 March 1986, 1,604 persons were held on remand awaiting trial in Australian prisons. They comprised 14.8 percent of all prisoners (10,813) held on that day. The corresponding figures three years later (on 1 March 1989) were 1,990 and 16.6 percent, indicating a continuing increase in the number of remand prisoners.

There are marked differences among the Australian jurisdictions with respect to the percentages of remand prisoners. The relevant 1988 figures range from 7.5 percent of Queensland's prison population to 24.1 percent in New South Wales.

All jurisdictions use bail as an instrument to keep a substantial number of persons charged with offenses out of prison. However, in New Zealand a recent *Prison Review* (1989) has pointed out that bail appears to be insufficiently used and recommends that "there is a need for more community-based information to be provided to courts prior to bail decisions" (p. 243). In both countries, many persons who are placed on bail are subject to rigorous requirements as part of that bail, including reporting, morning and night, to their local police station. A variation in South Australia is provided in the Bail Act of 1985, which allows for conditions of bail to include a requirement that such persons place themselves "under the supervision of an officer of the Department of Corrective Services and [agree] to obey the lawful directions of that officer."

Broadly speaking, the vast majority of bailed persons do appear for trial. No statistics are available for those who abscond from bail, but they would constitute a very small percentage of all those bailed.

Discontinuation of Crime Proceedings

In Australia, a very small number of criminal proceedings are discontinued following decisions to do so made by directors of public prosecutions, who are independent functionaries now established in most jurisdictions.

Some other criminal offenders are diverted from the court process in both countries by particular police programs. Many jurisdictions have specific procedures for dealing with youthful offenders, who are officially cautioned or placed before an aid or a screening panel, which may deal with the offense in a more informal way.

A particular diversionary program for adults that has caused the discontinuation of some criminal proceedings is the Shopstealing Warning Program run by the Victoria Police in Australia. It commenced in 1986 and, under certain conditions, allows persons caught stealing from shops to be officially cautioned by police rather than taken through the formal justice process. At one level it is unlikely that shop thieves who met the criteria for the program would have been sentenced to prison if they had gone to court. However, such a sentence is a theoretical possibility.

Trial Stage

Introductory Comments

Sentencers in Australia and New Zealand now work under a general instruction to use imprisonment sparingly. That instruction has received some legislative embodiment. For instance, the Victorian Penalties and Sentences Act of 1985 requires, in section 11, that a court must not pass a sentence of imprisonment on a person unless the court, having considered all other available sentences, is satisfied that no other sentence is appropriate in all the circumstances of the case.

A further requirement is placed on sentencers in the lower (magistrates) courts by section 12, which states:

Where a Magistrates' Court passes a sentence of imprisonment on a person, the Magistrates' Court—

a. must state in writing the reasons for its decision; and
b. must cause those reasons to be entered in the records of the court.

Those two requirements impress upon sentencers the necessity to consider alternatives to imprisonment in a considered and conscientious way. Implicit in the legislation is the notion of a hierarchy of sentences, and that has been most recently addressed by a Victorian government committee on sentencing, which makes the following recommendation in this regard:

It is recommended that the following be a list of sentences in order of severity:

- A term of imprisonment
- A term of detention in a Youth Training Centre
- A term of imprisonment (whether suspended or not) combined with a Community Based Order
- A bond under division 3 of part 4
- A wholly or partly suspended sentence of imprisonment
- A Community Based Order containing a community service condition
- A Community Based Order that does not contain a community service condition
- A fine that is substantial to the offender; an order requiring the offender to pay an amount of compensation that is substantial to the offender
- A fine that is moderate to the offender; an order requiring the offender to pay an amount of compensation that is moderate to the offender
- A fine that is small to moderate to the offender; an order requiring the offender to pay an amount of compensation that is small to moderate to the offender
- A fine that is small to moderate to the offender with no conviction recorded
- A discharge without conviction

[Note] The Committee believes that it is not possible to define fines and compensation orders in more exact detail than using the terms small, moderate or substantial. This is so because the principle which applies to the fixing of fines is that the financial circumstances of the offender must be taken into account when doing so. The Committee expects that the courts through guideline judgments, and the (proposed) Judicial Sentencing Board through guidelines, will assist the courts in determining the meaning of moderate, substantial or small for these purposes. (Victorian Sentencing Committee 1988, p. 364).

While alternatives to imprisonment are now widespread in Australia, in the words of Chan and Zdenkowski (1986), "Apart from probation and parole, many of the so-called community-based sentencing and release options have had a rather limited history." The table those authors provide to support that proposition is shown here as table 8.4.

Table 8.4   Australia—Community Based Options by State/Territory (Approximate date of introduction)

Opt.	Probation[a]	Parole/ Licence	Work Release	Periodic Detention	Community Service
FED	1960	1967/1960	-	1982[b]	1982[b]
NSW	[1961][c]	1966/1900 or earlier	1969	1970	1979
VIC	1958	1958	1975	1973[d]	[1982]
QLD	1959	[1959]	1969	1970[e]	[1981]
SA	1913	1969	-	-	1981
WA	[1965]	1963	1970	-	1976
TAS	1973	1975	-	-	1971
NT	[1972]	1971	-	-	[1979]
ACT	1929[c]	1976	-	-	1985

Note: The dates refer to the year the relevant legislation was passed or dates of commencement (which are noted in square brackets).
[a] In the sense of supervised release. Distinguish from legislation providing for "good behavior" bonds, which has a much longer history.
[b] Not proclaimed, except in the ACT, where periodic detention centers are not currently available.
[c] Probation orders based on bond legislation.
[d] Never implemented; restyled as attendance center orders.
[e] Repealed May 15, 1984.

Chapter 8

Short-term Imprisonment and Alternatives

There is no restriction on the minimum length of imprisonment that an Australian or New Zealand court can impose. In most, it is still possible for a person to be detained "until the rising of the court," which effectively leads to an offender's detention for a matter of hours. However, that option is very selectively used.

Some indication of the extent of short-term imprisonment is provided by the fact that, at any time, around 1 percent of Australia's prisoners are serving sentences of a month or less. At any time, sentences of three months and less provide around 4 percent of the prison populations in both Australia and New Zealand. This occurs despite the fact that some jurisdictions operate under legislation explicitly requiring courts to impose imprisonment only as a "last resort."

Mechanisms to allow for a finding of guilt without the imposition of a substantial penalty are available in the courts. It is possible for sentencers to formally admonish offenders before returning them to the community without their being subject to active official oversight or supervision. This is achieved through a range of possible findings by the court, including formal dismissal of the case, discharge (either absolute or conditional), adjournment, good behavior bonds, and recognizances.

All those require offenders to agree to conform to certain conditions, the chief of which is not to offend again. Failing to meet the conditions set by the court can lead to further court action.

An Australian example of such a mechanism is section 556A of the New South Wales Crimes Act of 1900, which allows the court,

> having regard to the character, antecedents, age, health, or mental condition of the person charged, or to the trivial nature of the offense, or to the extenuating circumstances under which the offense was committed, or to any other matter which the court thinks it proper to consider, [to decide that] it is inexpedient to inflict any punishment, or any other than a nominal punishment, or that it is expedient to release the offender on probation, the court may, without proceeding to conviction, make an order either (a) dismissing the charge; or (b) discharging the offender conditionally on his entering into a recognizance, with or without sureties, to be of good behavior and to appear for conviction and sentence when called on at any time during such period, not exceeding three years, as may be specified in the order.

A person convicted of an offense in New South Wales may also be re-placed on a bail order, with rigorous conditions, pending formal sentence. This possibility is established under common law and basically allows an offender's behavior under community-based supervision to be assessed.

After some period of time, the offender appears in court for formal sentencing, and his or her behavior while on that order is very relevant to the final sentence.

In early 1988, the Northern Territory commenced, as a sentencing option, a home detention program specifically to keep appropriate offenders out of prison. The program involves a complex assessment phase involving welfare personnel, police, and thorough lifestyle checks, after which offenders assessed as suitable have their prison terms suspended in favor of home detention with conditions imposed by a court or the director of Correctional Services. These conditions may include full or partial abstinence from alcohol, counseling or treatment for substance abuse, or any reasonable condition as the authorities see fit. Offenders and others concerned by the imposition of a home detention order are consulted, and offenders' consent must be freely given before they can participate in the program.

While it is intended that home detention be used for offenders who pose no known threat to others, it is nevertheless intended to be a punitive sanction. All offenders on home detention are subject to strict, and random, face-to-face surveillance, both at home and at their places of employment, by paid part-time surveillance officers recruited from the local community. Surveillance is now supplemented, but not replaced, by electronic monitoring.

Many community and government bodies are involved in supporting the operation of home detention and in assisting offenders to comply with conditions and successfully complete the order. Health, welfare, and law enforcement personnel are consulted for advice and assistance. Offenders subject to tests or conditions have the necessary support mechanisms put in place according to their needs. Police officers are required from time to time, upon receiving information from Correctional Services, to conduct formal breath tests on offenders.

The legislation establishing this program was passed in late 1987, and, by early March 1990, 127 offenders had been placed on the program in lieu of imprisonment. Home detention is managed very carefully as a direct alternative to prison, and offenders who breach their residential or other conditions are dealt with swiftly.

Fines

As indicated earlier, fines continue to be the most frequently used noncustodial sentencing option in Australian and New Zealand courts of summary jurisdiction. A further monetary penalty that can be imposed, and that may help avoid a prison sentence, relates to penalties by way of compensation and reparation.

In Australia, these may be in the form of (a) a restitution order, which refers to the power of the criminal court to order the return, *in specie*, of property to its proper owner; (b) a compensation order, which relates to the provision of monetary or other compensation for loss, damage, or injury sustained as a consequence of crime; (c) compensation for criminal injuries, which is not necessarily connected with the court process in which conviction is obtained or dependent on the obtaining of a conviction; (d) an order to pay costs to reimburse the informant or the prosecutor for the expense of the proceedings (Fox and Freiberg 1985, pp. 178–79). In New Zealand, reparation orders are becoming increasingly used. In 1987, 18 percent of convicted property offenders were also sentenced to reparation.

While most fines are paid, there are still a number of fined persons who, for one reason or another, do not pay. This has led to some recent legislative action in Australia to reduce the number of persons being sent to prison in default of payment of their fines. Mostly, this has been directed to creating alternative default mechanisms for nonpayment of fines. A number of jurisdictions now have fine-option orders that require offenders to complete some community service in lieu of payment of the fine. The success of these schemes to divert offenders from prison can be seen from the fact that in October 1988, 388 Australians were received into prison for nonpayment of fines, compared with 1,000 two years earlier. (New South Wales' figures dropped from 327 to 12 in that period.) Notwithstanding that, at any given time the prison populations still include some persons who have only failed to pay fines. The Australian National Prison Census for June 1987 shows 2.2 percent of the sentenced population being imprisoned for fine default only. The comparable figure in the New Zealand Prison Census of November 1987 was 1.6 percent.

Suspension of Sentence or of Enforcement, Including Probation

Criminal courts in New Zealand are able to conclude a case by ordering the offender "to come up for sentence if called upon," and this can be seen to be a variation of a suspended sentence. Such sentences are available in some Australian jurisdictions but are as yet fairly modestly used. It is possible for sentences to be partially suspended, or for supervision to be ordered as a condition of suspension. Overall, Australian courts still favor the use of either unsupervised release or supervised release through probation or other orders.

Probation has long been a mainstay of Australian sentencers, as indicated in table 8.2, which shows that 49 percent of all offenders under some form of supervision or detention order were on probation. There are no features that distinguish Australian probation practice from that around the world.

On the other hand, probation in New Zealand has undergone some change since the Criminal Justice Act of 1985. That act introduced the concept of "supervision," which replaced probation. Supervision places limited restrictions on offenders' freedom and is directed toward the social reintegration of offenders, often through their being required to undertake specified courses of education or training.

A further New Zealand program introduced in the 1985 act is the community care order. It aims to provide opportunities for offenders to receive treatment for diagnosed problems, to encourage the social integration of offenders, and to increase the responsibility taken by community groups for offenders. In practice, the order has been underutilized by sentencers, as can be seen from table 8.3.

Community care includes the distinctly New Zealand initiative of Maatua Whangai, which reflects the partnership between Maoris (the indigenous New Zealanders) and the Pakeha (white or Euro–New Zealanders). It allows the use of the Maori extended family system, the Whanau, to take greater responsibility for their families or children, who often become involved with the state agencies.

Corrective or Compulsory Labor

No jurisdiction in Australia or New Zealand employs corrective or compulsory labor as practiced in some Eastern European countries. There are, however, obligations to work inherent in community service orders (see the next section).

Community Service

As table 8.4 indicates, all Australian jurisdictions now have community service orders, and New Zealand introduced them in 1981. While there are variations in actual procedures, basically offenders placed on such orders are required to attend work sites for a fixed number of hours over a fixed period of months. Many offenders find that work is a positive experience, but breaches of the orders are dealt with firmly by the courts.

Other Alternatives

In an attempt to simplify the sentencing task, the Australian state of Victoria has recently established the community-based order, which brings the elements of probation, community service, and the attendance center program under one general heading.

The order is legislatively defined in section 29 of the Penalties and Sentences Act of 1985. It sets out the following six "core" conditions:

a. That the offender does not commit another offense during the period of the order

b. That the offender reports to a community corrections center

c. That the offender reports to and receives visits from a community corrections officer

d. That the offender reports any change of address or employment

e. That the offender does not leave the state without permission

f. That the offender obeys all lawful instructions of community corrections officers

The act also provides eight optional "program" conditions, which give sentencers considerable flexibility. In practice, the Victorian Office of Corrections provides professional staff at the court, and, after interviewing the offender, they recommend which if any, of the following eight conditions are appropriate for that offender:

1. Attendance for educational and other programs for a period of one to twelve months, with up to two attendances, or up to eight hours, per week, and an aggregate period of attendance of between twenty and four hundred hours

2. Unpaid community work for between ten and five hundred hours, to be performed within twelve months

3. Supervision by a community corrections officer

4. Assessment or treatment for alcohol or drug addiction, or medical, psychological, or psychiatric assessment or treatment

5. Testing for alcohol or drug use

6. Residence at a specified place

7. Nonassociation with specified persons

8. Any other condition that the court considers necessary or desirable

Postconviction Stage

Semiliberty or Semidetention

Work release from prison is available on a limited basis in some Australian prisons. Under such programs, prisoners are released during the day (usually toward the latter part of their sentence) to perform work outside the prison in jobs that are not connected with prison industries. The evenings and weekends are spent in prison. However, work release is applicable only in the states of New South Wales and, to a much lesser extent, Queensland. Some other jurisdictions have legislative provisions for work release, but it has not been used for many years in any other state.

New South Wales also has available periodic detention, whereby prisoners are required to return to prison at the end of the working week and spend the weekends there. This permits offenders in employment to retain their jobs. In December 1989, 667 prisoners were detained under this arrangement.

Most jurisdictions have the power in their prison legislation to grant temporary leave for specified purposes such as attending a funeral or seeking medical treatment. However, in two states, Queensland and South Australia, these leave provisions are utilized to enable home detention of some prisoners in the last weeks of their sentence.

The Queensland program has been going longest and is built upon the existing leave-of-absence provisions. It commenced in May 1986, and in its first six months of operation 123 offenders had been released from prison to serve their remaining sentence in home detention.

Prisoners are required to make formal application to be placed in the program. They have to satisfy various criteria, the most critical of which are that they have less than four months of their sentence to serve and that they have a definite place at which to reside. They have to agree to random personal supervision, which is undertaken by prison officers dressed in civilian clothes and driving unmarked government cars. Telephone supervision is also used.

In addition, prisoners (for that is their legal status) on the program have to participate in prescribed activities depending upon their individual problems, needs, and goals. These include family, drug, and alcohol counseling, self-development workshops, and fitness and recreational activities. The program is thus designed to provide prisoners with positive incentives and opportunities to reestablish their lives in a practical and supported manner in the community. In recent times, the program has been underused, despite the fact that failures on the scheme have been few and relate to failure to meet conditions of release rather than the commission of further criminal activities.

The South Australia program was formally established by special legislation in 1986. It does not incorporate the program component that is a critical part of Queensland's program, but apart from that it is similar. To date, almost two hundred prisoners have been placed on the program, which may utilize electronic monitoring equipment in the near future.

A number of jurisdictions have aftercare probation, which results from a split sentence of a prison sentence with a specified nonprobation term.

Conditional Release or Parole

Parole continues to be made available to many Australian and New Zealand prisoners. All parole boards are granted power to release an offender prior to the expiration of the full (or maximum) sentence imposed by the court.

In some jurisdictions, courts can fix minimum sentences that must be served before parole can be granted. However, despite the apparent success of those on parole—over 70 percent do not reoffend—parole procedures are under review in some jurisdictions, mainly reflecting a public disillusionment with what is seen as the eroding of prison sentences through early release.

Western Australia has recently introduced changes that allow sentencers to say whether offenders should be eligible for parole but without saying how long the nonparole period should be. In any event, the maximum period of parole is legislatively restricted to two years, after which the remainder of the original sentence is effectively canceled.

A wide range of activities involving temporary release on parole of New Zealand prisoners is available, although activities are restricted for those convicted of violent offenses.

In Victoria, a formalized prerelease scheme was introduced in 1985. Under it, the parole board is empowered to grant a prerelease permit to a prisoner serving a sentence of twelve months or more, provided that at least three, but no more than twelve months of the prisoner's sentence remain to be served and that the permit period does not exceed one-third of the sentence being served. Conditions as to place of residence and reporting to a corrections center are usually required.

In some jurisdictions, there is an executive power to release an offender on license (subject to certain specified conditions) prior to the expiration of the full sentence specified by the court. New South Wales, for instance, has a release on license board as well as a parole board.

Other Measures

New Zealand and all Australian jurisdictions have the ability to pardon or exercise a royal prerogative of mercy. This power is normally exercised by the governor in council, which in practice involves the governor acting upon the advice of the relevant cabinet.

References

J. Chan and G. Zdenkowski. "Just Alternatives—Part 1." *Australian and New Zealand Journal of Criminology,* vol. 19 (1986), pp. 67–90.

R. Fox and A. Freiberg. *Sentencing: State and Federal Law in Victoria.* Melbourne: Oxford University Press, 1985.

Prison Review, Te Ara Hou: The New Way, Report of the Ministerial Committee of Inquiry into the [New Zealand] Prisons System (Chair: Sir Clinton Roper). Wellington: Government Printer, 1989.

Victorian Sentencing Committee. *Sentencing.* Melbourne: Government Printer, 1988.

9

An Australian Case Study: The Northern Territory Home Detention Scheme

Dennis Challinger

For many years, the Northern Territory of Australia has had an imprisonment rate many times the Australian rate. By way of example, in October 1988 the Northern Territory had an imprisonment rate of 231 per 100,000 population, compared with a figure of 72 per 100,000 for Australia as a whole. However, the Northern Territory rate is now actually declining, the respective rates for October 1987 being 271 and 74, for October 1986, 271 and 70, and for October 1985, 264 and 68. The decrease in rates is a result of a commitment by Northern Territory Corrective Services (NTCS) to reduce imprisonment rates in the territory.

Some remarkable successes have already been achieved in this area. Receptions into territory prisons declined by 25 percent in two years from 1986, specifically as a result of conditional liberty programs, with the fine-default program having the most dramatic result.

That program allows fine defaulters to satisfy monetary penalties by carrying out unpaid work in the community under the community service order (CSO) program instead of undergoing a prison term. It also permits the use of the CSO program by persons who do not have the resources to pay their fines and who therefore are potential fine-default prisoners.

In addition, great emphasis has been placed on diverting offenders from prison through providing sentencers with a range of viable noncustodial sentencing options. Sentencers are assisted in using those options by the provision of court-based correctional staff to give professional advice. This approach reflects the NTCS view that it is better to reduce the number of people entering the prison system by action at the "front end" of the sentencing process. So-called back-end responses aimed at reducing the number of people in prison include early release schemes for prisoners, but they can be seen as interfering with the judicial process through reducing a prisoner's sentence. It is the basic philosophy of avoiding imprisonment at all that explains why home detention is available to Northern Territory courts quite specifically as an alternative to prison.

Home Detention in Australia

There are other home detention schemes operating in Australia, but generally they can be seen as "back-end" solutions to prison crowding problems. In the state of Queensland, a home detention program operates, and it allows selected prisoners to serve up to the last four months of their sentences at home. Over a thousand prisoners have been placed on the program, which involves daily contact by supervising prison officers in plain clothes. Only 5 percent of those on the program have technically breached conditions, and only 1 percent have been charged with offenses while on the program.

The state of South Australia enacted specific legislation in 1987 that allows for "the release of selected prisoners at the discretion of the Chief Executive Officer into approved residences in the community where they are subject to intense supervision, special conditions and curfew." Over two hundred prisoners have been placed in this program in the final stages of their prison sentences. South Australia was the first Australian jurisdiction to use electronic supervision in the program. As with the Queensland program, this home detention is not available to a sentencing court but administered by the correctional agency.

The Northern Territory Home Detention Order (HDO) is, by contrast, only available to a court. That the HDO is an alternative to prison is evidenced by section 19A(1) of the Criminal Law (Conditional Release of Offenders) Act. It states:

> Where an offender is convicted of an offense against a law of the Territory, the court by which the offender is convicted may, if it thinks fit, by order sentence that offender to a term of imprisonment but direct that the sentence be suspended on the offender entering into a home detention order.

Clearly then, a sentencer has to not only decide that a prison term is required or warranted, but actually pass such a sentence before suspending it in favor of a home detention order. This not only reduces the chance of net widening, but also clearly establishes the consequences of breaching the HDO.

Making a Home Detention Order

A court cannot make a home detention order unless the offender gives consent and the director of NTCS provides a report. Section 19B(1) of the legislation requires this report to state that

1. suitable arrangements are available for the offender to reside at the premises or place specified in the report;
2. the premises or place specified in the report is suitable for the purposes of a home detention order; and
3. the making of the home detention order is not likely to inconvenience or put at risk other persons living in those premises or at that place or the community generally.

For the purposes of making that report, the director may "take into account the views of those members of the community who, in the opinion of the Director, may be affected by the making of the home detention order." The two groups in the community who would be most affected by an offender's being placed on a home detention order are the offender's own family and the victim (if any) of the offense.

One criticism of home detention is that it places an unfair burden on offenders' families to themselves act as jailers. In the Northern Territory, great efforts are made to ensure that families understand and are comfortable with the concept of home detention. To date, the offenses for which home detention has been used have not involved angry victims. However, the director's report acknowledges that victims of an offense might have real concerns if the prison sentence were not activated, and their views can be considered in the assessment process. Great care is taken in the assessment process to eliminate the possibility of net widening, and advice is provided to courts in a similar way to a presentence report. Home detention assessments usually take a week to prepare and must include

- welfare checks to ensure that problems of child abuse and domestic violence are canvassed,
- previous convictions are recorded by the police,
- acknowledgment of the offender's obligations,
- the full consent of those others resident at the place of detention, and
- consent of the employer to random checks at the workplace.

Surveillance

The surveillance of those on HDOs is an important and vital part of the program, and the powers given to the officers by the legislation reflect this. Section 19G(2) reads:

A surveillance officer may, at any time

a. without a warrant
    i. enter premises or a place in or at which an offender is in accordance with a home detention order, residing; or

269

> ii. search those premises or any building at that place, or the
> offender, for the purposes of determining whether the offender is
> in breach of the order; or
> b. require the offender under a home detention order to undergo
> such tests as the Surveillance Officer thinks fit to determine
> whether the offender is in breach of the order.

The tests referred to in (b) above may include a test to determine the presence of alcohol or any other drug in the offender's body. In practice, surveillance officers (or police) can, on a regular or random basis, use hand-held breath-testing apparatus to test whether home detainees have been drinking alcohol, although a formal breath test administered by the police is necessary to provide evidence for a court. Random urine tests can be required where a home detainee is suspected of using drugs. (Regulation 3 [k] provides that home detainees are not to consume alcohol or any other drug without approval from the director of NTCS.)

In early 1988, thirty-three surveillance officers were recruited and trained. These paid, part-time officers were selected from over 250 applicants. Their selection was largely based on maturity and reliability, and the selection process included Northern Territory police security and character checks. A further nine surveillance officers were recruited and trained in early 1989, slightly decreasing the average age of forty from the first intake. Approximately a quarter are female.

Most of these officers have past involvement in discipline-oriented occupations or are still so employed, while others have no current careers, due to family commitments or retirement. Surveillance officers are paid on contract rates and are reimbursed for the use of their private vehicles and telephones.

The surveillance process involves senior staff preparing a roster of face-to-face visits in advance and, depending on availability, selecting a surveillance officer to carry out the visits. Visits are made to places of residence and work and to other places where the offender is permitted to be, and telephone checks are also made. Since January 1990, electronic monitoring of offenders has been available.

Surveillance rosters are assisted by computerized random selector, and visits now average three in any twenty-four-hour period. The minimum is two visits, while up to six have been made in cases where a home detainee's behavior or movements have raised suspicions about his or her activities. Offenders are regularly visited in close succession and frequently between midnight and dawn.

Surveillance officers carry out visits by themselves, using a specially prepared contact book for each offender. The book is countersigned by the offender at the time of the visit. Surveillance officers are expected to carry out visits at the times allocated and are themselves checked on to ensure compliance. They are expected to report any suspicious circumstances immediately. No home detainee is aware of which officer will visit, or when or where.

Only in exceptional circumstances will home detainees now be given the necessary written permission to consume alcohol during the course of their HDOs. In the early months of the program, many home detainees were permitted to consume alcohol in their own homes only and to never exceed 0.08 percent blood-alcohol concentration. The 0.08 percent blood-alcohol content level was used to teach offenders to control their alcohol intake to within legal driving limits (although in practice that proved to be virtually impossible). The first offender who tested at a level higher than 0.08 percent was breached immediately, resulting in his being in custody within ten minutes for an appearance in court the next morning. The swiftness of breach action is a most important feature of the program.

Electronic Monitoring

The Northern Territory government now considers the electronic monitoring of home detention offenders as a realistic adjunct to face-to-face surveillance for suitable offenders. One problem with face-to-face visits is that they often invade the privacy of other residents at the offender's home and, due to their random nature at all hours, can wake children and neighbors.

There is no intention to replace face-to-face surveillance with an electronic alternative but to balance the use of

- face-to-face surveillance,
- one-to-one counseling,
- active electronics (e.g., random phone calls), and
- passive electronics (e.g., radio transmitters).

The mix of the four will naturally be dependent on the circumstances of each offender, and the formula will be commensurate with program objectives and offender needs.

As the Northern Territory Department of Law has advised that the placement of any device on an offender (even with his or her consent) could be construed as a technical assault and, at the least, an invasion of privacy, relevant legislation is being prepared to specifically permit the use of electronic surveillance devices. For the present, participation in electronic monitoring is on a strictly voluntary basis.

Chapter 9

The Use of Home Detention

The home detention program started in February 1988 and has shown steady progress. By March 1990, 127 persons had been on the program, and 102 had successfully completed their periods of home detention. This constitutes a success rate of over 90 percent. There was a total of forty-three breaches amongst these 127 cases, but in only 9 cases was the HDO revoked.

As a guide to its cost-effectiveness, should the home detention program involve one hundred offenders per year, with an average of seventy actual prison days each after remissions, then the saving in prisoner days will be more than 5 percent.

The main offenses for which HDOs are imposed are alcohol-related driving offenses (68 percent) and driving while disqualified (15 percent). Males predominate among the home detainees to date (90 percent), 54 percent are single, and 50 percent are aged 27 or under. The average period of a home detention order is 3.15 months.

A Positive Sentence

The possible real benefits of placing an offender on a home detention order are illustrated by the following, not atypical, actual cases provided by NTCS.

Bill Jones, a home detainee looking at six months' imprisonment should he breach his home detention order (of the same length), resented being placed on restrictions by the home detention team. In addition, he did not consider he needed the alcohol education and control counseling he was directed by the court to undertake.

Jones, during the first months of his order, was rude and resentful when told he would not be granted permission to go to the park with his dog, visit a friend, or engage in other activities clearly not permissible for a person detained at home. He had constant excuses for failing to attend the arranged appointments at the counseling center. When told that no further excuse would be accepted for failing to comply with this particular condition, Jones requested a change of agencies and suggested a different counseling arrangement. Not only was this a perfectly acceptable alternative, he was commended for his initiative.

After "behaving like a child" in the first two sessions, Jones related to his counselor and accepted a number of premises he had rejected out of hand until that stage. He started to find the truth in the statements offered to him in that, if one adopts a positive attitude when relating to others, one will be treated in a more positive and friendly manner oneself. He also accepted that considering others is most helpful in personal relationships and, indeed, that one benefits from accepting responsibility for one's own behavior and predicament when attempting to influence future directions.

The change in Jones's attitude was dramatic and noticed by all involved in his case, not the least his spouse. His final comment to NTCS was, "Home detention has been the best thing that could happen to me."

Fred Smith (age forty-four) was convicted of a fourth offense of driving with a blood-level exceeding 0.08 percent and was sentenced to two months' imprisonment suspended upon entering a home detention order for the same period. He has served prison terms in the past and has one breach-of-bond conviction. Smith is a married man, lives in a Housing Commission home, has two dependents, and owns a small business that employs two others. He has been assessed as having a middle-order alcohol dependence. Mrs. Smith was stressed by personal and business financial problems, which were a contributing factor to an expected family breakup. She stated, however, that she would support her husband on home detention during the HDO to try to keep their lives together.

Smith commenced the HDO and received random surveillance and regular breath testing and alcohol counseling. During the term of the HDO, eviction proceedings were commenced for rent arrears but were stayed after representations from NTCS.

Although the HDO was only for a two-month period, some positive results were evident at its conclusion. Smith's financial position had improved, his employees received back pay, the Housing Commission was paid, and Mrs. Smith had decided to stay on and try to keep the marriage together. Smith now claimed to know how much he could drink before he exceeded the driving limit. He also claimed that his health (high blood pressure) had improved and that he wished it to continue to improve. An unofficial contact with Smith, three months after the HDO was complete, confirmed the above.

Smith's case indicates that even in the early stages of a program such as home detention, resources and support can be provided that are not possible in a prison environment. If home detention had not existed, then at best the offender's situation would be the same after his imprisonment, and the worst (and most likely) scenario would have included no home, no family, and no business.

Home Detention for Indigenous People

The Northern Territory faces a unique problem in prison management, as the majority of its prisoners (70 percent) are of Aboriginal descent. In addition, prisoners tend to serve comparatively short periods of incarceration, and alcohol is often a related factor. The difficulties posed by indigenous prisoners are a cause for concern in many parts of the world. In the Northern Territory, where indigenous Australians often live in remote communities, a sentence of imprisonment simply removes them further from their community.

A high priority has therefore been placed on further establishing home detention in remote Aboriginal communities, and recruitment of surveillance officers is currently underway in Groote Eylandt, an island off the coast but part of the Northern Territory and peopled entirely by Aboriginals.

Two traditional Aboriginal men, both of whom had severe alcohol problems, have successfully completed HDOs. The first man, from Yirrkala (a community on the Gulf of Carpentaria), completed the Alcohol Dependence Treatment Unit's three-week residential program, followed by weekly follow-up meetings as part of his HDO. This man had a long history of alcohol-related crime, including nine offenses of driving while disqualified, and completed an HDO of six months' duration, the last six weeks of which were served back at Yirrkala.

The other Aboriginal was from Bagot (an Aboriginal community near Darwin). He served a four-month order for driving offenses, conditional upon spending the first two months at a hostel for Aboriginals with alcohol abuse problems. In the event, arrangements made for supervision back at Bagot proved unsuitable, and the order was completed back at the hostel.

A further six Aboriginals have been placed on HDOs, but all have been residents of Darwin. Nevertheless, it is the intention of the NTCS to examine every possible avenue for Aboriginal involvement, in both urban and rural areas. Few major problems exist with residential or surveillance provisions in urban areas, and the use of hostels is also currently being examined. Rural communities, however, do pose greater logistical obstacles, especially through peer group pressure, residential problems, and the lack of substance abuse programs or established surveillance procedures.

The process of trying out the program in a rural community will take time and a good deal of community cooperation, in order that program credibility is not placed in jeopardy. It may well result in being viable in some, but not all, Aboriginal communities. (In fact, one Euro-Australian is currently serving a home detention order in a remote Aboriginal community where he is working on a building project.)

Summary

In effect, home detention is an offender treatment program whereby certain types of offenders can undergo their "prison" sentences at home. Home detainees undertake to comply with conditions that severely restrict movement and activities beyond attending employment, rehabilitation programs, and so on. Notwithstanding these restrictions, "exit interviews" with home detainees and their families often indicate that the HDO has been a positive and beneficial experience for them.

Fundamental to the success of the home detention program is the perception on the part of courts, police, offenders, and the community at large that home detainees will be subject to strict surveillance under a system that cannot be circumvented.

Surveillance officers are employed to monitor home detainees, and while they have certain powers, essentially their function is checking that home detainees are at home. Any breach of home detention conditions leads to a prompt return to court.

As public confidence in the program grows, it can be expected that sentencers will be more likely to use the sanction. But the legislation prevents the program from being used for offenders who do not merit a prison sentence. Any increase in numbers of offenders with home detention orders will have to come from those who would have otherwise gone to prison. It is therefore undeniably a valuable alternative to prison.

Part V
Europe

Noncustodial Sanctions in Europe: Regional Overview

Matti Joutsen and Norman Bishop

There is wide consensus in Europe that certain offenses and certain types of offenders merit imprisonment.[1] Even so, all European governments consider imprisonment to be a sanction that has serious negative effects on the prisoner and his or her social situation. It is also a costly sanction to administer. For these reasons alone it should not be used with offenders for whom an alternative sanction would serve as well.

Skepticism concerning the prison as a place of treatment has now become a part of formal criminal policy in virtually every European country. In the almost totally unanimous replies to a questionnaire from the Helsinki Institute for Crime Prevention and Control affiliated with the United Nations (HEUNI), imprisonment is repeatedly described as a sanction that cannot achieve any improvement in the great majority of prisoners or in their social situations. On the contrary, there is widespread awareness that the prospects for satisfactory adjustment in society are frequently made worse by imprisonment.[2]

The respondents to the HEUNI survey also make reference to the high costs of running a prison system—both the running costs and the costs of a large-scale prison building program. Today, the economic resources available for necessary public services are subject to severe constraints. Moreover, to the extent that the prison system is required to take in more prisoners than it can deal with, overcrowding results, further hampering attempts to ease the negative consequences of imprisonment.[3]

The Current Use of Noncustodial Sanctions[4]

Of measures that imply considerable supervision and control of the offender (suspended or conditional imprisonment with supervision, probation, community service, reformative and educational labor, special forms of treatment, and local banishment), the most common in Europe are probation and suspended or conditional incarcerative sanction with supervision or the condition of treatment. Of all the countries responding to the questionnaire, only Finland and Romania did not indicate that such measures were available in their criminal justice system.[5]

Community service, as a separate sanction, is a fairly recent European innovation. It was first introduced in England and Wales in 1975. The sanction involves performance of a certain number of hours of unpaid work for the good of the community. Its use has spread to the Federal Republic of Germany, France, Ireland, Italy, Luxembourg, Northern Ireland, Portugal, and Scotland, and in an experimental stage to Denmark, the Netherlands, and Norway. Belgium, Cyprus, Finland, Sweden, and Switzerland are presently considering its adoption.[6] A corresponding sanction exists in Bulgaria, the German Democratic Republic, Hungary, Poland, and the USSR. The main difference between the two is that community service is performed during leisure hours, while the latter sanction is performed at the normal place of work (and thus relies heavily on the supportive and supervisory input of co-workers).[7]

Open, ambulant, or contract treatment was noted in less than one-half of the countries: Bulgaria, Denmark, France, the Netherlands, Poland, Portugal, Sweden, Switzerland, the USSR, and Yugoslavia. *Suspension of driving or other license* as a principal sanction was noted by Bulgaria, Denmark, France, Hungary, Ireland, Italy, the Netherlands, Poland, Scotland, Sweden, and the USSR. *Deprivation of certain rights and/or removal of professional status* was noted by Bulgaria, Denmark, Finland, France, Hungary, the Netherlands, Norway, Poland, Scotland, Sweden, and the USSR.

In addition, the majority of countries reported that they had measures involving control and supervision that could not be fitted into the above categories (see the Annex).

The state is less intervenient in the noncustodial alternatives, which in essence have the character of a penal warning. These are customarily used where the offense is not grave and especially where the offender is of previously good character. They are known by a variety of names, among them *admonition, absolute discharge, conditional discharge, conditional sentence without supervision,* and *simple suspension of sentence.*[8]

The most common penal warnings were *findings of guilt with no sanction imposed* (all except Austria, Belgium, Bulgaria, the Federal Republic of Germany, Greece, Italy, Norway, Romania, and Switzerland) and *conditional or suspended sentence with no supervision or control* (all reporting countries with the exception of the Federal Republic of Germany, the German Democratic Republic, Malta, Scotland, and Yugoslavia). *Admonitions* were possible in somewhat over half of the countries. Seven countries reported other sanctions involving monetary payments or penal warnings.

State intervention in the offender's life is at a minimum where monetary payments are concerned. All European countries use *fines*, which are the best known and most used of this category of sanction.[9] *Compensatory payments* (compensation orders and the like) were noted by Bulgaria, Cyprus, Denmark, England and Wales, the German Democratic Republic, Greece, Ireland, Malta, the Netherlands, Northern Ireland, Poland, Scotland, Sweden, and the USSR. Somewhat over half of the countries noted *confiscation of personal property* as an independent sanction.[10]

There are wide provisions for the combination of custodial with noncustodial sanctions and the combination of different noncustodial alternatives. Where the offense is of a certain seriousness or where the offender's criminal record is serious, a single noncustodial sanction may be considered insufficient or otherwise inappropriate.[11]

Noncustodial Sanctions and Practice

It is difficult to make generalizations regarding the extent to which the potential for noncustodial sanctions is being used in practice. However, the very fact that all European states agree that wider use should be made of these sanctions suggests that courts continue to sentence offenders to prison even though a noncustodial sanction would be available and appropriate.[12]

In the responses to the HEUNI questionnaire, many European countries noted that they have amended their legislation in order to expand the use of fines as an alternative to imprisonment. In Austria, for example, the court is required to impose a fine instead of imprisonment for up to six months where the offense is punishable with imprisonment for at most five years.[13] A similar effort in the Federal Republic of Germany has been only partly successful.[14] Responses from Greece, Portugal, Belgium, France, and Switzerland cited other examples.[15]

Problems with Noncustodial Sanctions

A number of problems have been pinpointed in the effort to encourage wider use of noncustodial sanctions in Europe.

One is related to sentencing. The court must make a choice among a number of alternatives, using multiple criteria that relate the seriousness of the offense to what are deemed to be the relevant characteristics of the offender and the penal value of the noncustodial sanctions available, either singly or in combination.[16] Also, courts frequently work under pressure of time and therefore tend to favor sanctions that do not require time for the collection, presentation, and assessment of social inquiries about the offender and his or her situation. Furthermore, judges are more familiar with assessing juridical information than with assessing data drawn from the social sciences.[17]

A second problem relates to the availability of resources to implement the sanction. If the court lacks confidence in the operational efficiency of the services responsible for the implementation of noncustodial sanctions, it will probably be less inclined to make use of those sanctions.[18]

A third area concerns the attitudes of various parties (including the public, the courts, professional groups, and the victim) toward noncustodial sanctions. In view of the results of research, there is reason to think that precedents, general guidelines, and sentencing conferences are not fully adequate. It is important to involve professional groups in the drafting and introduction of new legislation on sanctions from the outset.[19]

A fourth area of concern relates to the possible dysfunctions of wider use of noncustodial sanctions, in particular the so-called net-widening effect. Statistical evidence from various countries clearly suggests that noncustodial sanctions either are used far less than they might be or, when used, are substitutes for other noncustodial sanctions and not for imprisonment. In addition, when suspended sentences are pronounced, the period of imprisonment imposed may be longer than if an unconditional sentence to imprisonment were to be used. In the event of activation of the original sentence, the offender can therefore go to prison for longer than would otherwise have been the case.[20]

Promotion of Noncustodial Sanctions

The European countries reported a number of different ways to promote the greater use of noncustodial sanctions. Mention was made of the role of court precedents in guiding the practice of lower courts; this method was preferred over legislated guidelines in order to maintain the division of power between the executive and the judiciary. Other references were to sentencing guidelines and other means to clarify relevant offense and offender criteria;[21] guidelines to prosecutors; judicial conferences; and the arrangement of training. Various statutory tools were also mentioned.[22]

Other strategies that were mentioned focused on drawing the attention of the courts to the official policy of favoring noncustodial sanctions or of increasing the credibility of such sanctions.[23]

Conclusions and the Need for Further Research

In Europe as elsewhere, the problems associated with the use of imprisonment have led to a stronger interest in noncustodial sanctions.

Noncustodial sanctions are expected to do many things. For example, they are generally expected to help in reducing the prison population and the overall costs of the system. They are also believed to be more conducive to social reintegration, thus decreasing recidivism.

Actual experience in the different European countries cannot be taken as a clear-cut demonstration that noncustodial sanctions have these benefits. For example, even when noncustodial sanctions do replace imprisonment, they generally replace quite short sentences, thus having little effect on the size of the prison population. At the same time, other circumstances (such as increased crime) could lead to more, and/or more severe, imprisonment sentences, thus giving the impression that the reform has on the contrary led to greater use of imprisonment.[24]

The second goal mentioned was cost reduction. Here, again, the evidence is ambiguous, largely due to the fact that the concept of costs itself can be variously defined and measured. What is generally implied is that the wider use of noncustodial sanctions would allow the state to administer the enforcement of sanctions more cheaply. However, an assessment of the success achieved in reaching this goal requires an estimate of the savings that might be made with various kinds of changes in the rate with which different sanctions are used.[25] Comparisons of per-diem costs alone are oversimplifications. Fines and penal warnings are cheap (fines even bring in revenue) but probation and community service require an organized, skilled, and professional corps of workers to ensure their proper use.[26] Second, minor cuts in prison rates would not reduce the costs of running prisons. Third, net widening may increase costs. Fourth, it would be unwise to concentrate solely on financial criteria as a measure of effectiveness; we should also note the humanitarian and ethical factors involved, as well as the social costs of reliance on imprisonment as the "normal" punishment. These, however, are beyond the venue of the empirical researcher.

Part of the eagerness to associate the greater use of noncustodial sanctions (and the correspondingly lesser use of imprisonment) may be due to a misapprehension that there is a close link between the use of sanctions and the structure and level of crime in society. In fact, however, it can be argued that the degree of the use of custodial sanctions does not appear to be decisive for the general level of crime control in society. It may be that high rates of imprisonment do not in fact curtail crime in general, or that low rates do not in fact encourage crime. Other intervening factors such as the likelihood of detection and certainty of punishment are probably more important in determining the level of crime.[27]

Perhaps the most ambiguous goal of the greater use of noncustodial sanctions is the promotion of social rehabilitation. It is argued that noncustodial sanctions do not hinder readjustment to society and may in fact facilitate this. Thus, noncustodial sanctions may reduce recidivism.

Regrettably, it is difficult to define and measure recidivism, to say nothing of rehabilitation.[28] The HEUNI report concluded that "recidivism is a measure of effectiveness which has to be handled with caution. Studies on the amount of recidivism at the end of a follow-up period following different disposals do not suggest that noncustodial alternatives lead to a significantly greater degree of recidivism than custodial sentences."[29]

Noncustodial sanctions are not the panacea that will solve the many serious problems faced in criminal justice today. They will not necessarily reduce the rate of crime, promote rehabilitation, or lead to significant savings. To require that noncustodial sanctions "prove their worth" by doing all of this is to ask the impossible. The use of noncustodial sanctions should be compared to the alternative of placing the offender in prison. The available evidence is that noncustodial sanctions are at least as successful as sentences of imprisonment on several important counts, and that they lack many of the drawbacks of imprisonment. There is considerable scope for expanding the use of noncustodial sanctions. This scope should be used.

Notes

This chapter is largely based on Norman Bishop, *Non-Custodial Alternatives in Europe*, HEUNI publication no. 14, Helsinki, 1988. See also W. Rentzmann and J. P. Robert, *Alternative Measures to Imprisonment*, Seventh Conference of Directors of Prison Administration (Strasbourg: Council of Europe, 1986).

1. Imprisonment is considered to be necessary with serious offenses against life, health, and well-being, serious trafficking in drugs, aggravated thefts, gross fraud, serious economic crime, serious offenses against the environment, and offenses that seriously endanger national security. Legislation often provides that noncustodial sanctions are not appropriate, or are prohibited, when the offense in question is punishable by imprisonment for two years or more. In some countries the limit is placed at three years or more. However, the time periods can be much shorter; for example, in Italy a sentence to imprisonment for one month or less can be replaced by a fine, and imprisonment of up to three months can be replaced by "supervised liberty." Bishop, *Non-Custodial Alternatives in Europe*, p. 50.

Imprisonment is also considered to be necessary for certain kinds of offender. The characteristics of such offenders are often denoted in a wide and vague manner. The list of those for whom noncustodial sanctions are considered to be unsuitable in various countries includes, e.g., vagrants, habitual offenders, recidivist asocial persons, drug offenders, and violent, sadistic, perverted, and mentally ill offenders. The most common limitations relate to previous criminal history and record. Bishop, *Non-Custodial Alternatives in Europe*, p. 51.

2. Ibid., p. 47.
3. Ibid., p. 48.
4. In the following, the classification scheme is based on the degree to which

the state intervenes in the life of the offender. Clear-cut classifications are impossible, since states use a seemingly limitless variety of measures that may have the same name, while different names may be used for essentially the same measure. Also, people will undoubtedly disagree on the extent to which any particular measure, such as suspended imprisonment with supervision, community service, or even a fine, intervenes in the life of the offender. See, e.g., Anton M. van Kalmthout and Peter J. P. Tak, *Sanctions-Systems in the Member States of the Council of Europe, Part I, Deprivation of Liberty, Community Service, and Other Substitutes*, Deventer, Antwerp, London, Frankfurt, Boston, and New York, 1988.

5. Bishop, *Non-Custodial Alternatives in Europe*, pp. 63–68. See, e.g., K. Kloeck and H. van Geel, *Probatie als vorm van prépenitentiaire "hulpverlening" aan sociaal gehandicapte volwassenen* (Probation as a pre-prison "treatment" for socially handicapped adults), rapport 3, deel V, Project marginalisering en welzijnszorg (Leuven: Nationaal Ondersoeksprogramm in de sociale wetenschappen, 1978).

6. Bishop, *Non-Custodial Alternatives in Europe*, pp. 68–71. This development was encouraged in part by resolution (76) 10 of the Council of Ministers of the Council of Europe.

The Netherlands is the only country in which the sentencing judge is required to make explicit what sentence the community order replaces; see Peter Tak, "The Community Service Sentence in the Netherlands," *Research Workshop Document*, UNICRI, 1990.

For other literature, see, e.g., Peter Tak, "A Comparative Survey of the Use of Alternatives to Imprisonment in the Member States of the Council of Europe," in *Community Service as an Alternative to the Prison Sentence*, IPPF publication no. 28, Bonn, 1987, pp. 101–14; H. J. Albrecht and Wolfman Schädler, ed., *Community Service: A New Option in Punishing Offenders in Europe*, Criminological Research Report by the Max-Planck Institute for Foreign and International Penal Law, vol. 25, Freiburg im Breisgau, 1986; G. Duguid, *Community Service in Scotland, The First Two Years*, Central Research Unit Papers, Scottish Office, 1982; *Proveprosjekt med samfunnstjeneste* (Report on an experimental project with the community service order), NOU 1982:4; Ken Pease, "Community Service Orders," in Michael Tonry and Norval Morris (ed), *Crime and Justice: An Annual Review of Research*, vol. 6 (Chicago: University of Chicago Press, 1985).

7. See Károly Bárd, "Work in Liberty under Surveillance in Hungary," *Research Workshop Document*, UNICRI, 1990.

8. Bishop, *Non-Custodial Alternatives in Europe*, 72–79.

9. Imprisonment for nonpayment of fines is a serious problem in certain countries. In Ireland, for example, 50 percent of all receptions into prison are made up of fine defaulters. Such nonpayment is not a serious problem in countries applying the day-fine method (Austria, the Federal Republic of Germany, Finland, Hungary, Portugal and Sweden, and proposed in Belgium), where the size of the fine in itself is related to the ability of the offender to pay. In Sweden, for example, no fine-defaulters at all were sent to prison from 1984 on. Ibid., pp. 82–83.

In Scotland, a new program has been introduced into sheriff courts after an initial experimental phase. The Fines Officer Scheme is designed to reduce the number of persons going to prison because of inability to pay their fines. Fines officers visit defaulters at their homes to inquire about reasons for nonpayment and to obtain financial information in the light of which fine installments may be adjusted, and they may advise offenders how best to order their financial affairs so that their obligations may be met. The experimental scheme was evaluated by departmental researchers, and on the basis of the findings a national program was introduced. A. R. Millar, response to HEUNI questionnaire; citation is to idem, *The Experimental Introduction of Fines Enforcement Officers into Two Sheriff Courts*, Central Research Unit Papers, Scottish Office, 1984.

For other research on fines, see, e.g., P. Softley, *Fines in Magistrates' Courts*, Home Office Research Study no. 46, HMSO, 1978; idem and D. Moxon, *Fine Enforcement: An Evaluation of the Practices of Individual Courts*, Research and Planning Unit Paper no. 12, Home Office, 1982.

In Bulgaria, Italy, and the USSR, nonpayment of fines cannot lead to imprisonment. In the USSR, nonpayment can result in work duty. In the Federal Republic of Germany, nonpayment can lead to community service.

10. Bishop, *Non-Custodial Alternatives in Europe*, pp. 79–89. England and Wales, and Scotland, are unique in that their legislation provides for compensation orders as independent noncustodial sanctions. Ibid., p. 87; see, e.g., G. Maher, *The Use of Compensation Orders in Scotland*, Central Research Unit Papers, Scottish Office, 1987. Compensation orders are also being considered in the Netherlands.

11. Bishop, *Non-Custodial Alternatives in Europe*, pp. 89–96.

12. A study in Belgium suggests that very little use was made of the possibilities to impose noncustodial alternatives; of possible cases, only 7 percent received a suspended sentence, 2 percent were put on probation, and 17 percent were subjected to a conditional custodial sentence. According to a later study, 73 percent of short-term prisoners could have been sentenced to noncustodial alternatives instead. Cited in ibid., p. 104.

13. This is possible as long as imprisonment is not deemed necessary for individual or general prevention; article 37 of the Penal Code. Bishop, *Non-Custodial Alternatives in Europe*, pp. 79–80.

14. Article 47 of the Penal Code; Bishop, *Non-Custodial Alternatives in Europe*, pp. 79–80, 102.

15. In Greece, imprisonment for up to six months should normally be converted into a monetary sanction; in 1984, conversion became possible for sentences up to eighteen months. Only about 3 percent of custodial sanctions that fall within the scope of the legislative limitations are in fact enforced. Bishop, *Non-Custodial Alternatives in Europe*, p. 80.

In Portugal, article 43 of the new Penal Code that entered into force in 1982 stipulated that sentences of imprisonment for up to six months must be replaced by a fine unless deprivation of liberty was essential for reasons of general prevention. In 1982, 73 percent of such sentences were replaced with a fine; by 1985, this proportion had fallen to 61 percent. Ibid., pp. 80–81; Helena Parada Coelho, "The Need for a Wide Understanding of Non-Custodial Alternatives Imposed by the Courts," in *Alternatives to Custodial Sanctions*, Proceedings of the European Seminar, HEUNI publication no. 15, pp. 143–164, at 150.

Since 1983 it has been possible in France to impose up to 360 days of day-fines for certain offenses (délit) punishable by imprisonment. As yet, however, this sanction is not used very widely (2,300 cases in 1985). Bishop, *Non-Custodial Alternatives in Europe*, p. 81.

16. Bishop, *Non-Custodial Alternatives in Europe*, pp. 98–99.

17. Ibid., p. 110; Bishop cites Portuguese and Belgian studies on this on p. 112.

18. For example, in Portugal, with the adoption of probation and community service, it proved difficult to set up a wholly new probation service. This led to an overburdening of the probation services, which in turn decreased court confidence in these services. Ibid., pp. 112–14; Coelho, "The Need for a Wide Understanding," pp. 146–47.

19. Bishop, *Non-Custodial Alternatives in Europe*, p. 117. Eliaerts reports that judges who are more oriented toward resocialization or reintegration of delinquents will be more favorable to noncustodial sanctions. In contrast to the classical (punitive) way of thinking, they will spend more time with the defendant, his or her lawyer, and probation services. They attach importance to full—not only juridical—information of the court, as a means of individualizing the sanction. Research in Belgium shows that judges granting probation will less automatically resort to imprisonment in case of recidivism or violation of probation. More classically oriented judges regard noncustodial sanctions as a favor to occasional delinquents guilty of less serious crimes—a favor that can seldom be granted twice. Christian Eliaerts, "The Use of Non-Custodial Alternatives to Imprisonment: The Point of View of the Court," in HEUNI publication no. 15, pp. 194–227, at 202–3; Eliaerts cites S. Snacken, "L'application de la courte peine de prison en Belgique," *Revue de droit pénal et de criminologie* (1986), pp. 555–75, at p. 572.

Research on attitudes toward community service has been undertaken, for example, in the Netherlands. According to the results, community service was considered "real" punishment by two-thirds of the prosecutors, judges, probation officers, and offenders interviewed; 85 percent of the places in which community service was carried out had a positive view of the sanction; 90 percent of the prosecutors, judges, and probation officers considered the experiments at least reasonably successful; 90 percent of the offenders said that it had been a positive experience. Bishop, *Non-Custodial Alternatives in Europe*, p. 122; Menke W. Bol, *CSO's in the Netherlands*, Report No. 76, Research and Documentation Centre, Ministry of Justice, 1985; idem and J. J. Oerwater, *Dienstverlening, Eindrapport van het onderzoek naar de vervanging van de vrijheidsstraf in het strafrecht voor volwassen*, Wetenschappelijk Ondersoeken Documentatie Centrum (WODC), rapport no. 47, 's-Gravenhage, 1984; idem, *Recidive van dienstverleners* (Recidivism among offenders sentenced to community service), WODC, rapport no. 73, 's Gravenhage, 1986.

On public opinion in general, see Jan van Dijk and Phillipe Robert, "L'opinion publique relative à la criminalité et à la justice pénale," in Council of Europe, *Etudes relatives à la recherche criminologique*, vol. 17 (1979).

20. For example, in Poland, restriction of personal freedom was introduced in 1969 in order to reduce the rate of imprisonment. In fact, this sanction replaced fines and suspended sentences. Bishop, *Non-Custodial Alternatives in Europe*, p. 103. A somewhat similar experience is recorded from Portugal; ibid., pp. 103–4. More

encouraging experiences have been reported from England and Wales, where extensive research has been carried out on this phenomenon in connection with community service; ibid., p. 104–7.

21. An example here comes from England, where the Home Office regularly updates its handbook, *The Sentence of the Court* (London: HMSO, 1986). Guidelines have also been issued in Norway in connection with the introduction of community service. Belgium is considering the introduction of sentencing guidelines. Bishop, *Non-Custodial Alternatives in Europe*, pp. 100–101.

22. These include a statutory requirement of justification for the use of imprisonment; the elimination or relaxation of limiting conditions on the use of noncustodial sanctions; the abolishment of imprisonment for certain offenses; the elimination of imprisonment below a certain length of sentence; a restriction of the use of imprisonment in cases of recidivism; the establishment of a legal minimum term for imprisonment (e.g., one month); and the widening of the applicability on noncustodial sanctions.

23. This official priority given to noncustodial sanctions can be underlined either explicitly or implicitly—for example, through the imposition of restrictive conditions on the application of custodial sentences, or even through the encouragement of short custodial sanctions, in the hope that this will raise the threshold to longer sentences. The attractiveness of noncustodial measures, in turn, can be increased, for example, through the adoption of the possibility of inserting additional requirements in, e.g., probation orders (Bishop, *Non-Custodial Alternatives in Europe*, pp. 113–14), the improvement of the flow of information to courts (as noted in the responses from the Federal Republic of Germany, the German Democratic Republic, Ireland, the Netherlands, and Romania), and through closer control over the enforcement of the sanction (as noted in the responses from Norway and Sweden). Ibid., pp. 114–15.

24. Ibid., pp. 126–28; Bishop cites statistics from England and Wales and the Netherlands. Consequently, the effectiveness of noncustodial sanctions cannot be judged solely on the basis of whether their use reduces the size of a prison population. Ibid., p. 129.

The greater use of noncustodial sanctions may also be used in an effort to reduce the number of persons entering prison. This is valuable not only as a policy goal, but also in decreasing the work load of the prison administration. Ibid., pp. 130–31.

25. Ibid., p. 131.

26. When a new noncustodial sanction is taken into use, this in itself requires an infrastructure and financial means over and above what is currently going into imprisonment (Eliaerts, "Use of Non-Custodial Alternatives," p. 205). The financial costs of the infrastructure itself are not the only possible costs. In connection with community service, for example, administrators shall have to consider questions such as insuring offenders against injury, the bearing of responsibility for injury, the possible need for an initial medical examination, the possible right to social security, and the obtaining of the appropriate jobs.

27. Bishop, *Non-Custodial Alternatives in Europe*, pp. 53–55, citing *Criminal Justice Systems in Europe*, HEUNI publication no. 5, p. 3; Knut Sveri, "Om användning av straffrättsliga påföljder i Norden, Västtyskland, och Enland" (On the use of penal sanctions in Scandinavia, the Federal Republic of Germany, and

England), in an appendix to the *Om straffskalor, påföljdsval, straffmätning och villkorlig frigivning, m.m.* (English summary: Proposals by the Swedish Committee on Imprisonment on sanctions for crime, scales of penalties, sentencing guidelines, and conditional release, etc.), *SOU* (Stockholm), vol. 13 (1986), p. 77.

28. The response from England and Wales observes that "in general, research studies have failed to show that one type of sentence is more likely to reduce the likelihood that an offender would commit further offences than any other. The only measures which have been found to be consistently more effective than others were financial (usually fines, but sometimes compensation orders)." Cited in Bishop, *Non-Custodial Alternatives in Europe*, p. 136.

A Dutch study compared offenders given community service in 1981 with those given short-term unconditional imprisonment for similar offenses in 1980. The findings were that 42 percent of the community service group and 54 percent of the matched custodial sanctions group were reconvicted during the follow-up period of three years. Bishop, *Non-Custodial Alternatives in Europe*, p. 136; C. Eliaerts and Peter Tak, "De korte gevangenisstraf en de alternatieve sancties" (Short-term imprisonment and alternative sanctions), *Panopticon* vol. 3 (1984), pp. 199–212; see also idem, *Beslissig over en vormgeving aan de korte vrijheidsberovende en vrijheidsbeperkende straffen.* Eindrapport underzoeksproject Nationaal Fonds voor Wetenschappelijk Onderzoek, Brussel, Leuven, 1985.

29. Bishop, *Non-Custodial Alternatives in Europe*, p. 138.

Annex

Independent Noncustodial Sanctions Available in Europe, 1987

Table 10.1 is based on the responses to the HEUNI survey of noncustodial sanctions carried out in 1987. The respondents were asked to note on a list the *independent* noncustodial alternatives involving some degree of control or supervision, or respectively involving monetary payments and penal warnings, that were available in the respondent's country. Only those alternatives were to be marked that can be ordered *independently* of a custodial or other sanction *for adults*; combinations of sanctions were dealt with separately.

The classification given in Table 10.1 is that given by the individual respondents. Several respondents noted that some sanctions (in particular, treatment or deprivation of certain rights) were possible (if at all) only for limited categories of offenses and offenders.

Independent Control/Supervision Sanctions.

1. Probation
2. Suspended or conditional sanction with supervision or condition of treatment
3. Community service
4. Open, ambulant, or contract treatment

5. Suspension of driving or other licenses
6. Deprivation of rights
7. Removal of professional status
8. Local banishment (Scotland: exclusion order)
x. Other

> *Bulgaria:* Work service
> *Cyprus:* Recognizance to keep the peace and be of good behavior with or without sureties, recognizance to come up for judgment within 12 months.

Table 10.1

	control/supervision									monetary payments					penal warnings				
	1	2	3	4	5	6	7	8	x	1	2	3	4	5	6	7	8	9	x
Austria		2		4						1					6				
Belgium		2								1					6				
Bulgaria	1	2		4	5	6			x	1	2	3		5	6			9	x
Cyprus	1	2							x	1	2		4	5	6			9	
Czechoslovakia								8	x	1		3	4		6				x
Denmark	1	2	3	4	5	6	7			1	2	3	4		6	7	8		
England & Wales	1	2	3						x	1	2		4	5	6		8	9	
German FR	2									1									x
Finland						6	7			1			4			7			
France	1	2	3	4	5	6	7	8	x	1		3	4	5	6			9	
German DR	1		3						x	1	2		4			7			x
Greece										1	2	3			6	7			
Hungary	1	2			5	6	7	8	x	1		3	4	5	6	7			
Ireland	1		3		5				x	1	2	3	4	5	6		8	9	x
Italy	1	2	3		5				x	1		3			6				
Luxembourg		2	3						x	1			4	5	6				
Malta	1									1	2	3	4	5		7			
the Netherlands		2	3	4	5	6	7		x	1	2	3	4		6			9	
N. Ireland	1		3							1	2		4	5	6	7	8	9	x
Norway		2					7			1		3		5	6				
Poland	1	2	3	4	5	6	7		x	1	2	3	4		6		8	9	
Portugal	1	2	3	4					x	1			4		6	7		9	
Romania									x	1					6	7			x
Scotland	1		3		5	6		8	x	1	2	3	4	5		7	8	9	
Sweden	1			4	5	6	7			1	2	3	4		6	7			
Switzerland		2		4					x	1					6				
USSR	1	2	3	4	5		7			1	2		4	5	6	7			
Yugoslavia	1	2		4						1			4			7			

Czechoslovakia: Prohibition of certain activity

England and Wales: Attendance center orders

France: Exécution par fractions

German Democratic Republic: Educational measures imposed by social courts, such as community service

Hungary: Reformative-educational labor, severe reformative-educational labor

Ireland: Recognisance permitting treatment for drug abuse, supervision on deferment of penalty

Italy: Semi-liberté, détention à domicile, liberté surveillée, semi-deténtion, conversion en peine pécuniaire

Luxembourg: Suspension simple du prononcé de la condamnation, suspension probatoire du prononcé de la condamnation, cure de désintoxication, exécution par fractions, semi-liberté

The Netherlands: Weekend prison

Poland: Preduptsreditelnyi nadzor, uslovnaja otsrochka istsolnenija nakazanija s nadzorom ili poruchitelstvom

Portugal: Emprisonnement pendant les weekends, semi-détention, mesures spéciales applicables à des jeunes adultes

Romania: Travail en liberté dans les entreprises socialistes, placement sous garantie

Scotland: Caution for good behavior

Switzerland: Semi-détention, exécution par journées séparées, travail et logement en externat (il n'appartient pas au juge mais à l'autorité d'exécution de décider l'application de ce régime)

Monetary Payments and Penal Warnings as Independent Sanctions

1. Fines
2. Compensatory payments
3. Confiscation of personal property
4. Finding of guilt but no sanction imposed
5. Finding of guilt but no sanction imposed, providing no further offense committed during some stated period
6. Conditional or suspended sentence; no supervision of the offender ordered
7. Admonition
8. Acceptance of the offender's undertaking to be of good behavior for some stated period in the future
9. Decision on sanction deferred for some stated period
x. Other

Bulgaria: Social admonition

Czechoslovakia: Reformatory measure, forfeiture, expulsion

Federal Republic of Germany: Admonition together with suspended fine (''admonition under reservation'')

German Democratic Republic: Educational measures imposed by social courts, such as fines, public reprimand and compensatory payments

Ireland: Adjourn generally with liberty to re-enter, marked ''taken into consideration''

Northern Ireland: Recorded sentence

Romania: La remontrance

11

Work in Liberty under Surveillance in Hungary

Károly Bárd

As is the case in the majority of European countries, crime has been on the increase in Hungary over the last few decades. The number of criminal acts registered by the police amounted to approximately 120,000 fifteen years ago and had risen to almost 190,000 by 1987. The statistics relating to offenders identified in the same period indicate a more moderate change (81,045 in 1975 and 97,645 in 1987), illustrating that in Hungary also the major problems facing crime control are rising crime rates and decreasing police efficiency in clearing up crimes and identifying their perpetrators.

As a result of diminishing clearance rates, the number of offenders convicted by the courts also shows a relatively slight increase (59,422 in 1975 and 66,337 in 1987), as does the number of individuals sentenced to imprisonment (25,358 in 1975 compared with 26,780 in 1987), while in relation to unconditional prison sentences the number of adults actually sent to prison has actually dropped, from 14,592 in 1975 to 14,500 in 1987.

These figures should not, however, lead to the conclusion that the overall degree of punitiveness of the Hungarian courts has lessened and that deprivation of liberty has lost its central position within the sanction system. On the contrary, repressive tendencies in the judicial sentencing practice of the Hungarian courts seem to have become even stronger. Undoubtedly, short-term prison sentences (imprisonment of up to six months) have decreased to a considerable extent over the last decade, from approximately 13,000 in 1978 to 8,716 in 1987. On the other hand, imprisonment of five years or more today constitutes 1.8 percent of all prison sentences, while ten years ago it represented only 0.8 percent.

Increasing severity and the dominance of imprisonment is also reflected in the growing number of inmates per one hundred thousand members of the total population, a particularly important indicator of the overall degree of punitiveness. Since 1980, the respective figures have been as follows: 157 (1980), 164 (1981), 185 (1982), and 212 (1987), revealing a clear trend of a reduction in the chances of offenders' avoiding incarceration and an increase in the degree of punitiveness.

Part of the explanation certainly lies in growing crime rates and particularly in the rapid increase in the number of serious violent crimes and recidivism. The more serious of the two forms of criminal behavior under the present Hungarian penal law made up 27.8 percent of total criminality in 1980, while the respective proportion is over 34 percent today.[1]

On the basis of international comparison it is evident, however, that the harshness of the sentencing practice of the Hungarian courts cannot be explained solely by the spreading of more dangerous forms of criminality. Only comprehensive empirical research can reveal the causes and the part they play in shaping judicial sentencing patterns. One of the possible reasons could be the lack of proper alternatives to imprisonment. At first sight this assumption seems absurd, since it is well known that the criminal codes of the Eastern European region dispose of a number of sanctions in order to ensure proper tailoring of the sentence, the most well-known of them being the various sanctions of a social nature and those including work obliga-tions. Unlike many other socialist penal laws, there are no measures of social pressure in the Hungarian Criminal Code, but even so, the catalogue of criminal sanctions not entailing the deprivation of liberty is quite impressive and includes three types of sanctions involving the obligation to do some sort of work. Why then do courts not make use of the available alternatives? What are the main barriers to the further reduction in the use of imprisonment? What prevented legislators and courts from implementing to a greater extent the Resolution of the Sixth United Nations Congress on the Prevention of Crime and the Treatment of Offenders, which called upon Member States to examine their legislation with a view to removing legal obstacles to the utilization of alternatives to imprisonment and to the identification of new ones?

The search for the answer to these questions forms the topic of the present paper. Our purpose is to assist decision makers in other countries in identifying the preconditions that have to be present in order that noncustodial sanctions become credible alternatives to imprisonment. Therefore, the case study is necessarily critical and perhaps even one-sided. It focuses on describing both the legal and the organizational deficiencies as a result of which noncustodial sanctions involving work obligations have failed to become effective alternatives to imprisonment so far.

A Brief Survey of the Sanction System in Eastern European Countries

It is commonly assumed that the laws of the countries in Eastern Europe form one of the major legal families. Common basic principles of social structure, as well as similarities in historical evolution, have had an impact on legal institutions, so that, in spite of growing differences, penal law in the various countries still shows numerous common traits.[2] Therefore, it seems appropriate to provide a brief overview of the main characteristics of the sanction system in Eastern European countries to improve understanding of the development, and the present regulation, of Hungarian penal law.

The first, and perhaps basic, general trait of criminal law in Eastern European countries is its pragmatism and utilitarianism[3]: the institutions of criminal law (both substantive and procedural) are expected to be useful. This principle stems from the optimistic approach shared by criminal policymakers in these countries as regards the outcome of the fight against crime. As for the system of sanctions, the pragmatic approach explains the emphasis placed on the efficiency expected of criminal sanctions. At the level of legislation, efficiency is the primary criterion when deciding on whether a given sanction should be introduced or not. At the sentencing level, efficiency means the priority given to prevention (primarily to individual prevention) over the other functions of punishment.

Utilitarianism and efficiency call for a flexible reaction to crime. Therefore the system of sanctions is subjected to relatively frequent changes. The striving for flexibility is also reflected in the fact that legislators in the region tend to abandon the traditional differentiation between punishment and penal measures. Besides, the formal distinction between principal and supplementary punishment (if upheld at all) is of limited significance in many countries, since provisions on sentencing usually empower courts to replace principal forms of punishment by supplementary ones.[4]

The high number of sanctions not entailing deprivation of liberty is a further common trait of the sanction system in the Eastern European region. Among noncustodial sanctions, it is certainly reformation through work duty that is most frequently associated with Eastern European criminal law.[5]

The origins of this type of sanction go back to Soviet law in the period following the revolution,[6] and, as indicated in decree number 3 of 20 July 1918 on the court, it was intended to serve as an alternative to short-term imprisonment from the very beginning.[7]

With the exception of Yugoslavia, all Eastern European countries have adopted this type of sanction. Even if it is known under various names, the central elements, namely, work duty and a strong emphasis on reform, are similar in all such legislation. Basically, reformative work in terms of such legislation means that the offender is placed under the supervision of a work collective or a trustworthy individual who should exert a beneficial impact on him or her. In addition, the carrying out of work is required, and a certain percentage of the offender's salary is deducted. At the ideological level, reformative work is justified by the presumed individual preventive value of education through work. It is also assumed that reformative work is particularly suited to the conditions of socialist societies, where, as a result of the lack of extensive unemployment, economic pressure does not represent sufficient motivation to work.[8]

As to the legal technicalities, the differences in the various legislations are considerable. In Hungary and in Romania, for instance, reformative work is an independent, separate sanction, while in the German Democratic Republic, the obligation to remain at a designated workplace is part of the duties imposed upon the offender sentenced to "conviction on probation." The differences are even greater if one compares the frequency with which reformative work is used, as well as the obligations the offender is expected to fulfill in addition to work duty, in the various countries.

At one extreme, we encounter the Romanian solution. No statistical data are available from this country, but it is reported that reformative work is widely used as an alternative to imprisonment.[9] The scope of application of reformative work is relatively broad under Romanian law: With the exception of a few criminal offenses, it may be used as a substitute for imprisonment in those cases where the maximum prison term prescribed by the law for the given crime does not exceed ten years, provided that in the particular case the court would not impose a prison sentence of more than five years.[10] In addition to the duty to work, numerous constraints are imposed upon the convict, and he is placed under tight social control. From 15 to 50 percent of his salary is retained by the state, the term of punishment is not taken into consideration when fixing the amount of his pension, he may leave the locality of the workplace only with the permission of the militia, and so on.

In contrast to Romania, reformatory work in Czechoslovakia, Poland, and Hungary involves, in practice, the sole obligation of paying a certain amount of one's salary, while in the latter two countries, in particular, reformative work is used relatively rarely by the courts.

Work in Liberty under Hungarian Law

Brief Survey of the Sanction System with Special Attention on Alternatives to Imprisonment under Hungarian Criminal Law

Hungarian penal law was first systematically and comprehensively codified in the second half of the nineteenth century. The code of 1878 was a product of the classical school of criminal law, thus its sanction system contained only punishments (capital punishment, imprisonment, and fines as the principal forms) and no penal measures. It was in the twentieth century, under the impact of the modern school of criminal law, that penal measures serving aims other than retribution were introduced. Penal measures for preventing deviant juveniles and children from committing further offenses were introduced in 1908. This was the same year in which the institution of the suspended sentence found its way into Hungarian law. In 1913 an act on publicly dangerous vagrants and work-shy individuals was enacted, and workhouses were set up. In this way, the institution of security measures was introduced into Hungarian penal law. From 1928 onward, professional and habitual criminals could be sent to the so-called "severe work-house." No maximum term was set for this type of punishment, and convicts could thus, in theory, remain in the severe workhouse for life.

The only alternative to noncustodial sanctions before World War II was fines. The scope of application of fines was enlarged in 1928, and courts were called upon by the legislature to consider the offender's means when fixing the amount to be paid.

After World War II, a new general part of the Penal Code was constructed, characterized by the efforts to simplify the sanction system as well as to enhance its flexibility. The strict distinction between principal and supplementary sanctions was brought to an end. The most remarkable innovation of the new general part was, however, the introduction of reformatory-educative labor, clearly intended to replace imprisonment.

The first comprehensive Penal Code after World War II was Act V of 1961. In the area of sanctions, the only remarkable change concerned the return to the former strict separation of principal and supplementary punishment.

Following several amendments in the sixties and the seventies, Parliament enacted a new penal code in 1978 that brought about considerable changes in the system of sanctions. Legislators were concerned with the search for genuine substitutes for imprisonment; the day-fine system was introduced, the rules on reformatory-educative labor were modified, and the number of criminal offenses for which, besides imprisonment, noncustodial sanctions could be imposed was raised to a considerable extent. The replacement of imprisonment with sanctions not entailing deprivation of liberty was envisaged by the provision permitting the courts to impose, under certain conditions, a supplementary form of punishment or a penal measure as the only sanction.

As part of the campaign against work-shy individuals who represent a danger to the public, a previously unknown sanction, so-called "severe reformatory-educative labor," was introduced into Hungarian law in 1984. Through the latest amendment to the Penal Code, a new form of implementing reformatory-educative labor, which comes very close to community service, was introduced in 1987.

Reformatory-Educative Labor—Its Rise and Fall

Following the Soviet model, reformatory-educative labor was introduced into Hungarian penal law in 1950. Perhaps the introduction was premature—at least certain contradictions and ambiguities in the provisions relating to it seemed to indicate that the drafters had but a vague idea about what the new sanction actually entailed. Reformatory-educative labor was declared to be a penal measure and not a punishment. According to the argument in favor of this solution, the exclusive objective of the new sanction was education in contrast to punishment, which was intended to serve additional functions. On the other hand, the preconditions under which reformatory-educative labor could be imposed clearly showed that it was actually a type of punishment. Reformatory-educative labor could be imposed in relation to offenses punishable with up to five years' imprisonment, provided that the offender's social position and the circumstances under which the offense had been committed indicated that the objectives of punishment could be attained without depriving the offender of his or her freedom.

Besides the uncertainty as to the legal nature of reformatory-educative labor, other factors impeded its extensive use, primarily the Supreme Court's decision that it could be used only in respect of offenders employed at state firms or institutions. Not only did this decision violate the principle of equal treatment before the law, it also limited the scope of application of reformatory-educative labor to a considerable extent by excluding a broad strata of offenders.

It is therefore hardly surprising that the practical significance of reformatory-educative labor fell short of the legislators' ambitious expectations and failed to make any substantial impact on the number of prison sentences imposed, the proportion of its application ranging from 4.5 to 10.0 percent of all sanctions imposed in the fifties.[11]

The drafters of the first comprehensive postwar Penal Code (1961) seemed to identify the consequences of these legislative deficiencies and made an attempt to remove the barriers to the more frequent use of reformative-educative labor. In the code of 1961, reformatory-educative labor was accurately defined as a principal form of punishment, and the scope of its application was extended. According to the motivation behind the Penal Code, reformatory-educative labor was a sanction that could be used theoretically with any offender. Thus the decree on the implementation of the Penal Code set up the possibility of enforcing reformatory-educative labor in cooperatives and at a new workplace designed by the court (in terms of the previous law, the sanction had to be implemented at the offender's actual place of employment).

In the first years following the enactment of the Penal Code of 1961, reformative-educative labor seemed to meet the drafters' ambitious expectations, the proportion of its use out of the total of all sanctions imposed reaching 15 percent. In the second half of the sixties, however, a crisis in the institution became evident when the number of cases where reformatory-educative labor was imposed represented but a negligible fraction of all sentences imposed by the courts. This fact indicated that legislators had failed in removing the barriers to the wide use of reformatory-educative labor. Even if the motivation behind the law declared that reformatory-educative labor was a punishment of general applicability, a large group of offenders was then excluded. In practice, reformatory-educative labor was not used on people in a number of professions where a clean record was required for employment. Furthermore, it could not be imposed on individuals in positions of authority, as this could have led to the absurd situation of the convict being in charge of directing the members of a given unit who are at the same time meant to be guiding and educating the convict.

The apparent fiasco of reformative-educative labor led some experts even to suggest its abolition in the sixties.[12] However, in 1971 legislators made a further attempt to save the institution and extended the scope of its applicability. They realized that the expected reformative and educative activity of work collectives had turned out to be a mere illusion. Not only had the idea of collectivism lost much of its credibility, but production units with members who had been working together for years had become a rarity as a consequence of the liberalization of the labor market and employees' increasing mobility in the sixties. Therefore, the legislators introduced a new form of reformatory-educative labor, namely, the implementation of the sanction within specific work colonies. The minister of justice was authorized to take care of the detailed rules of implementation in a separate decree. However, the decree never materialized. It was perhaps the lack of clear concepts as to which group of offenders should be sentenced to serve reformative-educative labor at the work colonies, the failure to provide proper facilities, and the organizational shortcomings that explain why the only provision of the 1971 amendment that has never entered into force was the one on the work colonies.

In the course of the preparatory works to the present Penal Code (dating back to 1978), the majority of the experts involved in the drafting activity agreed that the retention of reformative-educative labor in its traditional form was senseless. It therefore came as a complete surprise to them when they saw that the final draft of the Penal Code prepared by the Ministry of Justice adopted the provisions of the 1961 code in a basically unchanged form. The draft was then sanctioned by Parliament, but the legislators' liking for reformatory-educative labor (which might perhaps be explained by ideological considerations) could not stop the institution's slow death. In 1987, only 2,944 out of the total of 59,682 convicts were sentenced to reformatory-educative labor. The vehement debates of the sixties and seventies did not reappear in the legal periodicals this time. No further discussions were needed, as theorists, practitioners, and policymakers all knew that reformative-educative labor in its traditional form, as introduced in 1950, had failed totally to become a serious alternative to imprisonment in Hungary.

Severe Reformative-Educative Labor

In 1984 severe reformative-educative labor as an independent sanction was introduced into Hungarian penal law. The introduction of this new form of principal punishment was part of the campaign against work-shy individuals, who, according to the evaluation of the crime-control agencies, represented a danger to the public. (According to official information, there are approximately fifteen thousand to twenty thousand cases per year where various measures of a penal or administrative nature are imposed by the authorities for publicly dangerous work-shyness.) The amendment to the Penal Code in 1984, besides introducing severe reformative-educative labor, raised the maximum prison term for publicly dangerous work-shyness from one to two years, while the sanctions for the corresponding administrative infraction were also strengthened.

Severe reformative-educative labor, which must be performed at a workplace within a locality designated by the court, with the additional obligation to live in a "semiopen" institution, was partly intended to fill the gap between imprisonment and reformative-educative labor, which had come to be filled by the payment of a fine in installments over the years.

In 1987 the scope of application of reformative-educative labor was broadened, and in addition to work-shy individuals, perpetrators of certain property crimes were eligible.

As far as the restrictions attaching to the liberty of the convict are concerned, this new sanction may certainly be regarded as a credible alternative to imprisonment. However, the rules regarding its implementation make it doubtful whether there are any significant differences between the two types of sanction at all: inmates may only leave the institution in their leisure time and the locality over the weekend with the permission of the institution's management. As far as the choice of work to be done is concerned, it is economic interests that dominate. Convicts, predominantly males, are forced to do hard, physical work in areas where there is a permanent shortage of workers. The hard labor frequently does not correspond with the physical conditions of the target group. It has, for instance, been reported that in one of the localities where convicts serve their sentences, 80 percent of the 127 inmates were regarded as alcoholics, and one-quarter of them had been subjected more than once to long-term medical treatment prior to sentencing for alcohol-related problems.[13]

Many convicts perceive severe reformative-educative labor as a particularly hard prison regime and force the courts to commute their sentences to imprisonment by breaking the work obligations or violating the restrictions attached to the sanction (in 1987, in about 18 percent of cases, sentences were converted into imprisonment).[14]

According to the law, one day's severe reformative-educative labor corresponds to one day of prison, indicating that legislators also regard severe reformative-educative labor as a sanction coming close to incarceration as far as the harm inflicted upon the convict is concerned. For all of these reasons, it is doubtful whether severe reformative-educative labor could be defined as a genuine alternative to imprisonment. The obligations placed upon convicts, the hard working conditions, and the extent to which their personal liberty is restricted actually make it a specific form of imprisonment imposed upon a particular target group.

Severe reformative-educative labor will thus most probably never become a genuine alternative to imprisonment. Through Act XXIII of 1989, the Hungarian Parliament abolished the criminal offense and the administrative infraction of "work-shyness representing danger to the public." According to the motivation behind the act, the penalization of a work-shy way of life is contrary to Hungary's international obligations, as it violates the prohibition against forced labor as set down in the International Pact on Civil and Political Rights, as well as in the ILO pact on forced and mandatory work. Furthermore, so the argument runs, the penalization of the so-called work-shy way of life lacks any rational basis under present economic conditions, when unemployment has become a significant social problem in the country. The penalization of work-shyness would only open the way for the even more oppressive treatment of individuals who live on the periphery of society, without contributing to the solution of the social problem itself. Since severe reformative-educative labor is tailored above all to control work-shy individuals, the decriminalization of this category is likely to lead to the abolition of severe reformative-educative labor.

The Obligation to Perform Unpaid Work for the Public as a Specific Form of Implementing Reformative-Educative Labor

In 1987 there was introduced in Hungary a new form of implementing reformative-educative labor that is practically identical to the community service to be found in the legislation of numerous countries. The rules follow the Western European pattern, although, formally, community service is not an independent sanction but rather, as it is in Poland, a specific form of implementing reformative-educative labor. The useful work performed for the community has to be done by convicts on their day off or during their holidays. According to the law, the court dealing with the case decides only the type of sanction to be imposed, while the place and type of work is assigned by the so-called "court of corrections," presided over by a single judge. The bulk of the work, however, rests with the probation officers who assist the judge in finding appropriate work.

The procedure resulting in the designation of the place of work and the determination of its type runs as follows: the local authority departments in charge of collecting information on available jobs generally present the courts with a regular list of firms and institutions willing to provide work for persons sentenced to undertake community service. Probation officers then visit these workplaces and make inquiries as to the type of work offered. If they find the work suitable, they will contact the convicted person and inform him or her of the work available. The discussions with the convict are formalized in writing and presented to the court along with the probation officer's recommendation as to which workplace should be designated. When making the recommendation, the probation officer should consider the convict's condition, skills, and previous training. On the basis of the recommendation, the judge will decide on the place and type of work, paying due regard to the convict's state of health, obtaining the opinion of a medical expert if necessary.

Apart from the work obligation, the convict's personal liberty is not restricted. As in the case of "ordinary" reformative-educative labor, the violation of the work obligation or a serious breach of work discipline may lead to community service being commuted into imprisonment. While two days of "ordinary" reformative-educative labor correspond to one day in prison, the respective relation in the case of community service is one to one. The rules on commuting into imprisonment indicate that community service is regarded by legislators as the more severe sanction in comparison with "ordinary" reformative-educative labor. On the other hand, the rules on exemption from the detrimental consequences of conviction show that community service is the sanction that carries the least stigma. The offender sentenced to community service is exempted from the detrimental consequences of conviction on the day the court's decision becomes final. Thus the offender remains a person with a clean record and may keep his or her job even where a clean record is a precondition of employment. In the case of "ordinary" reformative-educative labor, the offender is exempted from the detrimental consequences of conviction on the day he completes his sentence.

Undoubtedly, it was the legislators' intention to extend the applicability of community service to all types of offenders, independent of social status, job, and position. The legislators' expectations, however, have not yet been fulfilled. In 1988 (the year in which community service was introduced), 70 percent of all convicts were unskilled workers, many of them unemployed.[15]

In contrast to severe reformative-educative labor, the introduction of community service met with general approval among experts, and the first eighteen months following its introduction gave some positive indications. However, the reservations of those who had called for longer and more thorough preparatory work prior to the introduction of community service seem to have been confirmed by the practice of the courts.

In 1988 there were only thirty-six cases in the whole country in which offenders were sentenced to community service. No research findings are yet available capable of revealing the causes of the courts' reluctance to impose the new sanction more frequently. We are therefore forced to confine ourselves partly to a repetition of the arguments voiced prior to the introduction of community service by experts within the framework of the discussion about the new provisions of penal law.[16] The country's present economic situation and the lack of proper jobs do not favor the extensive use of community service: in practice, only institutions operating under the supervision of the local authorities (such as hospitals) are willing to provide work opportunities. As a result of increasing unemployment, factories are becoming more and more reluctant to provide work for individuals sentenced to community service. In a number of cases in 1988, community service simply could not be implemented, for the lack of openings. As a result of certain negative historical experiences in Hungary, when the work obligation was used as a sanction against minorities and political opponents of the regime, the public is inclined to perceive community service as an extremely defamatory sort of sanction. The same holds true for the convicts themselves. Out of the thirty-six persons sentenced to community service, six did not even take up the post or complete the work, because they perceived the tasks to be performed (mainly cleaning work) as humiliating and preferred to spend a few days or even weeks in prison. Due to poor preparation and sensitization, the public and the managers of factories who should provide work possibilities have but vague or false ideas about what the institution of community service is actually all about.

Conclusion

The gloomy picture drawn of the difficulties involved in replacing incarceration with alternatives involving work duty performed under conditions of liberty should not lead to the belief that sanctions containing work obligations are inappropriate as alternatives to imprisonment. The fiasco of reformative-educative labor and the problems concerning community service in Hungary should be interpreted as a warning to decision makers in other countries to refrain from introducing alternatives to prison without making the proper organizational preparations, undertaking a thorough analysis of the economic and social conditions in their country, and testing the intellectual and psychological state of the population or adequately informing and preparing the public.

Chapter 11

Notes

1. K. Györgyi and S. Lammich, "Entwicklung des Strafrechts, der Kriminalität, und der Strafzumessungspraxis," Ungarn seit dem Inkrafttreten des Strafgesetzbuches von 1978, ZStW 100 (1988), pp. 990, 992.

2. I. Andrejew, *Zur vergleichenden Darstellung des Strafrechts der sozialistischen Staaten*, ZStW 99 (1987), pp. 152–161.

3. K. Bárd, *Some General Traits of the Criminal Justice Systems of the Socialist Countries, with Special Reference to Hungary*, HEUNI publication no. 7, Helsinki, 1986, pp. 1–12; M. Filar and E. Weigend, "Die Entwicklung des Strafrechts", den sozialistischen Staaten Europas, ZStW 98 (1986), p. 247.

4. Filar and Weigend, "Die Entwicklung des Strafrechts," p. 250.

5. I. Andrejew, *Zur vergleichenden Darstellung*, p. 160, and N. Bishop, *Non-Custodial Alternatives in Europe*, HEUNI publication no. 14, Helsinki, 1988, pp. 69–71.

6. Filar and Weigend, "Die Entwicklung des Strafrechts," pp. 250 et seq.

7. I. Andrejew, *Le droit pénal comparé des pays socialistes*, Paris, 1981, p. 129.

8. Ibid., p. 161.

9. V. Papadopol and C. Turianu, "Strafen und Maßnahmen ohne Freiheitsentzug im rumänischen Strafrecht," *Jahrbuch für Ostrecht*, vol. 28 (1986), pp. 349–76.

10. Papadopul and Turianu, "Strafen und Maßnahmen," p. 358.

11. K. Györgyi, *Punishment and Penal Measures* (in Hungarian) Budapest, 1984, p. 56.

12. Ibid., p. 92.

13. On the problems related to severe reformatory-educative labor, see Gy. Vokó and Gy. Sáfrán, "On the experience concerning the implementation of severe reformatory-educative labour" (in Hungarian), *Bulletin of the Prosecution Office*, no. 1 (1988), pp. 32–36.

14. See ibid., p. 33.

15. The data on community service were provided by the Hungarian Ministry of Justice.

16. "Discussion on the amendment of the provisions in penal law" (in Hungarian), *Criminological Review*, no. 16 (1987).

12

Community Service Sentence in The Netherlands

Peter J. P. Tak

The history of Dutch sentencing law is characterized by an endeavor to reduce the use of short-term imprisonment. An important step will be taken in this direction in the very near future when the sentence to do unpaid work will be incorporated into the Penal Code as a new principal sentence alongside the existing principal sentences of imprisonment, detention, and fines. After almost ten years of experiments with this new sentence, it will finally get its legal basis. It is far beyond the scope of this report to give a detailed description of the development of the Dutch sanctions system since the enactment of the Penal Code in 1886, but it is possible to indicate moments in time when this reduction process manifested itself in the introduction of statutory measures.

It is necessary to look back briefly on the developments in sanctioning law to provide a frame of reference for a detailed discussion of the new sentence of unpaid work. The frame of reference is determined not only within the Netherlands but also internationally. Therefore, this chapter begins by looking at influences from abroad that have affected the national process of reducing short-term imprisonment by using unpaid work as a penalty. Then it outlines the national frame of reference, including a discussion of the experiments with the community service order as sentence. Next it concentrates on the empirical research with regard to the practical application of the community service. Finally, it provides an outline of the draft bill on the sentence to do unpaid work, which has been under discussion in Parliament since 1987.

Community Service Penalty from an International Perspective

For over a hundred years there has been a trend toward reducing short-term imprisonment. Franz von Liszt, especially, and those who with him established the Internationale Kriminalistische Vereinigung—the forerunner of the

International Association of Penal Law—have given this development an international dimension.

As time has gone by, the authorities who determine and shape the criminal policy have become convinced of the very limited usefulness of short-term imprisonment. The short-sharp-shock effect of this sanction seems insignificant when set against the damaging effects of short-term imprisonment upon the offender, upon his or her home environment, and eventually upon the community, too.

This realization has led to the situation that in almost all Western European countries far-reaching changes in the sanctions systems have been implemented with a view to drastically reducing short-term imprisonment as a judicial response.

Legislators have tried to achieve this reduction in short-term imprisonment by

- abolishing principal prison sentences of less than one month,
- radically restricting the opportunity to pass short unconditional prison sentences,
- widening the applicability of the suspended sentence,
- strongly emphasizing noncustodial sentences,
- restructuring the fines system by introducing day fines and widening the applicability of pecuniary sanctions, and
- introducing new sanction modalities, such as the declaration of guilt without imposition of a punishment and the warning.

It seems only right to point out that none of these legal measures aimed at reducing short-term imprisonment has had the desired effect. The short prison sentence still seems to be the preferred sentence for indictable offenses in the middle order of criminality. It is for these reasons that much creative and energetic work in the last few decades has been put into creating sanctions with the same punitive value as the short-term prison sentence, and comparable in terms of purpose, but without the damaging consequences of short-term imprisonment. These newly developed sanctions are therefore also known as "alternative sanctions."

In recent years European nations have been confronted with rising crime rates and a hardening of criminality, which has often given criminal courts little choice other than to impose prison sentences. This has resulted in almost all countries struggling with a shortage of prison capacity. Numerous solutions have been brought to bear upon these problems. We name a few of them:

- Automation of the administration of the prison system in order to optimize the occupation rate in prisons (Sweden)
- Building new penal establishments and reopening establishments that were closed in the past (The Netherlands)

- General amnesty or pardon (France, July–August 1981, twelve thousand prisoners; Italy, December 1986, approximately eight thousand prisoners)
- Downgrading of property offenses, reducing the maximum prison term by a quarter (Denmark, 1973 and 1982)
- Doubling cell occupation (Austria, France, Belgium)
- Increased use of conditional release (the Netherlands and Denmark)

Although these measures have alleviated the problem, it appears that they are still insufficient to resolve the estimated longer-term shortage of prison capacity. Also, in many countries, expanding prison capacity by building new prison facilities encounters political resistance based on financial and humanitarian considerations. The economic recession therefore has also played a part in compelling governments to look for alternatives to the short-term prison sentence.

Major impetus for the development process of these alternative sanctions came from the Council of Europe. In 1976 the Committee of Ministers of the Council of Europe adopted resolution (76)10 based on the Report of the European Committee on Crime Problems, "Certain Alternative Penal Measures to Imprisonment." In this resolution the governments of the Member States are asked:

> 3. to study various new alternatives to prison sentences with a view to their possible incorporation into their respective legislations and in particular c. to look into the advantages of community work and more especially the opportunity it provides:
>
> - for the offender to make amends by doing community service
> - for the community to contribute actively to the rehabilitation of the offender by accepting his cooperation in voluntary work.

Of worldwide importance has been resolution 8 of the Sixth United Nations Congress on the Prevention of Crime and the Treatment of Offenders, in which member states are called upon "to examine their legislation with a view to removing legal obstacles to utilizing alternatives to imprisonment, to identify various new alternatives to prison sentences that could be implemented without undue risk to public safety, to encourage wider community participation in the implementation of alternatives to imprisonment . . . and to make efforts to inform the public of the advantage of alternatives to imprisonment and to encourage public acceptance of these measures."

The secretary general's report *Alternatives to Imprisonment and Measures for the Social Resettlement of Prisoners* for the Seventh United Nations Congress on the Prevention of Crime and the Treatment of Offenders (Milan, Italy, 1985) indicates that community service, under different names and modalities, is carried out in the United Kingdom, France, Luxembourg,

Denmark, and The Netherlands. To this list may be added West Germany, Portugal, and Italy. In a few other countries, including Finland, Belgium, Norway, and Switzerland, the introduction of community service is currently under discussion or legislation is in the preparatory stages.[1]

Community Service from a National Perspective

The fundamental principle underpinning the Dutch Penal Code of 1886 was that a deprivation of liberty in the form of a prison sentence or detention was the indicated sanction for intentional and negligent crimes, respectively. In principle the imposition of a fine was possible for some crimes, but this kind of penalty was regarded as being in an entirely different class and was only considered appropriate for the least serious offenses. Originally prison sentences could only be imposed unconditionally, and the criminal judge had a large measure of freedom to determine the duration of the sentence. Unlike the laws of many countries, Dutch penal law does not lay down a minimum sentence for each type of criminal offense; there is a general minimum sentence of one day for all offenses punishable with a custodial sentence. There are separate statutory maximum sentences laid down for all offenses punishable with a custodial sentence.

The prison sentence is fixed term or lifelong. The minimum fixed-term prison sentence is one day, and the maximum is fifteen consecutive years. If a crime carries either a fixed term or a life sentence, to be decided by the judge, then the maximum sentence that can be imposed is twenty years. A life sentence means, in practice, imprisonment for about twenty-five years.

The Penal Code has included provision for parole since 1886, but up to 1915 this was only rarely used. The parole regulations were changed in 1915, allowing convicted offenders to be paroled after serving two-thirds of their sentence with a minimum of nine months. The rules were changed again in 1987. Now a convicted prisoner serving a sentence of one year or less is automatically released after serving six months and when one-third of the remaining sentence has been served. Convicted persons serving sentences longer than one year are released after serving two-thirds of their sentence. No conditions are attached to the early release, and it cannot be revoked. With a small number of exceptions, all persons convicted to serve more than seven months in prison are released early.[2]

Since 1915 the suspended sentence has been included in Dutch penal law. Initially only prison sentences of less than one year could be completely or partially suspended. Since 1987 judges have been able to suspend up to one year of a sentence that does not exceed three years in total. Conditions can be attached to suspended sentences. Besides the general condition attached to the suspended sentence, that the accused will not commit new offenses during the probationary period, the court may impose special conditions concerning the conduct of the sentenced person. The Penal Code does not give any further specification of admissible conditions. However, the code expresses one restriction: a conduct order may not restrict the right to freedom of religion or conviction, nor may it restrict civil and political liberties. The aim of the conduct order is to challenge a convicted person to behave well and to avoid a bad way of life. The definition of a special condition is left to the discretion of the judge; in appeal, however, a court may decide a condition to be inadmissible.

The Fines Act of 1925 took another step toward reducing the use of the prison sentence. It enabled judges to impose fines for offenses where the only statutory penalty laid down was a prison sentence, provided the custodial sentence he or she would have imposed did not exceed three months. This act also empowered judges to impose a higher fine than the maximum statutory fine laid down for a particular offense. From this time on, fines up to a maximum of f.20,000 could be imposed, depending upon the seriousness of the offense.

The relative proportion of prison sentences and fines imposed has changed radically over the years, especially since the Second World War. Of sentences imposed in 1895, 71 percent were unconditional prison sentences and 29 percent were fines; in 1935, the figures were 65 percent and 24 percent, and in 1970, 34 percent and 66 percent. Between 1970 and 1980 the percentage of prison sentences continued to go down, to reach approximately 25 percent, and the percentage of fines rose to about 75 percent. Since 1980 there has been a slow turnaround, and by 1986 prison sentences made up about 30 percent, and fines, about 70 percent. To put this in context, it needs to be pointed out that the absolute numbers of persons convicted to prison sentences and fines has risen steadily (table 12.1).

It has been stated in quite a number of publications by foreign researchers that the Dutch penal climate is a mild one. This is based on a comparison of the incarceration rate in The Netherlands to that in the

Table 12.1

	All fines & prison sentences	Uncond. prison sentences %	Part.susp. prison sentences %	Suspended prison sentences %	Fines %
1970	43,894	19.1	10.4	4.5	66.0
1975	51,581	19.2	8.9	4.9	67.0
1980	72,712	13.8	8.6	3.4	74.2
1986	73,571	14.5	7.4	7.9	70.2
1987	71,718	15.9	7.5	8.7	67.9

Table 12.2

	Prison sentences	<2w <1m	>2w <3m	>1m <6m	>3m <1y	>6m <3y	>1y	>3y
1980	16,325	2,158	7,320	2,789	2,054	1,157	847[a]	
1981	18,059	2,069	7,673	3,383	2,473	1,385	1,076[a]	
1982	19,093	1,918	8,022	3,834	2,599	1,473	1,247[a]	
1983	17,849	1,601	6,703	3,933	2,748	1,535	1,329[a]	
1984	18,626	1,372	6,511	4,293	3,009	1,821	1,618[a]	
1985	17,164	1,194	5,775	3,910	2,861	1,902	1,318	204
1986	17,123	1,233	6,009	3,572	2,749	1,915	1,258	387
1987	17,534	1,030	5,795	3,953	2,884	2,040	1,409	423

*Includes all sentences of one year or longer.

countries in question, and, in fact, the Dutch incarceration rate seems to be one of the lowest in Western Europe: 36 inmates per 100,000 inhabitants (as of 1 February 1988). However, two critical remarks should be made concerning this statement:

- Although the incarceration rate is still rather low it has increased considerably over the last five years (from 24 per 100,000 in 1980 to 36 in 1988). This increase is due both to a general increase in the crime rate and to the fact that, in recent years, on average almost 15,000 sentenced persons have had to wait a considerable period of time before being able to serve their prison sentences, due to a lack of prison capacity. The average number of prisoners rose, as the cell capacity went up from 3,224 in 1980 to 4,599 in 1986 and 5,291 in the first quarter of 1987. In 1981 the shortfall in prison capacity was 800 cells. This will increase to 2,200 cells by 1990 if the prison policy remains unchanged. A prison building program has been started, and some prisons that were closed down are being reopened. From 1981 to 1985, prison capacity was increased from 3,900 to 4,900 places. The required prison capacity for 1990 is estimated at 7,508.
- Although the incarceration rate is still rather low, there is a significant difference in the percentage of prison sentences imposed in The Netherlands as compared, for example, with Germany or Sweden. The percentage of persons sentenced to imprisonment is much higher in The Netherlands. In 1987, 17,534 prison sentences were imposed on a total of 71,718 sentenced persons. In The Netherlands, however, the length of prison sentences is much shorter than in the other countries mentioned. Short-term imprisonment (i.e., prison sentences of less than six months) plays an important role in the Dutch penal sanctions system, as table 12.2 shows.

Two Policies Applied for Reducing Sentencing to Prison

In the sixties there was a general tendency in northwestern Europe to reduce the use of short-term prison sentences because of doubts about its general deterrent value. In fact, the Dutch Penal Code contained only a single alternative to imprisonment at this time, the fine. A committee was asked to propose ways of extending the legal possibilities of imposing fines instead of short-term imprisonment in appropriate cases. The proposals made by this committee have led to the introduction of new regulations on the imposition of fines in the Penal and Procedural Codes. They can be summarized as follows:

- Since 1983 the public prosecutor has been able to settle a case out of court if the offender voluntarily pays a certain sum of money. This settlement applies to minor offenses and to crimes punishable with a maximum penalty of six years' imprisonment. This extension of the possibility for settlement is a means of, on the one hand, reducing the role of the custodial penalty and, on the other hand, sparing the offender a public court session for a nonserious crime and saving court time for the adjudication of serious crimes. Guidelines have been laid down by the attorneys-general for settlement by transaction in cases where a court would usually impose a fine. Every year approximately 12 percent of all offenses reported to the prosecution service are dealt with by transaction. About half of these cases concern drunken driving (with a blood-alcohol level of between 0.5 and 1.30/00), simple theft, and hit-and-run cases.
- Over the one hundred years since the Penal Code was enacted, new fines at contemporary money values have been introduced for new offenses, but there has never been a comprehensive reorganization and modernization of the whole fines system. Consequently the level of fines laid down for various offenses is chaotic and uneven. It was now proposed to divide fines up into categories and lay down a rate of fine for each criminal offense. This was effected by the act of 10 March 1984. All criminal offenses in the Penal Code and a number of other acts are divided up into six fine categories: f.500 (category I), f.5,000 (II), f.10,000 (III), f.25,000 (IV), f.100,000 (V), and f.1,000,000 (VI). All infractions come under categories I, II, and III, and crimes fall into categories II, III, IV, or V. Where a corporate body is convicted, the fine imposed may be one group higher than would normally have been the case. These two acts conclude, for the time being, the expansion of the role of the fine as a penal sanction.

The emphasis upon the fine as the first choice of sentence, as a means of reducing short-term imprisonment, must be viewed with a fair amount of skepticism in the light of developments in recent years. Both fines acts rested on the idea that because of increased welfare the accused would be able to pay a quite substantial fine that would have a punitive value equivalent to a short prison sentence of about two weeks. However, even before the two acts had been introduced, there were already indications that their effect would be less marked than had originally been thought. The ideas behind the two acts had developed during a period of economic growth, but they are now being operated under conditions of decreasing welfare and massive unemployment and where there is an ever increasing number of citizens with very limited financial resources. By the early 1980s the economic crisis had resulted in a situation where a growing number of convicted persons failed to pay their fines. In such cases the Penal Code provides for the enforcement of a fine-default detention. However, this has not happened in practice, due to a shortage of places in remand centers. If default detention were enforced on a large scale, this would frustrate the criminal policy aim of using fines instead of short prison sentences. Because the Dutch sanctions system has little to offer as an alternative to short-term imprisonment other than fines, new alternative sanctions needed to be developed. Such sanctions would have to be equivalent to short-term imprisonment in punitive value but must not, sooner or later, end up as a deprivation of liberty and, equally, must not involve the undesirable negative side-effects of imprisonment.

It was a sentence made by a magistrate in Arnhem in 1971 that provided the impetus for the development of alternative sanctions. Three juvenile offenders found guilty of overt violence (section 141, Penal Code) were given a suspended prison sentence with the condition that they do unpaid work on weekends, over a three-month period, in a nursing home or institution caring for the disabled. This sentence led to a flood of legal arguments about the admissibility of such a far-reaching condition. The stream of literature that followed contributed to a growth of awareness in government and Parliament. The alternative sanction had become a political issue, and in 1974 a committee was set up to advise the government on the desirability of diversifying the sanctions system in the Penal Code. In 1978 the committee recommended experimentation with community service orders. Then in 1980 a working party was set up to do the necessary preparatory work: to indicate under what legal framework the experiments could be carried out and how community service could be supervised in practice. On 1 February 1981, experiments were initiated in eight of the nineteen court districts. The experiments were to be conducted over a two- to three-year period and would be evaluated. At the end of this time a decision would be made as to whether a statutory regulation for community service was desirable. In 1982 the experiments were extended to all districts.

The experiments had to comply with a number of basic principles and conditions drawn up by the justice minister and the working party and laid down in circulars. The most important were:

- The offer to do community service must be initiated by the accused. If neither the accused, his advisor, nor his probation officer makes such a proposal, then community service is usually not possible.
- In order to be considered for this sanction, the person concerned must have confessed his or her guilt.
- Community service can function as an alternative only to an unconditional prison sentence of six months or less. Because of practical constraints this was reduced to three months in August 1983.
- The number of hours must be between 30 and 150.
- Community service may not conflict with the constitutional rights to freedom of religious and political conviction. To avoid problems relating to provisions prohibiting forced labor, community service may only be imposed with the consent of the person involved. Concern that the forced labor prohibition should not be contravened also lies behind the provisions that the work has to be seen as useful by the person doing it, that it must have some social value, and that the accused should offer to do it.
- The work has to be unpaid and noncommercial. It must be work that would otherwise not be carried out and for which there is no paid work force available.
- In principle no category of offense or offender is excluded. This means that recidivists can also be sentenced to community service.
- The organization and coordination of community service is to be carried out by the probation service. These responsibilities include finding projects, writing community service proposals (this is usually part of a social enquiry report), supervising the person on community service, and supplying the court authorities with a report at the end of the community service period. The probation service also has a duty to take out accident and third-party insurance on behalf of the person on a community service order.

Unlike in England, no separate statutory arrangements were made for community service in The Netherlands, but ministerial guidelines stated that the experiments were to take place within the existing statutory frameworks. Various forms of waiver of prosecution were named: unconditional waiver of prosecution, postponement of prosecution, conditional waiver of prosecution, and also the form whereby the public prosecutor settles a case without a court hearing. Conditional suspension of pretrial detention and suspension of the hearing with postponement of sentencing were also among the proposed judicial modalities. Later, partly as a response to practical pressures, community service within a pardon and suspended sentence were also added.

In all the above modalities, community service appears in the form of a special condition. However, what happens when the community service has been completed varies considerably. Under the various forms of waiver of prosecution and the pardon, the person knows exactly where he stands; completion of the community service means that the criminal case is definitely closed. In the case of a suspended sentence, what happens depends upon whether any other conditions were attached to the sentence and upon the length of the probationary period. In the case of conditional suspension of pretrial detention and postponement of sentencing, further court proceedings and a conviction almost always follow. However, provided the judge follows the guidelines, the person should not be given an unconditional prison sentence. All these modalities are based on guidelines that do not have the power of law. In practice they are frequently not adhered to, which has led to numerous juridical and practical problems.

Assessment of the Experiments

From the outset the community service experiments have been assessed by the Research and Documentation Center of the Ministry of Justice. The assessment study covered the period from February 1981 to May 1983. Three provisional reports were produced, followed by the final report in 1984.[3] During the period of the community service experiments, from February 1981 to the date on which the act on the penalty of unpaid labor will come into force, far more than ten thousand people were given community service sentences. In 1988, 4,913 community service sentences were imposed, of which 89 percent were for less than 150 hours, 8 percent were for between 150 and 250 hours, and 3 percent were for more than 250 hours of work. However, the evaluation study only looked at 450 cases. The information that we give below therefore relates only to a very small group of individuals who did community service.

What are the most important conclusions from the evaluation study?

- Over 90 percent of the community service work was completed successfully. The failures can be ascribed partly to circumstances beyond the person's control and partly to uncooperativeness or being brought up before the courts for another offense.
- The average length of community service was 100 hours. In 7.5 percent of cases, community service far exceeding the recommended upper limit of 150 hours was imposed.
- Community service was mainly imposed for property offenses (48.6 percent) and traffic offenses (23.8 percent). Almost 8.6 percent concerned aggressive offenses, and 3.0 percent, sex or drug offenses.
- Of persons sentenced to do community service, 93.4 percent were male and 4.6 percent were female (2 percent, not known); 25.3 percent were between eighteen and twenty years old; 22.4 percent, between twenty-one and twenty-four years old; and 17.5 percent, between twenty-five and twenty-nine years old.
- Of persons sentenced to do community service, 93.4 percent were male and 4.6 percent were female (2 percent, not known); 25.3 percent were between

eighteen and twenty years old; 22.4 percent, between twenty-one and twenty-four years old; and 17.5 percent, between twenty-five and twenty-nine years old.

- Of persons sentenced to do community service, 63 percent had previous convictions, while 37 percent were first offenders.
- Almost 60 percent of persons sentenced to do community service were unemployed and dependent upon social security benefits.
- The type of work involved in over 50 percent of cases was maintenance, repair, and painting, usually for institutions in the welfare sector. Housework and forestry and gardening made up a further 14 percent and 12 percent, respectively.
- There seemed to be enough institutions prepared to participate in the experiment, but canvassing for projects and maintaining contacts cost probation officers a great deal of time.
- A sound organizational structure is needed for this alternative sanction to function properly, and extra funds need to be set aside for this.
- It was noticeable that initially community service agreements were made with the prosecution service in 50 percent of cases and with judges in 50 percent of cases, but as time went by there was a shift in the direction of the judicial modalities.
- Judges and prosecutors tended to consider 150 hours' community service to correspond to about three months' imprisonment instead of six months' as originally proposed by the committee.
- There was a tendency to impose more hours of community service on unemployed offenders than on employed ones.

As well as the evaluation study of the application of the community service penalty, research was also undertaken into re-offending by persons doing community service. This study was published in 1986.[4] It compared re-offending by persons doing community service with those who had been sentenced to unconditional short-term imprisonment. The prisoners with whom the comparison was made had been convicted in the year preceding the start of the experiments. For the validity of the comparisons the prisoners and persons doing community service were matched for the nature of their offense, their age, the district where the sentence was imposed, their criminal past, their sex, and suspicion of drug use and according to the section of the Penal Code that they had breached. The study examined whether re-offending was more or less frequent by persons on community service than by prisoners serving short-term sentences. Re-offending by persons who had been sentenced to community service was looked at in terms of both the severity of the new offense and how soon it occurred within a three-year period after the first conviction. A distinction was made between reoffending in general and committing a further offense of the same type as that for which the person had originally been convicted. Significant differences were found only in relation to recidivism in general. Of those who had done community service, 42 percent re-offended, whereas 54 percent of those who had served short-term prison sentences re-offended. Property offenses account for most of this difference. Significant differences were found within this broad group of property offenses. For example, out of those convicted under section 311 of the Penal Code for certain types of theft, especially breaking and entering, 50 percent of those who were given community service re-offended, whereas 82 percent of the prisoners re-offended. Also worthy of note is that, among young offenders (eighteen to twenty-four years, inclusive) re-offending following a community service order is virtually absent, both for first offenders and for those with previous convictions. Among those convicted for traffic offenses, especially driving under the influence of alcohol, no difference in rates of re-offending was found at all.

Legal Regulation on Sentence to Unpaid Work

After an eight-year experimental period and over twenty thousand community service orders, the statutory regulations governing the penalty of community service (sections 22b–22j) were taken up into the Penal Code on 1 December 1989. A draft bill had been under discussion in Parliament since September 1987.

The intention behind these regulations is to reduce the use of the short unconditional prison sentence as far as possible. Short-term prison sentences are custodial sentences of six months or less. Six months is accepted internationally as the boundary between short and long prison sentences.[5] The aim of the new regulations is founded on the conviction that short-term imprisonment is often an inappropriate response to criminal conduct. Objections to short-term imprisonment are that it does not afford the delinquent any opportunity to serve a sentence in a purposeful way, it places the detainee outside the community, thus restricting his rehabilitation opportunities, and often also takes away the offender's existing social roles. It became clear during the experiments with community service that this alternative sanction overcomes most of the objections to the enforcement of short-term prison sentences. Community service does not isolate the convicted person from the community, and it reinforces self-respect, thereby increasing the person's chances of rehabilitation. An additional advantage is that it takes some of the pressure off the prison system.

The main points of the statutory regulations are as follows. In addition to the custodial sentences (the prison sentence and detention) and fines, there is now also the sentence to carry out unpaid work. This sentence is lighter than the sentences involving deprivation of liberty and more severe than the fine. The sentence to do unpaid work is deemed to be a sentence that restricts a person's liberty. The maximum number of hours of unpaid work that can be imposed as a penalty is 240 hours. The work must be completed within six months if the number of hours is less than 120, and within twelve months otherwise. A judge may only impose a community service penalty if the sentence he would otherwise impose is an unconditional prison sentence of six months or less or a part-suspended/part-unconditional prison sentence of which the unconditional part is not more than six months. Furthermore, a judge can impose this penalty only in response to an elaborated proposal from the accused that he is willing to carry out nonrenumerated work of a nature and in work project as stated in the proposal; the accused must also consent to the proposed sentence. The "compulsory consent" was taken up in the Penal Code to avoid contravening four international conventions forbidding forced labor, which The Netherlands has signed. To ensure that the penalty of unpaid work is used only as an alternative to an unconditional prison sentence, the judge has to state in his sentence the prison sentence he considered imposing for which the community service is a substitute. The sentence also specifies the number of hours' work to be carried out, the period within which it has to be completed, and the nature of the work.

The prosecution service is responsible for supervising the manner in which the work is carried out. Information can be requested from individuals and organizations involved in probation work for this purpose. If the prosecution service considers that the convicted person is not completing, or has not been able to complete, the work entirely in accordance with the agreement, then it can make changes to the agreement without going back to the court. Changes may be made in respect to the completion period and the nature of work being done. The convicted person will be informed of these changes and may make objections within eight days to the judge who imposed the sentence.

If the judge feels that the convicted person has not carried out the imposed work properly, and if the prosecution service demands this, the judge can actually impose the prison term mentioned in the sentence and order that all or part of it be enforced. He does take into account that part of the work that has been properly carried out. The prosecution service has to make its demand in this connection within three months after the end of the completion period for the community service.

When the prosecution service is satisfied that the work imposed has been carried out properly, it must inform the convicted person as soon as possible. In order to discourage unfair competition, regional review committees have been created to check whether workplaces are being used for community service.

Every probation officer has a duty to see that, where cases are suitable for the penalty of community service, this is brought to the attention of the accused, the prosecution service, and the judge, so that a community service proposal is actually made and the judge is given the opportunity of imposing a community service penalty.

The probation service is responsible for the practical implementation of the community service order. In the probation service a coordinator has been appointed for each of the nineteen jurisdictions. His job is to canvass for projects, maintain a project bank, maintain contacts with the project institutions, and write the final reports. The coordinator decides on the nature of the work to be carried out by the offender. In his decision the coordinator takes into account the skills, education, and vocational training of the offender. In case the work is part of teamwork, the coordinator has also to decide whether the offender fits in the team. When during the carrying out of the community service the place of work or the nature of work must be changed, the coordinator contacts the prosecution service, which is vested with the power to make these changes.

Unlike, for example, in the Federal Republic of Germany, community service cannot be used as an alternative to a suspended prison sentence, a fine, or a fine-default detention.

The statutory regulations make no distinction between employed offenders and those who are unemployed. The underlying principle is that community service will be carried out in free time, and the maximum number of hours of community service is based on this assumption. Nine or ten hours of community service on top of a thirty-eight-hour regular working week is deemed workable. However, the Penal Code does not lay down a maximum number of hours of community service that may be worked in a week.

The work being proposed for community service projects must be of benefit to the community. It can be with public bodies like the government or private organizations in the field of health care, the environment and the protection of nature, and social and cultural work.

No criminal offenses are specifically excluded from punishment with an alternative sanction either in the Penal Code or in practice. However, given the boundary of the six-month prison sentence, community service operates mainly in the very widespread middle range of criminality and is not used for the more serious offenses unless there are mitigating circumstances.

It is expected that in 1991 more than five thousand community service sentences will be imposed. In approximately 15 percent of these cases the community service will not be completed successfully. The community service sentence as a principal sentence saves at least 265 prison places a year. On average each community service sentence costs Dfl. 2,000 but saves sixty days of imprisonment, which would have cost Dfl. 13,800.[6]

Notes

1. P. J. P. Tak, "A Comparative Survey of the Use of Alternatives to Imprisonment in the Member-States of the Council of Europe," I.P.P.F. publication no. 28, Bonn,

1987, p. 101; A. M. van Kalmthout and P. J. P. Tak, "Sanctions-Systems in the Member-States of the Council of Europe," Kluwer, Deventer, 1988.

2. P. J. P. Tak, "Concepts of Conditional Release in Western Europe," *Netherlands International Law Review* (1989), pp. 19–49.

3. M. W. Bol and J. J. Overwater, "Dienstverlening, Eindrapport naar de vervanging van de vrijheidsstraf in het strafrecht voor volwassenen," Staatsuitgeverij, 's-Gravenhage, 1984.

4. M. W. Bol and J. J. Overwater, "Recidive van dienstverleners in het strafrecht van volwassenen," Staatsuitgeverij, 's-Gravenhage, 1986.

5. United Nations, Sixth United Nations Congress on the Prevention of Crime and the Treatment of Offenders, *Alternatives to Imprisonment and Measures for the Social Resettlement of Prisoners: Report of the Secretary-General* (A/CONF.121/13 and Add.1).

6. Proceedings of Parliament, 15 February 1989, p. 4,981.

Part VI
North America

13

Intermediate Sanctions in Canada

Department of Justice
Sentencing Team, Policy Programs and Research Sector

Why Intermediate Sanctions?

The two most recent reports in the correctional field, *Sentencing Reform: A Canadian Approach* (the Report of the Canadian Sentencing Commission) and *Taking Responsibility* (the Report of the Standing Committee on Justice and the Solicitor General) make extensive recommendations respecting the increased use of community alternatives. A listing of these recommendations is annexed.

"Imprisonment is still, throughout the world, the backbone of the system of criminal sanctions."[1] Prison and jail overcrowding in nearly every American jurisdiction has focused policymakers' attention on punishments that fall between prison and probation. These include various types of intensive probation, financial penalties, house arrest, intermittent confinement, "shock probation," community service, electronic monitoring, and treatment conditions.

Much of the pressure that has led to the current interest in intermediate sanctions concerns prison overcrowding and the related political and economic needs to devise alternative punishments that can credibly be imposed on people for whose imprisonment the state would rather not pay. Policymakers are caught between the perceptions that the public wants criminals to be punished for their crimes but that it does not want to pay for the construction and operation of additional prisons to increase overall prison capacity.

In the United States, intermediate sanctions are said to reduce pressure on prison resources. They permit the offender to retain family and community ties. They don't unduly jeopardize community security or safety. Many programs are fully or partly supported by fees charged to offenders. They are said (although here the evidence is much less clear than the conventional wisdom suggests) to free up prison space and thereby save substantial public monies.

Norval Morris[2] describes the way in which intermediate sanctions should be applied:

1. Intermediate punishments should be applied to many criminals now in prison and jail and to many criminals now sentenced to probation or a suspended sentence.
2. Intermediate punishments must be rigorously enforced if they are to be effective and credible sanctions. Adequate resources for their enforcement are essential.
3. Breaches of conditions of intermediate punishments must be taken seriously by the supervising authority and, in appropriate cases, by the sentencing judge if these punishments are to become credible sanctions.
4. The use of fines should be greatly expanded, in amount and in frequency, both as a punishment standing alone and as part of a punishment package. Fines must be adjusted to the offender's financial capacity (to be achieved by a system of "day fines") and must be collected; this requires innovative assessment and enforcement arrangements, since, at present, fines are set too low, do not sufficiently match the means of the offender, and are too often not collected.
5. The use of community service orders, standing alone or as part of a punishment package, should be greatly increased. Such punishments are applicable to the indigent and to the wealthy; they have much to contribute, provided, as for other intermediate punishments, they are vigorously supervised and enforced.
6. Intensive probation is a mechanism by which reality can be brought to all intermediate punishments. Allied to house arrest, treatment orders, and residential conditions up to house arrest, buttressed by electronic monitoring where appropriate, and paid for by fees for service by the offender, where that is realistic, intensive supervision has the capacity both to control offenders in the community and to facilitate their growth to crime-free lives.
7. Current sentencing reforms, both those developed and those proposed, have devoted inadequate attention to intermediate punishments. Sentencing guidelines, legislative or voluntary, shaped by a sentencing commission or by a court system, must provide better guidance to the judiciary in the use of intermediate punishments if a comprehensive sentencing system is to be developed. In particular:

   a. There is a range of offense-offender relationships in which incarcerative and intermediate punishments are equally applicable.
   b. There is a range of offense-offender relationships in which intermediate punishments and lesser community-based controls are equally applicable.
   c. The sentencing judge requires adequate information about the offender and his or her financial and personal circumstances to decide on the applicability to each convicted offender of a fine, of a community service order, of a treatment or residential order, of intensive probation, or of a split sentence involving incarceration and an intermediate punishment—or a mixture of several of those punishments.

    d. The judge should retain ultimate responsibility for the decision on the "backup" sentence, that is to say, on what should be done if the conditions of an intermediate punishment are not adhered to.

8. As intermediate punishments become part of a comprehensive sentencing system, it is desirable that their efficacy be critically evaluated so that, in time, an effective treatment classification will emerge.

What Are the Concerns?

To skeptics, intermediate sanctions represent "net widening." If 30 percent of convicted offenders in a jurisdiction where the rate of incarceration remains constant receive incarcerative sentences, and 70 percent receive probation, creation of new punishments more punitive than simple probation necessarily means that more offenders will experience relatively more punitive sanctions than before. Experience and empirical research suggest that "alternatives to incarceration" often are imposed on people who would otherwise not have been incarcerated. To others, the gross disproportion of minority and low-income people among convicted offenders will be exacerbated by development of intermediate sanctions, whether by diverting white offenders from prison or by increasing the number of people under stringent state control. Finally, some opponents of intermediate sanctions see their development as a manifestation of punitive attitudes that they oppose and that they fear will stifle humane strategies of rehabilitation and reformation.

Some types of sanctions provide alternatives by name only, as they lead back to prison too swiftly. Imprisonment may be indispensable as a backup threat against willful noncompliance with obligations imposed by alternative sentencing. But care should be taken lest inadvertent or minor violations of conditions of probation or mere nonpayment of fines more or less automatically subject the offender to imprisonment.

The development and increased use of alternatives to imprisonment should not deflect from the continued necessity of trimming back substantive criminal law where it covers conduct that can no longer be regarded as dangerous to society.

Especially in diversion programs, there sometimes occurs a suspicious quid pro quo between offering an alternative to imprisonment and the defendant's foregoing his or her procedural right to have guilt proved beyond a reasonable doubt. The opportunity to avoid imprisonment should generally not be made dependent on submitting to conviction without trial.

Most claimed cost-savings associated with development of intermediate sanctions do not bear up under scrutiny, especially when they involve comparisons of per-capita costs in community-based sanctions.

Chapter 13

What Works

House arrest and intensive supervision programs targeted on prison-bound offenders have been successfully implemented and institutionalized in a number of jurisdictions. Evaluators have concluded that they have diverted substantial numbers of offenders from prison at sizable net savings to the state.

The European experience with the use of fines as the primary sanction for low- and moderate-severity crimes demonstrates that fines can serve as credible intermediate sanctions in industrialized countries.

Community service sentences in the United States are most commonly used as adjuncts to other sanctions and seem at present seldom to be imposed as substitutes for incarceration.

Electronic monitoring programs in many jurisdictions are being used for offenders who present little to no risk of involvement in crimes that cause fearfulness; in IPS programs they are being used to appropriately increase surveillance intensity for higher-risk offenders liable to reoffend or abscond.

There is, throughout the correctional community, increasing political and organizational sophistication in developing, implementing, institutionalizing, and evaluating new programs.

Situation in Canada

Incarcerated Populations

The number of inmates in federal establishments increased by 25 percent over the five-year period beginning in 1982. The number of admissions as a ratio of the number of releases was 1.09 in 1986, up slightly from 1.08 in 1985. In other words, slightly more inmates are admitted than are released.[3]

Female offenders comprised 3 percent of total federal admissions, although this varies between 2 percent in New Brunswick and 6 percent in British Columbia. Native offenders comprised 10 percent of total federal admissions in 1986. East of Manitoba, not more than 3 percent of all federal admissions were natives. In the West, between 13 and 34 percent of all admissions were natives in Manitoba, Alberta, British Columbia, and the Yukon. Over 60 percent of admissions in Saskatchewan and the Northwest Territories (NWT) were natives. The average age on federal admission was thirty years.[4]

At the provincial level, female offenders comprised approximately 7 percent of total provincial admissions. Native offenders comprised about 18 percent of admissions. This percentage varies widely across the country, with less than 10 percent of admissions in Newfoundland being natives, while over 50 percent of admissions in Manitoba and Saskatchewan were

326

natives. The median age on admission is twenty-seven years. The median age of the Canadian population is thirty-eight years.[5]

The development of community correctional programs and services has been emphasized in recent years, particularly in light of the high costs and uncertain benefits of custody for certain offender groups.[6] While noncustodial services are not limited to probation, probation is the primary community-based alternative to incarceration.

In 1985–86 there were, on average, 109,815 offenders on the Canadian corrections caseload. This represents an increase of 12 percent since 1982. The majority of these, 82,243, were under some kind of community supervision, while 27,572 were held in custody. During the five-year period 1981–82 to 1985–86, between 82 and 85 percent of the total caseload was managed by provincially operated facilities. Over two-thirds of the total caseload were offenders on probation under provincial supervision.[7]

The proportion of cases carried by the federal correctional establishment is small in comparison to the provincial caseload. Additionally, the proportion supervised in the community at the federal level differs from the proportion supervised in the community at the provincial level. In 1986 there were 7,317 offenders under federal supervision in the community—50 percent under full parole, 31 percent under mandatory supervision, and 19 percent on day parole.[8] This compares to 11,214 in federal custody. By way of contrast, 82,243 offenders were under provincial community supervision as opposed to 27,572 in provincial custody. In short, by far the most "action" in terms of the number of offenders handled in the community is found at the provincial level.

Sentence Length

Provincial sentences are, of course, shorter than their federal counterparts. As can be seen in figure 13.1, provincial sentences are heavily skewed toward the lower end.[9] The median sentence length for provincial sentences in 1985–86 was thirty days. Seven provinces had median sentence lengths that were shorter than the national average. Nearly half of the admissions to provincial custody were for less than thirty days. Fully one-third of this group were sentenced to less than fifteen days.[10]

The actual time served is even less than the sentence awarded due to remission. Put another way, 98 percent of provincial inmates serve one year or less. This affects the bed space of provincial corrections significantly. The 61 percent of inmates who served up to thirty-one days to release took up only 12 percent of the bed space; the 2 percent who served longer than one year took up 16 percent of the available beds.[11]

Intermittent sentences, which seem to cause particular problems in respect of provincial correctional officials, represent 6 percent of all provincial admissions. This compares with 5 percent of admissions in 1982. The use of this sanction varied from 4 percent in Manitoba to 14 percent in British Columbia.[12]

Figure 13.2 shows federal sentence lengths, which vary generally between two and five years. The average sentence length has remained fairly

Figure 13.1: Provincial Sentence Lengths, 1985–1986

Figure 13.2: Federal Sentence Lengths

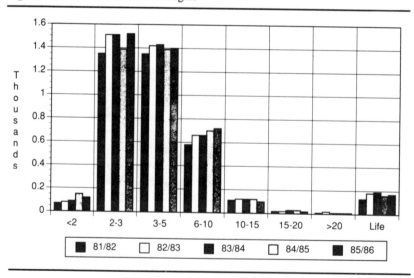

constant over the five-year period 1981–82 to 1985–86, at about forty-five months: 64 percent were sentenced to less than four years, 38 percent were sentenced to between two and three years, 3 percent were for sentences of ten years or more. Lifers and indeterminate sentences account for 4 percent of admissions.

Offenses and Dispositions

While the above information provides an overview of the structure of sentences and the gross options used, it is instructive to examine the nature of the offenses for which offenders were sentenced, to understand the context in which alternatives to incarceration, or "intermediate sanctions," can be considered. As can be seen in figure 13.3, the distribution of all offenses suggests that driving offenses and property offenses represent nearly 75 percent of admissions.[13] Violent offenses represent about 14 percent of admissions. The nature and extent of the violence problem varies from region to region. The problem is clearly more acute in the Prairies and in the NWT and less critical in the Atlantic and the Quebec regions. Criminal Code offenses comprise about 70 percent of all admissions. Provincial offenses, which include alcohol-related offenses, represent about 21 percent. Figure 13.4 suggests that noncustodial options are used in about 52 percent of all cases.[14]

Figure 13.3: Violence as Proportion of All Offenses (Distribution of offenses)

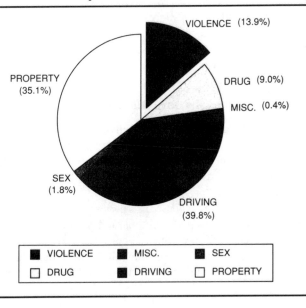

Figure 13.4: General Disposition for All Offenses (Type of disposition)

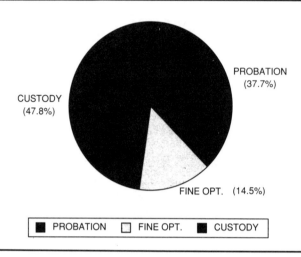

CUSTODY
(47.8%)

PROBATION
(37.7%)

FINE OPT. (14.5%)

| ■ PROBATION | □ FINE OPT. | ■ CUSTODY |

In general, this suggests that noncustodial offenses are used in over half of all dispositions and that a large number of dispositions are for offenses that would be viewed as being less serious (property and driving offenses).

The emergence of less secure institutions began in the 1950s and has increased steadily since then. In 1985–86 there were 170 provincial custodial facilities, of which 129 were designated "secure" and 41 were designated "open." These more open institutions tend to be much smaller than the more secure institutions. Many jurisdictions purchase these less secure facilities through the private sector.[15]

Resource Allocations

In 1985–86, federal expenditures on adult corrections totaled some $744 million, a 1 percent increase from the previous year. The Correctional Service of Canada spent $730 million, and $14 million were spent by the National Parole Board. Custodial facilities account for 76 percent of federal correctional expenditures.

The major operating expense is salaries and benefits for the staff. There were slightly more than eleven thousand persons employed in federal corrections, 75 percent of whom provide custodial services, while 9 percent were employed in parole offices. Community supervision functions, comprised of the sixty-two parole offices and their staff, account for 92 percent of the operating costs of community services, while purchased supervision accounted for 8 percent.

As would be expected, the provincial responses to the problems in their regions also vary. In 1985–86, $622 million were spent on provincial adult corrections.[16] This was an increase of 3 percent over the previous year's expenditures. Of this money, 81 percent was spent on custodial services, while 12 percent was spent on probation and parole. Compared to the federal level, much more is spent provincially on community supervision. The provinces, however, spend less on administration than do federal corrections. General provincial expenditures, per capita, can be seen in figure 13.5.[17]

For all the provinces, 0.6 percent of overall government expenditures were for corrections. The actual amounts of money spent are evidently a reflection of the size of the jurisdiction. Ontario spent a total of $265.6 million on corrections, an amount that represents 43 percent of the overall provincial total. The Yukon spends 1.5 percent of its budget on corrections, while Quebec spends 0.3 percent. When expenses are broken down by category, 71 percent is for the salaries and benefits of the fourteen thousand workers in the systems.

The percentages of the provincial budgets spent on community programs can be seen in figure 13.6. While the majority of correctional

Figure 13.5: Provincial General Expenses on Corrections (Per capital custody expenses by region)

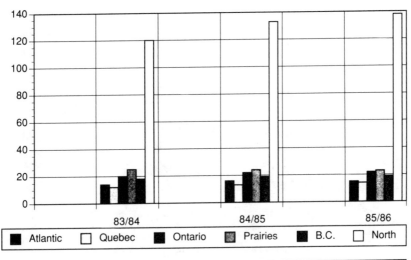

Figure 13.6: Provincial Choices for Community Expenditures (Types of community expenses)

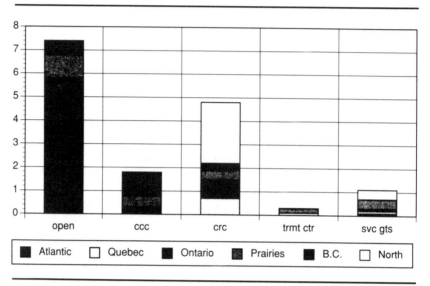

Figure 13.7: Provincial Expenditures on Community Programs (Per capita community expenses by region)

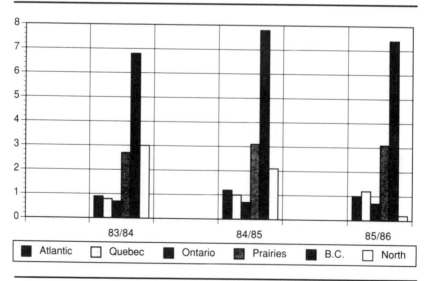

expenses are for custody services, the proportion of the provincial budget expended for community supervision varies between 7 percent in Newfoundland and 24 percent in the Yukon. Within expenditures for community services, 88 percent of provincial expenditures in the community are for government-operated facilities, while 5 percent are for purchased services. Grants and contributions are used for community supervision and account for 7 percent.[18] By far the greatest per capita expenditures on community programs are made by British Columbia, as can be seen in figure 13.7. The ways in which the provinces choose to spend their community monies may be indicative of the values they place on various aspects of the programs. As is indicated in figure 13.6, most monies are spent on open custody.

Overcrowding

There were sixty-two federal facilities in 1986. These facilities had a normal capacity of 9,681 beds plus 2,071 special-purpose beds available for dissociation and institutional health care. There was a total of 11,752 federal beds available in 1985–86. The average count of inmates within federal facilities in 1985–86 was 11,214, or 95 percent of normal capacity.[19]

For the provinces in 1985–86 there were some 19,000 beds available. This is made up of 17,480 operational beds in provincial custodial facilities plus 1,677 special-purpose beds for temporary detention, isolation, medical purposes, emergencies, etc. The average inmate count in 1985–86 was 16,358, an increase of 1 percent from the previous year. In short, there appears to be an overall availability of provincial operational beds on the order of 1,000 across all provinces.

Intermediate Sanctions in Canada

A useful historical overview and discussion of the objectives of alternative sentencing programs is found in the research report of the Canadian Sentencing Commission on the subject.[20] A number of alternatives to incarceration exist in Canada. The three best known are the community service order programs, fine option programs, and restitution programs. To this list can be added reconciliation programs, attendance programs, temporary absence programs, intermittent sentence programs, and prison industries.[21] For the purposes of this discussion, no mention has been made here of temporary absence, intermittent sentences, or prison industries, since it is felt that these are really more in the context of potential alternatives, within the definition used by Ekstedt.[22]

Community Service Orders[23]

In general, community service order programs are intended to provide an alternative to incarceration and to engender a sense of responsibility in the offender. The offender may be eligible for such programs if he or she is a nonviolent offender; the court awards a probationary sentence with a condition of doing community service if the offender is willing to participate.

In addition to the general questions about this type of program, indicated below, there is a general question as to what degree of community involvement in this type of alternative is possible and appropriate.

Fine Options[24]

This type of program is in use to try to deal with the large number of individuals who are incarcerated for not paying their fines. Three types of programs are currently operating: point of sentence programs, where the offender is informed at the time of sentence that the possibility exists to discharge the fine through community service work; point of default programs, where the offender is notified either on default or when default becomes imminent; and preinstitutional programs, where participation is limited to eligible nonincarcerated offenders.

Common objectives of such programs include avoidance of the use of incarceration, reduction of the cost of incarceration, provision to offenders of the opportunity to discharge their fines through community work, and encouragement of community participation in the criminal justice system. Common eligibility criteria include the participant having been levied a fine and given time to pay, the fine not being greater than $1,000, and the offender being willing to participate.

Policy questions common to this type of program include the issue of the offender's ability to pay—that is, if the offender can pay, should he or she be eligible for this type of program? Of interest to the jurisdictions receiving monies from such fines is the potential impact of the loss of this revenue.

Restitution Programs[25]

Programs of restitution exist in the formal sense in Saskatchewan only, but in both more or less formalized ways in other provinces as well. The common objectives of such programs are to increase victim satisfaction with the criminal justice system and to decrease the use of incarceration for property offenses in particular through increasing the number of restitution orders.

The outstanding policy questions respecting restitution include the role of the victim in the process, the ability of the offender to pay, and the assessment of the level of harm (by whom and according to what standards).

Victim-Offender Reconciliation Programs[26]

The major purpose of reconciliation programs is to reduce the complexity of the situation that arises when a minor offense has occurred and to assist in the reparation of the community identity. These programs are focused upon an attempt to personalize and humanize the criminal justice system. They provide a community-based mechanism for resolving minor conflicts at the postcharge or pretrial stages.

Attendance Programs[27]

A variety of rehabilitative and reintegrative programs are considered to lie within the attendance program grouping, including sociological and psychological therapies, life skills training, and counseling. Most jurisdictions have some or all of these types of programs available. A number of provinces have established impaired-driving programs, having as their objectives to educate the convicted impaired driver on the negative effects of impaired driving, to heighten awareness, appreciation, and understanding of the problem, and to induce long-range attitudinal changes.

Therapy for assaultive males has increased greatly in the recent past. There are now over thirty such programs. In addition, safe houses for women victims have received considerable publicity. The objectives are aimed at recognizing and confronting the violent behavior and ultimately replacing it with appropriate nonviolent and interactive responses. Six of ten provinces have established sex offender treatment programs. There is wide variability in the programs, some dealing with nonviolent, nonhabitual offenders, while others deal with all sex offenders. The general orientation is toward psychophysiological assessment techniques, conditioning, impulse control, and self-management approaches to therapy. The majority are conducted in a hospital setting and have strict referral criteria.

Programs for shoplifters have been established in various jurisdictions and operate under a variety of administrative arrangements. The aims of such programs are to help offenders, mainly women, to deal with underlying social and psychological problems that are presumed to be manifested in the shoplifting behavior.

Work Camp Programs (Yukon)

In the Yukon Territory a program has been created that has proven to be advantageous to both the community and the inmate. The Corrections

Branch of the Department of Justice has instituted a work camp program aimed at carrying out worthy public projects that would not otherwise take place due to lack of funding or local initiative. The current work program is viewed as an annex to the main correctional facility in Whitehorse. There are three basic principles underlying the move to work camps and community work placements for inmates:

1. A clear rehabilitative value in having inmates develop a working routine and work ethic
2. A means by which the offender makes restitution to the community at large
3. A means by which the offender is reminded that there is a significant consequence for his or her misconduct

Common Policy Questions

With such a diversity of programs, in a wide number of jurisdictions it is not surprising that there has been concern expressed about the consistency of these programs, the consistency of the policy bases, and the potential for disparity, not only between jurisdictions, but between judges and officials in the same jurisdiction. There is a lack of clarity respecting the objectives of the correctional system (retribution, deterrence, rehabilitation, or incapacitation) in respect of the use of these alternatives. Additionally, there have been questions respecting the amount of supervision that is appropriate.

Ekstedt[28] questions the goals of the programs and notes that the obvious purpose of relieving prison overcrowding has not happened in general. Indeed, other programs such as temporary absences have been used effectively to deal with prison population pressures. It is not clear who constituted the clientele for alternatives. The move to privatization poses difficulties in terms of standards and in respect of agencies' continuous need to seek additional funds from government or other sources as a result of government cutbacks.

There have been few cost/benefit studies. Finally, there is a question of who should be responsible for the information systems necessary to properly administer such programs, and how costs should be arranged.

What Are Canadians Saying?

The Canadian Judicial Council says the implementation of the Archambault recommendations (see the Annex) concerning full parole and the reduction of earned remission should be deferred until the system and facilities for community services sanctions have been provided and put into use for a sufficient period of time to indicate their effectiveness as sanctions for the purpose of reducing the use of incarceration.

The Supreme Court of Ontario, in its submission respecting the Archambault Report, says that it does not accept the development of specific guidelines for specific community sanctions. This would be inflexible. They agree that the judiciary should maintain primary control over the nature and conditions of community sanctions.

Some provincial representatives with whom we spoke claimed that there was no rehabilitation at the provincial level. The offender was much better off to get federal time. Some provinces have no funds to develop programs—particularly treatment for sex offenders and drug offenders. There is more need of treatment programs—the "nothing works" dictum is not accepted. Respecting community sanctions, they reject the idea that there is a vast potential for increased community sanctions. Pushing more people into the community would risk the programs that are currently in place by putting inappropriate people in the community. Community sanctions don't need to be sanctions in their own right. What is needed is better management and better continuity. They state that it's not true that more community programs imply less expense. As the Archambault Report is written, the key recommendation is 12.1, respecting cost. This is because of the similarity to the YOA provisions, which imposed considerable extra cost on the provinces.

The current situation in British Columbia appears to be different. They claim that provincial prison populations are "capped." Bed space in the institutions has been progressively reduced over the past several years, and there is greater reliance on the community. The "infrastructure" is in place, and expansion of community-based programs has been done. There is some concern respecting community exposure to dangerous persons through the use of community alternatives. There is clear necessity to evaluate the capacity of the community to absorb more. If all of the Sentencing Commission report recommendations were implemented, there would be a huge expansion of the requirements of federal/provincial exchange-of-services agreements as a result of the increase in the number of federal inmates who would have to be absorbed by the province.

In the Northwest Territories, the lengthy time and expense that would be required for travel would have major effects in respect of increased use of intermediate sanctions. There is no indication in the Archambault Report of implementation considerations for the provinces. The emphasis on the community is good, but the concept of automatic diversion of funds from the corrections field to the community is false. If judges had more alternatives, they would incarcerate less.

The Canadian Association of Elizabeth Fry Societies says that those communities that reported good relationships between volunteer court workers and judges had the greatest success in using community-based sanctions. Public opinion polls suggest that respondents think that the criminal justice system should be a priority for the government and that they were not opposed to spending money on it. A poll in Toronto also suggests that people do not want a "tougher" system, rather they want one that works properly and provides appropriate protection. Participants did not favor longer sentences or keeping offenders incarcerated for longer periods, and they indicated support for alternatives to incarceration. They suggested that there should be greater use of fines, restitution, community service orders, and other community alternatives (Decima, Toronto, April 1988). Canadians do not think that the courts work well and feel that some "fundamental change" is needed. Canadians were almost equally divided as to what the aims of the penal system should be, with 46 percent feeling that it should be rehabilitation and 45 percent feeling that it should be punishment.

Conclusions

A number of tentative conclusions can be drawn from the above material. By far the greatest number of offenders are handled by the provincial jurisdictions. Additionally, the provinces have a major part of the jurisdictional responsibilities in areas where intermediate sanctions could be developed. Accordingly, if major undertakings in respect of the development of intermediate sanctions are pursued, the provincial jurisdictions have to be leading players.

Pressures for development of intermediate sanctions may flow from the development of statements of purpose and principle, guidelines, or revised sentence maximums. There does not, however, appear to be reason to believe that severe population pressures exist at either the federal or the provincial level. Until the availability of incarceration is seriously limited for some reason, such as serious overcrowding or cost pressures, there is little likelihood of real movement toward the development of intermediate sanctions.

There do not seem to be the same pressures of overcrowding in Canada as in the United States. Accordingly, perhaps the lesser emphasis on community services is understandable. Both federal and provincial jurisdictions seem to place much greater emphasis on the custodial aspect of their operations than on the community aspect.

The problems in the various jurisdictions are different in nature, and the solutions adopted to date are different. Accordingly, any solutions that are sought will have to be tailored to the nature of the problems that can be identified in the particular jurisdiction, unless it can be determined that a national solution should apply.

In view of the number of nonviolent offenses, and in view of the small proportion of resources allocated to the community, it may be that there is an overuse of incarceration for offenses for which other alternatives could be considered. The value we place on the rate of incarceration in Canada as opposed to other countries needs to be reexamined in view of the short sentences that are served. This is particularly so when our rate of incarceration is compared to the United States, which has five times the rate of violent offenses in Canada. While it may be true that the incarceration rate in Canada is high on a per-capita basis, if those persons serve a shorter period of time incarcerated in correctional facilities, the potential negative impact of incarceration is reduced. The need to "improve" the rate should be examined in a new light.

Care must be taken in developing any alternative sentencing programs in view of the potential impact on provincial incarcerated populations that comes about as a result of the short sentences that are the current "norm." There appear to be clear and major differences in the availability of community services and the extent to which they are used. This may be so because of demonstrable regional sociological differences. More information needs to be gathered on this issue.

Annex

Archambault Recommendations[29]

Chapter 12—Community Involvement.

12.01 The Commission recommends that the federal and provincial governments provide the necessary resources and financial support to ensure that community programs are made available and to encourage their greater use.

12.02 The Commission recommends the development of mechanisms to provide better information about sentencing objectives to sentence administrators.

12.03 The Commission recommends that a transcript of the sentencing judgment be made available to the authorities involved in the administration of the sentence.

12.04 The Commission recommends that court officials, corrections personnel and other sentence administrators meet and discuss the parameters of authority in criminal justice administration, sentencing objectives and other issues in sentencing.

12.05 The Commission recommends the development of mechanisms to provide better information about alternative sentencing resources to the judiciary.

12.06 The Commission recommends that feedback to the courts regarding the effectiveness of sanctions be provided on a systematic basis.

12.07 The Commission recommends that prior to imposing a particular community sanction, the sentencing judge be advised to consult or obtain a report respecting the suitability of the offender for the sanction and the availability of programs to support such a disposition.

12.08   The Commission endorses the general policy in the Criminal Law Reform Act, 1984 (former Bill C-19), that community sanctions be developed as independent sanctions. The Commission recommends that the federal government enact legislation which reflects the sentencing proposals in the Criminal Law Reform Act, 1984 (Bill C-19). The Commission further recommends that additional proposals be examined by the Permanent Sentencing Commission and by the federal and/or provincial governments for further review, development and implementation.

12.09   The Commission recommends that community sanctions be defined and applied as sanctions in their own right.

12.10   The Commission recommends that specific guidance be developed, either by the Permanent Sentencing Commission or by a body specifically mandated to study this issue, respecting when particular community sanctions should be imposed.

12.11   The Commission recommends that the Permanent Sentencing Commission consider the feasibility of developing criteria and principles which permit the comparison of individual community sanctions and which attempt to standardize their use (e.g., X dollars is the equivalent of Y hours of community service).

12.12   The Commission recommends that the judiciary retain primary control over the nature and conditions attached to community sanctions.

12.13   The Commission recommends that the Permanent Sentencing Commission include in its review of community sanctions both those dispositions imposed by the judge at the time of sentencing and administrative programs in the custodial setting which affect the degrees of incarceration to which an inmate is subject.

12.14   The Commission recommends that the Criminal Code be amended to permit the imposition of a fine alone even for those offenses which are punishable by a term of imprisonment of more than five years.

12.15   The Commission recommends that fines be available for all offenses (except life sentences) regardless of the maximum penalty provided and in spite of the fact that some offenses would have presumptive "in" designations. Where the imposition of a fine would constitute departure from the presumptive disposition, it should be justified with reasons.

12.16   The Commission recommends that for those offenses for which a judge has decided to impose a community disposition, a pecuniary sanction such as a fine be considered as a first alternative for the more serious offenses and for the more serious instances of the lesser offenses.

12.17 The Commission recommends that a restitution order be imposed when the offence involves loss or damage to an individual victim. A fine should be imposed where a public institution incurs loss as a result of the offence or damage caused to public property.

12.18 The Commission recommends that where the offence carries a presumptive "out" disposition greater use be made of fines where the offender has benefitted financially from the commission of the offence.

12.19 The Commission recommends that the Permanent Sentencing Commission should consider ways of assisting the courts in the determination of equitable fines on offenders of varying means so as to maximize equality of impact.

The Swedish day-fine system is an example to be studied. Meanwhile, the provinces should be encouraged to institute pilot projects on the use of day-fine systems.

12.20 The Commission recommends that once it has been decided that a fine may be the appropriate sanction, consideration must be given to whether it is appropriate to impose a fine on the individual before the court. The amount of the fine and time for payment must be determined in accordance not only with the gravity of the offence, but also with the financial ability of the offender. Further to the above principle, prior to the imposition of a fine, the court should inquire into the means of the offender to determine his ability to pay and the appropriate mode and conditions of payment.

12.21 The Commission recommends that where the limited means of an offender permits the imposition of only one pecuniary order, priority be given to an order of restitution, where appropriate.

12.22 The Commission recommends a reduction in the use of imprisonment for fine default.

12.23 The Commission recommends that a quasi-automatic prison term not be imposed for fine default and that offenders only be incarcerated for wilful breach of a community sanction.

12.24 The Commission recommends that section 648 of the Criminal Code be retained.

12.25 The Commission recommends that the payment of fines be enforced in accordance with the model for fine default described on pages 382—384.

12.26 The Commission recommends that the following national conversion table be used for the assessment of default periods where incarceration is imposed for wilful non-payment of a fine. [Table not included here.]

12.27 The Commission recommends that the Criminal Code clarify the distinction between compensation and restitution by providing a definition of restitution which is used consistently throughout the Code.

12.28 The Commission recommends that restitution in the Criminal Code be understood to include the return of property obtained by the commission of the offence, the payment of money for the ascertainable loss, damage or destruction of property and/or the payment of money for the ascertainable loss or injury suffered as a result of the commission of the offence, by the offender to the victim.

12.29 The Commission recommends that compensation be understood as contribution or payment by the state to the victim of the offence for loss or injury suffered as a result of the commission to the offence.

12.30 The Commission recommends that its fine default model also apply to the enforcement of restitution orders.

12.31 The Commission recommends that the Criminal Code provisions be expanded and permit an order of restitution to be imposed as a separate sanction or in combination with other sanctions.

Prior to the imposition of an order of restitution, the sentencing judge shall inquire, or cause to be conducted, an inquiry into the present or future ability of the offender to make restitution or to pay a fine.

An order of restitution shall include consideration of:

i) property damages incurred as a result of the crime, based on actual cost of repair (or replacement value);

ii) medical and hospital costs incurred by the victim as a result of the crime; and

iii) earnings lost by the victim (before the date of sentencing) as a result of the crime including earnings lost while the victim was hospitalized or participating in the investigation or trial of the crime.

As between the enforcement of an order of restitution and other monetary sanctions, priority should be given to restitution.

Daubney Recommendations[30]

Sentencing Alternatives.

RECOMMENDATION 13
The Committee recommends that legislation be enacted to permit the imposition of a community service order as a sole sanction or in combination with others, provided that the judge is satisfied that a discharge, restitution, fine or simple probation order alone would not achieve the purpose of sentencing proposed by the Committee;

RECOMMENDATION 14
The Committee recommends that guidelines for the number of hours of community service which should be imposed in various circumstances be developed to decrease sentencing disparity;

RECOMMENDATION 15
The Committee recommends that a legislated ceiling of between 300 and 600 hours (over three years) be established for community service sentences for adult offenders, provided that judges be permitted to exceed the ceiling where a greater number of hours is agreed to by the offender as a result of victim-offender reconciliation or an "alternate sentence plan" proposal and reasons are provided by the judge;

RECOMMENDATION 16
The Committee recommends that legislation be adopted to exclude sexual and violent offenders from eligibility for community service orders unless they have been assessed and found suitable by a community service program coordinator.

Funding.

RECOMMENDATION 17
The Committee recommends that the federal government, preferably in conjunction with provincial/territorial governments, provide funding to community organizations for alternative sentence planning projects in a number of jurisdictions in Canada on a pilot basis;

RECOMMENDATION 18
The Committee recommends that the federal government, preferably in conjunction with provincial/territorial governments provide funding and technical exchange to community organizations to promote sound evaluation of such projects.

Victims.

RECOMMENDATION 19
The Committee recommends that the federal government, preferably in conjunction with provincial/territorial governments, support the expansion and evaluation throughout Canada of victim-offender reconciliation programs at all stages of the criminal justice process which:

    (a) provide substantial support to victims through effective victim services, and

    (b) encourage a high degree of community participation;

RECOMMENDATION 20
The Committee recommends that section 653(b) of the Criminal Code (contained in Bill C-89) be clarified to ensure that restitution for bodily injuries may be ordered in an amount up to the value of all pecuniary damages;

RECOMMENDATION 21
The Committee recommends that the federal government enact legislation and/or contribute support to provincial/territorial governments, to enhance civil enforcement of restitution orders with a view to relieving individual victims of this burden;

RECOMMENDATION 22
The Committee recommends that the following recommendations of the Sentencing Commission be implemented:

    (a) that a restitution order be imposed when the offence involves loss or damage to an individual victim. A fine should be imposed where a public institution incurs loss as a result of the offence or damage caused to public property (Rec. 12.17); and

    (b) that where the limited means of an offender permits the imposition of only one pecuniary order, priority be given to an order of restitution, where appropriate (Rec. 12.21).

Probation.

RECOMMENDATION 23
The Committee recommends that probation be replaced by seven separate orders (good conduct, reporting, residence, performance, community service, restitution, and intensive supervision), which might be ordered separately or in conjunction with one or more others or with some other type of order;

RECOMMENDATION 24

The Committee recommends that the Criminal Code be amended to provide a more efficient mechanism than is now the case for dealing with breaches of probation or other orders in a way which respects the offender's due process rights;

RECOMMENDATION 25

The Committee recommends that more extensive use be made of group work in community correctional programs and that adequate resources be provided so that these might be made available to offenders on a voluntary basis or pursuant to a performance order;

RECOMMENDATION 26

In particular, the Committee recommends that greater use be made of probation conditions or performance orders which require assaultive spouses to participate in specialized treatment or counselling programs;

RECOMMENDATION 27

The Committee recommends that consideration be given to the New Zealand sentence of community care and the Gateway Correctional Services model of intensive supervision;

RECOMMENDATION 28

The Committee recommends that funding be made available to voluntary and charitable agencies to establish or expand community residential and related programs.

Home Confinement.

RECOMMENDATION 29

The Committee recommends that home confinement, with or without electronic monitoring, be made available as an intermediate sanction, probably in conjunction with other sanctions, for carefully selected offenders in appropriate circumstances;

RECOMMENDATION 30

The Committee recommends that legislative changes required to permit the use of home confinement as a sentencing option provide reasonably efficient enforcement mechanisms which do not infringe basic due process rights of offenders;

RECOMMENDATION 31

The Committee recommends that consideration be given to requiring the consent of the offender and his or her co-residing family members to an order of home confinement;

RECOMMENDATION 32
The Committee recommends that in making an order of home confinement, the court consider appropriate collateral conditions (e.g., addictions counselling where appropriate).

Intermittent Sentences.

RECOMMENDATION 33
The Committee recommends that intermittent sentences not generally be used with respect to sexual offenses, where public protection, when necessary, should be secured through incarceration or where denunciation might be secured through home confinement, community residential orders, or short periods of continuous incarceration;

RECOMMENDATION 34
The Committee recommends that community residential centres be used for intermittent sentences:

RECOMMENDATION 35
The Committee recommends that consideration be given to combining intermittent sentences with performance orders or probationary conditions which are restorative or rehabilitative in nature.

Fines.

RECOMMENDATION 36
The Committee recommends that the following recommendations of the Sentencing Commission be adopted and implemented:

(a) That once it has been decided that a fine may be the appropriate sanction, consideration be given to whether it is appropriate to impose a fine on the individual before the court. The amount of the fine and the time for payment must be determined in accordance, not only with the gravity of the offence, but also with the financial ability of the offender. Further to the above principle, prior to the imposition of a fine, the court should inquire into the means of the offender to determine his or her ability to pay and the appropriate mode and conditions of payment; (Recommendation 12.20)

(b) that where the limited means of the offender permits the imposition of only one pecuniary order, priority be given to an order of restitution where appropriate; (Recommendation 12.21)

(c) that the use of imprisonment for fine default be reduced; (Recommendation 12.22)

(d) that a quasi-automatic prison term not be imposed for fine default and that offenders only be incarcerated for wilful breach of a community sanction. (Recommendation 12.23)

Intermediate Sanctions.

RECOMMENDATION 38

(a) That federal and provincial authorities develop, support and evaluate alternatives to incarceration and intermediate sanctions;
(b) that greater recognition and financial support be given to non-governmental agencies to develop alternative programs;
(c) that greater linkages be developed between the criminal justice system and other social and mental health services in society.

Notes

1. Thomas Weigend, Report for the International Association of Penal Law, Criminal Justice Policies in Relation to Problems of Imprisonment, Other Penal Sanctions, and Alternative Measures. Provisional Agenda of the Eighth United Nations Congress on the Prevention of Crime and the Treatment of Offenders.

2. Norval Morris, "Alternatives to Custody: Some dogmatic propositions concerning intermediate punishment and their imposition." Notes for a paper delivered at the conference on the Reform of Sentencing and Parole, August 1988.

3. *Adult Correctional Services in Canada, 1985–86*, Statistics Canada, p. 119.

4. Ibid., p. 130.

5. Ibid., p. 82.

6. The extent and availability of services, the extent of supervision, and the degree of centralized service all serve to place limits on the comparability of systems across the country.

7. *Adult Correctional Services in Canada 1985–1986*, p. 30.

8. Ibid., p. 133.

9. Note that on all bar graphs, the regions are represented from east to west, from the left side of the graph. In figure 13.1, the leftmost bar represents the Atlantic region. Due to scaling, not all bar labels print properly.

10. *Adult Correctional Services in Canada 1985–1986*, p. 88.

11. Ibid., p. 89.

12. Ibid., p. 90.

13. *Custodial and Probation Offenses: 1984/85*, Overview Report, Programs and Research Section, Department of Justice.

14. Ibid., pp. 6–7.

15. Ibid., p. 72.

16. *Adult Correctional Services in Canada 1985–1986*, p. 65.

17. Note that the sixth bar in this figure, to the far right, represents the North (NWT) and the Yukon Territories.

18. *Adult Correctional Services in Canada 1985–1986*, pp. 69–70.

19. Ibid., pp. 117–18.

20. J. Ekstedt and M. Jackson, 1988, *A Profile of Canadian Alternative Sentencing Programmes: A National Review of Policy Issues*, a report written for the Canadian Sentencing Commission, Minister of Justice, pp. 4–11 and 17–18.

21. Ibid., pp. 19–39.

22. Ibid., pp. 3–4.

23. Research and Statistics Section, Policy Programs and Research Branch, Department of Justice, *Fact Book on Community Service Order Programs in Canada*, 1986, prepared under contract by Peat, Marwick and Partners; and Ekstedt and Jackson, *A Profile*, p. 19.

24. Research and Statistics Section, Policy Programs and Research Branch, Department of Justice, *Fact Book on Fine Option Programs in Canada*, 1986, prepared under contract by Peat, Marwick and Partners; and Ekstedt and Jackson, *A Profile*, pp. 20–23.

25. Research and Statistics Section, Policy Programs and Research Branch, Department of Justice, *Fact Book on Fine Option Programs*; and Ekstedt and Jackson, *A Profile*, pp. 26–30.

26. Ibid., pp. 30–31.

27. Ibid., pp. 32–36.

28. Ibid., pp. 182–89.

29. *Sentencing Reform: A Canadian Approach*, Report of the Canadian Sentencing Commission, Minister of Supply and Services, Canada, 1986.

30. *Taking Responsibility*, Report of the Standing Committee on Justice and the Solicitor General on its Review of Sentencing, Conditional Release, and Related Aspects of Corrections, August 1988, published under the authority of the Speaker of the House of Commons by the Queen's Printer for Canada.

14

An Overview of Intermediate Sanctions in the United States

Annesley K. Schmidt

Each year in the United States over 11 million offenders become involved with the criminal justice system (Bureau of Justice Statistics [BJS] March 1988). By the end of 1987, almost 300,000 adult offenders were in local jails, over 580,000 were in state and federal correctional facilities, 362,000 were on parole, and over 2.2 million were on probation (BJS April 1988, November 1988, December 1988). These figures reflect a continuing increase. Between 1983 and 1985, the probation population grew by 18 percent, and the prison and jail population, by 15 percent (BJS January 1987). These increases are causing continuing pressure on correctional resources. Thirty-eight states have court-ordered "caps" limiting their prison population and thereby apparently subverting the legislative and judicial intent.

The quandary presented by this situation was recently summarized: "Prisons are criticized because they cost too much and do too little. Community programs are under fire because they are perceived as too lenient and unsafe. The public wants more protection from crime and lower cost for the corrections system" (Johnson 1989, p. 10). As a result, "policymakers and managers across the country are looking for 'intermediate' or 'middle-range' sentencing options that are tougher than traditional probation but less stringent—and less expensive—than imprisonment" (Petersilia 1987, p. vi).

As illustrated by the quotations above, many people in the United States prefer the term "intermediate sanctions" to the term "alternatives to incarceration." First, intermediate sanctions is a broader term, describing

Most of the research described in this chapter was completed while the author was a research analyst at the National Institute of Justice, a component of the Department of Justice, United States of America. The opinions expressed herein are those of the author and do not necessarily reflect the official position of the Department of Justice of the United States of America or any of its components.

numerous mechanisms "annexed to a violation of a law as a means of enforcing the law" (*Webster's Ninth New Collegiate Dictionary* 1983, p. 1040) and includes sanctions that may involve a short period of incarceration. Secondly, the term "alternatives to incarceration" is perceived to include a politically liberal bias, while *intermediate sanctions* is seen as politically neutral.

Legal Basis for the Use of Intermediate Sanctions

The United States is a republic where the power to define and sanction criminal behavior is located in the federal government, the governments of each of the states, and local governments. A commission examining the functioning of the criminal justice system described it as "an adaptation of the English common law to America's peculiar structure of government, which allows each local community to construct institutions that fill its special needs. Every village, town, county, city and State has its own criminal justice system, and there is a Federal one as well. All of them operate somewhat alike. No two of them operate precisely alike" (President's Commission 1967, p. 7).

The criminal law in these jurisdictions is derived from various sources. State and federal constitutions establish the principles and standards under which laws are enacted and then reviewed by appellate courts for conformity. Laws are passed by the legislative bodies at all levels of government. Case law, derived from appellate court decisions, provides another source. In addition, official federal, state, and local governmental agencies develop rules that sometimes carry criminal penalties for violation (Cole 1989, pp. 75–76).

The goals to be achieved by sanctioning have been described in a number of ways. The federal criminal law says that the sentencing judge shall consider the need for the sentence "A) to reflect the seriousness of the offense, to promote respect for the law, and to provide just punishment for the offense; B) to afford adequate deterrence to criminal conduct; C) to protect the public from further crimes of the defendant; and D) to provide the defendant with needed . . . [services]" (United States Code, chapter 18, section 3553 [a] [2]). Other approaches have characterized the sometimes contradictory purposes or philosophies of sentencing as general or specific deterrence, just deserts or retribution, rehabilitation or treatment, and incapacitation (Gottfredson and Taylor 1983). In addition, the sentence usually incorporates the concept of limited risk control, to reflect simultaneous concern about the risk the offender poses to society and fair punishment (O'Leary and Clear 1984).

Jurisdictions differ in the ways in which they describe the purpose of the sentence. Also, penal "codes vary as to the structure of the sentences permitted. Each structure makes certain assumptions about the goals of criminal sanction, and each allocates discretionary authority" (Cole 1989, p. 477). Many new strategies were developed as solutions to problems perceived in the previous approaches.

One sentencing structure, indeterminate sentencing, is designed to support the goal of rehabilitation and support treatment of offenders by establishing a range from minimum to maximum, with the exact time of release dependent on the completion of treatment (Cole 1989, p. 477).

However, dissatisfaction with rehabilitation created support for the concept of deserved or determinant punishment, where the sentence specifies the precise length of imprisonment. At the end of that period (minus time subtracted for good behavior, work, etc.), the offender is released automatically, and participation in treatment programs does not affect the release date (Cole 1989, p. 478).

Closely related to determinate sentencing is mandatory sentencing, which developed out of the perception that "many offenders are being set free by lenient judges and that the objective of crime control requires greater certainty that criminals will be incapacitated" (Cole 1989, p. 479). Legislatures responded to the public concern with requirements that a person convicted of specific offenses, such as the use of a handgun in the commission of a felony, "must be confined a minimum of some specified amount of time. No consideration may be given to the circumstances of the offense or to the background of the individual" (Cole 1989, p. 480).

Another approach designed to ameliorate different perceived problems is sentencing guidelines, an approach that grew out of efforts to constrain judicial discretion. Sentencing guidelines provide the judge with an instrument, indicating the usual sanction given in the past in particular types of cases. While the precise nature of the instruments differs among the states, many construct a grid on the "basis of two scores, one related to the seriousness of the offense, the other to characteristics of the offender that indicated the likelihood of recidivism. . . . The judge locates the recommended sentence by finding the appropriate cell" (Cole 1989, p. 479).

In any particular state, the laws have usually been enacted at different times and thus frequently contain elements of various of these approaches, making attempts to compare offenses among the states difficult. In addition, states differ in the structure of corrections and particularly probation, which is responsible for the supervision of offenders in the community.

Each time an offender is found guilty, the judge reviews the available sanctioning options to establish the appropriate sentence. Available options differ depending upon the jurisdiction in which he or she is located. In some places the choices are almost dichotomous: incarceration in a prison or jail, where the offender remains in the facility at all times, or probation, which allows the offender to remain at liberty subject to conditions, but where the enforcement of conditions may be minimal at best. In other jurisdictions, intermediate sanctions are available between the two extremes.

The structure and application of the criminal laws of the state or federal jurisdictions provide the context in which sentencing occurs. Therefore, a particular intermediate sanction may be used in one state where the corrections department establishes a program. In another state, establishment of that same program might require legislation before it could begin. Thus, basically similar programs have been established in different ways in different states.

The Application of Sanctioning

Given the diversity of sentencing structures and the numerous foci of their establishment and application, it is not surprising that there is little information available about the nature and extent of the sanctions being applied in the various jurisdictions and effectively no information about the application of intermediate sanctions. A national summary of criminal sanctions applied is not available. In fact, only recently the Bureau of Justice Statistics presented "the first nationally representative data on felony sentencing in State courts throughout the nation," drawing on data from one hundred counties (BJS 1989, p. 1), including the "75 largest counties which comprise 37 percent of the U.S. population but account for about half of the Nation's reported crime" (BJS 1989, p. 2).

This study found that state courts sentenced an estimated 46 percent of convicted felons to state prison (usually reserved for those with sentences of one year or more), 21 percent to local jails (usually for a year or less), 31 percent to straight probation, and 2 percent to other nonincarcerative sentences (BJS 1989, pp. 1, 4). "An estimated 31 percent of all adults convicted of a felony in 1986 were sentenced to probation with no jail or prison time to serve" (BJS 1989, p. 4). None of the four categories of sentences in the study—to state prisons, to local jails, to straight probation, and other nonincarcerative sentences—was further subdivided. Therefore, no national statistical information is available about the application of the many intermediate sanctions.

Intermediate Sanctions and Their Effectiveness

Prison and jail crowding has focused policymakers' attention on the need to develop punishments that fall between probation and incarceration. These include intensive supervision probation, financial penalties, house arrest, intermittent confinement, "shock" probation and incarceration, community service, electronic monitoring and the use of treatment conditions. These punishments, commonly known as "intermediate punishments'' or ''mid-level punishments'' or ''intermediate sanctions,'' are beginning to fill the gap that is widely perceived to exist between probation and prison. (Tonry and Will 1988, pp. 1–2)

While intermediate sanctions of one kind or another exist in most jurisdictions, not all are available in any one jurisdiction. This paper presents brief descriptions of various alternatives that are operating in at least one jurisdiction in the United States.

Even though these alternatives exist, little is known about the effectiveness of these or other correctional programs. In 1979, a National Academy of Sciences panel reported:

> After 40 years of research and literally hundreds of studies, almost all the conclusions that can be reached have to be formulated in terms of what we do not know. The one positive conclusion is discouraging: the research methodology that has been brought to bear on the problem of finding ways to rehabilitate criminal offenders has been generally so inadequate that only a relatively few studies warrant unequivocal interpretations. The entire body of research appears to justify only the conclusion that we do not know of any program or method of rehabilitation that could be guaranteed to reduce the criminal activity of released offenders. Although a generous reviewer of the literature might discern some glimmers of hope, those glimmers are so few, so scattered, and so inconsistent that they do not serve as a basis for any recommendation other than continued research.

More recently, in a discussion of the intermediate sanctions of intensive supervision, house arrest, electronic monitoring, residential community corrections, and split sentencing, Byrne and Kelly (1989) summarized the research, saying, ''We actually know little about the effectiveness of these sanctions (i.e. crime control, comparative cost and diversionary impact)'' (p. 1).

Explaining the paucity of research, Tonry and Will (1988) suggest that the evaluation of intermediate sanctions is difficult for five reasons.

> First, the purpose of particular programs are seldom specified in any authoritative way, and different people often have different purposes in mind. . . . Second, it is difficult to disentangle cause and effect in assessments of most legal changes. . . . Third, efforts to isolate the effects of specific policy changes, for example, establishment of an ISP program, are complicated by the occurrence of other changes that affect the implementation and consequences of the policy changes under examination. . . . Fourth, although very few intermediate sanction programs have been evaluated carefully, many administrators believe their programs to be successful . . . [so that] in a field . . . in which few

rigorous evaluations have been conducted, the persuasive force of conventional but untested wisdom is great. . . . [And,] fifth, although there are important exceptions, much of the existing evaluation research is badly flawed . . . and cannot serve as a foundation for drawing meaningful conclusions. . . . [They conclude that] taken together, these problems make evaluation research on intermediate sanctions challenging and make it difficult to offer strong assertions about the effects of individual programs. (Pp. 27–29)

In addition, and further compounding the problems, common terms are used to describe intermediate sanctions, but, in different jurisdictions, programs having the same name may have substantially different elements. In this paper, three arbitrary categories of intermediate sanctions are defined: those that involve some incarceration, those that involve direct payment by the offender, and those that do not involve imprisonment or direct payment. Each category includes a number of variations. The programs, as implemented in diverse jurisdictions, differ substantially in program elements. Finally, while each of these is described separately here, they frequently occur in combination. Examples of the possible combinations include community service, which may be a required component of an intensive supervision program, or shock probation, which requires a period of incarceration prior to supervision in the community.

Sanctions Involving Some Incarceration

A short period of incarceration serves as a precursor to supervision in the community for many of those receiving intermediate sanctions. The most common application of this approach is the split sentence—a term of incarceration followed by a term of probation. "In 1984, nearly a third of those receiving probation sentences in Idaho, New Jersey, Tennessee, Utah and Vermont also were sentenced to brief periods of confinement" (BJS March 1988, p. 96). Even though split sentences have been used for years, their use "has not been systematically evaluated, and it is difficult to even determine whether this strategy is being used as an add-on to cases who would have traditionally received straight probation (or some other non-incarcerative sentence) or as a technique for reducing prison crowding (by using short-term incapacitation and probation in lieu of longer sentences)" (Byrne, Lurigio, and Baird 1989, pp. 35–36).

Two variations of split sentences—boot camp and shock incarceration—have recently received more attention. "In Georgia, Oklahoma and Mississippi, young first offenders are sentenced to 'boot camp' correctional facilities, where they are confined for short periods under rigid standards and strict military discipline. After they have completed their sentence, they return to their communities under intensive supervision'' (Petersilia 1987, pp. vii, viii). Similarly,

> Shock incarceration refers to programs in which the sentencing judge may release an offender from prison or jail after he has served some portion of his sentence and place him on probation or parole. The rationale for such programs is that an offender who is ''shocked'' by a brief prison or jail experience will be deterred from returning to crime. . . . Both shock incarceration and boot camps provide a means for courts to impress offenders with the seriousness of their actions without a long prison sentence. They allow courts to save money without appearing to be soft on crime, and they provide community-based treatment for offenders who can be rehabilitated, while imposing sentences that are severe enough to satisfy the demands of public policy. (Petersilia 1987, p. 61)

Boot-camp types of split sentences have now been established in twelve states, with ten additional states planning them (MacKenzie 1989). These prisons ''generally provide a highly regimented program involving strict discipline, physical training, hard labor, and some drill and ceremony, resembling aspects of military training'' (U.S. General Accounting Office [USGAO] 1988, p. 1). The young offenders who successfully complete these programs are placed on probation, and those who fail are sent to regular correctional facilities (Pagel 1986). However, ''available data are not sufficient to determine if boot camps reduce prison overcrowding, costs, or recidivism. The lack of evidence appears to be a result, principally, of the relatively short period of time that most boot camps have been operating and the lack of boot camp cost data compared to other prison costs'' (USGAO 1988, p. 3).

The more traditional split sentence ''consisting of a short period of incarceration followed by probation in the community'' (BJS 1988, p. 90) has been used for many years. One study in five states found that ''in 1984 nearly a third of those receiving probation sentences . . . were sentenced to brief periods of confinement'' (BJS March 1988, p. 96). The periods of incarceration and probation are usually fixed and stated at the time of sentencing.

Shock probation, one variation of this customary use of the split sentence, occurs where the offender is released after serving only a part of a previously specified term of imprisonment. Sometimes the offender is informed in advance that his or her sentence will change, but often the alteration comes as a surprise. An evaluation of Iowa's shock probation program concluded that ''differences in failure rates of the shock probationers and those sentenced to straight probation, parole, and residential facilities appear to be related more to the characteristics of the samples than the effects of 'shock' sentencing" (Boudouris and Turnbull 1985). When surveyed, judges, prosecuting and defense attorneys, and probation officers in Texas felt that shock probation was effective. Offenders, who were incarcerated for 60 to 120 days prior to placement on probation, felt the program was very effective, and the state saved a considerable amount of money as a result of the program (Texas Adult Probation Commission 1981).

A community corrections act is a totally different approach to incarcerative sanctioning. These acts use "economic incentive strategies for reforming local sentencing practices using reimbursement formulas" (Austin and Krisberg 1982, p. 390). Through these programs, enacted in several states, state funds are provided to localities that keep certain types of offenders locally rather than sending them to state prisons. "Although community corrections legislation may have redistributed correctional costs and shifted decision making from State to local levels, it is questionable whether it has made a long term contribution to reduced imprisonment" (Austin and Krisberg 1982, p. 406).

Short-term, local incarceration, such as that supported by community corrections acts, also occurs in states without those specific acts. Similar community-based correction facilities, described by names such as *prerelease centers*, *work release centers*, *halfway houses*, and *restitution centers*, provide local, minimum security confinement. The offender lives at the center, which usually provides treatment programs, such as those for alcohol or drug abuse. The offender continues in the job he or she held in the community or, if unemployed, is helped to obtain employment. The employed offender earns taxable income, continues to support her or his family, and is frequently charged a fee designed to at least partially offset the costs of program operation.

Sanctions Involving Direct Payments by the Offender

Fees charged to participants in programs such as work release are only one of the variety of intermediate sanctions that involve direct payments by offenders. Others include fines, restitution, and victim compensation. All require that the offender pay money or provide uncompensated work.

Offenders may be required to make direct payments through fees for services. Many jurisdictions, such as Georgia and Texas, now charge offenders a supervision fee as well as fees for drug testing and other special needs. Similarly, federal offenders staying in halfway houses are charged a fee equal to 25 percent of gross wages, up to the cost of the program. These fees offset the costs of services either directly, by adding to the appropriated resources of the probation department, or by being returned to the state treasury, where they are added to the general revenue.

Fines are direct payments of a court-ordered amount of money, frequently thought of only as a response to infractions, such as violations of traffic laws. Recent research has found that judges are positively disposed toward fines. However, their favorable attitude seems inconsistent with their sentencing practices. The research also found that the amount of the fine imposed is relatively low and that fines are rarely used as the sole sanction. Judges expressed concern about whether and how to use fines with poor offenders but supported the use of the European day-fine system in which the amount of the fine is determined by the offender's income and the severity of the offense (Cole, Mahoney, Thornton, and Hanson 1987; Hillsman, Mahoney, Cole and Auchter 1987). A pilot project on the use of day fines is presently being designed as the exploration of this option continues (Hillsman, Sichel, and Mahoney 1984).

Another way in which offenders are required to pay is through government seizure of property derived from or used in criminal activity (BJS March 1988, p. 93). In 1983, $100 million were forfeited to federal authorities, and subsequent legislation has expanded the federal forfeiture powers. Recent survey findings indicate that the use of this process is relatively limited. "Thus, the potential remains for greater state use of forfeiture to disrupt illegal drug trade by denying traffickers their profits, working capital and means of doing business" (Stellwagen 1985). Many state codes also contain forfeiture provisions applicable to offenses other than those that are drug related.

A different approach is seen in what Austin and Krisberg (1982) describe as the "reparative penalties," whereby "the victim and/or the community is symbolically restored to its pre-crime status" (p. 378). In the past, these have been used only for less serious offenders. Recently, efforts have been made to apply reparative penalties to more serious offenders, either as a sentence or as one element of a sentence, and to expand their application to those committing more serious crimes. "Sentences to community service stipulate that offenders must perform specified periods of uncompensated work for public or nonprofit agencies. Restitution requires that the offender reimburse the victim through service or money under the jurisdiction of the court. It may also require useful service to a community agency or monetary payment to a public fund" (Austin and Krisberg 1982, p. 378).

A community service sentence, in the beginning, "was used primarily to permit convicted offenders who could not pay fines to work off their obligation by working without pay for the community. Their hours were valued at the minimum wage and they worked until the total 'earned' equaled the amount of their fines. . . . Community service sentences were usually add-ons to probation, rather than sentences unto themselves, and the combination was considered a rehabilitative alternative to jail sentences" (Petersilia 1987, p. 73). Although these sentences are administered in different ways in different jurisdictions, the offender usually works in the community for either governmental agencies or private nonprofit community agencies. They pick up trash in public parks, clean roadsides, and provide manual labor for nonprofit agencies. Community service is a required component of several intensive supervision programs. The intensive supervision program in Georgia resulted in thousands of hours of community service being rendered (Erwin and Bennett 1987). Similarly, during 1986 the New Jersey program had an average of 366 participants, who performed 57,942 hours of community service (Pearson 1987).

While community service programs provide service to the community at large, restitution and victim compensation are more directly related to the victim of the crime. Restitution is direct compensation from a particular offender to a particular victim. However, a 1981 study in Pennsylvania found that only 34.4 percent of the ordered restitutions had been collected (Fulmer 1984). In addition, restitution may lack equity to the victims, since only apprehended offenders can be ordered to pay restitution, and many offenders are not apprehended (BJS March 1988, p. 68). Victim compensation programs, on the other hand, have a less direct relationship between the offenders and the victim. They are state-directed funds into which offenders pay and from which victims are compensated, often for injuries that resulted from a crime. Summarizing recent studies, Tonry and Will (1988) said that "in general, it appears that restitution programs tend to be inefficient and ineffective" (p. 171).

Sanctions Not Involving Imprisonment or Direct Payments

There are other kinds of intermediate sanctions that do not include imprisonment, many of which involve supervision in the community. O'Leary and Clear (1984) describe three levels of supervision intensity: intensive; regular, which is subdivided into close and medium; and reduced, divided into minimum and administrative. When supervision in the community is to be an intermediate sanction, it is generally more intense than that found on standard probation and places additional requirements and/or constraints on the offender.

The objectives of intensive probation or parole supervision, often referred to as "ISP,"

> are straightforward: to increase contacts with probation officers and other responsible members of the community, to hold the offender more accountable for his crime (e.g., through victim restitution, community service) and financially responsible for his supervision (through collection of supervision fees), to reduce opportunities for recidivism (e.g., by mandating curfews) and, in some programs, to reintegrate the offender into the community (e.g., through counseling, employment).

... While these general objectives are rather widely accepted, practices vary considerably among programs. The only thing ISP really means is "more than routine" supervision. (Petersilia 1987, p. 11)

In addition, some programs specifically target offenders that other programs specifically exclude (Petersilia 1987, p. 12).

ISP programs are now operating in forty states, even though research evaluating ISP does not "provide adequate answers to the ... policy dilemmas now facing legislators and correctional administrators.... Of course, lack of information has certainly not slowed the development of intensive supervision" (Byrne, Lurigio, and Baird 1989, pp. 68–69).

Compliance with conditions calling for abstinence from alcohol and drugs can be tested. Portable breath analyzers may be carried by an officer checking to assure that offenders have not consumed alcohol. Devices can also be retrofitted onto the vehicle of an offender convicted of drunk driving to assure that the person starting the car is sober. In addition, they will soon be available for use in conjunction with electronic monitors.

Testing urine for the residuals and metabolites of illegal drugs usually requires laboratory analysis. The specimen to be tested may be required on demand as a release condition. That specimen may be collected in the office of the supervising agency or by the officer making his or her rounds at the offender's home or place of employment. Random testing assures that the offender cannot return to use without the fear of being caught. The most recently developed equipment analyzes the sample in the field and requires less than five minutes to complete.

Another intermediate sanction in the community may be placement in a special program. One such program is TASC, Treatment Alternatives to Street Crime. These programs were designed to break the drug addict's cycle of addiction, arrest, release, readdiction, and rearrest through referral to community treatment resources and monitoring the offender's response to treatment. Some jurisdictions, such as Montgomery County, Maryland, have continued these programs with local funding after the initial federal funding ceased. Recently, after a five-year hiatus, federal support is again available for both existing programs and the development of new programs (Office of Justice Programs 1985, 1987).

"In Long Beach, California, probation officials are teaming up with police to provide greater surveillance of probationers. Police officers carry laminated cards listing the names and addresses of felony probationers residing in the community, along with their probation conditions. Police who observe any violations detain the offenders and immediately call the probation officer" (Petersilia 1987, p. vii).

In New Jersey and California, members of the community are being asked to sign formal contracts with probation and/or parole departments stating that they will serve as "community sponsors." Community sponsors assume some responsibility for assuring that the probationer is adhering to his or her court-ordered conditions and agree to notify the court if violations are observed (Petersilia 1987, p. viii).

Conclusions

Whichever theoretical, philosophical, or legal basis defines the purpose for which a sanction is given, there will always be some offenders who must be incarcerated. There are other offenders for whom the goals of sanctioning can be fulfilled without incarceration. This is possible particularly if there are a variety of options available to the sentencing judge.

This chapter has presented some of the various forms of intermediate sanctions presently in use in the United States. A combination of sanctions can be used in many programs, as is frequently the case. Obviously, the number of ways in which sanctions could be combined is almost endless, and the sanctioning combinations can be tailored to meet the needs of the offender and the requirements of the community safety.

Nationwide statistics show that prison populations are increasing. Thus, prison space is a scarce and costly resource to be used with discretion. At the same time, the probationer population is increasing. The needs of the communities in which these people live must be considered, above all the need for public safety and protection from victimization. In order to achieve these diverse objectives, it is necessary to have a system of classification to assist in the determination of the appropriate sanction and to have a variety of sanctioning options to be used in combinations that will maximize their effectiveness. Creative use of sanctions can not only widen the options available but increase the protection of the community as well.

References

All the cited publications of the National Institute of Justice, the Bureau of Justice Statistics, and the Bureau of Justice Assistance, as well as most of the other published and unpublished works, are available from the National Criminal Justice Reference Service, Box 6000, Rockville, MD 20850, or, in the continental United States but outside the Washington, D.C., metropolitan area.

Austin, J. and B. Krisberg. "The Unmet Promise of Alternatives to Incarceration." *Crime and Delinquency*, 28 (3) (July 1982): 374–409.
Baird, C. Report on Intensive Supervision Programs in Probation and Parole. Prison Overcrowding Project. Unpublished, July 1983.
Ball, R. A., C. R. Huff, and J. R. Lilly. *House Arrest and Correctional Policy: Doing Time at Home.* Newbury Park, Calif.: Sage, 1987.

Boudouris, J. and B. W. Turnbull. "Shock Probation in Iowa." *Journal of Offender Counseling, Services, and Rehabilitation*, 9 (4) (Summer 1985): 53–67.

Bureau of Justice Statistics (BJS). "Justice Expenditures and Employment, 1985." *Bulletin*, Government Printing Office, March 1987.

Bureau of Justice Statistics (BJS). *Report to the Nation on Crime and Justice*, 2d ed. March 1988.

Bureau of Justice Statistics (BJS). "Prisoners in 1987." *Bulletin*, Government Printing Office, April 1988.

Bureau of Justice Statistics (BJS). "Probation and Parole 1987." *Bulletin*, Government Printing Office, November 1988.

Bureau of Justice Statistics. (BJS). "Jail Inmates in 1987." *Bulletin*, Government Printing Office, December 1988.

Bureau of Justice Statistics (BJS). "Felony Sentences in State Courts, 1986." *Bulletin*, Government Printing Office, February 1989.

Byrne, J. M., and L. M. Kelly. Restructuring Probation as an Intermediate Sanction. Unpublished draft, January 1989.

Byrne, J. M., A. J. Lurigio, and C. Baird. The Effectiveness of the New Intensive Supervision Programs. Unpublished draft, March 1989.

Citizens Crime Commission of Connecticut, Inc. Connecticut Intensive Probation Supervision. Unpublished, Hartford, CT, March 1984.

Cole, G. F. *The American System of Criminal Justice*, 5th ed. Pacific Grove, CA: Brooks/Cole, 1989.

Cole, G. F., B. Mahoney, M. Thornton, and R. A. Hanson. The Practices and Attitudes of Trial Court Judges Regarding Fines as a Criminal Sanction. Unpublished, March 1987.

Description of the Electronic Surveillance Program, Jackson County, Medford, Oregon. Personal correspondence, April 1987.

Erwin, B. S., and L. A. Bennett. "New Dimensions in Probation: Georgia's Experience with Intensive Probation Supervision (IPS)." In *Research in Brief*, National Institute of Justice. Washington, D.C.: U.S. Government Printing Office, 1987.

Fulmer, R. H., Restitution as Part of the Criminal Justice System in Pennsylvania. Pennsylvania Association on Probation, Parole, and Corrections. Unpublished, Spring 1984, pp. 3–13.

Gottfredson, S. D., and R. B. Taylor. *The Correctional Crisis: Prison Populations and Public Policy*. National Institute of Justice. Washington, D.C.: U.S. Government Printing Office, 1983.

Hillsman, S. T., B. Mahoney, G. F. Cole, and B. Auchter. "The Fine as a Criminal Sanction." In *Research in Brief*, National Institute of Justice. Washington D.C.: U.S. Government Printing Office, 1987.

Hillsman, S. T., J. L. Sichel, and B. Mahoney. *Fines in Sentencing: A Study of the Use of the Fine as a Criminal Sanction*. National Institute of Justice. Washington, D.C.: U.S. Government Printing Office, 1984.

Johnson, P. "A Home as a Prison: Can It Work?" *Journal of Offender Monitoring* 2 (2) (Spring 1989): 10–18.

MacKenzie, D. "Boot Camp." Paper presented at the American Academy of Criminal Justice Sciences, Washington, D.C., March 30, 1989.

361

Morris, N., and M. Miller. "Predictions of Dangerousness in the Criminal Law." In *Research in Brief*, National Institute of Justice. Washington, D.C.: U.S. Government Printing Office, 1987.

National Institute of Justice, U.S. Department of Justice. Electronic Monitoring Equipment. Unpublished, February 1987.

Office of Justice Programs, Bureau of Justice Assistance, U.S. Department of Justice. *Program Brief. Treatment Alternatives to Street Crime (TASC)*. Washington, D.C.: U.S. Government Printing Office, February 1985.

Office of Justice Programs, Bureau of Justice Assistance, U.S. Department of Justice. "Guidelines for Implementation and Operation of TASC Programs." *NIJ Reports*, March/April 1987.

O'Leary, V. and T. R. Clear. *Directions for Community Corrections in the 1990's*. National Institute of Corrections. Washington, D.C.: U.S. Government Printing Office, 1984.

Pagel, A. "Regimented Rehabilitation, Doing a Tour of Duty in a 'Boot Camp' Prison." *Corrections Compendium*, November 1986.

Petersilia, J. *"Probation and Felony Offenders."* In *Research in Brief*, National Institute of Justice. Washington, D.C.: U.S. Government Printing Office, March 1985.

Petersilia, J. "Exploring the Option of House Arrest." *Federal Probation*, June 1986.

Petersilia, J. *Expanding Options for Criminal Sentencing*. N.p.: Rand Corp., November 1987.

Petersilia, J. and S. Turner. *Prison versus Probation in California*. N.p.: Rand Corp., July 1986.

President's Commission on Law Enforcement and Administration of Justice. *The Challenge of Crime in a Free Society*. Washington, D.C.: U.S. Government Printing Office, 1967.

Stellwagen, L. D. "Use of Forfeiture Sanctions in Drug Cases." In *Research in Brief*, National Institute of Justice. Washington, D.C.: U.S. Government Printing Office, 1985.

Tennessee Board of Paroles. *Intensive Parole Supervision Program*, 1987.

Texas Adult Probation Commission. Shock Probation Survey Executive Summary. Unpublished, 1981.

Tonry, M. and R. Will. Intermediate Sanctions. Unpublished draft report. November 1988.

U.S. General Accounting Office (USGAO). *Prison Boot Camps: Too Early to Measure Effectiveness*. GAO/GGD-88-125, September 1988.

U.S. Sentencing Commission. *Sentencing Guidelines and Policy Statements*. Washington, D.C.: U.S. Government Printing Office, 1987.

15

Electronic Monitoring in the United States

Annesley K. Schmidt

In the United States, there were more than 581,000 people in state and federal prisons at the end of 1987 and approximately 300,000 people in local jails. In addition, there were 2.6 million offenders in the community on probation and parole. These levels indicate a marked increase in the number of offenders under correctional control.

The changes prompted by population pressure and citizen concern about crime and public safety have led to the development of new approaches to the management of offenders in the community. New terminology denotes the options made available by new technologies. Thus, *home confinement* denotes a condition of release into the community that requires an offender to remain at home or at some other specified location during his or her nonworking hours. *Electronic monitoring* denotes the use of telemetry technology to assure the offender's compliance with a home confinement release requirement.

The requirement that an offender remain home during his or her nonworking hours has been used as a condition of probation for many years. It was often added in a pro forma manner with little hope or expectation that it would be enforced. It was felt that probation officers who had full-time daytime jobs were reluctant to spend uncompensated hours in undesirable neighborhoods assuring that offenders did not go out. This perception and similar ones had led to a lack of faith in probation as a meaningful sanction.

The introduction of electronic monitoring technology has changed the perception of home confinement, also known by other terms such as *house arrest*, to its being a meaningful sanction with far greater assurance of the

Most of the research described in this chapter was completed while the author was a research analyst at the National Institute of Justice, a component of the Department of Justice, United States of America. The opinions expressed herein are those of the author and do not necessarily reflect the official position of the Department of Justice of the United States of America or any of its components.

offender's compliance. This shift began in the United States in December 1984, when electronic monitors were first introduced as part of an ongoing correctional program.

Twenty years ago, the possibility of using technology to monitor offenders was discussed in the literature, and some experimental prototypes were developed and tested (Schwitzgebel 1964, 1968, 1969a 1969b). In the brief four years since the technology was introduced, it has stimulated discussion among criminal justice professionals as well as in the popular media. These commentaries describe the equipment or discuss its application in one or more programmatic contexts or raise issues about the applications. Some programs have prepared materials on their experiences using the technology. While all of these present descriptive information or opinion, none are based on sound empirical research studies, because none have yet been completed.

The Technology

The technology of electronic monitoring, presently available commercially in the United States, obtains information about the offender's presence in, or absence from, the monitored location and transmits it to a computer, usually over telephone lines. However, several different approaches are used to accomplish this. One approach is the "continuously signaling device," which constantly monitors the presence of an offender at a particular location. Another approach is the "programmed contact device," which telephones the offender periodically to verify his or her presence. The most recently developed approach is "hybrid" equipment, which combines these two technologies.

A continuously signaling device has three major parts: a transmitter is attached to the offender, usually on the ankle, and sends out a continuous signal. Transmitters produced by some manufacturers send an altered signal to alert officials if they are tampered with, while others do not. A receiver-dialer located in the offender's home is attached to a telephone and detects signals from the transmitter. It reports to the central computer when it stops receiving the signal and when it starts receiving it again. A central computer is programmed to accept reports from the receiver-dialer over the telephone lines, compares them with the offender's curfew schedule, and alerts correctional officials about any unauthorized absences. The computer also stores information about routine entries and exits of each offender.

"Programmed contact devices" are a technological alternative. They contact the offender at intervals to verify that he or she is at the required location. These devices all use a computer programmed to telephone the offender during the monitored hours, either randomly or at specifically selected times. The computer is also programmed to prepare reports on the results of the call. However, each uses a different method to assure that it is the offender who is responding to the call and is in fact at the monitored location as required. One system uses voice verification technology. Another system requires that the offender wear a wristwatch device that is programmed to provide a number unique to that offender at that time. This number appears when a special button on the device is pressed and is entered into a touchtone telephone in response to the call. A third system uses a "wristlet," a plastic module that is strapped to the offender's arm. When the computer calls, the wristlet is inserted into a "verifier box" connected to the telephone to verify the offender's presence. A fourth system provides visual verification when the offender being monitored activates and transmits a video image, like a snapshot.

Offenders are also monitored without electronic verification. Automatic equipment telephones the offender and records the response. With this approach, verification that the person responding is in fact the monitored offender occurs only when the recording is played by someone who recognizes the offender's voice.

Hybrid equipment has recently been introduced by several manufacturers. This equipment normally functions as a continuously signaling device. However, when the computer notes that the offender has left at an unauthorized time, it functions similarly to a programmed contact device, contacting the offender by telephone and verifying that the person responding is the offender being monitored, either by the use of voice verification technology or by the insertion of a "wristlet" into a "verifier box" attached to the telephone. If verification does not occur, notification is made that a violation has occurred.

In addition to the development of the hybrid equipment, a number of other changes have already been made. The transmitter of the continuously signaling equipment has been made smaller, and its signal has been made unique to one receiver-dialer so that if two offenders are in one location the signals can be distinguished. The computer programs now allow the offender's schedule to include leaving and returning several times in the same day and provides the supervising staff with a clearer picture of the offender's entries and exits.

The role of the telephone in the monitoring requires that offenders do not have some of the new telephone technologies on their telephones. For example, call forwarding, where the telephone will automatically switch the call to another number, or a portable telephone would make it easier for the offender to respond to calls when away from home, thus circumventing the program. Many programs also prohibit call waiting, which allows for more than one incoming call and would interfere with the equipment's effort to call the central computer or with the verifier box's being attached. The programs review the offender's monthly telephone bill to assure that the offender is not receiving these telephone services.

At present, most of the equipment limits participation in monitoring programs to those who have a telephone at home. However, one company produces equipment that allows an officer to drive near the offender's house and tune in to the frequency of the monitor and thus determine if the offender is home without the officer's leaving the car or the offender's being aware that he or she has been monitored. Other companies are investigating similar approaches.

Case Study—Electronic Monitoring in the United States

Research conducted in the United States identified locations where monitoring programs existed and provided one-day counts of the number of offenders being electronically monitored. The first count found 826 offenders were being monitored in twenty-one states on 15 February 1987. A year later, the number had tripled—2,277 offenders in thirty-two states were being monitored on 14 February 1988. It is estimated that the February 1989 study will find that the number has more than tripled again to about 7,200 offenders and that the number of states has increased to thirty-seven (Renzema 1989).

Monitoring programs existed in thirty-two states, in all sections of the country. However, 49.5 percent of the offenders were in two states, Florida and Michigan, where the monitoring activities were structured quite differently. Almost all (87.8 percent) monitored offenders in Michigan were monitored by the Michigan Department of Corrections, with the remainder monitored by small programs established by a local court, a sheriff, or private agencies. In contrast, there was greater diversity in Florida, where 57.8 percent of the monitored inmates were in programs sponsored by the Department of Corrections but 23.9 percent were monitored by city or county agencies, including sheriffs' offices, local departments of corrections, and police departments. An additional 16.9 percent were monitored by private monitoring service providers and 1.2 percent by a federal demonstration project.

Florida might be viewed as a microcosm of the country as a whole, in that monitoring activities were found there in large metropolitan areas, medium-sized cities, small towns, and rural areas. Monitoring programs had been established by all levels of government—federal, state, county, and city; they provided the service with their own staff or contracted for it. These public agencies represented all elements of the criminal justice system, including police departments, sheriffs, courts, correctional systems, and probation and parole agencies. In addition, monitoring services were provided by private entrepreneurs who contracted with governmental agencies or with offenders directly.

The large number of offenders being monitored in Michigan and Florida was not typical. In most states, the programs involve only small numbers of offenders. Responses were received from more than one locality in each of the thirty-two states with monitoring. Yet seven states were monitoring between twenty-five and forty-nine offenders, and twelve states were monitoring fewer than twenty-five offenders. In addition, two states had established programs but had no offenders being monitored on 14 February 1988, while one state program had not quite begun.

Offender/Participant Characteristics

The programs provided descriptive characteristics of the 2,277 offenders who were being monitored on 14 February 1988. These included age, sex, offense, and legal status of the offender as well as the date that the monitoring began. Of the offenders, 54.1 percent had been monitored for six weeks or less, their monitoring having begun in 1988. At the other extreme, approximately 5 percent of the offenders had been monitored for more than six months.

While three times as many offenders were being monitored in 1988 as had been in 1987, most characteristics of the two groups were similar. The average offender was thirty years old, and the vast majority of those being monitored both years were male. However, the one area where important differences were found was offense.

Those being monitored in 1988 included people convicted of almost every possible criminal violation. Table 15.1 provides the summary categorization of offenses. When these offenses are examined in more detail, the type of offender being monitored becomes clearer. For example, of the 25.6 percent of the offenders who were charged with major traffic offenses, 71.0 percent of them were charged with driving under the influence or while intoxicated. Most of the other offenses in this category are offenses that frequently reflect present or previous drunk-driving convictions, such as the 12.5 percent who were charged with driving on a revoked or suspended permit.

Drug law violations were another frequently reported offense category. Of the drug law violators, 53.2 percent were charged with possession of drugs. The remainder were charged with distribution.

Property offenses were another of the common offense group. These were concentrated in a few closely related offenses, with 28.0 percent being burglary and 39.6 percent being thefts or larcenies. Additionally, 16.6 percent of offenders were charged with breaking and entering.

Table 15.1   Offense by Year of Survey

| | 1987 | | 1988 | |
	Number	Percent	Number	Percent
Major traffic	275	33.4	583	25.6
Drugs	111	13.5	347	15.3
Against the person	46	5.6	220	9.7
Property	150	18.2	456	20.1
Sex	23	2.8	91	4.0
Weapons	10	1.2	29	1.3
Frauds	27	3.3	86	3.8
Multiple offenses	84	10.2	138	6.1
Other	97	11.8	324	14.2
Total	823		2274	

The offense distribution in 1988 was noticeably different from that found in 1987. The proportion of major traffic offenders decreased, and the other offense categories increased. This change in offense type was a reflection of the growth of programs run by state departments of corrections. These state offenses were generally more serious than those found at the local or county level. These programs tended to include prison-bound offenders or parolees/releasees from state institutions.

Program Characteristics

At present in the United States, there is no clearly established programmatic context in which the use of monitors is either appropriate or inappropriate. Present programs are operated by public agencies at all levels of government and by private agencies. The programs also differ in purpose and target population. Some focus on particular types of offenders, such as those who are "chemically dependent" or "deemed to be at high risk of failure." Others described the program as an "alternative" and mentioned the problem of jail crowding. Additional types of programs include:

- A pretrial program that monitors the release of defendants held in jail for two weeks or more pending trial who would have previously remained in jail
- A town's police department that monitors those charged with or convicted of violations of city ordinances who would otherwise have been held in a county jail that charges the town per-diem costs of custody
- A work-release program at a county jail from which offenders can "graduate" to living at home with an electronic monitor
- A program for "those at risk of failure" while on probation or parole
- A local jail with a court-ordered ceiling on its population that uses monitors

for less serious offenders in order to make jail space available for more serious offenders
- An intensive probation supervision program that uses electronic monitors to augment the efforts of the staff to assure compliance with the home confinement requirement of the program

Electronic monitoring devices have also helped correctional agencies handle difficult cases. For example, placement in a monitoring program enabled a seventy-year-old, who had repeatedly been convicted of drunk driving and whose health was very poor, to remain out of jail but at home where the community could be assured that he was not on the roads. Another jurisdiction monitored an AIDS victim who was charged with a criminal violation, avoiding the problems inherent in his confinement in the close conditions of the jail, and allowing him to continue to receive treatment from medical personnel familiar with the disease and with his care.

All of these programs use the equipment to assure that the offender abides by a home confinement condition and remains at a required location during specific hours. Hofer and Meierhoefer (1987) suggest three levels:

> *Curfew* is a type of home confinement that requires offenders to be at their residence during limited, specified hours, generally at night. . . . More severe than curfew, home detention requires that offenders remain at home at all times, except for employment, education, treatment, or other times specified for the purchase of food or for medical emergencies. . . . *Home detention*, if strictly enforced, is more punishing than curfew and affords greater control over an offender's activities. . . . *Incarceration at home* is the most severe form of home confinement; the home substitutes for prison. Offenders are to remain there at all times with very limited exceptions (e.g., religious services or medical treatment). . . . The goal is to punish and maintain control over the offender. (P. 6, emphasis added)

Most respondents charge offenders who participate in their monitoring program. Of the two largest programs, the Florida Department of Corrections does not charge offenders, but Michigan does. The majority of other programs assess fees. These charges were usually made on the basis of a sliding scale. The maximum fee charged by some programs was as high as $15 per day.

The in-program failure rates of the programs showed tremendous variation. Some reported that almost no participants had failed to complete the program successfully, while others reported that almost half of those admitted had failed to do so. Most failures were the result of infractions of program rules—primarily, failure to abide by the curfew or use of alcohol or drugs. These variations were the result of myriad factors, some known and many unknown. Some programs had a great deal of control over who entered the programs, and others had almost none. Some programs could refuse to accept into the program offenders they deemed inappropriate, and others could not. Some programs focused on a higher-risk target population than others and thus expected higher failure rates. Some program procedures required that an offender be returned to custody at the first violation, while others tried to work with participants who appeared to be starting to fail.

The failure rates were also probably affected by the coverage of the output from the monitoring equipment. Some programs reviewed the computer output only during "normal" business hours (e.g., 9–5, Monday through Friday). Others continuously review the reports from the computer and respond to the report of the violation immediately, at any time, day or night, weekdays, weekends, or holidays. Those programs with around-the-clock coverage were probably in a better position to prove to a court or paroling authority that a violation had occurred, when they requested revocation of an offender's release.

Problems Experienced by Monitoring Programs

Respondents mentioned a variety of problems that they had experienced and usually resolved successfully. Some programs initially had difficulty gaining acceptance of the equipment or of the program. This resistance might have come from either officers involved in implementing the programs or other parts of the criminal justice system. Many of the concerns were resolved by education and training. Confidence was also gained when offenders successfully completed the program. There was also a shakedown period during which they learned to use the equipment correctly and to interpret the printout. Some of these may indicate that a proper foundation was not established before the program was implemented.

Another difficulty was orientation and training of the offender and his family. The offender needs to handle the equipment properly and understand what is expected of him. The family needs to accept the fact that they must limit their use of the telephone, recognize the fact that the computer will call, and learn how to respond when it does. Problems could be created within the home by poor wiring, by telephones with "call waiting," or by the quality of transmissions over the telephone lines serving the home. Some were overcome by repairs or by using a radio-frequency filter.

Some programs also experienced unanticipated costs. These included the costs of extra telephone lines, special interconnections, and other supplies.

The Environment in Which the Programs Developed

Between 1983 and 1985, the probation population grew by 18 percent and the prison and jail population by 15 percent (Bureau of Justice Statistics 1987). These increases are continuing and creating pressure on correctional resources. Thirty-eight states have court-ordered "caps" limiting their prison population and subverting the legislative and judicial intent shown by the establishment of the penalties and in the imposition of sentences.

With these pressures, the judge who is seeking the appropriate sanction for a convicted criminal may find the available options limited. The choice often becomes dichotomous between two imperfect alternatives: incarceration, offering maximum control in crowded prisons; or probation, often viewed as providing little or no control.

The commercial development of electronic monitors occurred as the pressures of population were confronting questions about the credibility of probation. While monitors are seen by some as the resolution of these conflicting pressures, others see them as raising questions and issues without providing solutions.

One of the most frequently raised concerns is "net widening." The expression "net widening" is based on an analogy to a fisherman's net. If the net is opened more widely, more fish will be caught in it. Thus, in this context, it refers to sanctioning those who would not otherwise have been sanctioned or sanctioning someone more severely than would otherwise have been done. Some people are concerned that monitors may facilitate net widening. Others would argue that offenders presently are being sanctioned at a lesser level than is appropriate, because of prison crowding. They feel that if there is an increase in the level of sanctioning, it is an increase to an appropriate level. These questions will continue, because resolution is unlikely, given the differences in philosophies and in programs.

The idea of electronic monitoring, to a certain extent, raises the specter of George Orwell's *1984*—of equipment that can spy on people, reveal their secrets, and invade their privacy. While the technology is available that would transmit voices and "spy" on the wearer, the present equipment does not have that capacity. It also has been pointed out that prisons are not places where a great deal of privacy is possible. Alternatively, if the equipment replaces an officer entering the offender's home for a surveillance check, the equipment will reveal less than an officer is likely to learn about the activities in the house and the interaction of the members of the household.

Programmatic Questions That Remain to Be Answered

There are inherent tensions as monitoring programs are established. Monitors are an alternative or sentencing option, but an alternative to what and option for whom? Some feel that monitors should be used only as an alternative to incarceration and only for those who would otherwise be imprisoned. Others feel that some offenders are sentenced to probation in response to the pressure created by prison crowding and that the use of a monitor will increase an inappropriately mild sanction to a more appropriate level. Since this debate is part of the ongoing discussion of the purpose and application of sanctioning, an easy resolution will not be possible.

Monitors, at least in theory, could be used on any number of offender groups. They could be used on sentenced or unsentenced offenders. They could be used before sentencing, immediately after sentencing, or at a later point in the sentence when problems appear. They could be used to monitor house arrest, as an alternative to jail, as part of an intensive supervision program, or in the context of a work-release program. All of these program possibilities have been discussed, and most of them are presently operational. However, it is not yet known if monitors are effective in these program applications, much less where they are most effective.

Whether particular types or groups of offenders can be monitored in a given community will depend, in part, on what that community, its judges, and its elected and political officials consider acceptable and appropriate punishment. For example, in some communities there may be strong pressure to jail drunk drivers; other communities may be satisfied if drunk drivers are required to stay home during their nonworking hours with monitors used to assure that they are not on the roads.

Who can and should be monitored in the community may also depend on the type of equipment selected and the structure of the program in which it is used. Some equipment monitors the offender continually, while other types do so only intermittently. Some devices send a signal if tampered with, and some do not, so that removal of, or damage to, the equipment is only detected with visual inspection. And if the equipment indicates that the offender is not where he is supposed to be or that some other problem has occurred, the program may require an immediate response, or the program staff may review these indicators on weekdays during the day. Programs that have the base computer located in a facility that is staffed twenty-four hours a day, seven days a week, know immediately that a problem has occurred and can send staff to the offender's house to check and, if necessary, attempt to locate the offender. In contrast, other programs review the printout in the morning, and offenders are contacted for explanations when abnormal findings were made the previous night.

Next, how long should the offenders be monitored by the equipment? Here again the equipment is too new and the experience too limited to provide an answer. Officials at Pride, Inc., in West Palm Beach, Florida, believe that offenders can tolerate the monitors for about 90 to 120 days (Rasmussen and Rothbart 1986). After that, they feel, offenders begin to chafe under the restriction. Others (Garcia 1986) however, would argue that the purpose is to create new habits, and thus require six months or more. At a different level, this question must be answered in the context of why the program is being operated. The answer will be quite different if the goal is retribution as opposed to fulfilling the requirement of the law. In Palm Beach County, it has been decided that three days on the monitor is the equivalent of one day in jail to fulfill the required mandatory sentence for a second conviction for driving while intoxicated (Ford and Schmidt 1985). For other offenses, the prescribed sentence is a range, and therefore the appropriate length of time to be served on the monitor is not as clear.

Technological Questions

In addition to the questions about monitoring programs, there are also questions or potential problems that should be considered related to the functioning of the equipment itself. The technology is developing very rapidly, and problems are being solved almost as soon as they become apparent.

Telephone line compatibility is one problem that became apparent. Telephone lines carry electrical current, and the characteristics of that current can vary with different telephone systems. Additionally, some telephone exchanges use very modern switching equipment and can handle pulses such as those from touchtone phones. Others use older equipment that may have trouble handling the electronic signals transmitted by some of the monitoring systems. Whether this is a problem can be determined specifically only through a test of the local system and local exchanges and/or consultation with the local telephone company.

Another problem that has been addressed by some manufacturers is the effects of weather conditions. During windstorms and thunderstorms, both electric lines and telephone lines are whipped around and may come into contact with other lines. This may lead to arcing of the power and power surges. Now, these monitoring devices have surge protectors placed on both incoming electrical and telephone lines. In addition, uninterruptable power supplies are also provided by some manufacturers to guarantee that even during power outages power will be supplied to the system or to some components such as the central computer. Many devices use radio frequency signals for communication between components of the system. In some locations, radio landing beacons from airports and radio station broadcasts can interfere. Whether this is a problem is dependent on the other radio transmissions in the area where the equipment is being used and the radio frequency that the device uses.

Another issue is the effect of iron and steel, which may block signal transmission or create an electromagnetic field. This can occur in steel trailers or stucco houses. It can also occur in houses that have large appliances such as refrigerators and cast-iron bathroom fixtures. In some places, the problems can often be dealt with by moving the receiving equipment. In other settings, it may limit the offender's mobility to less than had been expected. At least one manufacturer provides repeater stations within the house, to forward and amplify the signal.

Some Issues to Consider When Establishing a Monitoring Program

The development of new technology has led to the possibility of a different approach to the supervision of offenders in the community. However, it has been only a short four years since the first program began, so there are many questions, the answers to which are yet to be learned. The fact that these unanswered and unanswerable problems exist must be kept in mind when a program is established. At the same time, the limited experience that has been gained during the short period that monitors have been available has revealed some of the issues that must be resolved when establishing a monitoring program. There are myriad decisions that must be made, few of which have known ''right'' answers.

The program needs to provide the context in which the equipment is to be used. If that is lacking, then there will be the inappropriate situation of equipment in search of a program. The program needs to be defined in terms of how an offender enters the program, who will make the decision, on what will the decision be based—risk, need, offender status—and how long people will remain in the program.

The program's statement of purposes and objectives should supply a clear rationale for the use of monitors, which means that at least one of the program goals should be offender surveillance or control. If this is not a goal, there seems little reason to use monitoring equipment. Given the political controversy and philosophical issues, clarity of purpose provides the potential for a rational response when these arise.

Then, the program needs to determine what type of equipment it will use, keeping in mind both the cost and the surveillance implications of their choice in the light of the program's goals. Does the program wish to monitor continuously or intermittently? Is tamper-resistance required, or is periodic visual inspection sufficient to determine if the offender has attempted to remove the monitor or damaged it? What is the nature and size of the equipment itself?

If equipment seems appropriate in the context of the program, the next questions are financial. What will be purchased? The usual choice is one of two possibilities—equipment and service. Either the agency obtains the equipment and uses its staff to provide the service, or the agency contracts for service with a company that will provide both monitoring equipment and monitoring. This may be done through a lease, purchase, or lease with an option to purchase.

The equipment is going to provide information that was previously unknown. This will range from simple facts, such as that the offender was probably late for work because he was late leaving, to information that the offender is not at home when he is supposed to be. The program needs to determine in advance how it will respond to as many of these as it can anticipate. For the minor issues, responses may be as simple as telephoning the employer to determine that the offender is in fact at work. In contrast, part of the response to violations may be by phone or in person, at the time when it first becomes known or during the next work day.

The decisions about response to violation have implications for costs and staffing. They must also be made considering what the responsible authorities—usually a court or parole board—are going to require as proof of violations. When planning the response to violations, the program should consider the possibility that false alarms may occur and that equipment may be damaged accidentally or purposely. In addition, the added information means that staff is now aware of failures that would have previously been unknown and may need to respond if the program is to maintain its credibility with the offenders and with the public.

Some of those establishing programs have felt that electronic monitors would alleviate their prison and jail crowding. However, this view is at best optimistic and more probably untrue, at least at present, for a variety of reasons. First, the population selected as the focus of monitoring programs may or may not be one that might otherwise be sent to jail or prison if monitors were not available. Second, consideration needs to be given to the likely impact on the total problem. In a thousand-inmate jail, the release of twenty monitored inmates would reduce the population by only 2 percent. One hundred monitored inmates would have to be released before the population would be affected by 10 percent. In a smaller jail, more impact would be achieved by a system the size of the typical initial purchase (twenty units), if all units were being used at the same time. In the prison systems of many states, with their much larger populations, more monitored inmates would have to be released before a significant reduction in population could occur. Furthermore, the cost of a monitoring program cannot be directly compared to per-diem costs of incarceration. The largest component of per-diem costs is staff salaries. Therefore, the only savings achieved are in marginal categories such as food, until the number of released inmates is large enough to affect staffing of the facility or reduce the requirement for construction of additional facilities.

Once these decisions, and many others, have been made, it is important that the program plan allows time to test and get acquainted with the equipment and to train staff.

As the program plan is being developed, there are a variety of other issues that need to be considered. All the elements of the criminal justice system need to be involved in the planning so that their issues and agendas can be considered. In addition, at least some elements of the broader community should be involved, such as the press and political action groups concerned about criminal justice issues, such as MADD (Mothers Against Drunk Driving).

Existing programs using monitors in the community function as part of the criminal justice system. Therefore, they require the cooperation of the courts, probation, and parole. Additionally, many times they also may involve the sheriff, other law enforcement agencies, and others. As with any multiagency effort, the lines of responsibility must be clear, and the cooperation between them, developed. For example, if the results of the monitoring are to be reviewed around the clock, then the base is optimally located where twenty-four-hour staffing is already present. This facility might be a jail operated by the sheriff. If the program, on the other hand, is being operated by the probation office, the division of responsibilities and expectations should be clearly specified, preferably in writing.

The establishment of a monitoring program in some areas has provided an opportunity for the agency to be proactive, reaching out to the public and the press. This contrasts with the reactive posture often assumed by corrections and may lead to the development of relationships with the press that may be useful in other contexts.

In summary, when starting a program, it is important to be realistic about why the program is being established and what it is expected to accomplish. In addition, it needs to be placed in a programmatic context that is well thought out, has consistent policies and procedures, documents the occurrences, and has specific expectations. Monitoring equipment should never be equipment in search of a program.

International Discussion of Monitors

Internationally, it appears that the interest in the use of monitors is growing. In addition to the United States, electronic monitoring has been used, or the use discussed, in the public media of Canada, Great Britain, Holland, and other nations.

There is a small electronic monitoring program in the Canadian Province of British Columbia, and interest has been expressed in the Province of Ontario as well. The national government is not, however, planning to use the equipment (Lilly 1989).

Great Britain has discussed "tagging," as they call electronic monitoring, since 1981, and the issue has become highly politicized. There are now several British manufacturers of the equipment, and the government has announced its intention to support three experiments during the summer of 1989, using private service providers (Lilly 1989).

The Netherlands has investigated monitors while avoiding politicizing the issue. The Ministry of Justice has sent its staff to international meetings, invited manufacturers to present demonstrations, and supported the development of a paper on the topic (Lilly 1989).

The Future of Electronic Monitors and Monitoring

In the short period of time since electronic monitors have been available commercially, there has been a growth in their use from the first offender monitored in December 1984 to about eight hundred in February 1987 and to about twenty-three hundred in February 1988. Discussions with the manufacturers indicate that this pattern of growth is continuing. Many have outstanding orders for equipment to be used in new programs or to augment existing programs. In addition they report receiving quite a few inquiries from those considering the establishment of a program. Internationally, also, it appears that the use of monitors is also growing. Thus, it seems reasonable to expect that, in the future, at least some of the existing programs will expand and that there will be more monitoring programs in more states and localities and possibly additional countries.

Present law enforcement technology makes it possible to track electronic signals emitted by a device as it moves (U.S. Congress, 1985 and 1988). While this kind of tracking is not presently used to monitor offenders, there is discussion of various approaches to locating offenders or following them as they move around the community. Satellites have been suggested, with the analogy drawn to the way that polar bears are monitored as they move around the Arctic. However, since satellites require line-of-sight transmission, the large buildings found in an urban environment raise questions about the feasibility of this approach. It is more technologically feasible to suggest triangulation from specially installed antennae, but the installation may prove prohibitively expensive. Another proposal would use a system such as the cellular telephone system. The questions about this approach include: What kind of device on the offender would transmit to the cell? How precisely could the transmitter be located within the cell? Would this approach be cost-effective?

When and if the technology progresses from monitoring the presence of an offender in one given location to tracking the offender as he moves about the community engaged in legal activities, both legal and ethical issues are apparent. How these issues will be resolved is hard to predict but will certainly determine the direction of future monitoring activities.

The technology is so new, and the research is, thus far, so limited, that there are many questions about monitors of all kinds, on all levels. Some of the questions are these: Can the equipment be used legally? On whom should it be used? Will the community accept it? Will it provide the community with additional protection? The National Institute of Justice is supporting experimental projects that will provide some answers to some of these and other important questions. As the research findings become available, more experience is gained with monitors, and more time passes, so that determination can be made of the effects of participating in a monitoring program, it seems likely that clearer indications will develop of the most appropriate use of monitors. A number of future scenarios seem plausibly related to different aspects of the questions: Who should be monitored? Why? Under what circumstances? Meanwhile, the programmatic, philosophical, and technological questions remain.

In summary, monitors are new technological devices that offer exciting possibilities for controlling offenders in the community. However, there are still many unknowns, many issues that should be considered by those establishing programs, and many questions yet to be both asked and answered.

Appendix

Some Preliminary Findings about the Use of Monitors

Some programs have conducted studies of their efforts, including statistical descriptions of all the offenders who had participated in their program, while others provided assessments. None have yet done a sound empirical study, although some are under way. The descriptive findings indicate that the programs are satisfied with what they are doing and feel that they are accomplishing their objectives.

One example of a statistical report was provided by Michigan Digital Surveillance (Denton 1988). They described the 145 offenders who had participated in their program since its founding on 1 October 1986, including the 8 in the program at the time the report was written but excluding five juveniles. Offenders in their program had come directly from court with sentences ranging from 14 to 365 days with an average sentence length of 68 days. Most participants were employed males who had paid the full cost of the program. They had been charged with drunk driving and were attending AA and/or counseling. Of the 145 offenders, 88.3 percent had successfully completed the program.

The failure rate for the Michigan program contrasts sharply with the report from one of the programs of the Florida Department of Corrections

(Williamson 1988). That program had a success rate of slightly less than 50 percent. They point out that they are serving felony offenders who have already served time on probation or community control without electronic monitoring and have failed.

Pride, Inc., of Daytona Beach, Florida, summarized the responses of sixty-four clients to complete a confidential exit interview form (McGowan 1987). Not surprisingly, most offenders rated house arrest far more positively than jail. Almost two-thirds of the participants reported that being on house arrest had altered their lifestyle. The program staff reported that those with short monitoring sentences, thirty days or so, responded that their social life was restricted but they were not really affected. On the other hand, those with sentences of ninety days or more were far more likely to respond that lifestyle changes had occurred. When asked the reason that they responded as they had, the explanations included such comments as "I learned to budget my time," "I no longer have the urge to constantly be going out somewhere and I will probably stay home more often now," and "It made me more happy about my home environment and now I find myself staying home more and enjoying it." Another offender described himself before monitoring as leaving work, going to a bar with the boys, and then sometime in the evening going home drunk. While being monitored, he had to omit the bar, so he went home and got to know his wife and son. He felt that his habit of the bar had been interrupted, so that after the monitoring ended he would continue to go home.

Pride updated that report in 1988 (McGowan 1988). They reported that they had saved the taxpayers of Volusia County, Florida, $449,064 to date with their program, compared to the $27 cost of one day in jail for one offender. Of the offenders in their program, 88 percent are male, and they average thirty years old. They have been placed in the program for an average of thirty-six days following conviction for drunk driving. The program now has a 7.6 percent failure rate. Responding to an exit questionnaire, most offenders had been previously incarcerated and rated the program as superior to jail. When asked if monitoring had altered their lifestyle, most offenders responded that it had and explained it by such statements as: "It made me think about all the things I do as a privilege" or "Because I never knew the seriousness of the offense." When asked if they had any comments that would help improve the program, most reported responses showed a positive reaction to the program.

An Orange County, California, report (Whittington 1987) describes the first six months of their program. They screened 133 inmates from the jail, which resulted in fifty-one participants, eleven of whom were people with handicaps or serious medical programs who would have been held in the jail's medical ward if not for the program. Of those placed in the program, 93 percent were male, 67 percent were nonminority white, and 26 percent were Hispanic. In addition, 95 percent had no prior felonies, 92 percent were employed seven or more months during the last twelve months, 80 percent were charged with driving under the influence, 89 percent were classified as having an occasional or frequent problem with alcohol abuse, and 95 percent were rated as "motivated to change." The Orange County program used a programmed contact monitoring device that telephones the offender, who verifies his presence by responding to questions and then inserting a wristlet into a verifier box. Initially, the instructions to the offenders were given only in English, but Spanish and Vietnamese have been added. One technical violation, possession of beer and a small amount of marijuana, occurred, but there were no new law violations.

Dr. Annette Jolin (undated) evaluated the electronic surveillance program in Clackamus County, Oregon, which has been operating for a longer time. The report provided statistical information on the first ninety-six offenders to complete the program, 52 percent of whom had been charged with drunk driving and 11 percent with driving while suspended. These offenders spent an average of thirty-three days under house arrest, with 53 percent being monitored by a program contact device and 40 percent by a continuously signaling device, and 8 percent switched from one system to the other. The report also discussed the problems experienced with the functioning of each type of equipment.

The Clackamus County report discussed the program outcomes for these offenders, which did not involve the loss or destruction of any equipment. Of these offenders, 90 percent successfully completed the program. Of the ten offenders who failed, only one was charged with a new crime. Postprogram recidivism was examined when the time since program termination ranged from six to eighteen months; 27 percent (25 of 95 offenders) had been rearrested in Oregon, most within six months after the end of the program.

References

Alpert, G. P. and J. Allison De Foor, II. "Florida's Invisible Jails." *Judges Journal*, 23 (Fall 1984): 33, 46.

"Anthropotelemetry: Dr. Schwitzgebel's Machine." *Harvard Law Review*, 80 (1966): 403–21.

Ball, R. A. and J. Robert Lilly. "Home Incarceration: An Alternative to Total Incarceration." Paper presented at the 9th International Meeting of the Society of Criminology, Vienna, Austria, September–October 1983a.

Ball, R. A. and J. Robert Lilly. "The Potential Use of Home Incarceration with Drunken Drivers." Paper presented at American Society of Criminology Meeting, Denver, 1983b.

Ball, R. A., and J. Robert Lilly. "A Theoretical Examination of Home Incarceration." Paper presented at the Annual Meeting of American Society of Criminology, Denver, CO, August 1984.

Berry, B. "Electronic Jails: A New Criminal Justice Concern." *Justice Quarterly*, 2(1), (March 1985).

Brydolf, L. "High-Tech to Cut Costs of Justice." *San Diego Transcript*, 5 February 1986, pp. 1A, 6A.

Bureau of Justice Assistance. Monograph: Electronic Monitoring in Intensive Probation and Parole Programs. February 1989.

Bureau of Justice Statistics (BJS), "Justice Expenditures and Employment, 1985." *Bulletin*, Government Printing Office, March 1987.

Bureau of Justice Statistics (BJS), *Report to the Nation on Crime and Justice*, 2d ed. March 1988.

Bureau of Justice Statistics (BJS). "Prisoners in 1987." *Bulletin*, Government Printing Office, April 1988.

Bureau of Justice Statistics (BJS). "Probation and Parole 1987." *Bulletin*, Government Printing Office, November 1988.

Bureau of Justice Statistics (BJS). "Jail Inmates in 1987." *Bulletin*, Government Printing Office, December 1988.

Bureau of Justice Statistics (BJS). "Felony Sentences in State Courts, 1986." *Bulletin*, Government Printing Office, February 1989.

Byrne, J. M., L. Kelly, and S. Guarino-Ghezzi. "Understanding the Limits of Technology: An Examination of the Use of Electronic Monitoring in the Criminal Justice System." *Perspectives*, Spring 1988, pp. 30–37.

Calvello, A., Assistant Public Defender. Memorandum to R. L. Jordan by Public Defender, Palm Beach County, Florida. "Electronic Monitors," 2 October 1985.

Christensen, C., Assistant Attorney General. Letter to William C. Vickery, Director, Division of Corrections, State of Utah. "Informal Opinion No. 83–81," 24 April 1985.

Clear, T., S. Flynn, and C. Shapiro, "Intensive Supervision in Probation: A Comparison of Three Projects." In B. R. McCarthy, ed., *Intermediate Punishments: Intensive Supervision, Home Confinement and Electronic Surveillance*, pp. 31–50. Monsey, NY: Willow Tree Press, 1987.

Contra Costa County, Adult Probation Department. Adult Home Detention Program, End of Project Report, December 1983 through April 1985.

Corbett, R., and E. Fersch. "Home as Prison: Use of House Arrest." *Federal Probation* (March 1985): 13–17.

del Carmen, R. V. and J. B. Vaughn. "Legal Issues in the Use of Electronic Surveillance in Probation." *Federal Probation*, June 1986.

Denton, M. Untitled statistical report. Harper Woods, MI, February 1988.

"Electronic Monitoring of Probationers on the Increase." *Criminal Justice Newsletter*, 16(20) (15 October 1985), 4–6.

Flynn, L. "Community Control 'House Arrest' . . . a Cooperative Effort Effectively Implemented." *APPA Perspectives* (American Probation and Parole Association) 9 (3) (Summer 1985): 1–4.

"Florida's Offenders Under House Arrest." *Corrections Today*, October 1985, p. 105.

Ford, D. and A. K. Schmidt. "Electronically Monitored Home Confinement." *NIJ Reports*, U.S. Department of Justice, National Institute of Justice, November 1985.

Friel, C. M., and J. B. Vaughn. *A Consumer's Guide to the Electronic Surveillance of Probationers*. Huntsville, TX: Criminal Justice Center, Sam Houston State University, 1985.

Friel, C. M., J. B. Vaughn, and R. del Carmen. Electronic Monitoring and Correctional Policy: The Technology and Its Application, Research Report. National Institute of Justice, June 1987.

Gable (formerly Schwitzgebel), R. K. "Applications of Personal Telemonitoring to Current Problems in Corrections." *Journal of Criminal Justice*, 14 (1986): 167–75.

Garcia, E. D., Lt. In-House Arrest Work Release Program, 15 February 1986, personal communication.

Goldstein, H. Administrative Office of the Courts. Personal communication, Trenton, NJ, March 1986.

Hofer, P. J. and B. S. Meierhoefer. *Home Confinement*. Federal Judicial Center, 1987.

Ingraham, B. L. and G. Smith. "Use of Electronics in Observation and Control of Human Behavior." *Issues in Criminology* 7(2) (Fall 1972): 35–53.

Inverson, W. R. "High-Tech Leg Irons Put to the Test." *Electronics Week*, 4 March 1985, p. 30.

Jolin, A. Electronic Surveillance Program, Clackamus County Community Corrections, Oregon, Evaluation. Clackamus County Community Corrections, undated.

Lilly, J. R. "An International Summary of House Arrest and Electronic Monitoring." Paper presented at the American Academy of Criminal Justice Sciences, Washington, DC, 2 April 1989.

Lilly, J. R. and J. Wright. "Home Incarceration with Electronic Monitoring in Kenton County, Kentucky: A Preliminary Report." Submitted to the Kentucky Department of Corrections, December 1985.

Lilly, J. R., et al. "Electronic Jail Revisited." *Justice Quarterly*, 1986.

Marx, G. T. "The New Surveillance." *Technology Review*, 45 (May–June 1985) 43–48.

Marx, G. T. "I'll Be Watching You." *Dissent*, Winter 1986, pp. 26–34.

McCarthy, B. R., ed. *Intermediate Punishments: Intensive Supervision, Home Confinement, and Electronic Surveillance*. Monsey, NY: Willow Tree Press, 1987.

McGowan, J. Letter to The Honorable Harrison D. Griffin, 11 February 1987.

McGowan, J. Letter to The Honorable Norton Josephson, 19 May 1988.

National Sheriff's Association. "Electronic Prison Less Costly." *Sheriff's Roll Call*, 2(2) (March 1985): 8.

Palm Beach County, Florida, Sheriff's Department. "Palm Beach County's In-House Arrest Work Release Program." In B. R. McCarthy, ed., *Intermediate Punishments: Intensive Supervision, Home Confinement and Electronic Surveillance*, pp. 181–87. Monsey, NY: Willow Tree Press, 1987.

Petersilia, J. "Exploring the Option of House Arrest." *Federal Probation*, June 1986, pp. 50–55.

Petersilia, J. "Georgia's Intensive Probation: Will the Model Work Elsewhere." In McCarthy, ed., *Intermediate Punishments*, pp. 15–30.

"Probation and Bracelets: The Spiderman Solution." *Corrections Magazine*, 1983, p. 4.

Ranii, D. "Ankle Signal Linked to Computer May Monitor Probationers in New Mexico." *National Law Journal*, 28 March 1983, pp. 3 and 38.

Rasmussen, F., and G. Rothbart. Pride, Inc., West Palm Beach, FL. Personal Communication, April 1986.

Renzema, M. Personal communication, 18 April 1989.

Rorvik, D. "Behavior Control: Big Brother Comes." *Intellectual Digest*, January 1974, pp. 17–20.

Schmidt, A. K. "Electronic Monitoring." *Federal Probation*, June 1986, pp. 56–59.

Schmidt, A. K. "Electronic Monitoring—Who Uses it? How Much Does It Cost? Does It Work?" *Corrections Today* 49(7) (December 1987): 28–34.

Schmidt, A. K. "Electronic Monitoring of Offenders Increases." *NIJ Reports*, no. 212 (January/February 1989): 2–5.

Schmidt, A. K., and C. E. Curtis. "Electronic Monitoring." In B. R. McCarthy, *Intermediate Punishments*. New York: Criminal Justice Press, 1987.

Schwitzgebel (now Gable), R. K., et al., "A Program of Research in Behavior Electronics." *Behavioral Science*, 9 (1964): 233–38.

Schwitzgebel (now Gable), R. K. "Electronic Innovation in Behavioral Sciences: A Call to Responsibility." *American Psychologist*, 22 (1967): 364–70.

Schwitzgebel (now Gable), R. K. "Electronic Alternatives to Imprisonment." *Lex et Scientia*, (S, 1968): 99–104.

Schwitzgebel (now Gable), R. K. "Development of an Electronic Rehabilitation System for Parolees." *Law and Computer Technology*, 2 (March 1969): 9–12.

Schwitzgebel (now Gable), R. K. "Issues in the Use of an Electronic Rehabilitation System with Chronic Recidivists." *Law and Society Review*, 3(4) (May 1969): 597–611.

"Spiderman's Net: An Electronic Alternative to Prison." *Time Magazine*, 14 October 1985, p. 93.

U.S. Department of Commerce. "Electronic Monitoring Devices." *Commerce Business Daily*, 11 February 1985, p. 21.

Vaughn, J. B. "Planning for Change: The Use of Electronic Monitoring as a Correctional Alternative." In McCarthy, ed., *Intermediate Punishments*, pp. 153–68.

Weintraub, D. M. "Some Convicts Will Serve Their Sentences at Home." *Los Angeles Times*, 5 February 1986.

Whittington, M. Supervised Electronic Confinement Pilot Program, Final Report, Orange County Probation Department, December 1987.

Williamson, J. A. Attachment to letter to A. K. Schmidt, dated 17 February 1988, Tampa, FL.

Woolard, A. "Comic Strip Inspires Electronic Surveillance Device for Parolees." *Engineering Times*, 7 (5) (May 1985): 16–17.

16

Alternatives to Imprisonment in Latin America and the Caribbean

Elías Carranza, Nicholas J. O. Liverpool, and
Luis Rodríguez-Manzanera

Part One: Status and Prospects for Corrections in Latin America and the Caribbean—The Need for Alternatives to Imprisonment (Elías Carranza)

The excessive use of imprisonment, with its consequent series of negative effects, has been persistently denounced by the United Nations and by many other criminological and human rights institutions. It has, therefore, been regularly included as a subject at the quinquennial United Nations Congresses on the Prevention of Crime and the Treatment of Offenders. To cite only the most recent of such important events, at the Fifth Congress on the Prevention of Crime and the Treatment of Offenders (1975), it was included under the title "The Treatment of Offenders under Custody or in the Community, with Special Reference to the UN-Approved Minimum Rules for the Treatment of Prisoners." At the Sixth Congress (1980), it was incorporated under the title "Non-institutionalized Correctional Treatment and Its Consequences for Inmates Who Remain under Custody." At the Seventh Congress (1985), a special resolution was adopted entitled "Reduction of the Correctional Population, Alternatives to Imprisonment, and Re-insertion of Offenders into the Society." And at the Eighth Congress (1990), the subject was again included under the title "Criminal Justice Policies Relative to the Problems of Imprisonment, Other Criminal Sanctions, and Alternative Measures." Additionally, a special research workshop was prepared on the subject of alternatives to imprisonment.

The deteriorating effects imprisonment has on those who are subjected to it, the transfer of the effects of the penalty to the family and relatives of the offender, and the negative results it has for the community, in addition to its high cost, are valid reasons for attempting to reduce its application in both developed and developing countries. However, in the case of the latter, particularly in Latin America and the Caribbean, these arguments are even more relevant.

Because of the deterioration of the regional economies and the enormous external debt affecting them, budget cuts have been made that seriously imperil the social welfare sectors (health, housing, education),[1] with very negative effects on the primary prevention of crime. Particularly within the criminal justice systems, the budgetary imbalance is intensified through the reduction in the amounts allocated to the judicial branches and correctional systems.[2]

The shrinking of the budget at the correctional level is very serious due to the contradiction it implies vis-à-vis the fast increase in the correctional population. Latin America is a region where the population grows rapidly[3]; thus, even if rates remained constant, the correctional population would grow considerably in absolute terms, which would require constant modification (something that is not done at present) of infrastructural capacity. However, the problem is further aggravated due to the fact that the correctional population is growing in most of the countries of the region at a much faster pace than the population in general; this intensifies not only the overcrowding in facilities but also its multiple negative consequences.

Table 16.1 shows a noticeable increase in correctional rates in some countries of the region.

The information contained in table 16.1 points to a worrying condition of deterioration not only in the correctional domain but also in the criminal justice systems in general. On this subject, a recent study sponsored by the Inter-American Institute on Human Rights provided very enlightening and detailed information, itemizing human rights violation problems affecting each of the subsystems.[4]

A particular cause for concern related to the correctional population is the situation of "inmates awaiting trial," an issue given special attention by the United Nations in general, and by the UN Latin American Institute for Crime Prevention and the Treatment of Offenders (ILANUD) in particular, regarding the Latin American and Caribbean region.[5] Theoretically, the inmates awaiting trial are protected by the principle of innocence and by the guarantee of due process, which must be expedited without impinging on the right to defense. In reality, however, in most countries of the region there is a large number of inmates awaiting trial who remain in prison for long periods and who may subsequently be found innocent and released. The number of cases initiated (with or without the holding of a prisoner) where a sentence is finally handed down is very low. As an example, in a study carried out in Costa Rica, only 35 percent of a sample of 468 prosecuted individuals were sentenced; the bulk, 65 percent, were acquitted because charges were dropped during the instructional phase, release after trial, or dismissal of complaint (see chapter 17, this volume). It is estimated that the percentage of convictions in the remaining countries of the region is not higher.

Table 16.1 Total Number of Inmates and Rate of Imprisonment in Some Countries of Latin America and the Caribbean

Country	Year	Inmates	Country Population (in thousands)	Rate (per 100,000)
Barbados	1981	247	254	97
	1984	367	265	138
	1989	462	275	168
Bolivia	1987	3,312	6,730	49
	1988	3,485	6,918	50
	1989	3,582	7,113	50
Cayman	1981	46	12	383
	1984	74	12	616
	1989	165	12	1,375
Colombia	1986	24,893	29,323	85
	1987	27,280	29,942	91
	1988	27,358	30,568	90
	1989	31,077	31,195	100
Costa Rica	1972	——	——	85
	1979	2,308	2,217	104
	1980	2,543	2,284	111
	1981	2,876	2,353	122
	1982	3,068	2,423	127
	1983	3,076	2,495	123
	1984	3,409	2,568	133
	1985	3,514	2,642	133
	1986	3,656	2,715	135
	1987	3,986	2,790	143
	1988	3,918	2,866	137
	1989	4,163	3,015	138
Chile	1972	9,505	——	108
	1981	12,876	11,294	114
	1983	18,051	11,665	154
	1987	23,044	12,536	184
	1988	25,148	12,748	197
	1989	24,933	12,961	192
Dominican Republic	1981	5,355	5,835	91
	1985	5,871	6,416	92
	1987	6,898	6,715	103
	1988	7,538	6,867	110
	1989	8,370	7,019	119
El Salvador	1981	3,402	4,582	74
	1985	4,525	4,767	78
	1987	5,119	4,933	104
	1988	4,799	5,031	95
	1989	5,374	5,137	105

Country	Year	Inmates	Country Population (in thousands)	Rate (per 100,000)
Guatemala	1981	4,367	7,113	61
	1985	3,926	7,963	50
	1989	6,051	8,935	68
Honduras	1987	4,076	4,679	87
	1988	6,263	4,829	130
	1989	6,757	4,982	136
Jamaica	1982	3,254	2,254	144
	1984	3,497	2,291	153
Mexico	1972	43,506	——	83
	1976	42,943	20,501	48
	1980	58,352	70,416	83
	1987	71,600	83,039	86
	1988	73,521	84,886	87
Montserrat	1984	24	13	176
	1989	34	14	243
Netherlands Antilles	1982	365	257	143
	1989	412	279	148
Saint Lucia	1981	161	120	134
	1984	192	126	152
	1989	270	135	200
Trinidad and Tobago	1989	2,325	1,171	199
Uruguay	1981	1,890	2,916	65
	1987	1,859	3,057	61
	1988	2,038	3,081	66
	1989	2,353	3,104	76
Venezuela	1972	13,920	——	127
	1974	16,654	——	151
	1980	12,623	15,024	84
	1981	16,552	15,457	107
	1982	16,268	15,902	102
	1983	19,329	16,361	118
	1984	24,044	16,832	143
	1985	27,229	17,317	157
	1986	27,650	17,792	155
	1987	28,567	18,272	156
	1988	28,607	18,757	153

Sources: Prepared on the basis of data furnished by the ministries in charge of correctional matters in each country, and from population data from CELADE, *Demographic Bulletin*, 20, no. 40. Population data for Cayman and Montserrat were obtained from "U.N. Selected World Demographic and Population Policy Indicators."

Tables 16.2 and 16.3 show the number of inmates awaiting trial, the percentage thereof with respect to the total correctional population, and the rate per one hundred thousand in countries of Latin America and the Caribbean.

As can be seen in table 16.2, the percentage of inmates awaiting trial in countries of Latin America with criminal justice systems of the European/Continental tradition, ranges from 45 percent to 91 percent of the correctional population. The rates per one hundred thousand inmates not yet convicted are also very high, even higher than the overall rates (of convicted and nonconvicted inmates) of many European countries.[6]

A comparison with table 16.3 shows that, with the exception of Cayman, in the Caribbean countries with Anglo-Saxon systems the percentages and rates relative to inmates not yet convicted are lower than those of the countries in table 16.2. However, the overall rates relative to the correctional population in these countries (table 16.1) are very high and are gradually increasing.

Table 16.2 Total Number of Inmates, Inmates Awaiting Trial, Percentages, and Rates in Countries of Latin America and the Caribbean with Criminal Justice Systems of the European/Continental Tradition

Country	Year	Total Number of Inmates	Inmates Awaiting Trial		
			Number	Percent	Rate per 100,000
Colombia	1989	31,077	16,780	54.0	53.8
Costa Rica	1990	3,917	1,738	44.3	57.6
Chile	1989	24,933	13,143	53.0	101.0
Dominican Republic	1989	8,370	7,152	85.0	102.0
Ecuador	1988	6,293	4,392	69.8	43.0
El Salvador	1989	5,374	4,901	91.2	95.4
Guatemala	1989	6,051	4,418	73.0	49.4
Honduras	1989	6,757	5,971	88.3	120.0
Martinique	1989	384	175	46.0	55.5
Mexico	1988	73,521	44,847	61.0	53.0
Netherlands Antilles	1989	412	197	48.0	76.7
Nicaragua	1990	4,310	1,946	45.0	50.2
Peru	1986	14,819	9,560	65.0	47.3
Uruguay	1989	2,353	2,137	91.0	69.0
Venezuela	1988	28,607	20,263	71.0	108.0

Sources: Prepared on the basis of correctional information furnished by the ministries in charge of correctional matters in each country and from population data from CELADE, *Demographic Bulletin*, 20, no. 40. The data for 1989 for Guatemala include 962 inmates who, it is estimated, were being held in police facilities. The information relative to Peru for 1986 was obtained from the National Correctional Census of April 7, 1986.

Adapted from *Sixth United Nations Congress on the Prevention of Crime and the Treatment of Offenders,* A/CONF. 87/7, 9 July 1980, p. 20.

Table 16.3   Total Number of Inmates, Inmates Awaiting Trial, Percentages, and Rates in Countries of Latin America and the Caribbean with Criminal Justice Systems of the Anglo-Saxon Tradition

| | | | Inmates Awaiting Trial | | |
Country	Year	Total Number of Inmates	Number	Percent	Rate per 100,000
Barbados	1989	462	41	9	15.0
Cayman	1989	165	27	16	225.0
Montserrat	1989	34	2	6	14.3
St. Kitts-Nevis	1989	97	20	21	29.4
Saint Lucia	1989	270	50	19	37.0
St. Vincent and Grenadines	1989	253	31	12	29.0
Trinidad and Tobago	1989	2,325	1,075	46	92.0

Sources: Prepared on the basis of correctional information furnished by the governments of each country and from population data from CELADE, *Demographic Bulletin,* Year 20, no. 40, for Barbados, Saint Lucia, and Trinidad-Tobago; population data for the remaining countries were obtained from "U.N. Selected World Demographic and Population Policy Indicators."

In other words, regardless of the juridical status, an uncontrolled increase in the use of imprisonment has been occurring in the countries of Latin America and the Caribbean. Particularly serious is the fact that, in many cases, the worst violations of human rights can be attributed to critical conditions in prisons.

During a recent seminar held at ILANUD with directors of correctional systems of Latin America and the Caribbean, it was determined that there are serious overcrowding problems in at least seventeen countries of the region. In some countries the correctional system displays exceedingly high global overcrowding indicators. In others, the problem affects certain units, with overcrowding of up to 200, 300, and even 900 percent.[7]

It is well known that prison, as a "total institution" of a punitive nature, generates violence and its own pathological situations that affect those who live in it, whether they be inmates or correctional personnel. In addition to such natural effects upon the individual, in the case of Latin America and the Caribbean it is also necessary to take into account the magnifying effect brought about by overcrowding and the frequent impossibility of satisfying basic needs such as health, food, and shelter.

The fact that most of those who constitute the correctional population belong to the most deprived sectors of society and are, therefore, the most susceptible to criminalization by the criminal justice system, helps to understand (but not, however, to justify) the lack of priority given to correctional systems in the programs of the different governments.[8] On very few occasions are individuals from the higher social strata and with a certain amount of power, even if perpetrators of offenses that cause serious social damage, sentenced to imprisonment. This is one of the weaknesses in the operation of these systems.

As cautioned above, the correctional problem in Latin America and the Caribbean is closely related to conditions of regional development.[9] For this reason the only chance of effectively dealing with the problem is to recognize that there are criminal policy actions that go beyond their domain and that should be integrated into national policies for development. However, much can be done at the specific level of the criminal justice systems and concurrent with such integrating actions; one priority measure would be to encourage the use of available forms of noncustodial sanctions and preventive measures.

We have observed that in the Latin American countries with European/ Continental criminal justice systems efforts are being made to introduce alternatives to pretrial imprisonment, since inmates awaiting trial constitute the vast majority in the correctional systems of all these countries.

In the case of the Caribbean countries with Anglo-Saxon systems, it appears from tables 16.1 through 16.3 that, without excluding the possibility of exploring for alternative measures to preventive imprisonment, immediate efforts should focus on the use of noncustodial alternatives as punishment, since the high correctional population rates for these countries relate mostly to convicted felons.

Part 2 of this study presents an overview of the different alternatives to imprisonment available in the Latin American countries with European/ Continental systems. Part 3 consists of an overview of the different alternatives to imprisonment available in the Caribbean countries with Anglo-Saxon systems. In addition, the results of a "demonstration project" (experimental research) on a specific alternative to preventive imprisonment—release on personal recognizance—are also presented in this volume (chapter 17). But release on personal recognizance is only one of the possible alternatives. It is necessary to search for and encourage many other forms, at the legislative, police, judicial, and correctional levels.[10]

Part Two: Overview of Alternatives to Imprisonment in Latin America
(Luis Rodríguez-Manzanera)

Much has already been written on the crisis of imprisonment, and consensus appears to have been reached on this subject. However, the problem is aggravated when a situation of crisis is arrived at within a context already in crisis, as is the case with the correctional systems in Latin American countries with serious economic and political difficulties.

Latin American criminal law is plagued with the penalty of incarceration. The excessive use of custodial measures has led to a noticeable deterioration of entire criminal justice systems. The selectivity of the system becomes even more evident in the overcrowded Latin American prisons, where the phenomena of associating the individual with characteristics of prison life, stigmatization, and labeling are intensified. Violence in the prisons of the region, with its high toll of casualties, is an alarm signal that indicates there is a need for change. (Examples of this are the bloody mutinies in Argentina, Colombia, Guatemala, Mexico, Peru, etc., or the sinister Brazilian "lottery.")

The entire criminal justice system appears to be in a state of crisis, with unprecedented legislative inflation, more repressive rather than preventive codes, and inadequately selected and improvised personnel, and, unfortunately, tainted by serious outbreaks of corruption. Justice is sluggish, expensive, inequitable, and inconsistent. All of this is reflected with greater cruelty in the prisons.[11]

The discussion of preventive custody would warrant a separate chapter, since it has become one of the hardest dilemmas to resolve. A double problem is being confronted: the need to abolish penalty to imprisonment—as the death penalty is being gradually abolished—and the imperative need to find a way to replace imprisonment and what to replace it with. This chapter will look into several possible solutions and at the results obtained in Latin America with their application.

Imprisonment as Penalty in Latin America

Concern about the correctional problem (an unequivocal cause of human rights violations, indignation, and distress) has led several countries of the region to legislate by constitutional means, making humane treatment mandatory and following the tendency of social readjustment, often referred to by names such as *reeducation, social readaptation, rehabilitation,* and *social reinsertion.* Such is the case in the constitutions of Argentina, Article 18; Brazil, Article 153; Mexico, Article 18; Panama, Article 28; Paraguay, Article 65; and Peru, Article 234.

Prison's responsibility for reeducating offenders is referred to substantially in the criminal codes. For instance, in the case of Bolivia, in Article 25; Columbia, Article 12; Costa Rica, Article 51; Cuba, Article 27; Ecuador, Article 53; Panama, Article 47; Peru, Article 132; and Uruguay, Article 26.

Provisions relative to both the application of penalties and imprisonment are also made in the procedural codes of Argentina (677 et seq.), Costa Rica (504 et seq.), Cuba (481 et seq.), Dominican Republic (297 et seq.), Guatemala (218 et seq.), Mexico (575 et seq.), Nicaragua (513 et seq.), Panama (223 et seq.), Paraguay (546 et seq.), Peru (329 et seq.), Uruguay (315 et seq.), and Venezuela (358 et seq.).

Some countries have application codes or statutes; these are Argentina (Law by Decree 412/58), Colombia (Decree 1817/64), Brazil (Law on the Application of Criminal Sanctions 7210/84), Bolivia (Law 11080/83), Costa Rica (Law on the General Directorate of Social Adaptation), Mexico (Law on the Establishment of Minimum Rules for the Social Readaptation of Convicted Felons, 1971), and Uruguay (Correctional Law 470/975).

In spite of the large number of provisions, "the dispersion of regulatory measures is astonishing, especially in those countries where it has not yet been possible to systematize the successive provisions into unified corpora. The laws, decrees, and proclamations that are adopted in addition to criminal and procedural provisions and constitutional precepts all represent a heterogeneous scenario where the overlapping of concepts, contradictions and technical gaps are not infrequent phenomena."[12]

In most countries of the region there is judicial control over the application of penalty to imprisonment. Although the application of penalty is the responsibility of the administrative authorities, the judging entity that in the first instance handed down the sentence becomes the judge that supervises the application thereof.

Exceptions to this rule are Costa Rica, with an autonomous judge responsible for the application of the penalty, and the Dominican Republic and Mexico, where the application of penalty to imprisonment is entirely the responsibility of the executive branch.

Preventive Imprisonment in Latin America

In 1976, a United Nations expert stated that "the admission that only 40 percent of the total population under custody in Latin America has been judged becomes a tragic reality."[13] Over 65 percent of the sentences passed against primary felons were terms of less than three years, and more than half were penalties of less than two years. Six years later, the percentage of convicted felons had dropped to 31.53 percent, which means that 68.47 percent of those under custody were prosecuted individuals awaiting trial.[14]

The data available indicate that the region's trend is toward an increase in the number of nonconvicted inmates. For instance, in Mexico in 1972 the percentage was 40.39 percent; by 1974 it had reached 48.9 percent,[15] and by 1988 it had soared to 61 percent. This is not only cause for alarm, but also proof that, as already asserted, preventive imprisonment in Latin America becomes the rule, while imprisonment as penalty is the exception. It also indicates that preventive imprisonment fully assumes the retributory and repressive role of a penalty that is applied in advance, that is to say, it becomes a penalty without the characteristics of either punishability or punishment.

In almost all countries of the region, there is a limit to the imposition of preventive imprisonment, depending upon the seriousness of the offense for which the individual has been prosecuted. In the following countries, the maximum terms applied are these: Argentina, Nicaragua, and Paraguay, two years; Haiti, Honduras, Peru, and Uruguay, three years; Bolivia, four years; Colombia and Guatemala, five years. The minimum terms applied in other countries of the region are these: Brazil, Uruguay, and Venezuela, two years; Ecuador, three years; Panama, five years.

Costa Rica, Chile, and the Dominican Republic do not indicate specific terms. The limits instituted in Cuba are capital punishment and maximum term of imprisonment. Mexico uses five years as the arithmetical average between the minimum and the maximum.

There are numerous exceptions: independently from the prescribed range, in Argentina, Brazil, Costa Rica, Cuba, Chile, the Dominican Republic, Peru, and Uruguay, the judge may decide on preventive imprisonment if it is considered convenient (e.g., if it is felt there is danger the accused may escape or commit another offense).

Likewise, in Bolivia, Brazil, Colombia, Chile, Ecuador, Guatemala, Haiti, Honduras, and Paraguay, recidivists and habitual and professional offenders must remain in prison.

In brief, preventive imprisonment is a problem for which a solution must be found with the greatest urgency in Latin America. This should be achieved without diminishing the importance of the problem of imprisonment as penalty, since in three of every four correctional institutions there is no real physical division between prosecuted prisoners pending trial and convicted felons. This means that anything that is done to improve and diminish (and, if possible, eliminate) preventive imprisonment would benefit directly the convicted inmates.

Transformation and Alternatives

Individualization. The individualization of an adequate alternative measure to confinement is of the utmost importance; it will, therefore, be commented on in relation to Latin America. In order to ensure the individualization of an alternative, it is necessary to have the required legislative, judicial, and executive mechanisms.

Legislatively, alternative measures and general possibilities for their application must be provided for. A sufficiently large range of alternatives should be made available to avoid numerous limitations that would result in imprisonment continuing to prevail. This makes it necessary for the legislators to become acquainted with available material and human resources; to know what, in theory, are the possibilities for the application of an alternative measure; and to benefit from assessments of the penalties and measures in

393

force. The first important obstacle to overcome in replacing imprisonment with an alternative measure is the lack of provisions in the legislation. (As we shall see later, where these exist, they are rather limited.)

Judicially, the alternative measure must be individualized. However, in order to do this, it is necessary for the judge

a. to be trained in criminology;
b. to have access, before the trial, to valid reports on the offender's biopsychological and social personality;
c. to be able to find, either in the Criminal Code or in any analogous set of provisions, a wide range of measures from which to select the most adequate to the individual circumstances of the offender; and
d. to have knowledge of the advantages and disadvantages of such measures as compared to confinement, as well as of the different ways in which they may be applied, the results obtained in the countries where they have been tried out, and the appropriateness of the application thereof in a given social context.[16]

At least in certain regions it is necessary to substantially simplify alternative procedures.

Administratively, it is also necessary to individualize the alternative at the level where sanctions are applied. This power has been given to the executive branch in some countries of the area, but for the most part it continues to be exclusively a prerogative of the judicial branch. Understandably, the biggest problem is the notorious lack of facilities, specialized personnel, and material resources, which additionally diminishes the level of attention that can be devoted to individual cases and makes it imperative to search for collective alternative means of control.

The Juridical Situation. While it is indispensable to include alternatives to imprisonment (whether preventive or punitive) in the criminal legislation, there is also an imperative need to make changes in procedural terms, since the Latin American procedural codes maintain a peculiar system where the initial phase is of an inquisitorial nature and the second phase is of an accusatorial nature. This is not only a source of violations of human rights, but also an obstacle to any desired reform.

One way of accomplishing a coherent application of a penalty—as well as facilitating the application of alternative measures—could be by "sectioning" the procedure as proposed by the Social Defense School, that is, dividing the criminal procedure into two phases: first, "determination of behaviour" (Gramática),[17] or "guiltiness process" (Ancel); and second, the "detection of delinquency" (Gramática) or "social defence" phase (Ancel).[18]

Another change is also indispensable to expedite the procedure: serious thought must be given to the replacement of the intricate written procedure with a more practical oral procedure.

Furthermore, criminal executive law is almost unknown in most developing countries (as well as in many developed countries). University curricula include criminal law and criminal procedural law under the assumption that the convict is, in civil terms, a "casualty," someone who does not have any rights. In our law schools and colleges the problem is not studied as a subject; could it be because convicted felons are not a source of income, and therefore lawyers are not interested in them?

Legislatively speaking, criminal executive law has subsisted outside the realm of the law, since there are no laws for the application of sanctions, and laws that do exist are noticeably deficient. In reality, old customs and obsolete regulations prevail.

It can be asserted that certain groups of specialists (idealistic minorities) have attempted to create a criminal executive law institution. Nevertheless, as one of them maintains: "Everybody knows how an improvement in the prison system, and even the commutation of a sentence, infuriates people."[19]

There is concern throughout Latin America about legislating on the application of sanctions, and there are a number of draft bills on this issue; some of the proposed laws are noteworthy (such as the Brazilian one). Criminal and correctional committees are studying the problem, and, although the solution appears to be yet remote, the progress made during the decade of the '80s is substantial.

It is necessary to legislate on the application and substitution of sanctions. We need laws to regulate primarily the application of sanctions, not only the penalty of confinement but the entire criminal gamut including alternatives. The power of legislating is not within the reach of most of us, but we can succeed in making our universities give more importance to this subject.

The Treatment Institution. Before dealing further with this subject, it is necessary to clarify the sense in which we use the term *treatment*. Treatment is construed as the intervention of a technical criminological team—in other words, an interdisciplinary team covering the psychological, social, pedagogical, and medical aspects that must be studied in order to provide the attention that the inmate requires.

The primary function of the technical team is to prevent the victimization of inmates induced by life in prison, to eradicate stigmatization, and prepare the inmate for possible impending labeling. Additionally, the technical team would do whatever was necessary to keep inmates profitably occupied by engaging them in something purposeful such as learning a trade, improving educational capabilities, or developing a working skill. In this sense, we believe that treatment could be acceptable even if applied to preventive imprisonment (or maybe we should turn the terms around, since it is during preventive imprisonment that the harmful effects of confinement can be prevented).

The ideology of treatment, that is, the "theory whose purpose is to adapt the penalty to a therapeutic 'treatment' making its duration contingent upon the presumed needs of such 'treatment,' regardless of the magnitude of the offence,"[20] has been harshly criticized. In fact, the ideology of treatment affects the principle of rationality of the punishment. It settles itself within an individualistic etiology that denies the social factor and may be the source of much abuse.

What we propose is something very different from such an ideology, and we defend our point of view with an argument that emerges from the Latin American reality: human rights have made their appearance in prisons, to a large extent, thanks to the technicians, the professionals in psychology, medicine, sociology, criminology, and pedagogy. Some of the attacks against treatment should be mistrusted, since what is being concealed behind such attacks in those cases is either simply "a fashion" or the desire to maintain the supremacy of security and repression. The removal of technical personnel from the prisons might mean the elimination of uncomfortable witnesses to the most violent arbitrariness or dirtiest corruption.

Therefore, one way of substituting for a prison is to transform it into a treatment institution. "The purpose of transforming a prison into a treatment institution is to strip it of its punitive character. As soon as the prison becomes a treatment institution, it is no longer a prison."[21] Ruiz-Funes had already asserted that "in justifying its failures and subsisting as a goal-seeking institution, the prison is forced to evolve from a more or less secluded confinement place into an authentic school for reform."[22] In turn, Pizzotti maintains that "it will be practically impossible to arrive at the readjustment of the convicted felons if the anti-natural, artificial atmosphere that prevails is not caused to disappear. In all certainty, one of the most important causes of the failure of imprisonment is such a negative atmosphere."[23]

We are sure that transformation is possible. Experiments carried out provide reason to be optimistic and to contemplate not great establishments of punishment, enormous cathedrals of fear or crime colleges, but, instead, small criminological clinics. A change in the structure of corrections from authoritarianism to a more democratic institution is of paramount importance. The style in most prisons is still a military style: uniforms, semimilitary terminology, the existence of "officers." All this largely thwarts the possibilities of prisons becoming therapeutic communities. The usual passive attitude of "waiting for treatment" must be exchanged for a new awareness that may enable the individual to participate in it actively.[24]

Without a doubt, the change of structure implies a change of facilities and personnel. It is not possible for treatment to take place as long as "ancient convents, senescent fortresses, ruinous residences, if not bare caverns and dungeons, are the seats of such alleged treatment centres known as prisons."[25]

As regards personnel, an absolute change in mentality is necessary, favoring inexperienced, but selected and trained, personnel without a correctional background rather than those who have become "specialists" in the prison and who have already been victims of the effects of life in prison.

The problem of evaluation should be anticipated: evaluation must be done in accordance with the objective data obtained by observing the individual's conduct (i.e., obedience to the institution's regulations), but it is criminologically valuable to study also the internal aspects of the individual's personality in order to know how he or she assimilates a given treatment and thus be in a position to assess its effectiveness.[26] Evaluation is not common in Latin America. Pinatel reminds us that "offenders, save for specific exceptions, are not generally ill individuals; for the most part, because of their circumstantial or chronic departure from their regulatory system, they have committed an aggression against the values of the group of which they are a part."[27] "Treatment in an institution is not more than one of the possible ways in which offenders may be treated."[28] Di Tullio, the great Italian master, asserts that "it is necessary to give those under custody the sensation that they are not merely numbers, convicts who are rejected by society, but human beings among humans."[29]

One of the problems that limits the possibilities for treatment along broad lines is the Latin American tradition of placing the prisons under the supervision of the military, who, in principle, are not specialists in therapeutic forms of treatment.

In general, the laws relative to the application of sanctions are vague as regards treatment. They rarely define it or describe its objectives, and on certain occasions they circumscribe it to "education and work." Thus, we must be careful, because it commonly occurs that "inside the velvet glove of therapy and treatment there lies in concealment the very iron claw of punishment."[30]

The scarcity in terms of personnel and material resources is more intensely felt in the developing countries, which have multiple and urgent needs and which, in some cases, regard as a superfluous expenditure any investment made in crime prevention and in the treatment of the offender.

In spite of all this, treatment is gradually being adopted in the region (in Argentina, Bolivia, Costa Rica, Mexico, Nicaragua, Peru, Uruguay, etc.), and it can be asserted that most inmates granted early release owe their advanced liberation to the benefits granted at the different stages of the process.

Diversification of the Prison. Another way in which it is possible to gradually eradicate the traditional punishment of imprisonment is to diversify the systems. In this context, "system" is construed as "the set of conditions and influences which are brought together in an institution with the purpose of seeking the specific objective assigned to the criminal sanction in relation to a criminologically integrated conglomerate of offenders."[31] In other words, it is construed as the type of life that, in general terms, must be adopted in the correctional institutions, without excluding special systems for those institutions that are in charge of certain types of inmate.[32]

Under this mode of operation, a number of "prisons" would become decreasingly vindictive. Harmful habits and defects of the traditional prison would be gradually eradicated, steadily becoming less prisonlike, step by step. A few possibilities are briefly mentioned below.

Open Prisons. Although important progress was made in this respect during the preceding century, it can be said that the open prison is a current development to which experts and congresses have devoted attention and that they have amply recommended. The First United Nations Congress on the Prevention of Crime and the Treatment of Offenders, held in Geneva in 1955, concluded, in its first resolution, that "the open establishment is characterized by the absence of physical means to prevent an escape, and by a system that is founded upon both a discipline that is accepted and a sense of responsibility on the part of the inmate vis-à-vis the community in which she/he lives. This system encourages the inmates to use but not abuse the privileges offered them. These are the characteristics which distinguish an open establishment from all other types of correctional establishments, which, in some cases, draw their inspiration from the same principles but do not totally apply them."

Open establishments represent an encouraging future, not only as one phase of the overall treatment, but as a form of prison that can be substituted for a "closed" prison.

The term "open prison," as Neuman notes, may appear to be an inconsistency or an antithesis; however, in spite of the fact that these establishments are located in fields where, generally speaking, agricultural work is carried out, near towns or cities, and with little or no vigilance, the following must be kept in mind:

a. Only the security system, that is, the physical or material containment mechanism, has been replaced by moral and psychological coercion; and
b. the prison as such has not disappeared, but, rather, has "evolved."[33]

Mannheim and Wilkins, in their "Prediction Methods," as well as Highfields, in his experiment,[34] have demonstrated that the open correctional institutions can be at least as effective as the closed institutions, and, although more data are required to verify this hypothesis, their opinion must be taken into account. Experiments carried out in the region have been satisfactory: Argentina, Brazil, and Mexico made surprising progress in this respect, although for a number of reasons results have not been consistent.

Penal Settlements. With an extensive background in the history of punishment, penal settlements have had incredible successes and failures. From the Portuguese exile to the French Devil's Island, from Australia to North America, from Mindoro to Tangier, penal settlements proliferated, at times becoming prosperous cities and at times degenerating into hell.

The current idea of the penal settlement has changed radically. It is no longer the Siberian "house of the dead" or the "dry guillotine" of Guyana. The idea at present is that of legitimate population centers, where life may be as similar as possible to life in any city, and where there can be production and treatment without separating the offenders from their families.

In spite of all of their defects, the results obtained with modern penal settlements seem to be satisfactory, and doubtlessly better than those obtained with the traditional prison, for which reason our experts have proposed their improvement and expansion.[35]

Evaluation. As a key element, evaluation should be the spinal cord of the entire system. Evaluation is needed not only to be able to assert that a sanction must be replaced, but also in proposing a substitute.[36] The lack of evaluation has caused the failure of the best prevention and treatment plans, and it is common for the state and the technicians to imagine they are preventing, when in reality they are wasting time and money. The imposition of dissuasive punishment without an interest in ascertaining its effects continues to be a bad habit.

It is true that there is a notorious lack of individuals with an interest in, and the training for, criminological research, as well as a shortage of sufficient funds for a task of this nature. But "such an excuse cannot be given by the high officials in the different correctional departments who use substantial community funds and considerable personnel forces for the treatment of offenders, without insisting too much on the type of research that will make possible an estimation of what they are doing."

Criminology, in its narrow and traditional sense, that is to say, as an institution that is only concerned with the causes of crime and the treatment of offenders, has been very much criticized. At present, however, having evolved from microcriminology to macrocriminology, it carries out studies on criminal justice systems.[37] In this modern perception, criminology is a science that can be broadly applied, mainly in criminological policy decision-making.

Researchers are greatly mistrusted. It is felt that they are hypercritical, their only desire being to expose the failures of the system. This is not true.

Like Morris, researchers feel that "the correctional functionaries must be like allies to the researchers, instead of typically irresponsible individuals who are not concerned with the problems and duties of the prison."[38] Also, as Brydensholt maintains, "researchers are interested in the application of their knowledge; those responsible for the decision-making process are interested in founding their decisions upon scientific knowledge."[39]

It is necessary, therefore, in planning for an alternative, to calculate the evaluation method, since "if a new reforming method is applied without an evaluation trial, it will most likely seem effective, for there will be a strong temptation to apply it on those offenders who already display the best aptitude for becoming rehabilitated."[40]

Alternatives with Control and Supervision

In this section are analyzed the alternatives to imprisonment that provide for some form of control or supervision of the offender. Not all of these forms are applied in Latin America, but reference is made to them in order to get a broader view of the matter. Not all experts would agree in regarding some of them (e.g., conditional freedom) as true alternatives to imprisonment, but they must be mentioned because of their importance in the region. Special emphasis will be placed on alternatives to preventive custody, since this is the most critical problem in this part of the world.

Conditional Sentence.

The Concept. The conditional sentence is "the criminal institution whose purpose, through the suspension of the sanctions imposed upon first-time offenders without a background of bad conduct, is to seek their reintegration into a pattern of honest life, under the influence of the moral force alone of the sentence."[41] For Goldstein it is "a sentence imposed, whereby the application of the penalty is left in suspension, in order to be able to eliminate the conviction from the record if the offender does not commit a new felony before the expiration of the term imposed. The conditional sentence is afforded only to first time offenders, and in the event of minor offences."[42] In Cuello-Calón's opinion, "the essential feature of the conditional sentence in its original form is the suspension of the application of the penalty. The offender is tried and convicted, but, instead of serving time, she/he is left in freedom. If, within the term prescribed respectively by the different legislations, she/he does not commit a new violation, the assumption is made that the suspended sentence was actually never imposed."[43]

In European countries there is what is known as SURSIS. It consists of a postponement of the penalty to be imposed upon a convicted felon, which can be eliminated if, in the course of the five years following conviction, she or he is not convicted for any other common felony. Otherwise, both penalties are applied.

The conditional sentence was initially viewed with great suspicion. Experts such as Ferri criticized it because it allegedly left society unprotected, and the victim, abandoned and mocked. However, it gradually became accepted, and the correctional congresses that initially gave it a cold reception finally approved and recommended it.

The advantages of this practice have been publicized by the top experts. Cuello-Calón says, "The conditional sentence is not only a substitute for confinement, but a means which displays a certain educational effectiveness, since, during probation, the convicted felon develops the habit of living an orderly life in observance of the law."[44]

Background. It is thought that the concept of the conditional sentence originates in canonical law, under the principle of "absolution ad reinsidentiam," although it is also found in Anglo-Saxon law (the Frank pledge) and in Germanic law (Cautio de Pace Tuenda). In its modern version, it can be found in the state of Massachusetts (USA) in 1859 and later in the Belgian criminal law of 1888, as well as in the French criminal law of 1891. In Mexico in 1901, Miguel S. Macedo prepared a proposal, with a complete set of articles on conditional sentence, as a draft bill for reforming the Criminal Code of 1871. It was first introduced in the Criminal Code of San Luis Potosí in 1920, having remained instituted into the Criminal Code of 1929 in articles 241 to 248. At present, it exists in Article 90 of the Criminal Code currently in force.

This concept is known throughout Latin America, although under a variety of names: conditional application sentence (Colombia, Costa Rica), conditional remission of the sanction (Cuba), conditional suspension of the application of penalty (El Salvador, Panama), conditional suspension of the penalty (Brazil), conditional conviction (Argentina), conditional remission of the penalty (Chile).

Conditions. The conditions for the application of this type of measure that are common to the different legislations are the following:

a. That the suspended penalty correspond to a nonserious offense
b. That the beneficiary be a first-time offender
c. That the personal characteristics of the offender be appropriate for him or her to live in freedom, and that they lead to the assumption that he or she will not become involved in criminal activities
d. That the offender comply with certain responsibilities during the term prescribed

Furthermore, in several countries there are other requirements, such as having to repair the damage, and the use of additional measures, such as the guarantee of noncommission of an offense, an amount deposited as bail, a prohibition against visiting certain places, and so forth.

The first requirement for the suspension of the application of a penalty is that the offense committed, or the protest expressed against it, be of a lesser magnitude, as measured by the applicable sentence, which is not to exceed a certain term—two years in the cases of Argentina (Article 26), Brazil (Article 77), Mexico (Article 90), and Panama (Article 77), and not more than three years in the cases of Colombia (Article 68), Costa Rica (Article 59), Cuba (Article 57), Guatemala (Article 72), and El Salvador (Article 87). In Ecuador the term prescribed is only six months (Article 53), as used to be the case in Peru (Article 286 of the Criminal Procedural Code, which has been changed to provide for a two-year term). In Brazil and Peru involuntary offenses are considered separately.

A clear requirement for obtaining a conditional sentence is being a first-time offender, that is, not having a previous conviction. The exceptions to this principle are rare. In Argentina, if eight years have elapsed, in the case of involuntary offenses, and twelve years, in the case of voluntary offenses, a second conditional sentence may be handed down. In Cuba (Article 57.2), it may be applied to recidivists under ''very qualified extraordinary circumstances,'' but in no event will it be granted to multirecidivists. Colombia does not specify the requirement of being a first-time offender.

The personal characteristics of the offender must be taken into account for granting a suspended sentence. The criminal codes contemplate several examples: background of an honest life, way of living, stable working relationships, and so on. In addition, consideration is given to the type of offense, the circumstances in which it was committed, the reasons for committing it, etc. Lastly, a convincing repentance and, in several cases, reparation of the damage are required (see below).

In order for the judge to be informed on the preceding, she or he must have access to the pertinent reports. In this sense, the Costa Rican code is noteworthy in that it mandates the participation of the Criminology Institute, which determines the possible degree of rehabilitation the offender may attain and the conditions that must be imposed (Articles 60 and 61). The Mexican and Venezuelan codes also provide for personality tests.

The conditions under which application occurs may be varied: Reparation of the damage, or a guarantee in lieu thereof, is compulsory in Mexico (Article 90-II), El Salvador (Article 88), and Panama (Article 78-3) and may be imposed by the court in Cuba (Article 57-5-a). Additional requirements could be a guarantee or bond, the obligation to reside at a given location, having a legitimate job, not using alcohol or toxic substances, and so on.

One peculiarity in Cuba is that the court provides the pertinent information to the police and to the body of social organizations of the work center and place of residence of the offender, in order for them to observe and orient her or him during the probation period. Conditional release is revoked if these organizations no longer endorse the individual (article 57-6 and -7).

Naturally, the basic requirement for granting a suspension of sentence is respect for the law and noncommission of a new offense. If the individual commits a new offense, the suspension is revoked, and application is made of the pending sentence in addition to the sentence applicable for the second offense.

The duration of the probation period is restricted and may be fixed or vary according to the discretion of the judge; for instance, in Argentina, the restriction is four years; Brazil, two to four years; Colombia, two to five years; Costa Rica, three to five years; Chile, three years; Dominican Republic, one year; El Salvador, two to six years; Cuba, one to five years; Mexico, three years; Panama, two to five years; Peru, five years. In all cases, the term starts as of the date the sentence is handed down.

Ecuador has a peculiar system that takes into consideration the term set for the termination of the sentence, plus two additional years (Article 84).

Conditional sentence is the alternative that is most widely used throughout the region. Thus, in Argentina, of the total number of convictions (2,567), 54.62 percent (1,402) resulted in suspended sentences.

In Cuba, 85 percent of the offenses provided for in the Criminal Code admit the granting of a suspended sentence. Of the sentences to confinement, 63 percent have been suspended or replaced by alternatives. In Chile, by the beginning of 1988, 13,650 out of a total of 25,551 convicted felons received the benefit of a suspended sentence. In Panama in 1986, 785 of 2,546 convicted offenders were granted a suspended sentence.

Probation. Probation has been used extensively and is deeply ingrained in the principles of English Common Law. It was instituted as "recognizance" in 1361 with properties similar to those of the modern versions of 1878 and 1887. The term *probation* comes from the Latin *provare*, which means "to test." At present much attention is devoted to the study of this institution; it is applied in various countries, in some cases with remarkable results.

Probation, which is granted in lieu of short terms in prison (custody), provides for freedom with the suspension of sentence or of its application, and, as in the case of release on personal recognizance, the individual is subject to observation and treatment. It is mainly based on the assumption that the offender is not dangerous and on the probabilities of his or her recovery, for which reason a preliminary study is carried out on the individual's personality. The main purpose of probation is to prevent the offender from coming in contact with the often corrupting correctional system. The restrictions imposed by this procedure generally consist of treatment and reeducation.

"Probation is a treatment process prescribed by the court to individuals convicted for offences against the law, during which the probationer lives in the community and regulates her/his own life as per the terms imposed by the court (or other designated authorities) and remains under the supervision of a probation officer."[45]

The United Nations defines probation as "a method for the treatment of especially selected offenders, which consists of the conditional suspension of the sentence, whereupon the offender is placed under personal vigilance through which she/he is afforded guidance and treatment."[46]

There are two basic differences between probation and a conditional sentence. The first difference is that, in the Anglo-American system (probation), "what is suspended conditionally is the pronouncement of the sentence; the case becomes suspended. In the European system (as well as in Latin America), the sentence is handed down, but the application or imposition of the penalty is suspended for the length of the probation period, and up to the expiration of the right to apply the penalty."[47] The second difference is the intervention of the probation officers in charge of vigilance over, and guidance of, the offender benefiting from this form of treatment.

The advantage of probation over conditional sentence is its state of true freedom, subject to observation. The basic difficulty is finding observation personnel with the required specific characteristics: halfway between a social worker and a police officer. In other words, not everybody can or should be a probation officer. In addition, there is a problem of cost. If applied massively, probation is undoubtedly less costly, in real and social terms, than prison, but the initial investment is, at present, out of reach for Latin American countries overburdened by external debt and serious economic problems.

Chile has adopted a system that resembles parole, whereby those sentenced to two- to five-year terms may remain under the vigilance of a delegate who reports to the Ministry of Justice. By the beginning of 1988, 614 persons had been placed under the vigilance of thirty-five delegates, with great success, since there has been only 4 percent recidivism.

Conditional Freedom. Conditional freedom, known also as "preparatory freedom," or "freedom under protest," is quite an institution in Latin America. In Mexico it has existed since the adoption of the Criminal Code in 1871; in Uruguay it appears in the 1889 code, and in Argentina, in that of 1891.

At present conditional freedom is treated in the following sections of the laws: Argentina, C.C., Article 13; Bolivia, C.C., Article 66; Brazil, C.C., Article 83; Colombia, C.C., Article 72; Costa Rica, C.C., Article 64; Cuba, C.C., Article 58; Chile, Decree 321/25; El Salvador, C.C., Article 94; Dominican Republic, Law 5635/61, Article 2; Ecuador, C.C., Article 87; Honduras, C.C., Article 76; Mexico, C.C., Article 84; Panama, C.C., Article 85; Paraguay, C.C., Article 70; Peru, C.C., Article 58; Uruguay, C.C., Article 131; and Venezuela, Correctional Law, Article 76, and C.C., Article 20.

Conditional freedom is granted to convicted individuals who, having served a portion of their term, have shown good behavior in the correctional institution. A number of conditions are imposed on the beneficiary, the main condition being not to commit a new offense; the violation of these conditions would result in a revocation.

The term to be served varies from one-third (Brazil) to three-fifths (Ecuador and Mexico) of the penalty. It is granted when half the penalty has been served in Costa Rica, Chile, El Salvador, Peru, and Cuba; and when two-thirds of the time has been served in Argentina, Bolivia, Colombia, Panama, and Venezuela. There are special cases: twenty years must elapse in the case of a life sentence, in Argentina; the sentence is reduced to one-third if the offender is under twenty years of age at the beginning of the term, in Cuba; and only half of the sentence is applied in the case of involuntary offenses in Mexico.

In most countries of the region the judicial authorities are responsible for the application of this measure, except in Chile, Mexico, and Panama, where the responsibility lies with the administrative authorities.

In El Salvador, Peru, and Venezuela, conditional freedom recipients are obliged to live in a designated place. They must demonstrate a legitimate means of subsistence, in the Dominican Republic, Colombia, and Uruguay. Both obligations are applicable in Argentina, Ecuador, Mexico, and Panama.

The requirement of holding a job has been harshly criticized as lying outside the possibilities of compliance on the part of the released individual— not only because of the high rates of unemployment in the region, but also because of the innumerable difficulties former prisoners encounter in being accepted once they have been released.

The general ban on the consumption of alcoholic beverages, which is found in Mexico, Colombia, and Argentina, appears not to be applicable in cases where there was no connection between the use of alcohol and the offense committed. The Ecuadorian precept (Article 88) is even harsher, in that it prohibits visiting a tavern or being accompanied by people "of ill repute"; a similar precept is found in the Paraguayan Code (Article 68).

Recidivists do not have the right to conditional freedom, in Argentina and Costa Rica; nor do multirecidivists and drug traffickers, in Mexico and Peru. The required term is extended in the case of recidivists in Brazil (one-half instead of one-third), and in Cuba (two-thirds instead of one-half).

The obligation to repair the damage, or at least to provide a guarantee to that effect, is a requirement in Argentina, the Dominican Republic, Ecuador, Mexico, Peru, and Panama.

In terms of peculiarities worthy of mention, in Brazil (C.C., Article 85) and in Peru (C.C., Article 59), the judge establishes the conditions to be applied to the released offender. In Costa Rica, the Criminology Institute, which presents the reports to the judge, has a substantial participation. In Mexico, the Technical Correctional Council sends its report to the Ministry of the Interior, which is in charge of making the final decision. Both countries apply a treatment-by-stages system with prefreedom or semifreedom measures.

The Chilean system is cumbersome, in that the members of the "weekly visitation department" receive a report from the warden of the correctional institution, which they use to request a pronouncement on the subject by the "Court of Conduct" (representatives from the Judicial Branch and the correctional institutions, social workers, and the professional associations of lawyers and physicians). The case is then referred to the Ministry of Justice for the issuance of a "Supreme Decree" (if the privilege is granted).

In Cuba, the Ministry of Justice can request the release, even if the term specified by the law has not elapsed. Furthermore, political, mass, social, and military organizations intervene in the supervision of the measure and may request its revocation.

In Bolivia, when half the term has been served, the judge may be requested to prescribe confinement only at night, or on weekends, or in an agricultural institution; when two-thirds of the sentence have been served, total freedom may be requested.

Conditional freedom has had notable success in several countries of the region, especially when some form of supervision is contemplated. For instance, in Argentina, out of 2,846 cases supervised by the Release Supervision Board, only 14 cases warranted a revocation (0.5 percent; in the federal capital, the percentage goes up to 1.33 percent).

Parole. Parole is similar to conditional freedom, except that it can be granted at any time while the offender is serving a sentence. Those released on their word remain under the vigilance and guidance of specialized personnel—generally speaking, social workers and criminologists. This measure can be described as treatment in freedom granted on the offender's word.

The word *parole* comes from the French for "word of honor," and it stands for a broadly practiced and widely applied measure. Parole is the conditional release of an inmate in a correctional institution after having served a portion of her or his term. During parole the offender continues to be under the control of the state and may be returned to the institution if she or he violates the terms of her or his release.

Parole is not regarded as clemency or a reward for good behavior in the institution; its purpose is to bridge the gap between confinement and total freedom in the community. This enables the authorities to choose the most favorable moment for granting the release. It protects society by offering a close watch over the offender's behavior during his or her release and helps the offender through the critical period of adjustment.

Parole is granted, in the first place, on indication by the criminological councils in the correctional institution, who suggest the time at which the offender is eligible for this benefit, and, second, by the parole officers (in a role similar to that of the probation officers).

In continental Latin America, because of the traditional application of conditional freedom, there is no parole. Certain attempts have been made to adopt freedom under vigilance, but the lack of vigilance personnel causes this measure to become freedom under "self-vigilance."

Service to the Community. The different tasks that are performed as service to the community have the following characteristics in common:

a. They are not remunerated.
b. They are performed outside regular working hours.
c. They are performed in a public or private charitable institution or in an educational establishment.
d. The characteristics for compliance are set by the judge.

Community service is an alternative to imprisonment in Brazil (C.C., Article 46), Colombia (C.C., Article 48, applicable only in the case of petty offenses), Costa Rica (C.C., Article 55), and Mexico (C.C., Article 27).

In Brazil, community service may be applied for terms of less than one year (or in the case of involuntary offenses) but not to recidivists with unsatisfactory social backgrounds. Work entails eight hours per week, and the institution benefiting from it must submit monthly reports. In Costa Rica, authorization must be granted by the Criminology Institute; work is remunerated, but the salary (totally or partially) is used to pay for the penalty. In Mexico, the term imposed must not exceed one year, and the work period cannot be longer than three hours per day nor more than three days per week. Each day of service counts for one day of confinement. Degrading or humiliating work may not be imposed.

In practice, community service in Latin America has been applied only with a certain discretion because of the lack of an adequate infrastructure. An evaluation would be premature, since this alternative has, in fact, only recently been instituted (Brazil and Mexico adopted it in 1984).

Compulsory Work. Penalty to compulsory labor, applied from ancient times, gradually grew to be considered ignominious and unacceptable to humanity. Roads, mines, and galleys caused the extermination of thousands of exhausted and destroyed individuals. Only in recent times has thought been given to labor as a substitute for confinement and, therefore, as something to be performed in freedom.

Compulsory work in freedom has multiple advantages, since the offender does not have to interrupt association with his or her family and participation in social life. In addition the penalty becomes not only inexpensive but also productive. It was recommended by the London International Correctional Congress and has been used widely in the socialist countries, thanks to the control the state maintains over the business establishment. This procedure has been found to be convenient.

In Cuba it is known as "correctional work without confinement" (C.C., Article 33), and it is applied when the penalty to confinement does not exceed three years and the personal characteristics of the offender are appropriate. The offender serves her or his term on the job or in the location specified by the court; she or he may not be promoted, obtain increases in salary, or hold executive or educational positions.

Therapeutic Measures. Therapeutic measures are applied in the case of physical or mental illness that requires medical treatment and that, on account of its seriousness and duration, renders correctional treatment impossible. In these cases the individual's sojourn in prison is useless, since curative facilities are not provided, nor is it the prison's objective to provide medical or hospital services.

Medical Treatment. Patients suffering from chronic or infectious diseases should be separated from the rest and treated; only a physician should be able to authorize their return to prison.[48] In cases in which the individual must remain in confinement while receiving medical treatment, the ideal solution would be a specialized center with adequate personnel, the necessary instruments, and sufficient security.

The Minimum Rules for the Treatment of Prisoners establish such obligations (Article 22), and, in general, all concerned are in agreement with this. In this sense the situation in Latin American is serious. On the one hand, there are no specialized institutions; therefore, medical services are generally provided in an adjacent building or clinic within the prison itself. On the other hand, these services are not always equipped with adequate or sufficient supplies or personnel.

Psychiatric Treatment. Judicial psychiatric institutions or recovery houses are undoubtedly needed. The time when mentally ill offenders were kept in prisons ended with Pinel's pronouncements on the subject at the beginning of the past century, although many mentally ill individuals, even today, are in prisons.

In their respective legislations, all the countries of the region are complying with the provision in Article 82 of United Nations Standard Minimum Rules for the Treatment of Prisoners that prescribes the confinement of the mentally ill in psychiatric establishments and prohibits their permanent confinement in prison (i.e., Argentina, C.C., Article 34; Brazil, C.C., Article 96; Colombia, C.C., Article 56; Costa Rica, C.C., Article 101; Panama, C.C., Article 112; Peru, C.C., Article 93; Venezuela, C.C., Article 58).

Reality, though, is very different. In general, neither the facilities nor the centers and specialists that the law calls for are available. It is not unusual, in provincial prisons, to see how the system is reversed: Prisons are used as places of confinement for the mentally ill since there are no other facilities where those regarded as dangerous can be kept. When circumstances are favorable, there is a separate psychiatric ward where the mentally ill are kept separate from the rest of the correctional population; otherwise, they are kept with the other inmates, with the consequences this implies. Furthermore, most legislations indicate that the mentally ill must be confined "until she/he is cured"; this being sometimes impossible, the practical result is the imposition of a life sentence.

Brazil (C.C., Article 96) and Mexico (C.C., Article 69) have imposed the rule that the security measure cannot last longer than a penalty for the same offense. Panama (Article 114) makes it mandatory that the measure of security be equivalent in duration at least to the minimum of the penalty, but not more than twenty years.

Residential Confinement. Residential confinement consists of the obligation to reside in a certain place and not being permitted to leave it. This can be done under vigilance of the authorities or without it.

In Mexico, the judge can substitute residential confinement for correctional confinement in the case of political offenses (C.C., Article 73). In Colombia, it is called "residential restriction" (C.C., Article 57); in Venezuela it is accompanied, accessorily, by the suspension of employment (C.C., Article 20); in both countries it is a principal penalty. In Cuba (C.C., Article 34), it is known as "limitation of freedom," and it is subsidiary to confinement when it does not exceed three years. It implies the suspension of promotion and raises in salary, and it is supervised by the mass and social organizations of the place where the offender is ordered to reside under house arrest.

Prohibition to Visit Specified Places. Visits to specified places are prohibited when it is assumed (on a sound basis) that there the individual may commit new offenses or that his or her safety might be in danger. Examples of this are places that may encourage the commission of an offense, such as gambling houses, bars, taverns, brothels, poolrooms, and so forth, or places where the offender may be in specific danger, for instance, the town where the victims of the felony or the relatives of the victim (or victims themselves) live, especially if it is likely that they would take revenge.

The measure has been applied with success in our milieu as a complement or condition to other alternatives, such as conditional sentence, prerelease, weekend release, and so on. In the Cuban Criminal Code (Article 41), it is regarded as a penalty, while in the codes of Costa Rica (Article 101) and Panama (Article 108) it is defined as a security measure. Mexico provides for it in Article 24, without referring to its nature.

Restriction or Withdrawal of Rights. With the exception of Brazil (C.C., Article 44), the restriction or elimination of rights (also known as "disablement" or "interdiction") is presented in Latin America as an accessory—generally to imprisonment—or principal sanction but not as an alternative.

The rights that can be limited or suspended are numerous and include the following:

Family Rights. Family rights, including custody of children and guardianship, can be limited or suspended in Costa Rica (C.C., Article 57), Cuba (C.C., Article 38), Panama (C.C., Article 54), and Peru (Article 33).

Right to Practice a Profession or Occupation. The limitations to the right to practice a profession or occupation may go as far as definitely withdrawing the professional license to operate. Generally speaking, when an individual is dangerous or harmful in the exercise of his or her profession, confinement is not essential to avoid risks. It may suffice to prevent him or her from performing work. Something that must be kept in mind is the fact that making it impossible for someone to perform her or his own work may induce this person to earn a living by illicit means.

The prohibiton against practicing a profession or occupation is found in almost all the Latin American codes. For instance, Argentina (C.C., Article 20), Brazil (C.C., Article 47), Colombia (C.C., Article 58), Costa Rica (C.C., Article 57), Cuba (C.C., Article 39), Panama (C.C., Article 53), Peru (C.C., Article 27), and Venezuela (C.C., Article 25).

Citizen Rights. These generally accompany the penalty of imprisonment.

Driving License. Suspension of driving license is provided for as an accessory in Cuba (C.C., Article 40), as a substitute or principal sanction in

Brazil (C.C., Article 47), and as a security measure in Panama (C.C., Article 108).

Special attention must be given to this measure in view of the large number of offenses committed with motor vehicles. In most cases this offense is perpetrated by individuals who live honestly and have honest jobs and who are dangerous only when driving a vehicle. It is useless to confine them to a correctional institution, because they do not require treatment and because they can be intimidated by applying other means.

Noncustodial Arrest.

Weekend Arrest or Limitation. This measure had already been applied in the countries of the region with a system of treatment by stages (Costa Rica, Mexico). It consists of the offender's obligation to spend the weekend in the correctional institution. Generally speaking, the cells that are left vacant on weekends by inmates who are at the prerelease phase and spend the weekends at home are used for this purpose.

Through application of this measure, the main problems of imprisonment are avoided. It also becomes possible to provide treatment to, and maintain control of, the accused while avoiding the loss of a job, the dismemberment of the family, stigmatization, the ill effects of imprisonment, and so on.

This measure has recently been adopted in Mexico and Brazil as an alternative to imprisonment. In Mexico it falls under the form of substitute semifreedom in lieu of imprisonment, which the judge may prescribe (C.C., Article 27), and continues to be applied as a form of prerelease granted by the administrative authorities (Article 8, Law on Minimum Rules for the Social Readjustment of Convicted Offenders). In Brazil it is called "weekend limitation" (C.C., Article 48), and the sentencing judge determines the characteristics thereof (place, hours, and activities).

Night Arrest. From a stage of transition in treatment-by-stages, night arrest has evolved in many places into an effective substitute for confinement.[49] What makes this solution more imperative is the lack of work opportunities within the correctional realm, which constrains inmates to remain idle or to manufacture curious but useless objects. In order to avoid this, it has been proposed that inmates whose dangerousness is minimal (or in some cases even of medium level) be allowed to work (or study) outside immediately, without having to wait for their prerelease stage, except in the form of a substitute.

In addition to being a stage in the system by stages, night detention is already regarded as an alternative to imprisonment in Mexico (C.C., Article 27) and may be granted by the judge from the beginning, in Brazil (C.C., Articles 33 and 36; Articles 113 et seq., L.E.P.).

House Arrest. House arrest is hardly used and could be applied only in small towns, since control would otherwise be very difficult. It is, furthermore, an inequitable penalty, in that someone living in a palace or in a sumptuous villa would not be subject to a punishment equal to that of someone living in a hut or in a row house. Nevertheless it is preferable to imprisonment and has been experimentally applied as a substitute for preventive imprisonment.

In Argentina and Costa Rica (C.P.C., Article 293) it is provided as an alternative to preventive imprisonment in the case of honest women, adults over sixty, and valetudinarians. In Mexico it has been tried in the case of involuntary offenses.

Police Vigilance. In the case of police vigilance, vigilance and guidance mechanisms are alternatives to confinement. Control may be exerted by a public institution (i.e., the police) or by a private entity, such as the family, to which the individual may be entrusted. This measure has been notably successful in the case of minors and other offenders who may not be tried.

The imposition of measures of control may be one of the most interesting ways of substituting for imprisonment, since many institutions (labor unions, schools, social groups, businesses, sport clubs, etc.) can help the state control, watch, and orient misfits who do not require confinement. In Latin America this measure is used as an accessory to other alternatives (Cuba, C.C., Article 45; Mexico, C.C., Article 50) or as a penalty subsequent to release (Ecuador, C.C., Article 61).

Alternatives without Control or Supervision

Alternatives where no control or supervision are involved will now be examined. It must be stressed, again, that there are considerable differences among the countries, therefore only the most common concepts are used as a basis.

Fines. Fines, like imprisonment, are the most widely used penalties and have been regarded as the ideal substitute for confinement.

But fines are far from being ideal penalties, mainly on account of the shocking differences in economic resources among offenders. The only way fines could be regarded as an adequate substitute would be through an adequate fines system.

The application of the provision whereby the judge may accept the payment of the fine in installments in accordance with the offender's financial condition has been gradually extending: Argentina (C.C., Article 21), Brazil (C.C., Article 50), Colombia (C.C., Article 47), Costa Rica

(C.C., Article 54), Cuba (C.C., Article 35), Chile (C.C., Article 64), El Salvador (C.C., Article 85), Guatemala (C.C., Article 54), Mexico (C.C., Article 39), Panama (C.C., Article 49 [with the deposit of a guarantee], Peru (C.C., Article 23), and Venezuela (C.C., Article 51).

A solution adopted by various countries in the region is the application of the system of fines based on wages earned, whereby the offender must pay in accordance with her or his daily wages, that is, day fines, which can be demonstrated by fiscal records.

In this way the judge sentences to the payment of a fine based on income instead of setting a fixed amount. An added advantage is that the codes are automatically updated in this context, and they do not have to be revised every time there are currency fluctuations or the currency loses purchasing power.

The system of fines based on earnings has been adopted, for instance, by Brazil (C.C., Article 49), Costa Rica (C.C., Article 53), Cuba (C.C., Article 35), El Salvador (C.C., Article 61), Mexico (C.C., Article 29), Panama (C.C., Article 48), Peru (C.C., Article 20), and Venezuela (C.C., Article 50).

In spite of the problems posed by the obligation to pay a fine, such as the problem of an insolvent individual, the event that a third party (generally the family or relatives) has to pay it (which causes it to become a penalty that goes beyond its bounds) is in every sense preferable to imprisonment.

A serious problem that must be mentioned in this study is the habit of substituting imprisonment for a fine in cases of insolvency or refusal to pay. "To give the offender the opportunity of choosing between the payment of a fine and a term of imprisonment is the negation of our judging responsibility."[50] For cases of nonpayment of fine, almost all the countries in the region prescribe confinement. Consequently, prison becomes a substitute for the fine and not the contrary, as it should be. This is the case in Argentina (C.C., Article 21), Brazil (C.C., Article 51), Colombia (C.C., Article 49), Costa Rica (C.C., Article 56), Cuba (C.C., Article 35), Guatemala (C.C., Article 55), El Salvador (C.C., Article 84), Panama (C.C., Article 51), Peru (C.C., Article 21), and Venezuela (C.C., Article 30). Mexico appears to be the exception. In its 1983 reform of the Criminal Code it eliminated the possibility of substituting imprisonment for a fine. In the case of insolvency, the offender serves one day of community work for each day of day fines imposed; if this is not possible, freedom under vigilance is applied. When there are assets but a refusal to pay, a coactive economic procedure is started.

In Ecuador there is a peculiar figure known as "poverty remedy," whereby an individual can justify his or her state of indigence and thus obtain suspension of the prison term.

The possibility exists of substituting work (not always remunerated) for the confinement that substituted for the fine in the following countries, among others: Colombia (C.C., Article 48), Costa Rica (C.C., Article 35), Cuba (C.C., Article 35), Panama (C.C., Article 50), and Peru (C.C., Article 24).

In several legislations the impact of substituting imprisonment for a fine is softened by establishing a limit. For instance, in Peru it cannot exceed three months (C.C., Article 23).

Fines in lieu of imprisonment are being used successfully in Cuba under the new code (1988). The former code did not allow it. In the first six months under the new code, fines in lieu of confinement have been applied in 84 percent of the cases.

Release on Bail. Release on bail, known also as "secured release," "liberation," or "temporary freedom on guaranteed recognizance," is the most usual substitute for confinement in Latin America, which is peculiarly important on account of the previously analyzed problems regarding nonconvicted inmates.

Bail is a cash deposit or assets pledged as a guarantee for securing compliance with an obligation. It is very frequently used in the criminal domain, and it is offered to ensure that someone who is being released from the prison will appear upon request. This mechanism has been among the most helpful for rescuing individuals from preventive imprisonment.

Without a doubt, like the other measures based on payment, this one is also defectively inequitable in view of the differences in financial status among the individuals. There are dramatic cases of individuals who remain in prison for long periods because they have neither a guarantor nor sufficient means to comply with the imposition.

The solution proposed in the discussion of fines, which consists of a system of day fines, could work satisfactorily also in this case and would eliminate the problem brought about by shocking differences in financial status.

Much has been done in the region to promote the application of release on bail, in order that only those accused of having committed very serious offenses be held in preventive imprisonment. With the exception of Nicaragua and Peru, all criminal procedural codes in Latin America provide for it: Argentina (Article 383), Bolivia (Article 208), Brazil (Article 321), Colombia (Article 329), Costa Rica (Article 297), Cuba (Article 255), Chile (Article 261), Dominican Republic (Special Law No. 5439), Ecuador (Article 77), El Salvador (Article 250), Guatemala (Article 558), Honduras (Article 433), Mexico (Article 556), Panama (Article 2099), Paraguay (Article 351), Uruguay (Article 141), and Venezuela (Article 320).

Although in essence cash, assets, or securities deposited are equally effective in ensuring appearance in court and the serving of a sentence, there are differences in the ways it must be done: (a) automatic application if the punishment for the offense does not exceed a certain term in prison or if the circumstances do not call for imprisonment; (b) dependence upon the personal circumstances of the individual; (c) the combination of the two preceding methods. In most systems the individual can deposit the guarantee; in others a third party must do so (Panama). There are cases where the guarantor complies through arrest (Paraguay).

Bail may be conditional or unconditional. In Mexico, provisional freedom is a constitutional concept (Article 20). Peru's system is peculiar: either release applies, or formal imprisonment is mandated. The preceding is handled on the basis of numerous clauses, since release may not be granted in the case of the offenses listed under Article 79 of the Criminal Code. In Nicaragua, the usual method is "fianza de la haz," whereby the guarantor endorses the alleged offender without having to deposit securities or cash.

Release on Recognizance of the Accused. Release on recognizance, known also as "release under protest," is, after secured release, the second most common way of avoiding preventive imprisonment. Its characteristics are very similar to those of secured release, and it is applied in the case of very slight offenses or in the case of extreme poverty of the accused, as well as where there are no indications of the possibility of an escape. The difference between this and secured release or release on bail is that no financial guarantee is required, and it is sufficient that the accused promises to appear before the judge as many times as required.

This notion appears in the procedural codes of Argentina (Article 382), Brazil (Article 350), Colombia (Article 439), Costa Rica (Article 301), Cuba (Article 255), El Salvador (Article 253), Guatemala (Article 591), Mexico (Article 552), Nicaragua (Article 106), Paraguay (Article 364), and Uruguay (Article 144).

Reprimand and Warning. The precedents of reprimand and warning are infamous as penalties, their main purpose being to humiliate the prisoner by shaming her or him and exposing her or him to public mockery. Among others, the pillory, branding, exposure, the mask, and the hood used to be very popular. At present other forms are used, such as special publication of the sentence and public reprimand. We have no knowledge that special publication of a sentence may have been used as a substitute for confinement; instead, it has on occasion accompanied the penalty of confinement.

In the opinion of Ceniceros, reprimand is a measure of a moral and comminatory nature. It has two concurrent characteristics:

a. It is a form of solemn and public repression or estrangement.
b. It is a notification, a warning, or a lesson for the future, whereby the judge prevents recidivism.[51]

Reprimand functions as an alternative in the case of minor offenses that generally do not call for confinement. In Cuba it can be used as a substitute only for a fine (C.C., Article 36). In Mexico (C.C., Articles 42 and 43) and Venezuela (C.P., Article 32), it is an accessory penalty.

Reparation of the Damage. Regarded by several codes as a penalty, reparation can be a valuable substitute for confinement, since most victims do not care so much about the offender being punished as they do about the reparation of the damage caused. Very often, the victim prefers the recovery of the stolen items, the indemnification for damages, or some sort of satisfaction, rather than the offender's simply going to prison. In the case of certain offenses, such as statutory rape, kidnapping, or theft of little value, the reparation of the damage cancels the penalty.

Reparation of the damage is taken into account in Latin America as a requirement to obtain some sort of benefit or as a proof of repentance, but it is not actually used as an alternative to imprisonment.

Recognizance for Noncommission of an Offense. Recognizance for noncommission of an offense is one of the oldest measures (*cautio de bene vivendo*) and was recommended already in the 1890 Criminal and Correctional Congress. It consists of the deposit of a certain amount with the authorities as a guarantee that something specific that is harmful for society will not be done. As an exception, a deposit can be made to ensure that something good that has been ordered will be done.

We have already commented on the psychological reaction of the victim, who prefers the reparation of the damage to the punishment of the offender. In this case, we have something similar, the victim prefers the assurance that she or he will not be attacked again, rather than a risky revenge.

It is important to consider this measure in spite of its clear limitations because it cannot be applied to certain offenders. In addition, it presents the same problems as penalties consisting of payments—basically, the tragedy of the dispossessed, who do not have sufficient cash to guarantee their future good behavior, thus causing this measure to be discriminatory, benefiting only those who are financially powerful.

In the region it is used as a complement to warning (Mexico, C.C., Article 44), as a guarantee of compliance with the terms imposed by the judge for other forms of release (Peru, C.C., Article 38), or as an accessory penalty (Venezuela, C.C., Article 31).

Confiscation and Forfeiture. "Of the two types of confiscation developed and applied since ancient times by criminal legislations, general confiscation, that is, confiscation of all current and future assets of the convicted offender—an exceedingly rigorous penalty indeed—does not deserve to be taken into account as an alternative to imprisonment since it is not consistent with either the expectations of modern criminal law or with the new theories relative to punishment and because it is, furthermore, severe and unjust in that it affects the entire family of the offender, and is harder in the case of a person who has saved for the future than in the case of a spendthrift."[52]

Seizure of property through confiscation and forfeiture has become obsolete in Latin America. Several countries have prohibited it by constitutional precept. The other form, known as "special confiscation, seizure, or forfeiture," is above all an accessory penalty that is not used as an alternative to imprisonment and that consists of the loss of the instruments of crime (*instrumenta sceleris*) and of the benefits of crime (*producta sceleris*).

Special confiscation is a peculiar measure in that it is aimed at the object of danger rather than at the subject of danger; if we have eliminated the object, what good is it to confine the subject? The assumption that the holder of the object is dangerous is to a certain extent ill founded, since the offender could be in a state of ignorance with respect to the dangerousness of the object, to its use, and so on.

Rico clearly points out that the measure must be applied even in cases where the accused is acquitted, which shows that this is a real, and not a personal, measure.[53] In fact, society is protected by destroying the object, and there is no need to destroy also the offender by placing her or him in confinement, unless there is proof of her or his dangerousness. It is necessary to bear in mind that truly dangerous objects are rare and difficult to obtain, and that their seizure may well sufficiently meet society's protection and safety requirements. However, special confiscation or seizure is used in the region not as an alternative to imprisonment but as an accessory penalty.

Closing of a Business. The measure of closing a business is of a patrimonial nature, in that it has an economic impact on the beneficiary or owner of the premises. It has been criticized because it affects the personnel, the family, and the creditors and because of the fact that, since it cannot be divided, it may be disproportionate. However, its intimidating power has been demonstrated, particularly in the case of white-collar or white-glove crime.

The reasoning in this case may be the same as that for special seizure, since, by eliminating the harmful industry or the dangerous establishment, protection is ensured for the social conglomerate, and criminologically speaking it is no longer necessary to imprison the offenders. In Latin America it is used also as an accessory penalty but not as an alternative to imprisonment.

Estrangement and Banishment. Through the measures of estrangement and banishment the offender is sent away from his or her country and may not return. These measures have been used since ancient times, mainly in the case of political offenses but not, however, for common offenders.

As an alternative to imprisonment, banishment has many and very clear advantages, and its effectiveness should be evaluated. Although it might be felt that the application of this measure is a way of only transferring the problem to another location but not a means of solving it, still some offenders are not responsive to other forms of treatment, and it would be cruel to hold them in confinement.

In Latin America, banishment has been used as an exceptional measure in the case of political offenders, and it is generally applied to undesirable aliens as an accessory sanction after compliance with the main sanction.

Exoneration: Amnesty, Pardon

Imprisonment may be terminated by having served the term imposed, by the passing away of the offender, and also by exoneration, amnesty, or pardon, which are worthy of discussion since they contribute to the solution of the correctional problem, although they must be regarded not as substitutes for imprisonment but rather as ways of avoiding permanent imprisonment.

We have included the concepts of amnesty and pardon in this study because of the importance they have for Latin America mainly in the field of political delinquency.

Amnesty and pardon are provided for in the criminal legislation of Argentina (articles 59 and 61), Brazil (article 107), Colombia (article 78), Costa Rica (article 80), Cuba (articles 61 and 62), Ecuador (article 99), El Salvador (articles 122 and 123), Guatemala (articles 104 and 105), Mexico (articles 92 and 97), Panama (article 91), Peru (article 118), and Venezuela (article 104).

Amnesty. Amnesty is an act of oblivion with respect to the offense (*a* = without, *mnemeo* = memory), that is, "formally decreed amnesia with respect to a certain occurrence."[54] It was known by the Greeks and the Romans, applied in the Middle Ages, and used in all the countries—in some cases as pardon and in others as indulgence. Generally speaking, it is regarded as a means for arriving at political reconciliation. In Antolisei's opinion, it is "a general procedure through which the State renounces the application of the penalty for certain crimes."[55]

Amnesty is commonly a legislative decision, and it is granted by means of a law.

Pardon. Pardon is the true judicial exoneration. "It is the power conferred upon the judges, once the prosecuted individual is proven guilty, to exonerate her/him of the penalty established by the law because of exceptional circumstances that concur in the specific case."[56] Pardon in the region is generally the prerogative of the executive branch.

Differences between Pardon and Amnesty. Novoa-Monreal, the Chilean scholar, points out the following differences[57]:

1. Amnesty totally extinguishes the criminal responsibility; exoneration only eliminates the penalty.
2. Under amnesty, the individual appears as never having committed an offense; under exoneration, she or he remains as a convicted offender for all legal purposes.
3. Amnesty may be granted at any time following the commission of the offense; exoneration or pardon may be granted only after the handing down of the sentence.
4. Amnesty is retroactive, since it is concluded that the individual who benefits from it never committed an offense; pardon applies only to the future and does not change the situation of the penalties or the portion of the penalty served.

Criticisms of Pardon and Amnesty. Several authors are against these measures. It has been said, for instance, that pardon is an actual abuse (Roeder) and the preservation of ancient jurisprudence applied in times of absolute monarchs (Concepción Arenal). If the penalty is necessary, it must not be condoned; if it is unnecessary, it must not be imposed. In the excitement of crime, offenders enter cities as wolves approach a flock of sheep after a long fast (Bentham, Ferri).[58]

In spite of the opposition presented by such qualified experts as those mentioned, and by others, such as Beccaria, Kant, Feuerbach, Barraud, and Florian, both pardon and amnesty are accepted by a considerable number of experts, such as Antón Oneca, Ceniceros, Vallado, Romagnosi, Arranz, Rodríguez-Devesa, Manzini (softening the inflexibility of the law), Liszt (reparation for judicial errors), Prins (reduction of the application of the death penalty), and so on.

Pardon and amnesty should be favored, not, however, as open doors to impunity or injustice or to the disregard of victims, but as relief for those offenders who are not in the least dangerous, who possess a noticeable amount of dignity, who do not need treatment, and for whom a conviction would be a totally useless affliction.

There are undoubtedly individuals who should never be sent to prison (just as there are some who should never be allowed to leave the prison).

When the criminological council or the criminology institute concludes, in a technical and interdisciplinary manner, that confinement is unnecessary, but there are no available substitute measures as a result of a legal technicality or material impossibility, there should be a way out, regarding one last possibility for saving the convict. This could well be the pardon.

Pardoning is perhaps the most sublime of all human acts; "he who pardons is more of a victor than he who takes revenge," said Juan Ruiz-de-Alarcón, and Cicero asserted that "nothing makes man resemble God more than to pardon."

If pardoning is difficult with respect to a superior who slanders us, it is almost impossible with respect to someone beneath us who harms us. The offender, especially the pariah who arrives at the sentencing stage, is below, inferior intellectually, socially, and economically—and therefore a propitiatory victim, the scapegoat upon which all social vengefulness will concentrate.

We must not be afraid to pardon, nor can we pardon all crimes. Rivadeneira said that "the prince must look over carefully before deciding which offenses to pardon, and whom and how to pardon, because both pardon and punishment must always have as a target and an objective the republic, and therefore must be regulated with that purpose in mind; if we punish when it is convenient to punish, and pardon when it is convenient for the republic itself, let us pardon." In one of Shakespeare's immortal works he said, "Pardon is almost always the father of recidivism"; in another work he asserted that "the first words the wet nurse of the king's son must teach him are 'I pardon.'"

With due caution and the necessary advice of the technical councils, the state should grant pardon in certain cases. Perhaps it would be possible to spread the habit, in certain countries of the region, of pardoning nondangerous convicts on special symbolic dates, such as those commemorative of independence, Christmas, or New Year, thus benefiting occasional offenders, the elderly, the infirm, expectant mothers, circumstantial offenders, or juvenile delinquents who were unlucky enough to become of legal age in the process and who one day earlier would have been referred to the paternal councils or juvenile courts.

Pardon and Consent of the Victim. There are some offenses that are prosecutable only upon request of one of the parties. In these cases, pardon by the party who has the right to set in motion the justice mechanism may apply. Generally speaking, this can be done only up to a certain point of the process, although in some countries it is possible to grant the pardon after the sentence has been handed down.

The current trend is to broaden the possibilities for complaint by one of the parties, which in turn extends the possibilities for pardon. Thus, a multitude of sentences to imprisonment could be avoided. Several codes in the region are being reformed in this direction.

Conclusions and Recommendations

In this last portion of part 2, some of the problems discussed will be reviewed in order to present, at the end, a number of recommendations.

Prison Crisis. We could agree with Fishman: "In their present state (speaking in general), the prisons are gigantic crucibles of crime. Without order or harmony, the older, the younger, those bearing guilt, the innocent, the ill, the healthy, the hard core criminals, and the scrupulous ones alike are tossed into it; there they remain to become mixed with the following ingredients which are subsequently added: filth, pests, coldness, darkness, fetid air, overcrowding, and defective piping; this is then cooked and brought to a boil on the fire of the most overwhelming idleness."[59] However, we must be fair with prisons: They are but the reflection of the general crisis that afflicts criminal justice.

Alternatives to Imprisonment. In the context of these conclusions, we must ask ourselves the same question Bassiouni asks in his general report to the Fourth Bellagio Colloquium: Must alternatives to imprisonment become the rule, and prison, the exception?[60] In our opinion this is the way it should be, although, according to the same author, this poses a number of questions:

a. How should the alternatives be legislated over and regulated in order to ensure the greatest juridical security?
b. What selection process should be used to choose the adequate alternative?
c. Which authority will be charged with the application of the substitute measure, who will apply it, and who will supervise and evaluate it?
d. What legal controls should exist?
e. Which authority or agency will provide the means for the creation of the programs?
f. How should the programs be supervised and controlled to ensure effective application?
g. How will the rights of the individuals be guaranteed under these programs?

Many more problems to be resolved could be proposed, but those cited are the most important. Some of the solutions could be the following:

a. The adoption of laws for the application of sanctions
b. The development of administrative (probably interdisciplinary) entities that would study the cases and propose adequate substitutive measures

c. The evolution of the traditional correctional system into more flexible forms where substitute measures may be applied

d. A greater rapport among the different justice administration organizations.

Nor can it be forgotten that "planning research cannot be simply professional research; those conducting the practice and the decision makers must become involved in it. We observe with too much frequency that research produces serious indicative results, but that these results are not applied because those who had to make the decision to apply them did not become involved in the research; such research should also be what we call action research, that is, research oriented toward a specific policy developed in specific situations."[61]

Evaluation. "If the abolition of the prison is to lead to the rational selection of the methods which collectively must adopt most of its functions in the evaluation of the criminal sanctions, an evaluation research program must be supported."[62] It is futile to continue using an enormous amount of financial, technical, and human resources in correctional programs without maintaining constant evaluation of the results. In the planning of alternative measures, the establishment of evaluation systems will be necessary.

Transformation of Prisons. Although prisons themselves cannot, at present, disappear, it is necessary to diversify prisons and transform them into treatment institutions, for which purpose it is indispensable to break the traditional militaristic and rigid structures and introduce a new mentality among both the correctional personnel and the inmates.

Stürrup (1968) suggests an interesting way: "There are two outstanding items with respect to which anyone involved or concerned with offenders should meditate and apply to practice. First, the fact that there is very little difference between those we send into confinement for the offences they have committed, and the individuals in charge of them. Except for accidental reasons—circumstances of birth or fortune—many of the prison guards could be the inmates. A certain amount of humbleness must characterize this approach, which is generally not found in the individuals in charge of the correctional order. The second one is that it is necessary to keep the therapist from intervening in the life of the inmate and changing her/his attitudes in order for them to match those of the therapist. The function of the latter consists, rather, of eliminating the barriers that prevent the prisoner from helping her/himself find a cure by her/himself, because in the last instance each one of us is or may be assisted to become her/his own therapist."[63]

Replacement by Penalties. The catalogue of penalties is (or should be) sufficiently broad to permit the judge to select penalties other than imprisonment.

Leaving aside the death penalty and corporal imprisonment as dark reminders of a past that should never return, there are some proposable plausible options whose effectiveness has been demonstrated in other countries.

Short prison terms can be replaced with weekend arrest, vacational detention, or night arrest. The few experiments made in this respect have been satisfactory.

The penalty of labor in freedom has to be tried; the assistance of private enterprise, public organizations, and the labor unions may be of essential importance for the success of this method.

Fines, presently one of the main substitutes for imprisonment, must be systematized in order to eliminate existing reprehensible differences as regards their effectiveness (i.e., depending upon the wealth of the offender); we propose that, to overcome this problem, countries that have not yet implemented this measure apply the day-fine system.

While fines can substitute for imprisonment, the opposite should never occur; fines should be substituted for by labor or other adequate penalties or measures. This is one of the problems in the region that require an urgent solution.

Conditional Release.

a. Conditional sentence, or conditional suspension of sentence. This is one of the basic substitutes for the penalty of imprisonment and, when feasible, must be extended and improved with an orientation toward more functional systems of freedom under vigilance.

   It is necessary to review the concept of recidivism. One plausible solution is to set the limit at five years before the commission of the offense.

b. Secured release, provisional release, or release on bail. These are widely used. Therefore, it is necessary to adjust them according to more flexible systems, as they are often limited by fluctuations in the value of currency. Guarantees or bail that are clearly over and above the possibilities of the accused must not be imposed. It is necessary, because of prevailing economic conditions in Latin America, to extend the possibilities of secured release or release on personal recognizance.

c. Preparatory release. Traditionally important in our region, preparatory release has the purpose of avoiding an individual's remaining in prison longer than is required. Together with the partial remission of penalty and prerelease systems, it provides for an application of a penalty that offers good opportunities for treatment.

The biggest problem is the need for assistance to released individuals, mainly as regards work and possibilities of self-support. If this aspect is not solved, the measure may fail.

Pardon. Whether granted by the authority (exoneration) or by the victimized party, pardon is not a substitute for, but a means to avoid the permanence of, the offender's being in prison. The possibilities for pardon by one party must be extended, and exoneration by the authorities must be applied in cases where the criminological councils so recommend.

The Latin American Situation. It is not easy to analyze the situation in Latin America as regards the application of criminal penalties and treatment toward social rehabilitation. In the course of this work, we encountered numerous difficulties. The lack of official statistics is an initial obstacle. With the exception of some countries, there are no objective data concerning penalties and their application, let alone alternatives and their effectiveness. The second obstacle is the lack of laws for the execution of sanctions; this is governed by obsolete regulations and custom. Third, there is no evaluation, therefore no information is available as to whether or not the alternative measures put into practice have been successful. The fourth factor, which may provide a clearer idea of the Latin American situation, is the lack of criminology institutes. Barring a few exceptions, there are no possibilities for carrying out studies. There are no qualified professionals in the field of application of penalties or treatment of the offenders. The few specialists that can be found are either self-taught individuals or professionals who graduated outside Latin America and who have formed a curious group of idealists who could be called "the Bohemians of criminology."

A piece of information that must, indeed, be taken into account and that is accessible to researchers, is the budget of expenditures of the Latin American nations. On examination of this information, it is clear that justice administration is the "ugly duckling," especially as regards application of the penalty and the treatment of offenders.

Examples of available literature on this subject, which describes a gruesome and depressing reality and which could provide partial orientation, include *Celda 16,*[64] *Anatomía de una prisión,*[65] *El Apando,*[66] *La Isla de los Hombres Solos,*[67] *Las Tumbas,*[68] *Islas Marías,*[69] *El Sexto,*[70] *La Negra Historia de Lecumberri,*[71] *Diario de Lecumberri,*[72] *Soy un Delincuente,*[73] *De Devoto a Coronda,*[74] *La Fuga del siglo,*[75] *Adiós Lecumberri,*[76] *¿Por qué no Dijiste Todo?,*[77] and lastly *Crónica de Muertes Silenciadas.*[78]

The technical literature available about alternatives to imprisonment is not abundant in the region. We might cite Elías Neumann,[79] Miguel Reale,[80] René Ariel Dotti,[81] Roberto Meana,[82] Luis Rodríguez-Manzanera,[83] Bocaranda Espinoza,[84] and Luis Bravo-Dávila.[85]

The Sixth National Correctional Congress (held in Hermosillo, Sonora, in 1976) and the Pan American Criminology Congress (held in Buenos Aires, Argentina, in 1979) devoted part of their time to the study of this problem. It must be remembered, as Szabó suggests, that at present "the social protection bodies are mentally and technically equipped to combat a type of criminality that is in the process of extinction."[86] López-Rey[87] has already pointed out what has not been done in Latin America in the fields of criminology and penology, and it is true that the great correctional administration projects only exist on paper. Correctional reforms have been attempted on many occasions. Success has been attained in some cases (as in Costa Rica), but, more often than not, progress and setbacks have alternated in a continuous manner (as in Argentina, Brazil, and Mexico).

The truth is that there is a general lack of coherent criminological, penological, and correctional policies, which, in addition to economic difficulties, hampers the use of resources for studying and resolving the problem, especially since it is not regarded as a high-priority item that is approached from the political point of view of security.

Epilogue

It is undoubtable that "the bounds of criminal repression must be established in relationship to the sociocultural evolution of the community, and when punitive law, with its detention or confinement resource, fails as a means for exerting social control of a problem, other forms or types of control must be used."[88] We are involved in this search, and, as Alpert points out in his extraordinary book, we are aware that "many of these new ideas are modifications of the old ideas. All of them follow the direction of the open institution, the reduction of restrictions, and the treatment of the individuals under confinement, both minors and adults, in a humane and non-oppressive manner."[89]

To conclude this study, and to paraphrase a contemporary penologist whose thoughts we share, "the public will grow increasingly ashamed of its vindictive howl, its persistent demand for punishment. This is its crime, our crime against the offenders, and, incidentally, our crime against ourselves. For, before we are able to diminish our suffering from the inadequately controlled aggressive attacks of our citizens, we must renounce the philosophy of punishment, the obsolete, vindictive punitive attitude. Instead, we should adopt a more understanding, more constructive social attitude, which in some cases would be more therapeutic, and in some cases, more restrictive, but which would be preventive in its overall social impact.

In the last analysis, this is a matter of personal values and morality. Regardless of how glorified or piously disguised we represent it, vengeance as a human motivation must be personally repudiated by each and every one of us. This is the message of both the old religions and the new psychiatric trends. Unless this message is heard, unless we, the public—the person in the street, the homemaker—can renounce the delicious satisfactions provided us by the opportunities we have to take revenge on a scapegoat, we cannot expect to preserve our peace, our public security, or our mental health. Can we do it? Shall we do it?''[90]

Recommendations.

1. It is necessary to establish theoretically and legislatively the objectives of the application of criminal punishment.
2. The application of criminal punishment must follow the principle of need.
3. Criminology, penology, and law on the execution of penal sanctions should be included in university curricula.
4. The application of criminal punishment must be individualized.
5. There can be a just application of penalties and adequate treatment only through the involvement of professional staff trained in criminology.
6. The application of criminal penalties must draw away from retributive criteria and come closer to prevention criteria.
7. There must be a revision of the concepts of ''readjustment,'' ''reinsertion into the society,'' etc., from the point of view of modern theories relative to criminal subcultures, stigmatization, marginalization, the effects of prison life, and deviation.
8. In reference to treatment, the following questions have to be answered: Who should be treated? Why? What for? Where?
9. The Latin American countries must look for their own paths and solutions.
10. It is necessary to recognize the serious crisis affecting corrections, but it is also useful to admit that this crisis is actually part of the overall crisis that currently affects the entire criminal justice administration apparatus.
11. Prisons cannot at present disappear, but it is necessary that they become treatment institutions and that adequate substitutes for imprisonment be found for all cases where confinement is not indispensable.
12. The most urgent problem is that of preventive imprisonment, since individuals who are awaiting trial and who are presumed to be innocent are deprived of liberty. Alternatives to imprisonment are of little use if those who should benefit from them have already served preventive imprisonment terms.
13. A study should be made of the possibility of separating those awaiting trial from those awaiting the conclusion of an appeal process, in order to be able to provide adequate treatment.
14. We wish to stress the urgency of establishing mechanisms to evaluate preventive and correctional programs in order to be able to determine their effectiveness and to justify the use of material and human resources and to have the possibility of planning the necessary changes on an informed basis.
15. A reform of the criminal and procedural codes is required, to provide for realistic alternatives to imprisonment.
16. More discretional powers must be given judges in order for them to be able to apply a wide range of alternative measures.
17. The legislative federal and local structures should create laws for the execution of criminal sanctions, providing for specific alternatives to imprisonment.
18. A study should be made of the concept of the sanctioning judge, which exists in some countries, in order to study the possibility of introducing this figure,

who would periodically review the penalty of imprisonment and, if applicable, alter it with a noncustodial sanction.

19. It is desirable to substitute weekend arrest, vacational detention, and/or night arrest for short prison terms.

20. The use of sanctions based on work or payment in lieu of imprisonment is recommended, provided a system is found to eliminate the marked differences in financial status among the offenders. One solution could be the adoption of the day-fine system.

21. It is indispensable to extend and improve the measures of conditional sentence, temporary freedom, and preparatory freedom, including, in all of these cases, the participation of an official, a functionary, or someone in charge of watching the individual released under these methods, which has proven to be effective in the parole and probation systems.

22. The use of the pardon must be extended for very special cases and upon request of the technical criminological councils. It is likewise recommended that the possibilities for complaints by one of the parties be broadened, in order to increase the possibilities for private pardon.

23. The collaboration of the entire community for the solution of the criminal and correctional problem is recommended, for which purpose a program of information, awareness, and proselytism must be developed. Efforts must be made to use volunteers in "freedom under observation" programs and to secure the cooperation of corporations and labor unions, social associations, or educational institutions for alternatives to imprisonment involving work, control, and services for the community.

Part Three: Overview of Noncustodial Alternatives in the Caribbean
(Nicholas J. O. Liverpool)

Although imprisonment is still a major form of punishment in the Caribbean, noncustodial forms of punishment are also used, especially where the offense is not a serious one. Under the provisions of the legislation in force, a juvenile may be punished in one or more of the following ways:

a. Reprimanding and discharging the offender
b. Discharging the offender on his or her entering into a recognizance
c. Discharging the offender and placing her or him under the supervision of a probation officer
d. Committing the offender to the care of a relative or other fit person
e. Sending the offender to a reformatory or industrial school
f. Ordering the offender to be whipped
g. Ordering the offender to pay a fine, damages, or costs
h. Ordering the parent or guardian of the offender to pay a fine, damages, or costs

i. Ordering the parent or guardian of the offender to give security for his or her good behavior

j. Dealing with the case in any other manner in which it may be legally dealt with

Classification of Noncustodial Alternatives

Certain noncustodial alternatives for both adult and juvenile offenders require some measures of supervision or control of the offender. This type of alternative can be seen as the most serious noncustodial alternative; it requires the offender to be put under the control of some person or department of government indicated by the court, for a specified period of time. Under this alternative the major form of punishment is placing the offender under the supervision of the probation department.

An offender may also be required to be of good behavior for a period of time without any supervision, or he or she may simply be admonished and discharged. This type of alternative can be classified as a penal warning, the essential element of which is the formal warning given by the court.

A further classification can be made for monetary payments. The major form of monetary punishment is the imposition of a fine, and this is usually reserved for minor criminal offenses and quasi-criminal offenses. Finally, the court may combine two or more noncustodial alternatives, or it may combine any of these alternatives with a term of imprisonment as a more severe form of punishment.

Following the classification given, these alternatives will now be considered in detail.

Legislated Noncustodial Alternatives

1. Noncustodial alternatives involving control or supervision of the offender
   a. Probation and suspended or conditional sentences with supervision
      The common factor in probation and suspended or conditional sentence with supervision is that a sentence of imprisonment is possible and contemplated, but the court permits the offender to remain at liberty and requires him or her to observe certain conditions, among which is to undergo supervision.
      1) Adult offenders
         Legislation dealing with the probation of offenders provides that where any person is charged with an offense that is punishable on summary conviction, and the court thinks that the charge is provided but is of the opinion that having regard to the circumstances, including the nature of the offense and the character and surroundings of the offender, it is expedient to release the offender on probation, the court may make a probation order.

The legislation makes provisions for a probation order to be made where a person is convicted for an offense that is not punishable on summary conviction and then sets out the requirements of a probation order. The order shall

a) have effect for a period of not less than one year and not more than three years from the date of the order;
b) require the probationer to be under the supervision of a probation officer; and
c) contain such provisions as the court considers necessary for securing the supervision of the offender and such additional conditions as to residence and other matters as the court, having regard to the circumstances of the case, considers necessary for securing the good conduct of the offender or for preventing a repetition of the same offense or the commission of other offenses.

2) Statistics for adult offenders for the years 1981–86 (Barbados)

In 1981, 52 offenders were placed on probation. Of these, 21 were charged with larceny and 10 with breaking and entering and larceny.

In 1982, 51 offenders were placed on probation, with larceny accounting for 25 of offenses charged.

In 1983, 76 offenders were placed on probation; with larceny (24), and breaking and entering and larceny (13) again accounting for the majority of the charges.

In 1984, there were 102 offenders directed to the probation department, 26 for larceny charges and 23 for breaking and entering and larceny charges.

In 1985, the adults who were subject to probation orders numbered 65, with 22 on larceny charges and 14 on breaking and entering and larceny charges.

1986 saw 54 offenders being directed to the probation department; 21 of these were charged with larceny, and 11 with breaking and entering and larceny.

3) Juvenile offenders

The Juvenile Offenders Acts provide for juvenile offenders to be placed on probation.

4) Statistics for juvenile offenders for the years 1981–86 (Barbados)

In 1981, 72 juveniles were the subject of probation orders. This number accounted for 58 boys and 14 girls.

In 1982, there were 56 orders made, 43 in respect to boys and 13 in respect to girls.

In 1983, 169 juveniles were the subject of probation orders, while 128 were placed on probation in 1984.

In 1985, 23 boys and 4 girls, at a total of 27 juveniles, were placed on probation; in 1986, there were 39 boys and 5 girls, a total of 44 juveniles, placed on probation.

b. Supervision by the Juvenile Liaison Program

The Juvenile Liaison Program was implemented in 1983 and is a special unit of the Barbados police force. Although this scheme is mainly preventive, in some cases the court may convict a juvenile and order him or her to be supervised by the program. When performing this function under the direction of the court, the program is very similar to that of the Probation Department. Even where the scheme is providing a preventive service, however, it may still be regarded as an alternative to imprisonment. In some cases, where an offender actually admits to the commission of an offense, the Juvenile Liaison Scheme intercepts the charging of the offender, and if the scheme can get the victim of the offense as well as the parent of the offender to agree, the juvenile liaison officer may advise the police not to proceed with charges against the juvenile and instead immediately undertakes supervision.

c. Community service

The essence of community service lies in the fact that an offender is sentenced to perform a certain number of hours of unpaid work for the good of the community. In Jamaica and Dominica, specific legislation exists for this purpose. In other countries, community service is imposed within the framework of a suspended or conditional sentence.

Statistics for community service are available for the years 1981–82 in Barbados only. During this period only five offenders were affected by this order. Under this program, offenders may perform the services on weekends or in their leisure time if they are employed.

This type of order has proved to be extremely successful in the first six years of its operation.

1) Juvenile offenders

Community service orders in the case of juvenile offenders operate in the same manner as for the adult offender.

d. Special measures

Special measures include making orders for the treatment of mental or behavioral disorders if certain circumstances are found to exist. The treatment may be ambulant and provided under open conditions, but it may also entail residence (possibly compulsory residence) in a mental hospital, in some other institution, or in a residential therapeutic community. This type of sanction may be used for the mentally abnormal, as well as for alcoholics and drug addicts.

1) Adult offenders

The Mental Health Act provides that where any person, while imprisoned or detained for any cause, in any prison or other place of confinement, appears to be a person of unsound mind, it shall be lawful for a magistrate and justice of the peace, with the aid of two registered medical practitioners, to inquire and adjudicate as to the mental condition of that person.

The legislation also provides that where a person is charged before a magistrate with an offense punishable on summary conviction, and the magistrate is satisfied that the person committed the offense and is of the opinion that an enquiry should be held into his or her state of mind, the magistrate may proceed to hold an inquiry in accordance with the provisons of the Mental Health Act.

2) Juvenile offenders

Treatment for mental behavioral disorders in the case of juvenile offenders is usually included as a special order under a probation order.

e. Local banishment

Local banishment as a form of punishment does not exist anywhere in the Commonwealth Caribbean.

f. Deprivations and interdictions concerning rights, licenses, professional status, and so on

The decision to impose a deprivation, removal, or interdiction is not always made by a court. An administrative authority or a professional association may make the decision after a court sentence. Although the court may use these sanctions as independent noncustodial alternatives, the tendency is to use them in conjunction with other sanctions, including custodial ones.

This power is given through various legislative enactments. For example, where a person is convicted of an offense under the Road Traffic Acts, the said acts give the court the power to suspend or cancel the license of the driver of the motor vehicle or to endorse upon the license particulars of any order the court makes under the section.

2. Noncustodial alternatives not involving supervision and control of the offender

a. Penal warnings

The penal warning is used where the offense is not grave and especially where the offender has not exhibited good behavior in the past. The warning may be imposed unconditionally, and called an "absolute discharge," or conditionally, and called a "conditional discharge.'' Another form of penal warning is when a sentence of imprisonment is decided upon, but its enforcement is suspended provided that the offender is of good behavior for the stated period.

1) Adult offenders—Binding Over to Keep the Peace

Magistrates are empowered, on the complaint of any person, to decide on entering into recognizance, with or without sureties, to make an order to bind the person over to keep the peace and be of good behavior. The legislation further provides that a magistrate shall have power on any information for a summary offense, whether the information be dismissed or the accused be convicted to bind the accused, with or without sureties to be of good behavior.

2) Juvenile offenders

The Juvenile Offenders Acts provide that a juvenile who has been convicted of an offense may be reprimanded and discharged, or discharged on his or her entering into a recognizance.

b. Deferred sentence

Deference of sentence amounts to a tacit agreement between the court and the offender that, provided the improvement in the offender's conduct noted at the trial continues, and no further crime occurs, no custodial sanction will be imposed at the end of the period of deferment.

1) Adult offenders

Where a person is convicted of an offense punishable with not more than two years of imprisonment and has no previous conviction, the court may order that he or she be released on entering into recognizance, with or without sureties. During such period the court may request the offender to appear and receive judgment when called upon and in the meantime to keep the peace and be of good behavior. When taking this course of action, the court should take into account the age of the offender, his or her character and antecedents, the nature of the offense, and any other extenuating circumstance under which the offense was committed. The legislation also provides that where the court that dealt with the original offense, or any court of summary jurisdiction, is satisfied by information on oath that the offender has failed to observe any of the conditions of his or her recognizance, it may issue a warrant for his or her apprehension, after which the offender must appear for judgment or answer as to his or her conduct since release.

c. Monetary payments
  1) Fines
    a) Adult offenders
      The imposition of a fine is regarded as a major noncustodial alternative. In most cases, nonpayment of fines leads to imprisonment, if steps taken to ensure that fines are in fact paid do not lead to success.
    b) Juvenile offenders
      The Juvenile Offenders Acts make provisions for either the juvenile offender or his or her parent or guardian to pay the fine.
  2) Compensatory payments
      A growing preoccupation with the plight of the victim and a desire to see restitution made have led to an increased interest in making the offender pay compensation. The payment of compensation is often ordered in conjunction with the imposition of a sanction, and the offender's willingness to make restitution is taken into account when determining the sanction to be imposed.
    a) Adult offenders
      The legislation provides that where any person has been summarily convicted of an offense that is also an offense that can be tried on indictment, the magistrate may make the same order for the restitution of property as might have been made by the court before which the offender would have been tried on indictment.
    b) Juvenile offenders
      The Juvenile Offenders Acts state that the juvenile offender or his or her parent or guardian may be ordered to pay damages.
  3) Confiscation and forfeiture
      The legislative provisions on confiscation and forfeiture have little to do with credible alternatives to imprisonment. The provisions are limited to ensuring that neither the materials nor the proceeds of crime are left in the ownership of the offender.
      The court is given the power of seizure under specific acts. These acts include those dealing with betting and gaming, smuggling, customs, larceny, and drug offenses.

3. Combination of sanctions
  a. Combining unconditional imprisonment with a noncustodial sanction
      This can be an important way to mitigate, if not always to avoid, the use of custodial sanctions. It may, however, also have the

opposite effect of providing further punishment. For example, a lengthy term of imprisonment for serious drug trafficking may be combined with confiscation and certain deprivations of rights.

b. Combining noncustodial sanctions

Where an offense is of too serious a nature to impose a single, particular, noncustodial alternative, one way of avoiding imprisonment is to combine one or more noncustodial alternatives in order to add to their penal weight.

1) Adult offenders

The Larceny Act provides that where any person is convicted of an indictable misdemeanor, punishable under that act, the court may, if it thinks fit, in addition to or in lieu of any of the punishments provided by the act, fine the offender and require him or her to enter into recognizance and to find sureties, both or either, for keeping the peace and being of good behavior.

2) Juvenile offenders

The Juvenile Offenders Acts set out the forms of punishment that may be imposed upon juveniles and list each one as an alternative form of punishment. However, one provision states that the court may deal with the case in any other manner in which it may be legally dealt with. This provision is an open provision that would enable the court to combine any of the state sanctions in sentencing a juvenile. For example, the court may order the offender to pay damages and place him or her under probation.

c. Additional noncustodial alternatives—juvenile offenders

Additional noncustodial alternatives for juvenile offenders include committing the offender to the care of a relative or other fit person and ordering the parent or guardian of the offender to give security for his or her good behavior.

Notes

1. CEPAL, "La dinámica del deterioro social en América Latina y el Caribe en los años ochenta," LC/G.1557, 1989. CEPAL, "Efectos sociales de la crisis económica," LC/R.522, 1986.

2. E. Carranza, "El rol del poder judicial en la investigación en casos de derechos humanos," pp. 3ff. Inter-American Institute on Human Rights, IIDH, 1990.

3. CELADE, "América Latina: proyecciones de población 1950–2025," *Boletín Demográfico*, vol. 20, no. 40.

4. Eugenio R. Zaffaroni, "Sistemas penales y derechos humanos en America Latina. Informe Final." IIDH, DEPALMA, Buenos Aires, 1986.

5. *El preso sin condena en América Latina y el Caribe. Estudio comparativo,*

estadístico y legal de treinta países y propuestas para reducir el fenómeno, ILANUD, 1983.

6. In this context, see the specialized Council of Europe bulletin entitled *Chronique Statistique Du Bulletin D'Information Penitentiaire*, no. 12 (Conseil De L'Europe), table 2.

7. Regional Seminar for Heads of Correctional and Detention Centers, organized by the Henry Dunant Institute, ILANUD, and the International Center of Criminal and Correctional Sociological Studies and Research of the University of Messina, INTERCENTER. San Jose, 14–18 May 1990. With respect to the correctional situation as regards human rights in the countries with Anglo-Saxon systems, see Vivien Stern, *Deprived of Their Liberty*. A Report for Caribbean Rights (Georgetown, Guyana: Demerara Publishers, February 1990).

8. See the work of the experts who attended the Regional Seminar for Heads of Correctional and Detention Centers, organized by the Henry Dunant Institute, ILANUD, and the International Center of Criminal and Correctional Sociological Studies and Research of the University of Messina, INTERCENTER. San Jose, 14–18 May 1990, particularly the work by E. R. Zaffaroni entitled "Filosofía del sistema penitenciario en el mundo contemporáneo."

9. See considerations on this issue in the document prepared by ILANUD as a contribution to Subject I of the Eighth United Nations Congress on Crime Prevention and the Treatment of Offenders, entitled "Prevención del delito y Justicia Penal en el Contexto del Desarrollo."

10. A very clear picture of the different alternatives and possibilities for noncustodial treatment may be found in the document entitled *Desinstitucionalización de la corrección y sus consecuencias para el preso que sigue encarcelado*. This is a working document prepared by the Secretariat for the Sixth U.N. Congress on Crime Prevention and the Treatment of Offenders, A/CONF/87/7. Also in Luis Rodríguez-Manzanera, "La crisis penitenciaria y los sustitutivos de la prisión," Cuaderno 13, INACIPE, Mexico, 1984.

11. For more information on this, see *Inter-American Institute on Human Rights, Sistemas Penales y Derechos Humanos en América Latina*, Final Report; coordinator: Raúl Zaffaroni. Depalma, Argentina, 1986.

12. IIDH, p. 200.

13. Jorge A. Montero Castro, *Problemas y necesidades de la Política Criminal en América Latina*. ILANUD, Costa Rica, 1976, p. 12.

14. Elías Carranza, Mario Houed, Luis Paulino Mora, and Raúl Zaffaroni, *El Preso sin Condena en América Latina y el Caribe*, ILANUD, Costa Rica, 1983, p. 25.

15. A. J. Acuña, R. R. Calvillo, F. F. Campomanes, and L. H. Sagal, *La Realidad Penitenciaria en México*. Aries. Mexico, 1974.

16. José M. Rico, "Medidas Substitutivas de la Pena de Prisión." *Yearbook of the Institute on Criminal and Criminological Sciences*, Venezuela, 1968, pp. 130–31.

17. Filipo Gramática, *Principios de Defensa social*. Montecorvo Publishers, Spain, 1974, mainly chapter 5.

18. Marino Barbero Santos, *Estudios de Criminología y Derecho Penal. La División en dos fases del Proceso Penal*, University of Valladolid, Spain, 1972.

19. Elías Neuman, *Las Penas de un Penalista*, Lerner Publications, Argentina, 1976, p. 37.

20. Zaffaroni, "Sistemas penales," p. 201.

21. Jean Pinatel, *La prison peut-elle être transformée en institution de traitement?* International Criminology Records, Paris, France, 1969, p. 78.

22. Mariano, Ruiz-Funes, p. 15.

23. Nelson Pizzotti Mendes, "O Fracasso da Pena Privativa de Liberdade," in *Criminología* (Sao Paulo, Brasil: University Law Press, 1973), p. 265.

24. Cf. Gunner Marmell, "The Prison Community," International Criminology Records, Paris, 1969, p. 25.

25. Javier Piña-y-Palacios, "Encuesta sobre las prisiones de la República." *Criminalia* (Mexico) 28 (1961): 175ff.

26. Pinatel, *La prison peut-elle?* p. 39.

27. Ibid.

28. Ibid.

29. Benigno Di Tullio, *Principios de Criminología Clínica y Psiquiatría Forense.* (Madrid, Spain: Aguilar Publishers, 1966), p. 436.

30. Jack Young, "Los Guardianes del Zoológico de la Desviación," in *Estigmatización y Conducta Desviada,* University of Zulia. Maracaibo, Venezuela, p. 219.

31. Carlos García-Basalo, "En torno al Concepto de Régimen Penitenciario," *Magazine of the School of Correctional Studies,* Madrid, Spain, 1975.

32. López-Rey and Arrojo, Manuel. *Presupuesto de Orientación Profesional Penitenciaria.* Caracas, Venezuela.

33. Elías Neuman, *Prisión Abierta* (Buenos Aires, Argentina: Depalma, 1962), p. 148.

34. Roger Hood and Richard Sparks. *Problemas clave en Criminología.* Guadarrama, S.A., Madrid, Spain, 1970, mainly chapters 6 and 8: "Eficacia de Castigos y Tratamientos" and "El efecto de la pena de prisión."

35. Juan José González-Bustamante, op. cit.

36. Hood and Sparks, *Problemas clave en Criminología.*

37. Cf. V. V. Stanciu, "Contribución a una Nueva Criminología," *Mexican Criminology Magazine,* no. 1, 1976, p. 63.

38. Norval Morris, op. cit., p. 48

39. H. H. Brydensholt, "Impact of Criminological Research on Decision Making." *Evaluation Research in Criminal Justice.* Rome, Italy, 1976, p. 153ff.

40. Morris, op. cit., p. 47.

41. *Diccionario de Derecho,* 3d ed., Porrúa publishers, Mexico, 1973, p. 108.

42. Raúl Goldstein, *Diccionario de Derecho Penal.* Omeba, Buenos Aires, 1962, p. 110.

43. Eugenio Cuello-Calón, *La Moderna Penología.* (Barcelona, Spain: Bosch, 1958), pp. 626ff.

44. Ibid.

45. Helen Pidgeon, *Probation and Parole in Theory and Practice.* Cited by Ricardo Rangel in *Cuadernos Panameños de Criminología* vol. 1, no. 2, p. 101.

46. United Nations, *Probation and Related Measures,* 1951, p. 4.

47. Carrancá and Carrancá-Rivas Trujillo, *Código Penal Anotado,* Porrúa Publishers, Mexico, 1972, p. 200.

48. See W.H.O. (World Health Organization), "Aspectos Sanitarios de los Maltratos Evitables Inflingidos a Presos y Detenidos," *U.N. Fifth Congress on Crime Prevention and the Treatment of Offenders* (Doc. 75–100375), Geneva, 1975.

49. Cf. Rico, "Medidas Substitutivas," p. 132.

50. Morris, p. 22.

51. Ibid., p. 269.

52. Rico, "Medidas Substitutivas," p. 82.

53. Ibid., p. 145.

54. Fausto Vallado Berrón, *Proceso a la Universidad.* El Caballito publications, Mexico, 1973, p. 90.

55. Francesco Antolisei, *Diritto Penale. Parte Generale* (Milano, Italy: Giuffré Publishers, 1963), p. 562.

56. Ceniceros, p. 268

57. Eduardo Novoa-Monreal, *Curso de Derecho Penal Chileno,* vol. 2 (Santiago, Chile: Juridical Publishers of Chile, 1966), p. 448.

58. Cf. Carrancá and Trujillo, *Derecho Penal Mexicano, General Section,* vol. 2, Robredo, Mexico, 1950, p. 232.

59. Joseph F. Fishman, *Crucibles of Crime* (New York: Cosmopolitan Press, 1923), p. 251.

60. Sherif Bassiouni, *Reporte General de la Asociación Internacional de Derecho Penal,* Report to the Fourth Bellagio Colloquium, Milano, Italy, 1975, p. 14.

61. C. S. Versele, *Primeras Jornadas de Defensa Social de América Latina.* Caracas, Venezuela, 1974, p. 202.

62. Morris, p. 48.

63. George K. Stürrup, *Treating the Untreatable* (Baltimore: Johns Hopkins University Press, 1968), p. 217.

64. Gregorio Cárdenas-Hernández, *Celda 16,* Diana, México, 1970.

65. Marcel Viveros, *Anatomía de una prisión,* Diana, México, 1972.

66. José Revueltas, *El Apando,* Era, México, 1969.

67. José León Sánchez, *La Tela de los Hombres Solo,* Novaro, Mexico, 1970.

68. Enrique Medina, *Las Tumbas,* La Flor, Argentina, 1972.

69. Martin Luis Guzmán, *Islas Marías,* General de Ediciones, Mexico, 1973.

70. José María Arguedas, *El Sexto,* Editorial Horizonte, Peru, 1974.

71. Aldo Coletti, *La Negra Historia de Lecumberri,* Editorial Contenido, Mexico, 1977.

72. Alvaro Mutis, *Diario de Lecumberri,* Utopia, Mexico, 1976.

73. Ramón Brizuela, *Soy un Delincuente,* Editorial Fuentes, Caracas, Venezuela, 1979.

74. Alberto Fernández, *De Devoto a Coronda,* Plus Ultra, Argentina, 1975.

75. Carlos Contreras, *La Fuga del Siglo,* Carnel, Caracas, Venezuela, 1973.

76. Gregorio Cárdenaz-Hernández, *Adiós Lecumberri,* Editorial Diana, Mexico, 1979.

77. Salvador Castañeda, *¿Por qué no Dijiste Todo?* Grijalbo, Mexico, 1980.

78. Elías Neuman, *Cronica de Muertes Silenciadas*, Bruguera, Argentina, 1985.

79. Elías Neuman, *Evolución de la Pena Privativa de Libertad y Regímenes Carcelarios*, Ediciones Pannedille, Buenos Aires, Argentina, 1971.

80. Miguel Reale, et al., *Penas e medidas de Segurança no novo código*, Forense, Brazil, 1987.

81. René Ariel Dotti, *Bases e alternativas para o sistema de penas*. Federal University of Parana, Brazil, 1980.

82. Roberto Meana, *Aspectos criminológicos de los sistemas alternativos a las penas privativas de libertad*. University of Panama, 1987.

83. Luis Rodríguez-Manzanera, *La crisis penitenciaria y los substitutivos de la prisión*, INACIPE, Mexico, 1984.

84. Bocaranda Espinoza, *El régimen legal venezolano de la libertad en prueba*, APSA, Caracas, Venezuela.

85. Luis Bravo-Davila, *La Ley de sometimiento a juicio. Suspención condicional de la pena y tratamiento en libertad*, J.C.V., Caracas, Venezuela, 1981.

86. Denis Szabó, "Sociedades de Masa e Inadaptación," *French Social Review* (France) no. 5, 1965, pp. 472–86.

87. Manuel López-Rey-y-Arrojo, *Criminología*. Aguilar, Spain, 1975, pp. 495ff.

88. Luis Fernádez-Doblado, *Sustitutos de la Pena de Prisión* presentation to the Sixth National Correctional Congress, Monterrey, Nuevo León, Mexico, 1976, p. 7.

89. Benedict S. Alpert, *Prisons Inside-Out (Alternatives in Correctional Reform)*. (Cambridge, Mass.: Ballinger, 1974), p. 71.

90. Karl Menninger, M.D., *The Crime of Punishment* (New York: Viking Press, 1966), p. 109.

17

Release on Personal Recognizance in Costa Rica: An Experimental Research Study

Elías Carranza,
Marion Houved, and
Luis Paulino Mora

With respect to release on personal recognizance,[1] the countries of Latin America and the Caribbean may be divided into three groups: (a) those in which release on personal recognizance is not provided for; (b) those in which it is provided for, together with other possible forms of release; and (c) those in which it is provided for as the only form of release (Peru, and the La Pampa province in Argentina).

Group b includes Argentina (Article 382, Criminal Procedural Code for Federal Justice, and the regular courts of the Federal Capital and National Territories[2]), Brazil (Article 350, Criminal Procedural Code[3]), Colombia (Article 439, Criminal Procedural Code[4]), Costa Rica (Article 299, Criminal Procedural Code[5]), Cuba (Article 255, Criminal Procedural Code[6]), Chile (Article 357, Criminal Procedural Code[7]), El Salvador (Article 257, Criminal Procedural Code[8]), Guatemala (Article 591, Criminal Procedural Code[9]), Mexico (Article 552, Criminal Procedural Code for the Federal District[10]), Paraguay (Article 364, Criminal Procedural Code[11]), and Uruguay (Article 144, Criminal Procedural Code[12]).

The regulation of release on personal recognizance is not consistent among the countries cited. In some, it is provided for with noteworthy broadness. In most countries, it is subject to considerable restrictions. A detailed analysis of this subject can be found in the book *El preso sin condena en América Latina y el Caribe* (Non-convicted Prisoners in Latin America and the Caribbean).[13]

Extent to Which Release on Personal Recognizance Is Used in Costa Rica

In the case of "minor offenses" (those punishable with not more than three years' imprisonment), release on personal recognizance is used to some extent in Costa Rica. These offenses fall under the competency of the so-called criminal lower courts.[14]

In strict terms, release at the level of the lower criminal courts is not necessary, since the law provides, as a general rule, exemption from imprisonment, that is, prosecution in liberty, since, according to the Criminal Procedural Code, preventive imprisonment is applicable only when the offense allegedly committed by the accused is punishable with confinement in excess of three years or when there are serious indications that the accused will either attempt to evade the action of justice or continue to commit criminal acts.[15] However, the investigative prosecutors normally release the accused under this category of offense, mostly by applying the release on personal recognizance procedure.

In the case of more serious offenses, punishable with more than three years' imprisonment, release on personal recognizance is provided for by the legislation but is actually nonexistent for all practical purposes in Costa Rica. The instructional state is under the responsibility of the (unipersonal) instructional lower instance courts, while the passing of judgment is up to the superior criminal courts (which are comprised of three judges). In some localities of the country, the instructional stage is initiated by the mixed courts,[16] and then referred for its completion to the instructional courts.

In order to have accurate knowledge about the extent to which release on personal recognizance is applied in the case of these offenses, an in-depth study was made that included all lower-jurisdiction and instructional courts for a one-month period (November 1980). An update was carried out nine years later (in December 1989).

The initial study revealed that release on personal recognizance had not been applied at all (table 17.1).

After having obtained such drastic results relative to the nonapplication

Table 17.1 Releases on Bond and on Personal Recognizance without Bond Granted in the Case of Offenses Punishable with a Maximum Term of Three or More Years Imprisonment, Costa Rica, November 1–30, 1980

Releases	Number	Percent
On personal recognizance	0	0
On bail (real and personal)	270	100
Total	270	100

Notes: Number of county and provincial courts that responded: 53 (of 76): 70%.
Number of county courts that responded: 16 (of a total of 27): 59%.
Number of provincial courts that responded: 37 (of a total of 49): 76%.

of release on personal recognizance in the case of offenses punishable with terms of more than three years' imprisonment, a study on the opinion of the judges was undertaken in order to obtain an explanation about the nonapplication of a concept that is provided for with the greatest broadness in the Costa Rican criminal procedural law.

The results of this new study were quite interesting. All the instructional and superior criminal court judges (in trial and adjudicating courts) were surveyed. Most of the releases are granted, logically, during the instructional stage, but the superior criminal courts also grant certain releases and additionally intervene as appellate or consultation courts in the case of resolutions on release adopted by the instructional courts. In other words, the total universe of judges having competency in this matter was covered by the survey ($N = 58$).

Table 17.2 shows the arguments used by the judges to justify their nonapplication of release on personal recognizance. Some of the reasons are objective, but others are rationalizations through which the judges attempt to explain and justify their own conduct.

The first reason given by the instructional judges, that is, that they do not grant release on personal recognizance "because the superior courts overrule this decision," is an objective reason. In the course of research work it was possible to ascertain that, in fact, the superior courts revoke the releases on personal recognizance granted by the instructional courts for this type of offense.

However, it must be kept in mind that the judges of the superior courts are not members of "a different race." It is true that they, as a general rule, revoke the few releases on personal recognizance that are referred to them by means of appeal, but the instructional judges do not grant them either. There is a vicious circle that allows the judges to sustain a restrictive attitude without legal support: in the first instance judges do not grant releases, alleging in advance that, if they did so, the superior courts would revoke them; the latter do not grant them because the former do not grant them, which makes it impossible to have a knowledge of such situations when the cases go up to a higher court by means of consultation or an appeal.

The second reason expressed by the judges is that release on personal recognizance is not used because "the defense lawyers do not request it."

In the course of the research it was found that this is actually so. In spite of their commitment to serve the accused during the process, the defense lawyers generally share the same cultural and juridical criteria as the rest of their colleagues and the Costa Rican society in general. This means that, although some of the defense lawyers interviewed said that release on personal recognizance should be more widely used, when the time comes to request it, they do not do it, except in very few cases, in order not to "ride against the windmills," or simply because they share the criteria of the

Table 17.2 Reasons for Not Applying the Release on Personal Recognizance Survey Covering All Instructional and Superior Criminal Court Judges of Costa Rica, April 1981

Reason	Number of Times Mentioned		Number of Times Mentioned As			
			Main cause		Second most important cause	Third most important cause
	Number	%	Number	%		
1. The superior courts overrule it.	7	12	3	5	4	–
2. The defense lawyers do not request it.	3	5	–		3	–
3. The accused will evade the action of justice by not appearing in court.	46	81	31	54	10	5
4. The legal requirements are not met.	27	47	34	25	7	6
5. The concept is new and not well known in the country.	11	19	2	4	7	2
6. There are ways to make release on bail easier, for which reason it is more convenient to use that method.	5	9	3	5	1	1
7. There are individuals with clear criminal inclinations, which makes it impossible to apply the release on personal recognizance liberally.	1	2	–		1	–
8. Its application by the judge in cases of serious offenses may be misunderstood.	2	4	–		1	1
9. The judges do not understand that some cases are affected by poverty. They have the wrong idea about socioeconomic conditions.	1	2	–		1	–
10. If release on personal recognizance were used, the beneficiaries would not feel they were being punished.	7	12	4	7	2	1
11. Not sure/don't know.	1	2	–	–	–	–
		57	37	16		

Notes: All instructional and superior criminal court judges of the country were surveyed (58). The percentages were obtained on the basis of the total of individuals who responded (57).

judges who deny it. In this respect, the experimental study showed how three private lawyers appealed against the releases on personal recognizance that had been granted to their clients and requested the application of release on bail—for a very high sum—to which the higher court responded favorably. The attitude of these defense lawyers could be explained through the fact that release on bail would serve a double purpose: it would have a manifest function of ensuring the presence of the accused in court, and a nonmanifest function—in Merton's terminology[17]—of ensuring the payment of the lawyers' fees.

With respect to reason number three, which bases the denial of release on personal recognizance on the allegation that "the accused will evade the action of justice by not appearing in court," no empirical evidence was found to support it.

With respect to the fourth reason ("the legal requirements are not met"), this is a rationalization on the part of individuals who simply want to deny the release on personal recognizance. In fact, Costa Rican legislation is very broad on this subject,[18] and ultimately the granting of release on one or the other type of guarantee is left to "the discretion of the judge." Proof of the assertion that there is such broadness and rationalization on the part of the judges, is that, during the experimental research, release on personal recognizance was granted, according to the law, to 179 accused individuals.

The fifth reason is that release on personal recognizance is not granted because "the concept is new and not well known in the country." Although at the time the survey was carried out, the new Costa Rican criminal procedural legislation had been in force for five years, it could be admitted that, since it is a legislation that introduces a novel concept whose application is left to the discretion of the judges, it was in fact a recent phenomenon. The allegation of those who responded this way is, thus, valid.[19]

At the same time, this argument justifies the need for a research project, which could serve to help activate the legislation that is not being applied. Such a need has been corroborated again by the results of the "Second Study on the Extent to Which Release on Personal Recognizance Is Used in Costa Rica," which was carried out fifteen years after the entering into force of the new code and which demonstrated that, although release on personal recognizance was somewhat used during the years that elapsed between the first and second study, it continues to rarely be applied (in only 6.5 percent of the cases).

The sixth reason is that release on personal recognizance is not applied because "there are ways to make the release on bail easier, for which reason it is more convenient to use that method." In the case of individuals whose social condition makes it possible for them to provide the financial means as a guarantee, the reason is somewhat valid. It is "somewhat valid" because if the circumstances are appropriate for granting a release on personal recognizance, which would be less costly for the accused who is being protected by the presumption of innocence and which would be more economical for the judicial branch (less red tape), it would be advisable to use this form of pretrial release instead of the other requiring a bail.

However, in the case of individuals whose social condition makes it impossible for them to obtain their release upon the payment of a certain amount of money—which is the general case of those who remain under preventive custody in spite of the fact that they have been entitled to release contingent upon a real or personal guarantee—the argument that "there are ways to make the release on bail easier" is not true.

The seventh reason deserves special attention. It indicates that "there are individuals with clear criminal inclinations, which makes it impossible to apply the release on own recognizance liberally." The correct thing to do in the case of such individuals would seem to be to deny outright any type of release, or, if their "clear criminal inclinations" cannot be proven as legal evidence (*id est* real recidivism), to subject them to the same criteria that are applicable for release purposes to the population in general. Otherwise, this argument introduces dangerous levels of arbitrariness. In this respect, it is possible that the attitude of the judges is to some extent influenced by "public opinion" that the media persistently transmit, which exerts pressure over them. This is an important subject that would deserve special research with a specific methodology.

The eighth reason is that "its application by the judge in cases of serious offenses may be misunderstood." From a sociological point of view, in the case of serious offenses, in Costa Rica, at present, this argument is to a certain extent valid, since the concept is not deeply ingrained, and the judge who grants it is in some way offering a benefit that goes beyond the expectations of society in general and the accused her- or himself. This is why it is of the utmost importance that the Supreme Court gave its support to this research project. However, if the issue is analyzed from the criminal juridical point of view, the argument subjects criminal law to social fear. The point under study bears a close relationship to the immediately preceding one and must also be related to the arguments expressed earlier under the fifth reason.

The ninth reason the judges have expressed indicates, in the form of an interesting self-criticism, that release on personal recognizance is not granted because "the judges do not understand that some cases are affected by poverty. They have the wrong idea about socioeconomic conditions." This argument could well represent a good amount of the truth.[20]

Reason number ten, which consists of the argument that "if release on personal recognizance were used, the beneficiaries would not feel they were being punished," is an evident juridical aberration, since it confuses a precaution, preventive imprisonment, with a punishment.[21]

However, it is a well-known fact that, in general, in the countries of Latin America, preventive imprisonment is far from being an exceptional measure. Instead, it is so widely used that it becomes evident that in practice it functions as a penalty in a distorted process whose stages have been reversed: During the instructional stage the sanction of imprisonment is dictated and applied, and during the trial stage the "sentence" dictated during the instructional stage is formally confirmed, although the release of the prisoner is simultaneously instructed because a very long time has already elapsed; because the individual is acquitted but only after having served her or his "sentence";[22] or because some benefit may have been afforded the individual that will bring him or her out of the system. This produces the paradox that, when the individual should be free because of the constitutionally guaranteed principle of presumption of innocence that protects her or him during the trial, the individual is under custody, and when the individual's freedom should be restricted because of having found her or him legally responsible, she or he is released. Costa Rica is no exception to this phenomenon, although comparatively among the countries of the region the number of "inmates awaiting judgment" in this country is not high.

It is interesting to note that not one, but seven, judges—12 percent of the sample—answered this way in this country, which is characterized by a high juridical culture. Although possibly the answer may be interpreted as a frank explanation that reveals, with neither hypocrisy nor juridical rationalizations, one of the mechanisms of the country's "real criminal law," and that, because of the reasons stated above, would be typical not only of Costa Rica but of the countries of the region in general.

Drawing on data in table 17.2 it would be possible to construct a "scale of attitudes" of the judges vis-à-vis release on personal recognizance.

At any rate, whatever the personal attitudes of the judges are with respect to this measure, an unequivocal conclusion can be drawn: even in the case of those judges who express themselves positively vis-à-vis release on personal recognizance, it is evident that there are powerful reasons that keep them from applying it. After a study of all the lower instance courts for one month, it became evident that it was not applied in any of the cases.

The judges were also asked what advantages they found in forms of release contingent upon a financial guarantee that could not be found in release on personal recognizance. The judges' answers were consistent with the former answers. Tables 17.2 and 17.3 are rather like a photographic print and negative; the advantages pointed out with respect to release on a financial guarantee are the disadvantages alleged with respect to release on personal recognizance.

It would be appropriate to caution that the "advantages" presented in tables 17.2 and 17.3 (as highlighted by one of the interviewees) are not feasible according to the Costa Rican legislation, since under no circumstances can the amount deposited as a real guarantee serve for the payment of damages relative to the offense investigated; such erroneous replies are, indeed, noteworthy. It is likewise interesting to observe that one of the judges interviewed abstained from commenting on the advantages that release secured by a financial guarantee would have as compared to release on personal recognizance.

Table 17.3 Advantages of Release on Bail as Compared to Release on Personal Recognizance—Survey of All the Instructional and Criminal Superior Court Judges, Costa Rica, November 1980

Advantage	Times Mentioned	
	Number	%
1. That there is a coercive financial security that ensures the presence of the accused. In the case of personal recognizance, the justice system has a very important and effective collaborator for ensuring the appearance of the accused (the guarantor).	71	86.58
2. That an amount of cash will have been deposited (in the case of real recognizance), which ensures the payment of damages in the civil case.	1	1.72
3. That release on real or personal recognizance imposes upon the accused a certain type of extra punishment for the offense committed, which forces her or him to become aware of her or his criminal conduct. As an exemplifying element it is more effective.	4	6.90
4. That the state can recover some of the cost of the action in case the accused does not appear in court when required, by using the guarantee.	4	6.90
5. Real and personal guarantees do not show, in practice, any advantages over release on personal recognizance.	1	1.72
6. Does not answer, does not know, is not sure.	1	1.72

Note: All instructional and criminal superior court judges of the country (58) were interviewed. The total is higher than 58 because each judge was allowed to mention up to three advantages.

Table 17.4 Releases on Bail and on Personal Recognizance in the Case of Offenses Punishable with a Maximum Penalty of Three or More Years of Imprisonment, Costa Rica, November 1–30, 1989

Releases	*Number*	*Percent*
On personal recognizance	13	6.5
On the guarantee of a surety (real and personal)	189	93.5
Total	201	100.0

Note: Number of county and provincial courts that replied: 39 (out of 79)—49%.
Number of county courts that replied: 13 (out of a total of 27)—48%.
Number of provincial courts that replied: 26 (out of a total of 52)—50%.

Second Study on the Extent to Which Release on Recognizance Is Applied in Costa Rica

As explained before, a second study was carried out in November 1989, nine years after the first study and fifteen years after the entering into force of the current Criminal Procedural Code, which provides for release on personal recognizance for crimes punishable with three or more years' imprisonment.

Some modest amount of progress was found in the use of the form of release under discussion. During a period of one month, it had been applied in 6.5 percent of the cases (table 17.4).

Experimental Research on Release on Recognizance (without Bond) as Compared to the Forms of Release Subject to Bond[23]

Purpose of the Research

On the basis of the corroboration that the judges, alleging the criteria shown on table 17.2, do not grant release on personal recognizance in the case of offenses punishable with more than three years' imprisonment, the purpose of the study was to measure, using a sample of individuals released on personal recognizance, how they complied with their procedural obligations, particularly the obligation of appearing in court, as compared to how another sample of individuals released on real or personal bail (with the guarantee of a surety). This specific objective was chosen, bearing in mind that 81 percent of the judges, as can be noted by the results in table 17.2, pointed out as the main reason for not granting releases on personal recognizance that the accused would evade the action of justice by not appearing in court when required.

Methodology and Design

A typical "laboratory experiment" was designed, using an experimental group of individuals released on personal recognizance and a "witness" group of individuals released on real or personal recognizance with the guarantee of a surety, as the usual manner in which the Costa Rican courts grant the pretrial release in cases of offenses punishable with three or more years' imprisonment.

Universe

The universe for the study consisted of all those accused of offenses punishable with a maximum penalty of more than three years' imprisonment who had been granted pretrial release at the first and third instructional courts of San Jose (the capital city) and Hatillo (a district of the central county of the province of San Jose).[24]

Sample Design, Control Variables, and Theoretical Framework

The research team devoted a considerable amount of discussion to the definition of the variables that should be maintained under control during the experiment. It was agreed that the basic variable to be controlled was the type of guarantee (whether subject to a payment or not) used for the release, and the probability sampling was employed.

Random sampling was developed in the case of the three courts in the following manner: An agreement was made with the judges and court secretaries of the three courts, to the effect that they would observe the following steps in all cases admitted: (a) to determine, by reading the record, if, in accordance with the procedural law, pretrial release could be granted to the accused, and whether or not they were going to grant it, regardless of the form of guarantee to be imposed for granting it; (b) if it was decided to grant the release, to look for the first time at the date the record was received at the court, and, if it was of an odd number, grant the release on personal recognizance (without financial obligation); (c) if the case was eligible for pretrial release, and the date was of an even number, grant the release as usual, subject to a real or personal guarantee.

Before adopting the randomization procedure explained, it was determined that there were no differences in quantity or quality among the cases admitted on even or odd days that could alter the representativeness of the sample thus selected. Through this mechanism, it was possible to control the main variable (financial guarantee—nonfinancial guarantee).

The research team made the following theoretical reflection: if an accused individual is released on bail and wishes to escape, the amount deposited as bail will be, for this individual, simply the price of the escape. There seem to be other reasons (in addition to financial guarantees) that keep individuals from escaping and that incite them to submit themselves to a criminal process, such as the inconvenience of living as an alleged criminal at large who is constantly evading the justice mechanism, the existence of a fairly efficient criminal system that reduces the possibility of remaining on the run without being captured, the fact that individuals so released maintain certain ties with the community, and so forth.

One of such variables, which has been controlled in classical studies on the subject, is whether or not there are ties between the released individual and the community, as measured by the "family" and "work" indicators.[25] In addition to information on the form of the guarantee, then, information was also gathered on a number of additional variables relative to the ties of the released individual with the community, to the offense committed, and to the judicial process.

The Moral Guarantor

It was deemed important to give consideration to the following point: The financial obligation complies with the manifest function—using Merton's terminology[26]—of serving as a guarantee in case the accused individual escapes. But in addition to such manifest function, the (personal or real) financial guarantee provided by a third party serves an important latent function, as demonstrated to a large extent by the replies of the judges to the survey: The third party who appears as a guarantor or who has deposited her or his money becomes a zealous watchdog with respect to the released individual and can contribute, to a considerable extent, to the appearance of the latter when required by the court, and especially at the time of the trial. This latent function of the financial guarantee is very important, and thought was given to compensating for the lack of it in the case of release on personal recognizance through the introduction of a "moral guarantor."

The moral guarantor was an individual who was related to the accused by blood ties or friendship and who voluntarily offered to participate in the formal release process by making a moral commitment to convince the released individual to appear before the court on its request. Her or his only relationship to the court and to the released individual in this context was of a moral nature, without any other financial or criminal responsibility. These individuals gave the court their addresses and telephone numbers in order to collaborate by making easier the appearance of the released individual. In many cases the good-will function of these third parties was very useful in saving the court time and work, and sometimes even in avoiding an unjust revocation that would have been ordered because of unforeseen circumstances.

A decision was made also to control the two variables that are explained in the following section through their transformation into two constants, in order for them to affect both groups equally.

Important Operational Issues

In granting the release to the individuals from the two sample groups, the personnel at the courts had to strictly control two variables that could affect the final results:

(1) Before being released, all individuals had to be fully informed about the terms under which the release was being granted and their respective obligations.

In order to make sure that all individuals of the sample groups received the same information, special information sheets were prepared for each of the three forms of release (on real guarantee, on personal guarantee, on personal recognizance), which had to be read and given to them by the personnel in charge of the procedures.

(2) All individuals from both sample groups had to be released with the obligation of appearing once a month (and not more than once) before the court or the authority the court would appoint for this purpose.

The reason this was resolved in such a manner was to make the requirement uniform for all those released. The country's procedural law (article 307) establishes that in the case of release on personal recognizance the judge must impose on the accused the obligation to appear periodically, but it leaves up to the judge the determination of the applicable periodicity. It does not impose the obligation of complying with this requirement in the case of release on bail. In practice, what occurs is that those released on personal recognizance are instructed to appear every fifteen days and in many cases every week, while those released on a real or personal guarantee are rarely instructed to comply with this requirement. Such an obligation is useless for preventing an eventual escape or the commission of new offenses by the accused but does weigh against the good results expected from the pretrial release method. Something that must be kept in mind is that a prosecution during which the accused has been released lasts two years on the average. This means that the accused who must appear every fifteen days would have to appear forty-nine times, and the individual who must appear every week would have to appear one hundred and four times, with permission from her or his employer, thereby endangering the individual's occupational stability and forcing her or him to suffer from the consequent stigmatization, which is a negative set of circumstances for the social reinsertion expected.

In spite of the fact that it was very important to establish the same requirement for the appearance of all those released not more than once a month without exception, the judges were not very observant of the requirement. In reality, those released on personal recognizance were forced by some of the judges to appear more frequently, which made their situation more difficult and could have caused the failure of this experiment.

Research Findings

An experimental research project was initiated, as per the above-described design, that lasted more than six years. It consisted of the follow-up of a sample of 468 cases, starting at the time of release by the instructional court and ending with the conclusion of the prosecution at the superior criminal court.

The number of cases studied for each court is shown in table 17.5.

The research produced valuable information in three respects: (a) concerning the specific subject of release on financial and nonfinancial guarantee; (b) concerning the actual mode of operation of the judicial system (on "law in action," or "law as a fact," according to Alf Ross's terminology); and (c) concerning methodological issues relative to criminological research in the criminal justice systems.

A corroboration was again made of the negative attitude of the judges toward release on personal recognizance, such as had been observed during the previous study. In the previous study, the reply given by the majority of the judges was that they did not grant release on personal recognizance because the accused would then evade the action of justice by not appearing in court for the trial. At this time, consistent with what they had previously expressed, and notwithstanding the authorization that had been received from the Supreme Court to carry out the experiment, the judges did the following:

Table 17.5 Experimental Research on the Release on Personal Recognizance, Number of Cases Studied, by Court, Costa Rica, 1982–1988

Court	Released	
	Number	*%*
Hatillo Instructional Court	156	33.3
First Instructional Court	160	34.2
Third Instructional Court	152	32.5
Total	468	100.0

a. They ignored the randomization mechanism established, and, in 31 percent of the cases where release on personal recognizance was applicable, they granted release on a financial guarantee. At the same time, and in a smaller number of cases (5 percent), they did not respect the randomization in the opposite sense by granting release on personal recognizance to some of the accused who should have been released on bail.

b. In relationship to the preceding, in general the judges granted the releases according to the criteria that the more serious offenses warranted a financial guarantee, while the less serious ones qualified for release on personal recognizance. In fact, by using Pearson's correlation coefficient it is possible to note the reverse correlation between both variables: The higher the terms provided for by the law, the smaller the number of releases on personal recognizance the judges granted (see the itemized information in table 17.6).

In considering the relationship between this information on the conduct of the judges and the fact that 81 percent of the penal judges had said that they did not grant release on personal recognizance in cases of offenses punishable with terms of more than three years' imprisonment because "the accused will evade the action of justice by not appearing in court" (see table 17.2), the following hypothesis was tested: "The risk of nonappearance of the released individual in court increases in direct relationship to the seriousness of the offense (such seriousness being measured by the magnitude of the penalty applicable as established by the law)."

Because of the fact that the judges ignored the established randomization mechanism, the sample was neither random nor intentional but, rather, manipulated. Nevertheless, it was possible to derive certain conclusions.

The research did not corroborate the hypothesis of most of the judges and functionaries, who maintain that the risk of an escape or nonappearance in court is directly related to the seriousness of the offense, measured according to the magnitude of the penalty applicable as established by the law. In fact, the releases revoked correspond to offenses whose applicable terms are distributed dispersedly, there being no correlation between the two variables. This can be noted in table 17.7.

Because of the methodological limitations pointed out earlier, it was not possible to verify the hypothesis maintained by the judges, but by taking the total number of releases granted and the total number of cases where the release was revoked for nonappearance in court or before the instructional judge, it was possible to form the correlation table, table 17.7, which does not corroborate such a hypothesis.

In relationship to the preceding section, it was revealed that there is a relationship between nonappearance in court and the nature of the offense. In fact, it can be noted that the largest percentage of revocations for noncompliance on the part of the released individual, regardless of the form of release employed, occurs in the case of offenses against property. In table

Table 17.6 Percentage of Releases on Personal Recognizance Granted in Relationship to the Penalty Applicable, Summary of Three Courts, San Jose, Costa Rica

Offense	Code	Applicable Penalty (years) Mean	Applicable Penalty (years) Maximum	Number of Cases	Percentage of Releases on Personal Recognizance Granted
Theft	208	1.54	3	6	0.33
Resistance	303	1.54	3	4	0.75
Robbery	209	1.63	3	25	0.12
False checks	243	1.75	3	2	1.00
Concealment	321	1.75	3	2	0.50
Breaking and entering	204	2.00	3	3	1.00
Violations relative to property being held in trust	311	2.25	4	1	0.00
Statutory rape	159	2.50	4	3	0.33
Aggravated resistance	304	3.00	5	28	0.68
Serious injuries	124	3.50	6	14	0.50
Simulation of marriage	178	3.50	5	2	0.00
Use of false documents	363	3.50	6	1	0.00
Carnal abuse	161	4.00	6	3	0.33
Extortion	214	4.00	6	8	0.50
Bribery	339	4.00	6	9	0.44
Embezzlement of public property	500	4.00	6	4	0.25
Voluntary manslaughter	117	4.25	8	3	0.00
False swearing	314	4.50	8	5	0.60
Slander	317	4.50	8	2	0.00
Forging of public documents	357	4.50	8	15	0.73
Falsehood	358	4.50	8	8	0.63
Forgery	361	4.50	8	5	0.60
Robbery, second degree	212	4.75	9	88	0.56
Concussion	346	5.00	8	2	0.00
Swindling	216	5.08	10	41	0.34
Fraud	217	5.08	10	6	0.83
Swindling with the use of checks	221	5.08	10	7	0.14
Fraudulent administration	222	5.08	10	5	0.60
Unlawful possession	223	5.08	10	13	0.31
Aggravated corruption	340	5.50	10	1	0.00
Very serious injuries	123	6.50	10	1	0.00
Serious injuries	126	7.50	10	1	1.00
Rape	156	7.50	10	7	0.14
Embezzlement	352	7.50	12	12	0.17
Cultivation of marijuana	374	7.50	10	1	0.00
Provision of marijuana to another individual	376	7.50	10	2	0.00
Trafficking of marijuana	377	7.50	10	17	0.29
Possessing marijuana	378	7.50	10	10	0.10
Arson, causing an explosion	244	8.00	12	1	1.00
Aggravated rape	158	9.00	12	2	0.00
Forgery of currency	364	9.00	15	3	0.00
Aggravated robbery	213	10.00	15	87	0.22
Homicide	111	11.50	15	3	0.00
Kidnapping with extortion	115	14.00	20	1	0.00

Number of offenses typified: 44
Number of releases: 464

Table 17.7   Releases Revoked by Type of Offense, According to the Mean
Penalty Applicable, Summary of Three Courts, San Jose, Costa Rica

Number of Revocations Number of, by Type of Offense[a]	Applicable[b]	Mean Penalty Offenses typified
0	5.60	33
1	2.60	7
3	1.58	1
4	1.60	1
5	5.87	2

[a] The "0" value indicates that there were no revocations in the case of the 33 typified offenses; the "1" value indicates that there was one revocation in each of the 7 typified offenses; etc.
[b] The "5.6" value is the average of the mean penalties for the 33 typified offenses; etc.

Table 17.8   Releases by Offense and Percentage of Revocations Offense

Offense	Total Number of Releases	Total Revocations	
		Number	Percent
Against life	21	1	4.8
Sexual offenses	15	0	
Against the family	2	0	
Against privacy	3	0	
Against property	287	20	7.0
Against good faith in business	2	0	
Against the security of the people	1	0	
Against the public authorities	33	1	3.0
Against the administration of justice	9	0	
Against the duties of the public function	25	1	4.0
Against public trust	32	1	3.1
Relative to Drugs	30	0	
Embezzlement of public property	4	0	
Not specified	4		
Total	468		

Table 17.9   Releases on Personal Recognizance and Contingent upon a Real or
Personal Financial Guarantee, and Number and Percentage of
Revocations—Instructional Court of Information on the First
Instructional Court of San Jose and the Hatillo Instructional Court,
Costa Rica, 1982–1988

Guarantee Revocations	Releases Granted		
		Number	Percent
On personal recognizance	102	3	2.9
On real and personal guarantee	214	6	2.8

17.8 it is possible to observe also the percentage of revocations corresponding to the remaining criminal categories.

With respect to the main variable studied (release with or without bail bond), the research produced very interesting results. In the case of the releases granted in the first court of San Jose, and the Hatillo court, ($N = 316$), where the methodological requirements for the processing of release procedures were more strictly observed, the two forms of release produced the same results. As may be noted in table 17.9, practically identical proportions of success and failure (revocation) were obtained in the two subgroups, those released on personal recognizance and those released on real or personal guarantee (2.8 to 2.9 percent).

In the case of releases granted at the third court of San Jose, where the methodological requirements were complied with to a lesser degree, and where, in addition, a number of abnormal occurrences affected the normal operation of the court,[27] the results were disproportionate as to the number of revocations under one and the other forms of release, with a very high percentage of revocations in the case of releases on personal recognizance: four times higher than in the case of the other forms of release (see table 17.10).

When one compares the courts, one can see that the first court of San Jose and the Hatillo court were quite similar. The difference is again noticeable between these two and the third court of San Jose. The following table reveals that the third court generated five times more revocations than the Hatillo court, almost three times more than the first court, and almost twice as many as those of the other two courts together (table 17.11).

In turn, also, the third court produced a disproportionately higher number of revocations in the case of releases on personal recognizance, than the other two together (this can be observed in table 17.12). As can be concluded from the table, the third court revoked four times as many cases as the other two courts together.

From the preceding discussion it is possible to draw the following conclusions. In 102 cases of offenses punishable with terms of more than three years' imprisonment, in two instructional courts in the country, release

Table 17.10   Releases on Personal Recognizance and Contingent upon a Real or Personal Financial Guarantee, and Number and Percentage of Revocations—Third Instructional Court of San Jose

Guarantee Revocations	Releases Granted	Number	Percent
On personal recognizance	77	12	15.6
On real and personal guarantee	75	3	4.0

on personal recognizance was applied with the same amount of success as the forms of release contingent upon the payment of a financial guarantee.

On the occasion of the first study made in the country on this subject (November 1980), it was found that release on personal recognizance had not been used in the country in any one case. At the time of the second study (November 1989), it was found that it had been applied in 6.9 percent of cases. On the occasion of the experimental study, it was used in two instructional courts in 32.5 percent of the cases (102 cases), with the same amount of success obtained as with the other forms of release. This indicates that release on personal recognizance could be more widely used in Costa Rica than it is at present. The itemization of the offenses for which releases on personal recognizance were recommended, and the number and percentage of cases where it was granted, have been shown in table 17.6.

The procedure for processing the release on personal recognizance, and the procedure for the subsequent follow-up of the case that the court undertakes, can be very important for the success or failure of pretrial freedom. The following aspects are of special importance in this respect:

a. The need to inform the released individual about legal conditions and the obligations imposed.
b. Maintaining contact with the accused in the case, through periodic (but not too

Table 17.11 Total Number of Releases Granted at the First, Hatillo, and Third Instructional Courts, and Number and Percentage of Revocations

| Court | Releases Granted | | |
Revocations		Number	Percent
First Instructional Court	160	6	3.7
Hatillo Court	152	3	2
Third Instructional Court	156	15	10
Total	468	24	5

Table 17.12 Releases on Personal Recognizance Granted and Revoked, Comparison Between the Third Court and the First and Hatillo Courts

| Court | Releases Granted | Releases Revoked | |
		Number	Percent
Third Court	77	12	15.6
First and Hatillo Courts	102	3	2.9

Table 17.13   Number and Percentage of Individuals Convicted and Not Convicted

	Number	Percent
Convicted	164	35
Not Convicted	304	65
Total	468	100

frequent) appearances for purposes of control, since an excessive number of appearances in this case could have a negative effect. It is estimated that appearances once a month would be appropriate.

Only 35 percent of the cases studied resulted in a conviction (table 17.13). In 65 percent of the cases (304), the conclusion was the dropping of charges during the instructional or the adjudicating stage or an acquittal. This should be kept in mind in order to make the release procedure as easy as possible, thereby avoiding harm to individuals who most likely will be declared innocent by the courts.

Recommendations for Wider Application of Release on Personal Recognizance

1. To extend the application of release on personal recognizance in cases of offenses referable to a superior criminal court (those punishable with terms of more than three years' imprisonment). The preceding comments show that the excessively restrictive manner in which release on personal recognizance has been applied in the case of these offenses is not justified.

2. To organize training activities with the participation of penal judges and criminal justice administrators in order to transmit the knowledge acquired, thereby contributing to the reduction in the number of inmates awaiting trial through the application of this form of pretrial release. Of great importance would be that the Supreme Court—which sponsored this study—also sponsor such activities through the Judicial School.

3. In the granting of this form of pretrial release, it is advisable to comply carefully with some practical requirements that have proven to be effective. Following are some of these requirements:

   a. To provide the individual with exhaustive information on his or her legal status and imposed obligations.
   b. To keep the accused in contact with the case through a schedule of periodic appearances before the court; it is felt that appearances once a month would be

appropriate (in addition to any other appearances required for case-processing purposes).

c. To obtain and keep updated information regarding the full address of the individual released, as well as that of relatives or acquaintances who may eventually help notify the accused about judicial notices, and entrust selected relatives or acquaintances with this responsibility.

d. Prior to the revocation of a pretrial release for nonappearance on the part of the accused according to the schedule of appearances or a special request of the court, it is advisable to inquire about the causes by phone, or to issue a second summons, or to seek the collaboration of the relatives or acquaintances. This is justified not only on humanitarian grounds, but also because it can economize in terms of the processing of the case. In numerous cases studied in the course of this work, it was possible to ascertain that nonappearance on the part of the accused had been due to an error in delivering the notice, the fact that for one reason or another the notice had not reached the addressee, or force majeure, such as the illness of an individual who was without the means to contact the court.

e. To keep always in mind the principle of humane treatment, in order not to aggravate unnecessarily, through a prison term imposed in advance, the situation of the accused, who is, furthermore, protected by the presumption of innocence.

4. To establish a system of periodic evaluation that may enable the Supreme Court to determine the extent to which release on personal recognizance is being used by the courts and the results of this measure in practice.

5. In the countries of the region with the same Roman-Germanic criminal juridical system, to keep in mind also the results of this study to the extent to which they could be useful, and to organize similar demonstration projects that would make possible further research on these and other possible forms of extrainstitutional treatment, in order to avoid, to the fullest extent possible, the use of imprisonment for nonconvicted individuals.

6. In the case of the countries of the region with Anglo-Saxon systems, and not excluding the possibility of encouraging research on pretrial release, to devote efforts to research on alternatives to imprisonment.

7. Lastly, a request is made to the United Nations, particularly its criminal justice and crime prevention branch, UNICRI (United Nations Interregional Crime and Justice Research Institute) and ILANUD, to continue encouraging this type of comparative study on serious problems of the criminal justice system.

Notes

The authors wish to express their appreciation for the outstanding support provided by the Supreme Court of Costa Rica, as well as by the judges, secretaries, and staff of the courts. They participated by explaining the actual mode of operation of the criminal justice system, without advocating the belief that is so widespread in the legal profession, that the law coincides with reality, or—worse still—that the law causes reality to become "what it should be." Special gratitude goes to Victor Dobles for the case follow-up and to Juan B. Chavarria for the statistical processing.

1. Release without bail, solely on the basis of the promise on the part of the accused that she or he will comply with the obligations pertinent to her or his pretrial liberty and will appear before the court whenever required.

2. Organized by Dr. Guillermo Navarro, Pensamiento Jurídico Publishers, Buenos Aires, 1987.

3. Juarez de Oliveira, Sao Paulo, Saraiva 1988.

4. Compiled by Jorge Ortega-Torres, Temis Publishers, Bogota, 1988.

5. Edition prepared by A. Vincenzi, Lehmann, 1978.

6. Official publication of the Ministry of Justice, vol. 13, Havana, 1977.

7. Official edition, to 31 August 1976, Juridical Publishers of Chile, Santiago, 1977.

8. Excerpt from the *Judicial Review of the Supreme Court*, San Salvador.

9. First Reserved Edition for the Congress of the Republic, Guatemala, 1973.

10. *Legislación Penal Mexicana*, Andrade Publishers, Mexico, 1978.

11. Ministry of Justice and Labor, María Auxiliadora Press, Asunción, 1977.

12. Annotated and with a concordance by Dr. Adela Reta and Dr. Ofelia Grezzi, FCU, Montevideo, 1988.

13. E. Carranza, M. Houed, L. P. Mora, and E. R. Zaffaroni, *El preso sin condena en América Latina y el Caribe—Estudio comparativo, estadístico y legal de treinta países y propuestas para reducir el fenómeno*, ILANUD, 1983.

14. The "criminal judges" do not hear cases where the applicable penalty to be imposed exceeds three years' imprisonment.

15. Criminal Procedural Code, Articles 291 and 406.

16. These are unipersonal jurisdictional bodies that hear "petty" criminal, civil, commercial, family, and labor cases. In places where there is no investigative prosecutor's office or instructional judge, the lower instance courts initiate the investigation of crimes (those whose prosecution is not contingent upon disclosure or request on the part of the victim) and send the respective documents for completing the process to the Office of the Investigative Prosecutor or the corresponding instructional court (see Articles 5, 6, 7, 8, et seq. of Special Law No. 5711 on the Jurisdiction of the Courts, of June 1975). The preceding was so provided for because of financial and budgetary reasons, since such mixed courts are in places with a low population density that are distant from the capitals of the provinces. However, the way in which they operate does not seem to be the most adequate. In order to have greater control over the work of such lower instance courts, the Supreme Court has, at different sessions of the full Court, issued several guidelines intended to ensure

that the criminal cases being incorrectly processed in such courts be referred to the pertinent offices (instructional courts or investigative prosecutor's offices) without delay, after having complied with the minimum indispensable procedural requirements (see, among others, the resolution of the full Court of 13 June 1983, Article 48).

17. Robert K. Merton, *Teoría y Estructura Sociales*, Fondo de Cultura Económica Press, Mexico, 1964. I wish to refer to the results of the research explained under 3., from which the conclusion can be drawn that this is an assertion that does not have any scientific support; a prejudice that appeared as a falsehood on the basis of the sample of cases studied.

18. Article 301, Criminal Procedural Code: Release shall be granted on personal recognizance under the following circumstances: (1) When it can be concluded prima facie that, in the case of a conviction, probation or a judicial pardon are applicable; and (2) when, in the opposite case, a release is applicable contingent upon a real or personal guarantee, and the judge resolves, on account of the poverty of the accused, that she or he cannot provide such a guarantee, but will nevertheless comply with her or his commitments. (Law No. 5377 of 19 October 1973, Criminal Procedural Code, edition supervised by A. Vincenzi, Lehmann, 1978).

19. It must be clarified, nevertheless, that although originally the 1910 Criminal Procedural Code did not contain the concept of release on personal recognizance, by virtue of a reform introduced through Law No. 4815 of July 1971 (which, under Section IV, changed in its entirety the chapter that referred to pretrial release) this form of guarantee was established in Article 342, having been defined as "the promise under oath of the accused to comply strictly with the terms imposed by the court." In spite of this, it was practically never applied. Later, the Criminal Procedural Code of 1973 (which entered into force 1 July 1975) maintained the concept of release on personal recognizance with the results herein discussed.

20. A previous research paper ("La clase política y el Poder Judicial en Costa Rica," Jorge Rhenán Segura, EUED, Costa Rica, 1982) refers collaterally to the subject. It would be interesting to examine it in greater depth, in order to determine to what extent pretrial release could be biased by the social characteristics of the members of the Judicial Branch.

21. In this respect, Julio B. J. Maier, "Cuestiones fundamentales sobre la libertad del imputado y su situación en el proceso penal," Lerner Associate Publishers, Buenos Aires, 1981, pp. 95 et seq. Also José I. Cafferata-Nores, "La excarcelación," Lerner Publications, Córdoba, Argentina, 1977, pp. 30 et. seq.

22. Carranza, et al., *El preso sin condena*.

23. This research falls under ·a large program at ILANUD, through which several avenues are being explored in order to help reduce the correctional population rates and the number of minors under custody. This is being done with support from UNDP (Project RLA/88/001/D/01/01) through demonstration projects in Venezuela (being developed by CENIPEC, at the University of the Andes), Costa Rica (with the Supreme Court and the Ministry of Justice), and Argentina (in the field of minors with the Secretariat of Human and Family Development of the Ministry of Health and Social Action).

24. In accordance with the labor distribution ordered by the Supreme Court per the powers conferred upon it by the Organic Law of the Judicial Branch, and the

Special Law on the Jurisdiction of the Courts, the instructional courts 1 and 3 of San Jose hear summary proceedings initiated in the following districts of the Central (First) County of San Jose: Carmen (District 10), Merced (20), Hospital (30), Cathedral (40), Zapote (50), San Francisco de Dos Ríos (60), Mata Redonda (80), Pavas (90). In turn, the Hatillo court hears summary proceedings initiated in District 10 (Hatillo) and cases instructed by the lower instance courts of Alajuelita (County No. 10, Province of San Jose) and San Sebastián (District 11 of the Central County, Province of San Jose). Source: "División Territorial Administrativa de la República de Costa Rica," Executive Decree No. 12,087 of 26 November 1980, published in the *Official Gazette* No. 238 of 12 December 1980.

25. It can thus be observed, for instance, in the Vera's Manhattan Bail Project, whose results led to the formation of a great reform movement relative to pretrial release in the United States, in the '60s. Steven Belenko, "Pretrial Services in Criminal Court: an Evaluation of the New York City Criminal Justice Agency," Criminal Justice Coordinating Council, 1980.

26. Robert K. Merton, "Teoría y Estructura Sociales"; manifest and latent functions, pp. 29–94, Fondo de Cultura Económica Press, Mexico, 1964.

27. During the time that the data on the releases was gathered for the research at the Third Lower Instance Court, six temporary judges, three court secretaries, and more than twenty clerical personnel were replaced. There was an intervention by the Judicial Supervision Department, and the Administrative Directorate of the Supreme Court was also present.

Contributors

Adedokun A. Adeyemi is Professor of Criminology and Public Law in the Department of Public Law at the University of Lagos, Nigeria. He is also Project Consultant for the Research Workshop on Alternatives to Imprisonment.

Mohamed Faleh Al-Sagheer is Professor at the Imam Mohammed Ibn Saud Islamic University in Riyadh, Saudi Arabia. He is also Consultant for the Arab Security Studies and Training Center (ASSTC).

Károly Bárd is Professor of Criminal Law at the Eotuos University in Budapest, Hungary. He is also Consultant for the Helsinki Institute for Crime Prevention and Control, affiliated with the United Nations (HEUNI).

Norman Bishop is Scientific Consultant at the Helsinki Institute for Crime Prevention and Control, which is affiliated with the United Nations (HEUNI).

Elias Carranza is Deputy Director of the United Nations Latin American Institute for Crime Prevention and the Treatment of Offenders (ILANUD).

Dennis Challinger is Assistant Director of the Australian Institute of Criminology (AIC).

K. Horiuchi is Professor at the United Nations Asia and Far East Institute for the Prevention of Crime and the Treatment of Offenders (UNAFEI).

Mario Houved is Consultant for the United Nations Latin American Institute for Crime Prevention and the Treatment of Offenders (ILANUD).

Matti Joutsen is the Director of the Helsinki Institute for Crime Prevention and Control, which is affiliated with the United Nations. He is also Scientific Consultant for the Research Workshop on Alternatives to Imprisonment.

Nicholas J. O. Liverpool is Consultant for the United Nations Latin American Institute for Crime Prevention and the Treatment of Offenders (ILANUD).

Ridha Mezghani is Professor of Criminal Law at the University of Tunis, Tunisia. He is also Consultant for the Arab Security Studies and Training Center (ASSTC).

Contributors

Luis Paulino Mora is Consultant for the United Nations Latin American Institute for Crime Prevention and the Treatment of Offenders (ILANUD).

Y. Nagashima is Professor at the United Nations Asia and Far East Institute for the Prevention of Crime and the Treatment of Offenders (UNAFEI).

Masakazu Nishikawa is Professor at the United Nations Asia and Far East Institute for the Prevention of Crime and the Treatment of Offenders (UNAFEI).

I. Nishimura is Professor at the United Nations Asia and Far East Institute for the Prevention of Crime and the Treatment of Offenders (UNAFEI).

N. Nishimura is Professor at the United Nations Asia and Far East Institute for the Prevention of Crime and the Treatment of Offenders (UNAFEI).

Elufemi Odekunle is Director of the United Nations African Institute for the Prevention of Crime and the Treatment of Offenders (UNAFRI).

Luis Rodríguez-Manzanera is Consultant for the United Nations Latin American Institute for Crime Prevention and the Treatment of Offenders (ILANUD).

F. Saito is Professor at the United Nations Asia and Far East Institute for the Prevention of Crime and the Treatment of Offenders (UNAFEI).

S. Sato is Professor at the United Nations Asia and Far East Institute for the Prevention of Crime and the Treatment of Offenders (UNAFEI).

Annesley K. Schmidt is Community Programs Specialist at the U.S. Department of Justice, Federal Bureau of Prisons.

Hiroyasu Sugihara is Director of the United Nations Asia and Far East Institute for the Prevention of Crime and the Treatment of Offenders (UNAFEI).

Peter J. P. Tak is Professor of Law at the Catholic University of Nijmegen, the Netherlands. He is also Consultant for the Helsinki Institute for Crime Prevention and Control, affiliated with the United Nations (HEUNI).

A. Yamaguchi is Professor at the United Nations Asia and Far East Institute for the Prevention of Crime and the Treatment of Offenders (UNAFEI).

Uglješa Zvekić is Research Coordinator of the United Nations Interregional Crime and Justice Research Institute and Scientific Coordinator for the Research Workshop on Alternatives to Imprisonment.

DATE DUE

NOV 2 1 1997		
DEC 1 5 1998		
MAY 1 8 1999		
DEC 1 2 1999		
NOV 2 6 '00		
DEC 1 4 '00		
MAY 09 '01		
MAY 2 1 2003		
GAYLORD		PRINTED IN U.S.A.